FIFTY-ONE KEY FEMINIST THINKERS

Collected here are fifty-one key thinkers and fifty-one authors, recognizing that women are fifty-one percent of the population. There are actually one-hundred-and-two thinkers featured in these pages, as each author is a feminist thinker, too: scholars, writers, poets, and activists, well-established and emerging, old and young, and in-between. These feminists speak the languages of art, politics, literature, education, classics, gender studies, film, queer theory, global affairs, political theory, science fiction, African American studies, sociology, American studies, geography, history, philosophy, poetry, and psychoanalysis. Speaking in all these diverse tongues, conversations made possible by feminist thinking are introduced and engaged.

Key figures include:

- Simone de Beauvoir
- Doris Lessing
- Toni Morrison
- Cindy Sherman
- Octavia Butler
- Marina Warner
- Elizabeth Cady Stanton
- Chantal Akerman
- Gayatri Chakravorty Spivak
- Audre Lorde
- Barbara E. Johnson
- Sappho
- Adrienne Rich.

Each entry is supported by a list of the thinker's major works, along with further reading suggestions. An ideal resource for students and academics alike, this text will appeal to all those interested in the fields of gender studies, women's studies and women's history and politics.

Lori J. Marso is Professor of Political Science and Former Director of Gender, Sexuality, and Women's Studies at Union College in Schenectady, New York, USA.

In *Fifty-One Key Feminist Thinkers* Lori Marso has brought together an excellent collection of accessible yet incisive, rich and original semi-biographical essays on key feminist thinkers, ranging from Sappho and Sojourner Truth to Nawal El Saadawi and Judith Butler. The volume is an invaluable resource for anyone interested in feminist thinking in all its variety and complexity.

Moya Lloyd, *Professor of Political Theory,*
Loughborough University, UK

Showing readers that feminist theory remains one of the most exciting sites for engaging questions of both political thought and action, *Fifty-One Key Feminist Thinkers* creates a remarkable conversation between feminist theorists past and present. Considering questions of identity, freedom, power, justice, desire, autonomy, inclusion, difference, and what 'counts' as feminism, *Fifty-One Key Feminist Thinkers* offers readers a thought-provoking vision of the past and future of feminist theory.

Cristina Beltrán, *Associate Professor,*
Department of Social and Cultural Analysis, New York University, USA

Lori Marso has done an artful job of selecting authors to tell the stories of feminism. This is a delightful collection of the intellectual contributions of a range of feminist thinkers.

Falguni A. Sheth, *Associate Professor of Women's,*
Gender and Sexuality Studies, Emory University

FIFTY-ONE KEY FEMINIST THINKERS

Edited by Lori J. Marso

Routledge
Taylor & Francis Group

LONDON AND NEW YORK

First published 2016
by Routledge
2 Park Square, Milton Park, Abingdon, Oxon OX14 4RN

and by Routledge
711 Third Avenue, New York, NY 10017

Routledge is an imprint of the Taylor & Francis Group, an informa business

© 2016 Lori Marso

The right of the editor to be identified as the author of the editorial material, and of the authors for their individual chapters, has been asserted in accordance with sections 77 and 78 of the Copyright, Designs and Patents Act 1988.

British Library Cataloguing-in-Publication Data
A catalogue record for this book is available from the British Library

Library of Congress Cataloging-in-Publication Data
Names: Marso, Lori Jo, editor.
Title: Fifty key feminist thinkers / edited by Lori Marso.
Description: Abingdon, Oxon; New York, NY : Routledge, 2016.
Identifiers: LCCN 2015050400 |
ISBN 9780415681346 (hardback) | ISBN 9780415681353 (pbk.) |
ISBN 9781315558806 (ebook)
Subjects: LCSH: Feminists. | Feminism–History. | Women's rights–History.
Classification: LCC HQ1123 .F55 2016 | DDC 305.42092/2–dc23
LC record available at http://lccn.loc.gov/2015050400

ISBN: 978-0-415-68134-6 (hbk)
ISBN: 978-0-415-68135-3 (pbk)
ISBN: 978-1-315-55880-6 (ebk)

Typeset in Bembo
by Cenveo Publisher Services

for Luci

Women can be angry, wild, passionate, powerful, loving, violent, frustrated, sad, truthful, hungry, tender. Women can change the world; women can be free.

CONTENTS

HISTORICAL TIMELINE

1. Sappho (c. 630–570 BCE)
2. Christine de Pizan (c. 1364–c. 1430)
3. Mary Astell (1666–1731)
4. Abigail Adams (1744–1818)
5. Olympe de Gouges (1748–1793)
6. Mary Wollstonecraft (1759–1797)
7. Sojourner Truth (1797–1883)
8. Margaret Fuller (1810–1850)
9. Elizabeth Cady Stanton (1815–1902)
10. Anna Julia Cooper (1858–1964)
11. Charlotte Perkins Gilman (1860–1935)
12. Ida B. Wells-Barnett (1862–1931)
13. Emma Goldman (1869–1940)
14. Rosa Luxemburg (1871–1919)
15. Gertrude Stein (1874–1946)
16. Virginia Woolf (1882–1941)
17. Zora Neale Hurston (1891–1960)
18. Margaret Mead (1901–1978)
19. Rachel Carson (1907–1964)
20. Simone de Beauvoir (1908–1986)
21. Edith Thomas (1909–1970)
22. Doris Lessing (1919–2013)
23. Betty Friedan (1921–2006)
24. Mary Daly (1928–2010)
25. Adrienne Rich (1929–2012)
26. Luce Irigaray (1930–)
27. Toni Morrison (1931–)
28. Nawal El Saadawi (1931–)
29. Kate Millett (1934–)
30. Audre Lorde (1934–1992)
31. Monique Wittig (1935–2003)
32. Christine Delphy (1941–)

33. Julia Kristeva (1941–)
34. Laura Mulvey (1941–)
35. Gloria Evangelina Anzaldúa (1942–2004)
36. Gayatri Chakravorty Spivak (1942–)
37. Angela Davis (1944–)
38. Donna Haraway (1944–)
39. Anne Fausto-Sterling (1944–)
40. Shulamith Firestone (1945–2012)
41. Catharine A. MacKinnon (1946–)
42. Marina Warner (1946–)
43. Susan Moller Okin (1946–2004)
44. Octavia E. Butler (1947–2006)
45. Barbara E. Johnson (1947–2009)
46. Jamaica Kincaid (1949–)
47. Iris Marion Young (1949–2006)
48. Chantal Akerman (1950–2015)
49. bell hooks (1952–)
50. Cindy Sherman (1954–)
51. Judith Butler (1956–)

CONTRIBUTORS

M. Jacqui Alexander (entry on Audre Lorde) authored *Pedagogies of Crossing: Meditations on Feminism, Sexual Politics, Memory and the Sacred* (Duke, 2005) and co-edited *Feminist Genealogies, Colonial Legacies, Democratic Futures* (Routledge, 1997) and *Sing, Whisper, Shout, Pray: Feminist Visions for a Just World* (Edgework, 2003). Professor Emerita of Women's Studies, University of Toronto, she is the founding director of the Tobago Centre for the Study and Practice of Indigenous Spirituality: www.latierraspirit.org

Amal Amirah (entry on Nawal El Saadawi) is an Associate Professor of English and World Literature at George Mason University. She is the author and co-editor of *The Factory Girl and the Seamstress: Imagining Gender and Class in Nineteenth Century American Fiction* (Garland, 2000), *Going Global: The Transnational Reception of Third World Women Writers* (Garland, 2000) and *Etel Adnan: Critical Essays on the Arab-American Writer and Artist* (McFarland, 2002).

Ariella Azoulay (entry on Olympe de Gouges) is Professor of Modern Culture and Media and Comparative Literature at Brown University. She is the author of *Civil Imagination: The Political Ontology of Photography* (Verso, 2012) and *The Civil Contract of Photography* (Zone Books, 2008), a documentary film director (*Civil Alliances, Palestine, 47–48*) and independent curator of archives and exhibitions.

Lawrie Balfour (entry on Toni Morrison) is Professor of Politics at the University of Virginia. She is the author of *Democracy's Reconstruction: Thinking Politically with W.E.B. Du Bois* (Oxford, 2011), *The Evidence of Things Not Said: James Baldwin and the Promise of American Democracy* (Cornell, 2001), and numerous articles and book chapters on race, gender, and democracy.

Ritu Birla (entry on Gayatri Chakravorty Spivak) is Associate Professor of History and Richard Charles Lee Director of the Asian Institute at the Munk School of Global Affairs, University of Toronto. She is the author of *Stages of Capital: Law, Culture and Market Governance in Late Colonial India* (Duke, 2009) and has published widely in venues such as *Comparative Studies of South Asia, Africa and Middle East*, *The Journal of Law and Society*, *Public Culture* and *Social Research*.

Renate Blumenfeld-Kosinski (entry on Christine de Pizan) is Distinguished Professor of French at the University of Pittsburgh. She is the author of over sixty articles and numerous books, including *Poets, Saints, and Visionaries of the Great Schism, 1378–1417* (Penn State, 2006) and *The Strange Case of Ermine de Reims: A Medieval Woman between Demons and Saints* (Pennsylvania, 2015). She also edited and translated (with Kevin Brownlee) *The Selected Writings of Christine de Pizan* (W. W. Norton, 1997).

Marla Brettschneider (entry on Jamaica Kincaid) is Professor of Political Theory at the University of New Hampshire with a joint appointment in Political Science and Women's Studies. She has long served as Coordinator of WS and is Chair of Political Science. Brettschneider is the author of numerous award-winning books including *The Family Flamboyant: Race Politics, Queer Families, Jewish Lives* (SUNY, 2006) and also *Jewish Feminism and Intersectionality* (SUNY, 2016). She has been publishing on Jamaica Kincaid for many years.

adrienne maree brown (co-author of entry on Octavia E. Butler) is the co-editor of *Octavia's Brood: Science Fiction from Social Justice Movements* (AK Press, 2015). She's a writer, sci-fi scholar, pleasure activist, healer and facilitator living in Detroit.

Michelle Chilcoat (entry on Edith Thomas) is Associate Professor of French and Francophone Studies and is co-director of Film Studies at Union College in Schenectady, NY. She is the author of numerous articles and reviews that have appeared in journals such as *boundary 2*, *NWSJ*, *French Cultural Studies* and *French Review*. Her translation of Edith Thomas's *Contes d'Auxois* (*Auxois Stories*) is currently under review for publication in the MLA Texts and Translations series.

Cynthia J. Davis (entry on Charlotte Perkins Gilman) is Professor of English at the University of South Carolina. She authored both *Charlotte Perkins Gilman: A Biography* (Stanford, 2010) and *Bodily and Narrative Forms: The Influence of Medicine on American Literature, 1845–1915* (Stanford, 2000), and co-edited both *Charlotte Perkins Gilman and Her Contemporaries* (Alabama, 2004) and *Approaches to Teaching Charlotte Perkins Gilman's "The Yellow Wallpaper" and Herland* (MLA, 2003).

Jodi Dean (entry on Rosa Luxemburg) is the Donald R. Harter '39 Chair of Humanities and Social Sciences at Hobart and William Smith Colleges in Geneva, NY. She is the author or editor of twelve books, including *Democracy and Other Neoliberal Fantasies* (Duke, 2009), *The Communist Horizon* (Verso, 2012), and *Crowds and Party* (Verso, 2016).

Lisa Disch (entry on Christine Delphy) is Professor of Political Science at the University of Michigan in Ann Arbor, MI. She is author most recently of *The Tyranny of the Two-Party System* (Columbia, 2002), co-editor with Mary Hawkesworth of *The Oxford Handbook of Feminist Theory* (Oxford, forthcoming), and editor of a special issue of *South Atlantic Quarterly* on "1970s Feminisms" (Duke, 2015).

Charlotte Eyerman, Ph.D. (entry on Cindy Sherman) is Director and CEO of the Monterey Museum of Art. She has published and lectured extensively on modern and contemporary art. Major exhibitions include *Courbet and the Modern Landscape* (Getty Museum, 2006), *Action/Abstraction* (Saint Louis Art Museum, 2008) and *Cubisti Cubismo* (Complesso del Vittoriano, Rome, 2013). Recent publications include "Museums and the Social and Redemptive Power of Art," *Clark Art Institute Journal*, December 2015.

Crystal N. Feimster (entry on Ida B. Wells Barnett) is Associate Professor in the Department of African American Studies and the American Studies Program at Yale. A scholar of US women's history and African-American history, her research focuses on racial and sexual violence, social movements, and citizenship. She is the author of *Southern Horrors: Women and the Politics of Rape and Lynching* (Harvard, 2009).

Kathy E. Ferguson (entry on Emma Goldman) is professor of political science and women's studies at the University of Hawai'i. She is author of *Emma Goldman: Political Thinking in the Streets* (Rowman and Littlefield, 2011), co-editor with Monique Mironesco of *Gender and Globalization in Asia and the Pacific* (Hawai'i, 2008) and co-author with Phyllis Turnbull of *Oh, Say, Can You See? The Semiotics of the Military in Hawai'i* (Minnesota, 1999).

Michaele Ferguson (entry on Iris Marion Young) is Associate Professor of Political Science at the University of Colorado, Boulder. She is author of *Sharing Democracy* (Oxford, 2012) and co-editor of *W Stands for Women* (Duke, 2007). She is currently working on a book entitled *Taming the Shrew: The Rise of Neoliberal Feminism in America* and an anthology of Young's work, co-edited with Andrew Valls.

Namulundah Florence (entry on bell hooks) is Professor of Education at Brooklyn College. She is author of *bell hooks' Engaged Pedagogy: A Transgressive Education for Critical Consciousness* (Bergin & Garvey, 1998); *From Our Mothers' Hearths: Bukusu Folktales and Proverbs* (Africa World Press, 2005); *Multiculturalism 101: The Practical Guide Series* (McGraw-Hill, 2009); *Immigrant Teachers, American Students: Cultural Differences, Cultural Disconnections* (Palgrave, 2011); *The Bukusu of Kenya: Folktales, Culture and Social Identities* (Carolina Academic, 2011); and *Wangari Maathai: Visionary, Environmental Leader, Political Activist* (Lantern, 2014).

Andrea Foroughi (entry on Elizabeth Cady Stanton) is Associate Professor of History at Union College in Schenectady, NY. She is author of *Go If You Think It Your Duty* (Minnesota Historical Society, 2007). She has published articles on depictions of masculinity and femininity in nineteenth-century political visual culture, and in the 2012 film, *Lincoln*. She teaches courses in US history on gender and on the Civil War.

Rosalind Galt (entry on Laura Mulvey) is Professor of Film Studies at King's College London. She is the author of *The New European Cinema: Redrawing the Map* (Columbia, 2006), *Pretty: Film and the Decorative Image* (Columbia, 2011), co-editor of *Global Art Cinema: New Theories and Histories* (Oxford, 2010) and co-author of *Queer Cinema in the World* (Duke, 2016).

Judith Grant (entry on Catharine A. MacKinnon) is a professor of Political Science at Ohio University in Athens, OH. She is the author of *Fundamental Feminism* (Routledge, 1993) and co-editor of *Political Theory and the Animal Human Relationship* (SUNY, 2016).

Lisa Guenther (entry on Angela Davis) is Associate Professor of Philosophy at Vanderbilt University. She is the author of *Solitary Confinement: Social Death and its Afterlives* (Minnesota, 2013) and *The Gift of the Other: Levinas and the Politics of Reproduction* (SUNY, 2006) and the co-editor of *Death and Other Penalties: Philosophy in a Time of Mass Incarceration* (Fordham, 2014).

Evelynn Hammonds (entry on Anne Fausto-Sterling) is the Barbara Gutmann Rosenkrantz Professor of the History of Science and Professor of African and African American Studies at Harvard University. She is the co-editor of *The Harvard Sampler: Liberal Education for the 21st Century* (Harvard, 2011), *The Nature of Difference: Sciences of Race from Jefferson to Genomics* (MIT, 2008) and *Gender and Scientific Authority* (Chicago, 1996).

Victoria Hesford (entry on Kate Millett) is Associate Professor of Women's and Gender Studies at Stony Brook University. She is the author of *Feeling Women's Liberation* (Duke, 2013), and co-editor of the *Feminist Theory* Special Issue on "Experience, Echo, Event: Theorizing Feminist Histories" (August, 2014). Her essay, "On Not Being Women: The 1970s, Mass Culture, and Feminism," was published in *South Atlantic Quarterly* (Fall, 2015).

Lynne Huffer (entry on Luce Irigaray) is Samuel Candler Dobbs Professor of Women's, Gender, and Sexuality Studies at Emory University. She is the author of *Are the Lips a Grave?* (Columbia, 2013), *Mad for Foucault* (Columbia, 2010), *Maternal Pasts, Feminist Futures* (Stanford, 1998) and *Another Colette* (Michigan, 1992). She also serves, with Shannon Winnubst, as co-editor of *philoSOPHIA: A Journal in Continental Feminism*.

Ayana A. H. Jamieson (co-author of entry on Octavia E. Butler) is the founder of the Octavia E. Butler Legacy Network. She is a science fiction, comparative mythology, and California history scholar living outside Los Angeles where she enjoys teaching, organizing, mothering, and gardening.

Deborah Jenson (entry on Barbara E. Johnson) is Professor of Romance Studies and Global Health, and Director of the Franklin Humanities Institute at Duke University. She completed her doctorate in Romance Languages and Literatures at Harvard University under the direction of Barbara Johnson. Jenson's books include *Trauma and Its Representations* (Hopkins, 2001), *Beyond the Slave Narrative* (Liverpool, 2012), *"Coming to Writing" and Other Essays by Hélène Cixous* (Harvard, 1991), *Unconscious Dominions* (with Warwick Anderson and Richard Keller, Duke, 2011) and *Poetry of Haitian Independence* (with Doris Kadish and Norman Shapiro, Yale, 2015).

AnaLouise Keating (entry on Gloria Evangelina Anzaldúa) is Professor and Ph.D. Director of Multicultural Women's and Gender Studies at Texas Woman's University. She is author, editor, or co-editor of ten books, including *Transformation Now! Toward a Post-Oppositional Politics of Change* (Illinois, 2013), *Teaching Transformation: Transcultural Dialogues in the Classroom* (Palgrave, 2007) and Gloria Anzaldúa's *Interviews/Entrevistas* (Routledge, 2000) and *Light in the Dark/Luz en lo oscuro: Rewriting Identity, Spirituality, Reality* (Duke, 2015).

Nancy Lutkehaus (entry on Margaret Mead) is Professor of Anthropology at the University of Southern California. She is author of

Margaret Mead: The Making of an American Icon (Princeton, 2008) and *Zaria's Fire: Engendered Moments in Manam Ethnography* (Carolina Academic, 1995) and co-editor of *From Romance to Reality: Representations of Pacific Islands and Islanders* (Special Issue of *Pacific Studies*, 2015), *Gendered Missions: Women and Men in Missionary Discourse and Practice* (Michigan, 1998) and *Gender Rituals: Female Initiation in Melanesia* (Routledge, 1995).

Angela F. Maione (entry on Mary Wollstonecraft) is Lecturer on Social Studies at Harvard University. She holds a Ph.D. in Political Science/Political Theory from Northwestern University. She is currently completing a book manuscript on the political thought of Mary Wollstonecraft.

Lori J. Marso (editor, and entries on Chantal Akerman and Simone de Beauvoir) is Professor of Political Science at Union College in Schenectady, NY. She is author of the forthcoming book, *Politics with Beauvoir: Freedom in the Encounter* (Duke), and co-editor with Bonnie Honig of *Politics, Theory, and Film: Critical Encounters with Lars von Trier* (Oxford, 2016). She is also author of *(Un)Manly Citizens* (Hopkins, 1999) and *Feminist Thinkers and the Demands of Femininity* (Routledge, 2006), and co-editor of *Simone de Beauvoir's Political Thinking* (Illinois, 2006) and *W Stands for Women* (Duke, 2007).

Susan McCabe (entry on Adrienne Rich) is a professor at the University of Southern California. Her publications include *Elizabeth Bishop: Her Poetics of Loss* (Penn State, 1994), *Cinematic Modernism: Modern Poetry and Film* (Cambridge, 2005), *Swirl* (Red Hen, 2003) and *Descartes' Nightmare*, awarded the Agha Ali Shahid Prize (Utah, 2008). She is finishing a literary cultural biography, *H.D. and Bryher: A Modernist Love Story*, contracted by Oxford University Press.

Patricia Moynagh (entry on Abigail Adams) is, with Lori Marso, editor and contributor to *Simone de Beauvoir's Political Thinking* (Illinois, 2006). She has written articles on Hannah Arendt, Howard Zinn and activism. She is author of "War is a Condition in Need of a Cure" in *Agitation with a Smile: Howard Zinn's Legacy and the Future of Activism* (Paradigm, 2013). She is Associate Professor of Government and Politics, and Director of the Gender Studies Program at Wagner College.

Laurie E. Naranch (entry on Sojourner Truth) is Associate Professor of Political Science and Director of the Women's Studies Minor at Siena College, NY. Recent publications include "women's rights" and "gender and identity" in Blackwell's *Encyclopedia of Political Thought* (2014) and "Cash or Credit? Sex and the Pursuit of Happiness" in *Mad Men and Politics: Nostalgia and the Remaking of American Politics* (Bloomsbury, 2015). Naranch contributes blog entries to the Hannah Arendt Center at Bard College.

Deborah G. Plant (entry on Zora Neale Hurston) is an Independent Scholar formerly associated with the University of South Florida. She is the editor of *"The Inside Light": New Critical Essays on Zora Neale Hurston* (Praeger, 2010) and author of *Zora Neale Hurston: A Biography of the Spirit* (Praeger, 2007) and *Every Tub Must Sit on its Own Bottom: The Philosophy and Politics of Zora Neale Hurston* (Illinois, 1995).

Rebecca Jo Plant (entry on Betty Friedan) is an associate professor in the History Department at the University of California, San Diego, the author of *Mom: The Transformation of Motherhood in Modern America* (Chicago, 2010) and co-editor of *Maternalism Reconsidered: Motherhood, Welfare and Social Policy in the Twentieth Century* (Berghahn, 2012). Currently, she is writing a history of underage soldiers with Dr Frances Clarke of the University of Sydney.

Krista Ratcliffe (entry on Mary Daly) is Professor and Head of English at Purdue University in West Lafayette, IN. She is author, co-author or co-editor of *Anglo-American Feminist Challenges to the Rhetorical Traditions: Virginia Woolf, Mary Daly, and Adrienne Rich* (SIUP, 1996), *Who's Having This Baby: Perspectives on Birthing* (Michigan State, 2002), *Rhetorical Listening: Identification, Gender, Whiteness* (SIUP, 2006), *Performing Feminist Administration in Rhetoric and Composition Studies* (Hampton, 2010) and *Silence and Listening as Rhetorical Arts* (SIUP, 2011).

Alice Ridout (entry on Doris Lessing) is Assistant Professor of English at Algoma University in Sault Ste. Marie, Canada. She is the author of *Contemporary Women Writers Look Back: From Irony to Nostalgia* (Continuum, 2011), and co-editor of *Doris Lessing's* The Golden Notebook *After Fifty* (Palgrave, 2015) and *Doris Lessing: Border Crossings* (Continuum, 2009). She is Past President of the Doris Lessing Society (2012–15).

Jana Sawicki (entry on Donna Haraway) is Carl Vogt '58 Professor of Philosophy at Williams College. Author of *Disciplining Foucault: Feminism, Power and the Body* (Routledge, 1991) and co-editor of Blackwell's *A Companion to Foucault* (Wiley-Blackwell, 2013) and a *Foucault Studies* issue on queer theory (September 2012), she is currently finishing a series of essays on the reception of Foucault's ethical writings in queer theory.

Birgit Schippers (entry on Judith Butler) is Senior Lecturer in Politics at St Mary's University College Belfast. She is the author of *Julia Kristeva and Feminist Thought* (Edinburgh University Press, 2011) and *The Political Philosophy of Judith Butler* (Routledge, 2014), and editor of the *Ashgate Research Companion to Rethinking Ethics in International Relations* (forthcoming). Her current research examines agonistic and performative approaches to human rights.

Susan Sellers (entry on Virginia Woolf) is Professor of English Literature at St Andrews University, UK. She is a general editor of *The Cambridge Edition of the Works of Virginia Woolf* and volume editor of *The Waves* (Cambridge, 2011), as well as author of *Vanessa and Virginia* (Harcourt, 2009), a novel about Woolf's relationship with her sister, the painter Vanessa Bell. She has also published widely in the areas of feminist literary theory and modernist and contemporary women's fiction.

Torrey Shanks (entry on Marina Warner) is Assistant Professor of Political Science at the University at Toronto. Her research is in modern political theory, feminist theory, and language and politics. She is the author of *Authority Figures: Rhetoric and Experience in John Locke's Political Thought* (Penn State, 2014). Her work has appeared in *Political Theory* and *Theory and Event*.

Fanny Söderbäck (entry on Julia Kristeva) is Assistant Professor of Philosophy at Siena College. She is the editor of *Feminist Readings of Antigone* (SUNY, 2010) and the co-editor of *Undutiful Daughters: New Directions in Feminist Thought and Practice* (Palgrave, 2012). Her work lies at the intersection between feminist and continental philosophy and is published in *Signs*, the *Journal of Speculative Philosophy* and the *Journal of French and Francophone Philosophy*.

Patricia Springborg (entry on Mary Astell) held a personal chair in political theory at the University of Sydney, but is now Guest Professor at the Centre for British Studies of the Humboldt University in Berlin. In addition to being a Hobbes scholar and historian of political thought, she edited three volumes of Mary Astell's writings, authoring *Mary Astell, Theorist of Freedom from Domination* (Cambridge, 2005) and several articles on Astell.

Jeffrey Steele (essay on Margaret Fuller) is Professor of English at the University of Wisconsin-Madison. He is a former President and current Executive Officer of the Margaret Fuller Society. He is the author of *The Representation of the Self in the American Renaissance* (North Carolina, 1987) and *Transfiguring America: Myth, Ideology, and Mourning in Margaret Fuller's Writing* (Missouri, 2001), as well as editor of *The Essential Margaret Fuller* (Rutgers, 1992).

Joan Tronto (entry on Susan Moller Okin) is Professor of Political Science at the University of Minnesota, Twin Cities. She is co-editor of *Women Transforming Politics* (NYU, 1996) and author of *Moral Boundaries: A Political Argument for an Ethics of Care* (Routledge, 1993), *Caring Democracy: Markets, Justice and Equality* (NYU, 2013) and *Who Cares? How to Reshape a Democratic Politics* (Cornell, 2015).

Lynda Walsh (entry on Rachel Carson) is Associate Professor of English at the University of Nevada, Reno. She conducts research on the rhetoric of science, specifically the science–public interface. Her monographs are *Sins Against Science: The Scientific Hoaxes of Poe, Twain, and Others* (SUNY, 2006) and *Scientists as Prophets: A Rhetorical Genealogy* (Oxford, 2013).

Kathi Weeks (entry on Shulamith Firestone) teaches in the Women's Studies Program at Duke University. She is the author of *The Problem with Work: Feminism, Marxism, Antiwork Politics and Postwork Imaginaries* (Duke, 2011) and *Constituting Feminist Subjects* (Cornell, 1998), and a co-editor of *The Jameson Reader* (Blackwell, 2000).

Penny Weiss (entry on Anna Julia Cooper) is Chair of Women's and Gender Studies and Professor of Political Science at Saint Louis University. She authored *Gendered Community: Rousseau, Sex, and Politics* (NYU, 1993), *Conversations with Feminism: Political Theory and Practice* (Rowman & Littlefield, 1998) and *Canon Fodder: Historical Women Political Thinkers* (Penn State, 2009), and co-edited *Feminism and Community* (Temple, 1995), *Feminist Interpretations of Emma Goldman* (Penn State, 2007), and *Feminist Interpretations of Mary Astell* (Penn State, 2016). She loves critters, great and small.

Barbara Will (entry on Gertrude Stein) is A. and R. Newbury Professor of English and Associate Dean of the Arts and Humanities at Dartmouth College. She is the author of two books on Gertrude Stein: *Gertrude Stein, Modernism, and the Problem of "Genius"* (Edinburgh, 2000), and *Unlikely Collaboration: Gertrude Stein, Bernard Faÿ, and the Vichy Dilemma* (Columbia, 2011).

Victoria Wohl (entry on Sappho) is Professor of Classics at the University of Toronto. She is author of books and articles on the literature, social relations, and psychic life of democratic Athens, including *Intimate Commerce: Exchange, Gender, and Subjectivity in Greek Tragedy* (Texas, 1998), *Love Among the Ruins: The Erotics of Democracy in Classical Athens* (Princeton, 2002) and *Euripides and the Politics of Form* (Princeton, 2015).

Linda M. G. Zerilli (entry on Monique Wittig) is Charles E. Merriam Distinguished Service Professor of Political Science and Faculty Director of the Center for the Study of Gender and Sexuality at the University of Chicago. She works in the areas of feminist theory, democratic theory, and Continental philosophy. Her books include *Signifying Woman: Culture and Chaos in Rousseau, Burke, and Mill* (Cornell, 1994), *Feminism and the Abyss of Freedom* (Chicago, 2005) and *A Democratic Theory of Judgment* (Chicago, 2016).

PREFACE

Feminism is a critical political perspective that helps us to see and name the wrongs of oppression based in gender and sex, but also interlinked with race, class, age, location, sexuality, and ability. Feminist thinking, exemplified in the essays within this book, opens up the possibility of a future where freedom is collective and concrete, where we can be *more* than we are now, where we can desire and act in freedom and in solidarity. Within each of their historical moments, articulated within their locations, as well as the discourses or idioms of their lives and life-work, the feminist thinkers in this book advocate creative resistance and engage in multiple kinds and strategies of struggles. They inspire our imagination for living differently: more boldly; with less shame and anxiety, more courage; within supportive communities. We must produce, and not assume, this future. It is not certain or guaranteed, but these thinkers inspire us to think and work together to make it possible.

The feminist thinkers in this book are the designated "fifty-one key feminist thinkers," historical and contemporary, and also the *authors* of the entries. Collected here are fifty-one key thinkers and fifty-one authors, as we note that women are fifty-one percent of the population. We truly have one hundred and two thinkers featured in these pages as each author is a feminist thinker, too: we are scholars, writers, poets, and activists, well-established and emerging, old and young and in-between. We speak the languages of art, politics, literature, education, classics, gender studies, film, queer theory, global affairs, political theory, science fiction, African American studies, sociology, American studies, geography, history, philosophy, poetry, and psychoanalysis. Speaking in all these diverse tongues, we introduce and engage in the conversations made possible by feminist thinking. These are conversations within history and across generations, between and across borders of class, race, identity, sexuality, age, ability, location, political affiliation and ideology. The book thus showcases several conversations, within and amongst the thinkers featured and their contemporary feminist authors. These are the conversations that make up the ongoing practice and collective action of feminist politics.

The thinkers are presented in alphabetical rather than historical order, but they are also listed by birth date to give historical context. This choice, to present the thinkers alphabetically, intentionally subverts linear narratives that either assure continued progress as feminism marches towards the finish line, or lament our inability to deliver on this promised future. The "waves" metaphor is often deployed to tell a story wherein the first wave culminates in suffrage; the second wave results in the right to abortion, and heightened consciousness about wage inequities, racial discrimination, and sexual freedom; and the third (or even fourth) wave is ongoing, and mostly focused on autobiography, choice, empowerment, and diversity. The waves metaphor not only reduces the complexity of the issues raised, contested, and still left unsettled within each wave; it also tends to layer a familial story within the movement of the waves. Daughters outdo their mothers, and mothers are forgotten or disavowed. We either arrive at a rosy future, albeit with hurt feelings along the way, or we lament our inability to get to the destination and assign blame to various bad actors—lesbians, angry black women, not-so-dutiful daughters, racist mothers—who have stood in the way of our better future. This book challenges the progression narrative, as well as origin stories, and dispenses with family squabbles between mothers and daughters.

Readers can dip in, to whet their curiosity about a select historical or contemporary feminist, to discover new thinkers, or see how old favorites are framed. Some readers will choose entries by following their interest in our feminist authors, themselves known and respected in and beyond their fields of expertise. Some readers may devour the book cover to cover. However readers choose to approach the entries, what I hope you will see is that you, too, might be transformed by or provoked to engage in the ongoing conversations of feminism.

What is clear in these entries is that feminism is a subversive discourse. The thinkers within—the fifty-one, and the fifty-one authors of the fifty-one—recognize and encourage the dissension and anxiety produced by feminist conversations. While feminist conversations and conversations about feminism(s) encourage solidarity and spark hope for a better future, they do not shy away from discord, ugly feelings, or bad examples. They are unsettling and unsettled. Feminist thinking provokes conversations that, when they unfold in a democratic spirit, undo our daily habits and deepest assumptions about biology, nature, norms, happiness, sex, fulfillment, love, and life's multiple meanings. That is the imagination and activity this book inspires.

Lori J. Marso (editor)

ACKNOWLEDGMENTS

Alyson Claffey at Routledge has been wonderful, answering all my many questions with efficiency and patience. I also thank the office of the Dean of Arts and Sciences and the Political Science Department at Union College for financial support. Two undergraduate research assistants, Perry Moskowitz and Sydney Paluch, helped me to attend to several details at key points and kept me sane.

My contributors deserve the credit for the truly amazing document this book has become. Reaching across time zones, generations, fields of study and work, and styles of writing, we collectively present this conversation about feminism's pleasures, frustrations, antagonisms, and dreams. I thank all of my authors for their incredible expertise, patience, generosity, brilliance, and the much appreciated notes of encouragement that seemed to come at just the right moments.

This book is for Luci whose "Women Who Changed the World" has always been an inspiration.

ABIGAIL ADAMS (1744–1818)

Patricia Moynagh

Abigail Adams is often held up as a feminist thinker and rightly so. Her most quoted line "Remember the Ladies" appears in a letter, dated March 31, 1776, written to her husband, John Adams, future president of the United States. But at this moment, the United States is not yet united. Just shy of 100 days from declaring its independence from Great Britain, the newly envisioned nation is a messy work in process, a battleground occupied by factious stakeholders. The idea of liberty is unquestionably in the air, expressed loudly in the call for independence from King George III and his occupying army, the redcoats. Yet many contenders express loyalty to the so-called "mother country," and some, even if they desire independence, fear that freedom for *all* could bring disorder. The prospect of expanding liberty electrifies some and terrifies others.

Like many, Abigail Adams was directly and adversely affected by these conditions, raising her four children in the war zone that Massachusetts had become. John's role as a delegate (representing his state) took him away to Philadelphia (often for long periods) where, as a member of the Continental Congress, he was a leading founder of self-proclaimed revolutionary forces formulating ideas about how to govern. In his absence, Abigail played deputy husband. To her role of running the family, finances and farming were added. Referring to the revolutionary movement of which John was increasingly becoming a major contributor, he implored Abigail in 1774 "to take Part with me in this struggle" [1774] (1975, 59).

Join him in struggle she certainly would. Little did he expect her to seek its logical conclusion through expansion of liberty for slaves and women. Their physical separation, while difficult for them, has left researchers a treasure trove. She in Braintree (later named Quincy in 1803) and he in Philadelphia, their only way to connect was through letter-writing. Reading their epistolary exchanges (they preserved 1,160 letters between them) provides great insight into their times and how they differently understood the future of the nation.

Abigail wants women to be positively positioned to live their lives more fully. She contests the many and various laws, barriers, and customs that diminish women to a vassal caste, a subordinate species, legally superfluous. With all this talk of liberty, what of women's, she asks. Yet even before she gets to her famous command to "be more generous and favourable" to women "than your ancestors," she

1

condemns slavery. She points to a blatant contradiction. Delegates who are beginning to fight for liberty from Britain are not doing the same for slaves:

> I have sometimes been ready to think that the passion for Liberty cannot be Eaquelly Strong in the Breasts of those who have been accustomed to deprive their fellow Creatures of theirs.
> [1776] (1975, 120)

As much as two years prior (1774), she had written to John on the same topic: "I wish most sincerely there was not a Slave in the province." She added:

> It allways appeared a most iniquitous Scheme to me—fight ourselfs for what we are daily robbing and plundering from those who have as good a right to freedom as we have.
> [1774] (2007, 47–48)

As the letter continues, it's clear she is thinking much more widely about liberty and beseeching her husband to do the same. She knows he opposes slavery. She also knows she is his most trusted advisor and confidante. A frequent salutation to each other is "Dearest Friend" and she invokes this appellation over that of "Master" whether in relation to slave or wife, telling him to "give up the harsh title of Master for the more tender and endearing one of Friend" [1776] (1975, 121).

Abigail herself was not oppressed by race or class, but by her sex. But when Abigail advocated on behalf of her sex, John dismissed her as a "rebel" by using the same adjective, "sausy," to describe her unruliness as he had to depict other "rebels" six years earlier in 1770. At that time, he defended British soldiers who shot and killed five "rioters," an event that would be dubbed the Boston Massacre. Maybe there was some lawyerly honor in his commitment to show that British soldiers could get a trial in his state (he never regretted this decision, calling it one of the most "gallant" and "manly" of his life), but there is no undoing his words [1773] (2008–2015). In the courtroom, he depicted the crowd that threw oyster shells and snowballs at the soldiers as "most probably a motley rabble of sausy boys, negroes and mulattoes, Irish teagues and out landish jack tarrs" [1770] (2008–2015, 12). Among the "jack tars" was the black seaman, Crispus Attucks. Five of the seven soldiers, along with their captain, were acquitted and the other two were eventually exonerated, while the murdered—those

2

who had acted out against the injustices of the British—could not tell their stories. To John, "rebels," the category into which John's wife was quickly descending, were dispensable, but not so the "revolutionaries." The rebels were the dispossessed, the forgotten, the non-stakeholders. Those who rebelled, rather than revolutionized, did not count in the same way. They counted not, in fact: the new nation would be for the haves.

Responding to Abigail's letters, John viewed her as impertinently out of line. If Abigail advocated for women she was with the "sausy boys," but if she kept to her class and race, she was a patriot. Attempting to reach him in yet another way, Abigail declares: "Men of Sense in all Ages abhor those customs which treat us only as the vassals of your Sex" [1776] (1975, 121). Upon reading her "extraordinary Code of Laws" [1776] (1975, 122–23), John replies: "I cannot but laugh" [1776] 1975, 122–23). After enumerating—in jest-like fashion—all the insubordinate groups such as Children, Apprentices, "Colledges," Indians and Negroes, that have become "disobedient," "grown turbulent," or otherwise "insolent," John says her letter was "the first Intimation that another Tribe more numerous and powerfull than all the rest were grown discontented" [1776] (1975, 123).

So close to power was this soon-to-be second first lady (the term had not yet been invented) when she told her beloved to be "more generous" to women than his ancestors had been, Abigail Adams had John's ear, but it did not matter. She warns him of the hardness of "arbitrary power" which is "liable to be broken" [1776] (1975, 127). Finally she capitulates, while also making her best attempt to save face, by proclaiming "not withstanding all your wise Laws and Maxims," women have "power not only to free ourselves but to subdue our masters" [1776] (1975, 127). Yet Abigail is not satisfied and reaches out to her friend and playwright Mercy Otis Warren, with whom she long corresponded. She complains about her husband's response. She suggests how they will together "petition Congress" [1776] (2015). From many a plea, she moves to petition.

What Abigail urged her husband to do in the spring of 1776 remains unfulfilled. A party of one, however close to power, won't carry the day, not when centuries' worth of practices and institutions to reinforce them have promoted the diminution of women. It was not then, and is not now, enough to plead with one's oppressors. Nevertheless, that she spoke up at all and left her letters for her like-minded descendants to read shows that even a party of one is better than a non-existent one. Speaking up should not be underestimated even if the hearer does not like the message.

That the idea to "petition Congress" did not come to pass does not diminish Abigail's aspiration to transform her party of one into a petition of two. She was on the right track. For women to come together for common cause remains essential for enacting change. Each time members of the "more numerous tribe" speak out and work together for women's greater freedom, we are that much closer to honoring this aspect of Abigail's legacy.

Note to readers

First, anyone who writes about the Adamses is confronted with how to refer to them. Scholarly convention holds that the last name is used. Yet they share a last name (she was born a Smith). I have opted to refer to them by their first names, but with some hesitation because women are so often referred to this way, men less so. Second, Eighteenth Century English is different from our own. I have kept the original letters intact, mistakes and all.

Adams's major writings

1975. *The Book of Abigail and John: Selected Letters of the Adams Family 1762–1784*, edited and with an introduction by L. H. Butterfield, Marc Friedlaender, and Mary-Jo Kline (Cambridge, MA: Harvard University Press).

2007. *My Dearest Friend: Letters of Abigail and John Adams*, edited by Margaret A. Hogan and C. James Taylor (Cambridge, MA: Harvard University Press).

2008–2015. Taylor, C. James (ed.). *The Adams Papers Digital Edition* (Charlottesville: University of Virginia Press, Rotunda).

2016. Taylor, C. James (ed.). *Founding Families: Digital Editions of the Papers of the Winthrops and the Adamses* (Boston: Massachusetts Historical Society). www.masshist.org/digitaladams/archive/letter/

Further reading

Gelles, Edith B. 2009. *Abigail and John: Portrait of a Marriage* (New York: Harper-Collins).

Gelles, Edith B. 1992. *Portia: The World of Abigail Adams* (Bloomington and Indianapolis: Indiana University Press).

Holton, Woody. 2009. *Abigail Adams: A Life* (New York: Free Press).

Jacobs, Diane. 2014. *Dear Abigail: The Intimate Lives and Revolutionary Ideas of Abigail Adams and Her Two Remarkable Sisters* (New York: Ballantine Books).

CHANTAL AKERMAN (1950–2015)

Lori Marso

Film *auteur* Chantal Akerman's *Jeanne Dielman, 23, quai du Commerce 1080 Bruxelles* premiered in 1975. Mostly silent and presented in what seems like "real time" proportions, the film centers on a Belgian widow going about her day—peeling potatoes, washing dishes, making coffee, brushing her hair, taking a bath, cleaning the bathtub, straightening linens on the bed, shopping for a button, breading veal cutlets, making meatloaf, putting evening meals on the table for her teenage son, caring for a neighbor's child, eating her lunch alone at the kitchen table, and servicing clients as a prostitute for a half hour on each afternoon of the three days that the film chronicles. The year of the film's release was, coincidentally, the same year that Silvia Federici published her influential essay, "Wages Against Housework." In this essay, Federici argued that "not only is wages for housework a revolutionary perspective, but it is the only revolutionary perspective from a feminist viewpoint" (1975, 16). That same year, Laura Mulvey published her influential, now-canonical and much criticized, essay, "Visual Pleasure and Narrative Cinema," arguing that classic Hollywood film conventions are predicated on, as well as reproduce, the male gaze as subject and the female body as object (Mulvey 1975). *Jeanne Dielman* seemed perfectly poised to answer both Mulvey and Federici. The film can be read as challenging cinema's male gaze in its breaking with Hollywood's conventions and instead utilizing long interior takes, very little dialogue, and a minimalist aesthetic that is narratively linear yet remarkably experimental. Some argue that it also provides visual content to rally us to Federici's feminist revolution by revealing the daily grind of housework on screen.

Born in Brussels, Belgium, to Holocaust survivors from Poland, Chantal Akerman dropped out of film school in the first term to create *Saute ma ville* (*Blow Up My Town*), a thirteen-minute film that centers on a young girl (played by Akerman) in her apartment. She puts away groceries, makes herself some noodles and eats them, tapes up the doorway, mops the floor, dances a little. Accompanied by her humming and singing, the film is a study in female exuberance, anxiety, boredom, and sensation, chronicling the young woman coming undone. She kills herself at the end by turning on the gas, leaning over the stove, and lighting a match. This was Akerman's first film, made when she was only 18 years old. The themes of female alienation and isolation, the break from conventional narratives, and the emphasis on ambiguity in meaning, dominate much of her *oeuvre*. Akerman shot over forty films in all, including several shorts as well as longer features such as *Je tu il elle* (1975), *News from Home* (1976), *One Day Pina Asked Me* (1983), *Night and Day* (1991), and her final film, *No Home Movie* (2015). *A Couch in New York* (1996) is her most commercial film, and stars William Hurt and Juliette Binoche. *Je tu il elle*, which she created in order to prove she could make a feature length film, contains a brilliant lesbian sex scene (also with one of the roles played by Akerman) that was made 38 years earlier and is far bolder than the much discussed lesbian sex in Abdellatif Kechiche's 2013 *Blue is the Warmest Color*.

No Home Movie features Akerman talking with her mother, Natalia, in her Belgian apartment. Akerman's mother survived Auschwitz, and while this history clearly weighs on the family, there is little direct talk of the horrific events she must have suffered and witnessed. Instead, we see the widow going about her days, eating, tidying up, Skyping with her daughter (Akerman) when she is off on set making films, and interacting with a caretaker as well as Chantal Akerman's sister, Sylviane. The film is stark, beautiful, and made especially poignant by the circumstances surrounding its release. Akerman's mother died shortly after the film was completed, and during the week of its premiere at the New York Film Festival in October 2015, Akerman herself was found dead in her Paris apartment, having taken her own life at the age of 65.

The formal mechanisms in *No Home Movie*, the long takes and sole focus on the interior of the home, as well as the subject matter, a widow living out her days in domestic space, echo the style and subject matter of Akerman's most famous film, *Jeanne Dielman*, the three and a half hour feature that she made when she was only 25 years old. In an interview included with the Criterion Collection release of *Jeanne Dielman*, Akerman says that she wanted to portray the rituals of housework that she witnessed her mother and aunts performing as a sort of replacement for the Eastern European Jewish rituals destroyed during World War II and that they longed to replicate. As the three days documented in Jeanne's life unfold, viewers come to see her tasks and her relationship to them not only as mandated and determined by oppression (her structural position as woman in the home) but also as providing pleasure (they are ritualistic, aesthetic, bodily, and even sensual).

By portraying the details and work patterns of her day as affirming or at least maintaining Jeanne's identity, Akerman's formal choices and narrative frame refuse the simple reading of her heroine's life that would show housework only as drudgery and the female protagonist as victim. Creating order in her day, and subsequently in her life, by tending to these jobs may keep more dangerous emotions and disorderly thoughts and feelings in check. Likewise, Akerman's film reminds us that although women are cast as "other" to male subjectivity, women's experiences nevertheless do not situate them *only* as victims. Akerman's camera captures the pleasurable, sensual, aesthetic, and satisfying dimensions of "women's" work in the way she films Jeanne massaging the meatloaf, tidying the bed sheets, and perfectly setting the table. Her filming of Jeanne's work draws our attention to its sensual dimensions, illuminating that some women get a sense of satisfaction, and even pleasure, from these tasks. We see her in iconic images, peeling potatoes, hovering over pots on the stove, straightening the cover on the bed, placing the money she earns from prostitution carefully in the pot on the dining room table. But after the second (there are three) client leaves the house, we notice a subtle but palpable shift in Jeanne's composure and routine. As she exits the bedroom, her bangs are just a bit out of place. This is the first time we see any small detail out of order in Jeanne's appearance or routine, and the small disruption portends impending chaos. Jeanne fails to return the lid to the pot in the middle of the dining room table where she keeps cash earned from her sexual service to clients. Minutes later, she lets the potatoes boil too long. Carrying the pot around the apartment searching for a place to flush the water, she looks like a madwoman, full of anxiety. As Ivone Margulies puts it:

> We see Jeanne from the kitchen as she appears by its door, and this first shift in the camera's habitual position announces the character's unraveling. In one of the funniest choreographies ever of domestic terror, Jeanne carries the pot around the house, not knowing what to do with this evidence of mistiming.
>
> (2009)

Asked directly about what precipitates the change in Jeanne Dielman's sense of composure and strict bodily comportment, Akerman replies that Jeanne has had her first ever orgasm with a john, and that this displaced sexual feeling sets her on a course wherein everything veers out of control (Interview, Criterion Collection). It is important to notice that it is a new and unexpected sexual feeling, the orgasm, which sets Jeanne on the path to murder. It is as if she were so used to unfeeling, to the deadening and deadened effects of her small and straightened life, or to the small bit of control that she had over her tasks, that this deadness and illusion of control kept danger away. For example, as she explains one night to her son, she never thought to marry for love, but only for a better situation. When her son asks her about sex, the mother cuts off the conversation, turns and abruptly puts out the light.

As viewers we feel the anticipation of bad things to come as Jeanne seems ever more unable to control her domestic sphere and keep dirt and grime, and its ally, chaos, at bay. Yet, she perseveres and finishes her chores ahead of time. As she sits in a chair with her feather duster, we see the anxiety building in her breathing and composed yet increasingly discomforting body. Nearing the end of the film, and the late afternoon hours of the third day, Jeanne receives her third client in her bedroom. This time again, the encounter produces an orgasm, and this time the viewer is privy to it. Jeanne gets up from the bed, slowly and methodically dresses, takes a scissors in her hand, walks over to the bed and stabs her client.

The next image, and indeed the last seven minutes of the film, are of Jeanne sitting at her dining room table, her blouse splashed with blood, as the light from the window flashes across the screen changing its contours as time passes. What are we to make of the distinctly disturbing feelings, the murderous agency, and the perverse version of action as presented on screen by Akerman? While the meaning of this film is deliberately ambiguous, *Jeanne Dielman*'s staging of the housewife-prostitute-murderess on screen is a rich resource for thinking feminist politics. Individual women living within the demands of femininity often rebel, exceeding imposed limits on their identities in various creative, and sometimes perverse or violent ways.

Simone de Beauvoir describes perversions turning to violence in the following passage in *The Second Sex*:

> Shut up in provincial monotony with a boorish husband, with no chance to act or to love, she is devoured by the feeling of her life's emptiness and uselessness; she tries to find compensation in romantic musings, in the flowers she surrounds herself with, in her clothes, her person: her husband interferes even with these games. She ends up trying to kill him.
>
> (1949, 515)

"She" is the "smiling Mme Beudet" (ibid.). Although Beauvoir does not reference director Germaine Dulac in this passage, she may have been referring to the 1922 short silent film considered by many to be one of the first feminist films.[1] Beauvoir goes on to say, "the symbolic behavior into which the wife escapes can bring about perversions, and these obsessions can lead to crime" (ibid.).

What Beauvoir alerts us to is the insight that even the tasks and situations that bind women to conditions of unfreedom provide surprising openings not only for pleasure, but also for agency, even if in perverted form, to emerge. Rather than deny or demean negative emotions, their somatic expressions, and women's assigned structural location and tasks, Akerman relentlessly shows them on screen in several of her films. Abandoning both moralistic and redemptive framings, Jeanne, for example, is depicted as neither victim nor as sovereign agent, and her strange behavior defies our ability to see her as a generic type. Instead, we are offered a singular character defying categorization, and a complex account of how the didactic poles (victim versus agent) operate. Dielman seems trapped somewhere between thwarted and clichéd agency. When she murders her john with scissors, she commits a too obvious, easily condemned and almost stereotyped violence; scissors are a quintessential feminine weapon, second only to knitting needles.

Note

1 See Williams (2014) for a reading of this film as a feminist classic that anticipates *Jeanne Dielman*.

Akerman's key films

1968. *Saute ma ville*.
1972. *Hotel Monterey*.
1975. *Je tu il elle*.
1975. *Jeanne Dielman, 23, quai du Commerce 1080 Bruxelles*.
1976. *News From Home*.
1978. *Les rendez-vous d'Anna*.
1983. *One Day Pina Asked Me*.
1996. *A Couch in New York*.
2015. *No Home Movie*.

Further reading

Akerman, Chantal, and Angela Martin. 1979. "Chantal Akerman's Films: A Dossier." *Feminist Review* 3: 24–47.

Beauvoir, Simone de. [1949] 2011. *The Second Sex*. Translated by Constance Borde and Sheila Malovany-Chevallier. New York: Vintage.

Federici, Silvia. [1975] 2012. "Wages against Housework." In *Revolution at Point Zero: Housework, Reproduction, and Feminist Struggle*, 15–22. Oakland, CA: PM.

Foster, Gwendolyne Audrey (ed.). 2003. *Identity and Memory: The Films of Chantal Akerman*. Carbondale: Southern Illinois University Press.

Margulies, Ivone. 1996. *Nothing Happens: Chantal Akerman's Hyperrealist Everyday*. Durham, NC: Duke University Press.
——. 2009. "A Matter of Time: *Jeanne Dielman, 23, quai du Commerce, 1080, Bruxelles*." *Current*, August 18. www.criterion.com/current/posts/1215-a-matter-of-time-jeanne-dielman-23-quai-du-commerce-1080-bruxelles
Marso, Lori. 2016. "Perverse Protests: Simone de Beauvoir on Pleasure and Danger, Resistance and Female Violence in Film." *SIGNS: Journal of Women in Culture and Society* 41(4).
McFadden, Cybelle H. 2014. *Gendered Frames, Embodied Cameras: Varda, Akerman, Cabrera, Calle, and Maiwenn*. Madison, NJ: Farleigh Dickinson University Press.
Mulvey, Laura. 1975. "Visual Pleasure and Narrative Cinema." *Screen* 16(6): 6–18.
Williams, Tami Michelle. 2014. *Germaine Dulac: A Cinema of Sensations*. Urbana: University of Illinois Press.

GLORIA EVANGELINA ANZALDÚA (1942–2004)

AnaLouise Keating

Born in south Texas to sixth-generation Mexican-American rancher-farmers, Gloria Anzaldúa had a rare hormonal disorder that triggered premature puberty, including monthly menses from the age of six. This physical condition marked her as a "freak" (Anzaldúa 2000, 91), profoundly shaping her philosophy and politics by fostering a deep empathy for other outsiders.[1] Anzaldúa's sensitivity to difference was heightened when she entered Texas' segregated educational system in 1948 and was treated as inferior because of her Mexican heritage. Despite this ostracism, Anzaldúa excelled in school. Believing that education provides an effective vehicle to enact progressive social change, she obtained her teaching certificate in college and, after graduating, worked in the Texas public school system, teaching students from preschool through high school while battling the same racist system she had experienced. During summers she attended graduate school, earning a master's degree in English and Education. In 1973 Anzaldúa moved to Indiana to work as the state's liaison between the public school system and migrant farm workers' children; and in 1974 she entered the doctoral program in Comparative Literature at the University of Texas, Austin. Throughout the 1970s Anzaldúa also participated in numerous political movements, including the Chicano movement, the farm workers movement, the anti-war movement, the civil rights movement, and the women's movement.

Disillusioned by the limitations in collective politics and the racism, sexism, and classism in formal education, Anzaldúa decided that social transformation must begin with the individual. Because she believed that art (which offers revolutionary, innovative perspectives and intimately impacts each person) provides the most effective pathway for radical social change, she resolved to devote her life to her writing and in 1977 withdrew from her doctoral program at the University of Texas, moved to northern California, and immersed herself in the San Francisco literary scene. Despite severe economic hardships, she took only part-time jobs in order to hone her literary skills.[2] In 1979, after experiencing repeated tokenization and erasure because of her Chicana working-class status, she began editing a collection of writings by diverse women feminists of color and invited Cherríe Moraga to join her. Their groundbreaking multigenre anthology, *This Bridge Called My Back: Writings by Radical Women of Color* (1981), made a lasting impact on U.S. feminism, demonstrating that feminism is not—and never has been—an exclusively white, middle-class movement. *This Bridge* also introduced the term "women of color" into feminist discourse, underscoring the diversity among women of color. Particularly important, for Anzaldúa, was the book's final section, "El Mundo Zurdo: The Vision," which moves beyond identity politics to showcase an inclusionary politics of spirit, or what she later named "spiritual activism." At a time when many social activists emphasized separatism, joining only with others in their particular identity-based groups, Anzaldúa offered an alternative:

> Third World women, lesbians, feminists, and feminist-oriented men of all colors are banding and bonding together to right that balance. Only *together* can we be a force. I see us as a network of kindred spirits, a kind of family.

> (1981, 208)

This emphasis on multiplicity and radical inclusiveness is a hallmark of Anzaldúa's work. Whereas most feminist theorists prioritize or focus exclusively on gender, Anzaldúa insists that gender must be examined relationally, in dialogue with other identity components, like culture, race/ethnicity, class, geography, health, sexuality, and religion/spirituality. She develops an expansive model of feminism that does not automatically center sexism but instead flexibly addresses a wide range of social-justice issues while challenging normative identity categories. In her most widely acclaimed book, *Borderlands/La frontera:The New Mestiza* (1987),Anzaldúa positions herself as a queer tejana-Chicana and thus emphasizes that lesbian identity cannot be defined exclusively in Anglo-American terms and that Chicano identity cannot be defined exclusively in heterosexual or male terms. A hybrid text that shifts seamlessly among prose, poetry, memoir, history, social protest, philosophy, and myth, *Borderlands* enacts a literary multiplicity that expands previous scholarship on border issues, the Borderlands, ethnic/gender/sexual identities, and conventional literary forms. Anzaldúa's innovative code-switching (transitions, sometimes within a single sentence or paragraph, from standard to working-class English, Chicano Spanish, Tex-Mex, Nahuatl) made a lasting impact on literary discourse.

Anzaldúa's second edited collection, *Making Face, Making Soul/Haciendo Caras: Creative and Critical Perspectives by Women of Color* (1990), further expands her attention to inclusive alliance-building. Its innovative combinations of poetry, fiction, scholarly essays, and memoir offer new models for coalition-building among non-academic and academic social-justice activists. In the preface, Anzaldúa rejects the elitism in mainstream critical theory and underscores the importance of inventing inclusionary, expansive methods—"mestizaje theories" that "create new categories for those of us left out or pushed out of the existing ones" (1990, xxvi). Her third collection, *this bridge we call home: radical visions for transformation* (Anzaldúa and Keating 2002), is even more radically inclusive, generating provocative visions of women-of-color consciousness for the twenty-first century. While centering women-of-color authors and theories, *this bridge* includes work by men, transpeople, and white women who have been profoundly impacted by women-of-color perspectives; by so doing, it develops transformational identity politics.[3] Unlike many feminist and social-justice theories, which define identity through an exclusionary logic, Anzaldúa adopts a radically inclusive approach. As she explains in her preface, "Many of us identify with groups and social positions not limited to our ethnic, racial, religious, class, gender, or national classifications. Though most people self-define by what they exclude, we define who we are by what we include" (2002, 3). Anzaldúa does not ignore how gender, ethnicity/race, class, sexuality, and other identity markers shape human life; however, she maintains that these categories are not as useful as they were in the twentieth century. She invites readers to rethink human identity in more expansive terms that embrace relational differences and complex commonalities.

Anzaldúa's theory-praxis of spiritual activism is both inspiration for and culmination of her inclusionary politics. While Anzaldúa did not invent the term "spiritual activism," she introduced it into feminist theory and interdisciplinary fields like Women's and Gender Studies, Chicana/o studies, and Ethnic studies—offering an alternative to the academy's unacknowledged secularity and normative whiteness.[4] Typically, "spiritual" implies an other-worldly, inward-looking perspective that ignores social injustices; and "activism" implies outward-directed interaction with the physical world—the exact world that spirituality seems to deny or downplay. Yet for Anzaldúa, the two are inseparable: spiritual/physical, inner/outer, and individual/collective constitute a larger, interwoven whole that can be harnessed to energize social change. She defines "spiritual activism" as an embodied, entirely political endeavor distinct from organized religions (which rely on leaders, texts, rules, and other externally-imposed authorities) and from mainstream "New Age"[5] spiritualities (which focus almost entirely on individual desires and ignore oppressive social structures).

Spiritual activism locates authority within each individual by synergistically linking self-change with social transformation. As Anzaldúa asserts in "La Prieta,"

> I believe that by changing ourselves we change the world, that traveling El Mundo Zurdo path is the path of a two-way movement—a going deep into the self and an expanding out into the world, a simultaneous recreation of the self and a reconstruction of society.
>
> (Moraga and Anzaldúa 1981, 208)

Self-change is not an end in itself but is rather part of a larger process empowering activists to effectively intervene in and transform injustice.

Anzaldúa's spiritual activism is a visionary, experientially-based ontology, epistemology, and ethics. Drawing on indigenous Mesoamerican philosophies, Eastern thought, psychic literature, and empirical experiences, Anzaldúa posits a cosmic force that embodies itself throughout—and as—all existence: "Spirit exists in everything; therefore God, the divine, is in everything ... it's in the tree, the swamp, the sea ... Some people call it 'God;' some call it the 'creative force,' whatever. It's in everything" (2000, 100).[6] By thus positing a spirit-inflected monism, Anzaldúa develops and enacts a metaphysics of interconnectedness and a relational epistemology that facilitate participatory knowledge production, or what she variously theorizes as "la facultad" (1987), "mestiza consciousness" (1987), and "conocimiento" (2015).

Anzaldúa offers the most extensive discussion of spiritual activism in her posthumously published *Light in the Dark/Luz en lo oscuro: Rewriting Identity, Spirituality, Reality* (2015), which distills her ontological and epistemological investigations into a sophisticated aesthetics of transformation. As in her previous work, Anzaldúa insists on a common identity factor which, when acknowledged, can inspire the development of new tactics for survival, resistance, and transformation on all levels. But in *Light in the Dark* she takes this commonality even further, developing a cosmic identity politics that includes but goes beyond human life:

> Your identity has roots you share with all people and other beings—spirit, feeling, and body comprise a greater identity category. The body is rooted in the earth, la tierra itself. You meet ensoulment in trees, in woods, in streams.
>
> (2015, 140)

This shared identity makes possible Anzaldúa's inclusionary model of alliance-building and identity formation, described above.

Notes

1 Anzaldúa discusses the impact of her early menstruation in the final interview in her *Interviews/Entrevistas* (2000).
2 Much of Anzaldúa's work from this time remains unpublished. Her manuscripts are located in the Gloria Evangelina Anzaldúa Papers, in the Nettie Lee Benson Library at the University of Texas, Austin.
3 See Keating 2013.
4 See Crowley 2012.
5 Typically the phrase "New Age" is used to signal pseudo-intellectual movements that appropriate indigenous cultures, focus exclusively on the individual, and/or adopt an entirely consumerist mentality. While some versions of New Age thought follow this trajectory, others do not.
6 See also Alma Levine, "Champion of the Spirit: Anzaldúa's Critique of Rationalist Epistemology" in Keating 2005.

Anzaldúa's major writings

1987/2014. *Borderlands/La Frontera: The New Mestiza*. San Francisco: Spinsters/Aunt Lute.
1990. (ed.). *Making Face, Making Soul/Haciendo Caras: Creative and Critical Perspectives by Women of Color*. San Francisco: Aunt Lute.
1993. *Friends from the Other Side/Amigos del Otro Lado*. San Francisco: Children's Book Press.

1995. *Prietita and the Ghost Woman/Prietita y La Llorona*. San Francisco: Children's Book Press.

2000. *Interviews/Entrevistas*. Ed. AnaLouise Keating. New York: Routledge.

2009. *The Gloria Anzaldúa Reader*. Ed. AnaLouise Keating. Durham, NC: Duke University Press.

2015. *Light in the Dark/Luz en Lo Oscuro: Rewriting Identity, Spirituality, Reality*. Ed. AnaLouise Keating. Durham, NC: Duke University Press.

2002. Anzaldúa, Gloria and AnaLouise Keating (eds.). *This bridge we call home: radical visions for transformation*. New York: Routledge.

1981/2015. Moraga, Cherríe and Gloria Anzaldúa (eds.). *This Bridge Called My Back: Writings by Radical Women of Color*. New York: Persephone Press.

Further reading

Alarcón, Norma. 1998. "Chicana Feminism: In the Tracks of 'The' Native Woman." In *Living Chicana Theory*. Ed. Carla Trujillo. Berkeley: Third Woman Press. 371–82.

—. 2013. "Anzaldúan Textualities: A Hermeneutic of the Self and the Coyolxauhqui Imperative." In *El Mundo Zurdo 3: Selected Works from the 2012 Meeting of the Society for the Study of Gloria Anzaldúa*. Eds. Larissa M. Mercado-López, Sonia Saldívar-Hull, Antonia Castañed. San Francisco: Aunt Lute. 189–206.

Barnard, Ian. 1997. "Gloria Anzaldúa Queer Mestisaje." *MELUS* 22(1): 35–53.

Bost, Suzanne. 2010. *Encarnación: Illness and Body Politics in Chicana Literature*. New York: Fordham University Press.

Crowley, Karlyn. 2012. "Secularity." In *Rethinking Women's and Gender Studies*. Eds. Catherine M. Orr, Ann Braithwaite, Diane Lichtenstein. New York: Routledge. 240–57.

Delgadillo, Theresa. 2011. *Spiritual Mestizaje: Religion, Gender, Race, and Nation in Contemporary Chicana Narratives*. Durham, NC: Duke University Press.

Keating, AnaLouise. 1996. *Women Reading Women Writing: Self-Invention in Paula Gunn Allen, Gloria Anzaldúa, and Audre Lorde*. Philadelphia: Temple University Press.

—. 2008. "'I'm a citizen of the universe:' Gloria Anzaldúa's Spiritual Activism as Catalyst for Social Change." *Feminist Studies* 34(1/2): 53–69.

—. 2013. *Transformation Now! Towards a Post-Oppositional Politics of Change*. Urbana: University of Illinois Press.

Keating, AnaLouise (ed.). 2005. *EntreMundos/AmongWorlds: New Perspectives on Gloria Anzaldúa*. New York: Palgrave Macmillan.

Keating, AnaLouise and Gloria Gonzalez-Lopez (eds.). 2011. *Bridging: How and Why Gloria Anzaldúa's Life and Work Transformed Our Own*. Austin: University of Texas Press.

Yarbro-Bejarano, Yvonne. 1994. "Gloria Anzaldúa's *Borderlands/La Frontera*: Cultural Studies, 'Difference,' and the Non-Unitary Subject." *Cultural Critique* 28: 5–28.

MARY ASTELL (1666–1731)

Patricia Springborg

Mary Astell, famous for her rhetorical questions concerning the enslavement of women, is both typical and atypical of early modern feminists. She is quite typical in coming from a middle to lower middle class family (her father was a journeyman with a diversified North of England company). Although one of the finest stylists of the English language, she is also typical in being largely self-taught (her clergyman uncle provided early tuition) and in profiting from membership in a circle of educated women, often of higher social status. She is typical in engaging in 'the battle between the ancients and the moderns', being hostile to classical education in Greek and Latin as a gate-keeper for elite culture from which women, who were not typically schooled, were excluded (in this way she is similar to Judith Drake, whose *Essay in Defence of the Female Sex* of 1696 was often taken to be Astell's work, including by Locke). She is typical in being Tory rather than Whig (the long Tory ascendancy of the eighteenth century looked unbroken going into the future and early modern feminists were not going to waste their time on what they saw as a lost cause). She is also typical in being involved in women's education (her first work, like that of Mary Wollstonecraft, was on women's education, and Astell's *Serious Proposal* (1694, 1697) succeeded in getting Princess, later Queen, Anne's approval, and very nearly her financial support).

Mary Astell is atypical, however, both in the range of her work and its wide contemporary reception, often extending to several editions, and sometimes the subject of lampooning and plagiarism. Beginning with a theological discourse with the famous Platonist John Norris,

Letters Concerning the Love of God (1695), and concluding with a theological work significant in the ecclesiology of the Church of England, *The Christian Religion as Profess'd by a Daughter of the Church of England* (1705), her corpus includes philosophical treatises important to the reception of Descartes, Malebranche and Locke; a history of the English CivilWar pressing the Tory view; and a range of political pamphlets with impressive print runs that featured in the looming debate on Toleration.

Astell in her lifetime was equally famous as a political pamphleteer. Among the first to provide a published critique of Locke's *Two Treatises of Government* (1689), in her *Reflections upon Marriage* of 1700, she also undertook a critique of the Whig version of history in *An Impartial Inquiry into the Causes of Rebellion and Civil War … and Vindication of the Royal Martyr*, of 1704. From 1703 to 1709, Astell had been engaged as a High Church Tory pamphleteer, producing two pamphlets important in the debate on the occasional conformity of dissenters: *A Fair Way with the Dissenters and their Patrons*, addressed to Daniel Defoe, and *Moderation truly Stated*, both of 1704. In *Bart'lemy Fair, or an Enquiry after Wit in which due Respect is Had to a Letter Concerning Enthusiasm* of 1709, Astell closed her career as a writer with an elegant philosophical response to Anthony Ashley Cooper, the third earl of Shaftesbury and grandson of Locke's mentor, the first Earl, whose *Letter Concerning Enthusiasm* (1708) it targets.

To summarize, the subjects Astell treated ranged, in chronological order, from, first, philosophical questions concerning human agency and the capacity for personal salvation that belong to the reception of Descartes and concern the standing of the Malebranchistes, Port Royal Jansenists and Cambridge Platonists; to, second, practical questions of women's education and the possibility of establishing a female academy along the lines of the Port Royal School; to, third, a critique of the *gentrification* of courtship and marriage practices which increasingly enslaved women in the private realm, just as the emergence of the party system around the Whigs and Tories was opening up politics in the public sphere; to, fourth, the political question of a Tory, as opposed to Whig, version of the English Civil War, as establishing precedents for the regime change that took place in 1688–1689; and to, fifth, the constitutional issues of religious toleration and occasional conformity for dissenters. No early modern feminist to my knowledge exhibited range like this, and no modern one either, for that matter.

It was as the promoter of women's causes, and particularly women's education, that Astell made her name. Locke's library contained her *Reflections upon Marriage* which, like her *Serious Proposal*, ran to five editions in her day. Daniel Defoe's 'An Academy for Women' in his *Essay upon Projects* (1697) was modelled on Astell's *Serious Proposal*, and the Anglican Bishop and philosopher, George Berkeley, paid her the compliment of plagiarizing some hundred pages of it in *The Ladies Library*, a compilation of works on women's conduct and education ostensibly 'written by a lady' but, in fact collected by Berkeley and published in 1714 by Richard Steele to promote Berkeley's grand educational project of 1729–30 to found a college in Bermuda for the joint education of the English settlers and 'natives' in the liberal arts and sciences. Steele redoubled the insult by lampooning Astell's plans for a women's college and mocking her as Madonella in *Tatler*, numbers 32 and 63. Thought at the time to be the work of Jonathan Swift, it was almost certainly the work of Steele, as Astell points out in the Preface to the second edition of *Bart'lemy Fair* (1722), given its timing, 'a little after [the first edition of] The Enquiry [*Bart'lemy Fair*] appear'd' in 1709.

Nor was Astell spared by women. Susan Centlivre satirized her in her play *The Basset Table* (1706) as Valeria, 'that little She-philosopher … founding a College for the Study of Philosophy where none but women should be admitted' (1761, 1: 210). And, as late as 1847, Lilia, heroine of Alfred Lord Tennyson's *The Princess*, dreams of a women's college cut off from male society. Astell's female academy was later famously lampooned in Gilbert and Sullivan's *Princess Ida*, widely recognized as being based on Tennyson's poem. Over its gates the inscription would read, 'Let no man enter on pain of death', a deliberately truncated version of the famous inscription that adorned the doors of Plato's Academy, 'Let No Man Enter Here Unless He Study Geometry'.

More serious than the satires that she did not live to see, were the attacks Astell endured in her lifetime. Damaris Masham, daughter of the Cambridge Platonist Ralph Cudworth and Locke's confidante, in her *Discourse Concerning the Love of God* (1705), echoing the title of the Astell-Norris discourse, which had in fact been attributed to her, assailed Astell's *Serious Proposal* as leading to 'as wild as an Enthusiasm as any that has been yet seen; and which can end in nothing but Monasteries and Hermitages; with all those Sottish and Wicked Superstitions which have accompanied them' (1705, 120).

Perhaps precisely because she was a High Church Tory, Astell was able to point to the absurdity of bourgeois proto-liberal rhetoric that was gaining traction as the market economy grew. How dare Milton and Locke, among those who entrenched the subjugation of women in the private sphere, trumpet freedom from arbitrary power in the public sphere?

For if Arbitrary Power is evil in itself, and an improper Method of Governing Rational and Free Agents it ought not to be Practis'd any where; Nor is it less, but rather more mischievous in Families than in Kingdoms, by how much *100000* Tyrants are worse than one

she declared in the *Reflections*. 'What tho' a Husband can't deprive a Wife of Life without being responsible to the Law, he may however do what is much more grievous to a generous Mind, render Life miserable, for which she has no Redress.' Yet, 'not Milton himself wou'd cry up Liberty to poor Female Slaves, or plead for the Lawfulness of Resisting a Private Tyranny' (1996, 17, 18, 46–47). Quoting Locke's *Second Treatise of Government* directly, as indicated by the italics, she goes on to put her famous rhetorical question: '*If all Men are born free*, how is it that all Women are born slaves? as they must be if the being subjected to the *inconstant, uncertain, unknown, arbitrary Will* of Men, be the *perfect Condition of Slavery?*' (1996, 18–19).

Astell as an early modern feminist and social commentator risked her reputation to venture something new: a fine sociological sensibility for the social consequences of gentrification accompanying the expansion of market society, the rise of the stock market, and increasing disposable income among the middle classes,[1] exposed in her critique of courtship and marriage practices in *Reflections upon Marriage*; and, throughout her work, in a general sensitivity to the political consequences of the public-private divide, and the battle between the sexes that characterized it.

Note

1 For the rise of market society in this period see Eisenberg 2013.

Astell's major writings

1694, 1697. *A Serious Proposal to the Ladies, Parts I and II. Wherein a Method is Offer'd for the Improvement of their Minds.*

1695. *Letters Concerning the Love of God between the Author of the Proposal to the Ladies and Mr. John Norris: Wherein his late Discourse, Shewing that it Ought to Be Intire and Exclusive of All Other Loves, is Further Cleared and Justified.*

1700, 1706. *Some Reflections upon Marriage, Occasion'd by the Duke and Duchess of Mazarine's Case; which is also Considered.*

1704a. *A Fair Way with the Dissenters and their Patrons.*

1704b. *An Impartial Inquiry into the Causes of Rebellion and Civil War … and Vindication of the Royal Martyr.*
1704c. *Moderation Truly Stated.*
1705. *The Christian Religion as Profess'd by a Daughter of the Church of England.*
1709. *Bart'lemy Fair, or an Enquiry after Wit in which due Respect is Had to a Letter Concerning Enthusiasm.*
1996. *Mary Astell (1666–1731): Political Writings, Cambridge Texts in the History of Political Thought,* ed. Patricia Springborg. Cambridge: Cambridge University Press.
1997. *Mary Astell: 'A Serious Proposal to the Ladies'*, ed. Patricia Springborg. London: Pickering & Chatto.
2002. *Mary Astell's A Serious Proposal to the Ladies, Parts I (1694) and II (1697),* ed. Patricia Springborg. Peterborough, Ontario: Broadview Press (enlarged edition).

Further reading

Broad, J., 2003. *Women Philosophers of the Seventeenth Century.* Cambridge: Cambridge University Press.
Centlivre, Susanna, 1761. *The Works of the Celebrated Mrs Centlivre* (3 vols.). London.
Defoe, Daniel, 1697. *An Essay upon Projects.* London.
Drake, Judith, 1696. *Essay in Defence of the Female Sex.* London.
Eisenberg, Christiane, 2013. *The Rise of Market Society in England, 1066–1800,* trans. Deborah Cohen. New York and Oxford: Berghahn.
Kolbrener, W. and M. Michelson (eds.), 2007. *Mary Astell: Reason, Gender, Faith.* Burlington, VT: Ashgate.
Masham, Damaris, 1705. *Discourse Concerning the Love of God.* London.
Perry, Ruth, 1986. *The Celebrated Mary Astell.* Chicago: University of Chicago Press.
Springborg, Patricia, 1995. 'Mary Astell (1666–1731), Critic of Locke', *American Political Science Review* 89(3): 621–33.
Springborg, Patricia, 1998a. 'Astell, Masham and Locke, Religion and Politics', in Hilda Smith (ed.), *Women Writers and the Early Modern British Political Tradition,* 105–25. Cambridge: Cambridge University Press.
Springborg, Patricia, 1998b. 'Mary Astell and John Locke', in Steven Zwicker (ed.), *The Cambridge Companion to English Literature, 1650 to 1750,* 276–306. Cambridge: Cambridge University Press.
Springborg, Patricia, 2002. 'Mary Astell, Critic of the Marriage Contract/Social Contract Analogue', in Anita Pacheco (ed.), *Companion to Early Modern Women's Writing,* 216–28. Oxford: Blackwell.

Springborg, Patricia, 2005. *Mary Astell, Theorist of Freedom from Domination.* Cambridge: Cambridge University Press.

Springborg, Patricia, 2008. 'Astell (1666–1731)', in Andrew Bailey, Samantha Brennan, Will Kymlicka (eds.), *The Broadview Anthology of Social and Political Thought*, Vol. 1, 564–74. Toronto: Broadview Press.

SIMONE DE BEAUVOIR (1908–1986)

Lori Marso

Beauvoir is best known for *The Second Sex*, the seven hundred plus page *magnum opus* she wrote in 1949 that has been recently retranslated in a new English language edition (2010, paperback in 2011).[1] Beauvoir is likewise renowned for never marrying (she was a lifelong partner of Jean Paul Sartre), never having children, and for most of her life living alone to enjoy a schedule of writing, performed mostly in public, particularly in cafés. Less discussed in the secondary literature is her intellectual and political collaboration with contemporaries such as Richard Wright, Frantz Fanon, Violette Leduc, Claude Lanzmann, Nelson Algren, and Albert Camus. Beauvoir travelled extensively—to the United States, Mexico, the Soviet Union, North Africa, Cuba, Brazil, China, Japan, Egypt, and Israel—and in each place was involved in political conversations, and offered support to opposition and revolutionary movements. Her activism included opposition to France's war in Algeria, participation on the 1966 Russell Tribunal to bring war crimes charges against the United States' actions in Vietnam, work with young French Maoists in the 1970s, and penning and signing the Manifesto of the 343 for abortion rights in France in 1971.

Beauvoir never claimed to be a political activist or a philosopher, in spite of her extensive involvement in politics and her reworking of several central philosophical themes within existentialism, particularly freedom and ambiguity. She preferred instead to be known simply as a writer. Although enormously successful as a writer (she won the Prix Goncourt for *The Mandarins* in 1954), she was often described as being in Jean Paul Sartre's shadow. When she came to the United States on a four-month lecture tour in 1947, for example, a *Vogue* article said she was "the leading disciple of Jean-Paul Sartre's *Existentialist* philosophy" (Bauer 2015, 37). As several feminist philosophers have shown, however, Simone de Beauvoir was always the author of her own work (and had a hand in Sartre's as well) and indeed, her own life (she considered her autobiography a creative construction).

Beauvoir was a prolific writer in several genres: essays, novels, a play, short stories, philosophy, political theory, and sociology. These genres cover topics ranging from: gender, race, solitude, loneliness, old age, war, violence, vengeance, and the ethical responsibility of writers, to name a few. Her multiple essays were sometimes responses to historical circumstances, such as "An Eye for an Eye," on the trial of Robert Brasillach, executed for treason for revealing the hiding places of Jews during the Occupation. Other times they were on surprising topics such as the ethical perspective revealed in the Marquis de Sade's (considered to be misogynist) sexual practices. One of her most popular essays explores the depictions of femininity in film images of Brigitte Bardot. Although most of Beauvoir's writings have long been available in English (and several languages), The Beauvoir Series (a collaborative international project to translate into English several of Beauvoir's untranslated writings and re-translate others) is being published in seven volumes by the University of Illinois Press under the direction of Margaret A. Simons and Sylvie Le Bon de Beauvoir, adopted daughter and literary executor of Beauvoir.

The thread that runs through all of Beauvoir's writing is her emphasis on the central ethical and political importance of freedom. By freedom, she does not mean the sovereignty and power of the unencumbered individual. Influenced by Marxist and Maoist political movements, and deeply engaged with historical-political circumstances during her life in France, Beauvoir believed that freedom is experienced rather than utilized or owned, and it is realized only in encounter with others rather than in isolation. As recorded in her autobiography and novels, sometimes in frustration but other times in acceptance or even exhilaration, Beauvoir recognized that there is *always* an "other" (whether a person, object, ontological fact, or historical circumstance), and indeed several varieties and forms of others, in interaction and relationship with one's self. She sees these encounters as the central fact of existence. To fantasize complete independence and autonomy is a dangerous denial of the ontological fact of ambiguity, that we are both self and other, transcendence and immanence, free and trapped by circumstances, at the same time. To deny others the possibility of freedom by freezing them in a position of immanence, such as is done to women when they are associated only with home and hearth and to the colonized when spoken of as lesser than Europeans or as naturally suited to manual tasks, is to participate in the evil of oppression. According to Beauvoir, the situation of women provides a good example for disclosing one particular aspect of freedom's relationship to ambiguity: as humans, we are subject not only to the constraints of embodiment universally—we age, we get sick, we die—but some individuals and groups are interpreted through biological "data" infused with political and social meaning. As Beauvoir says of women: "[a woman is] like all humans, an autonomous freedom, [but] she discovers and chooses herself in a world where men force her to assume herself as Other" (2011, 17).

This primary emphasis on freedom has led some scholars to mistakenly associate Beauvoir with liberal individualism. However, Beauvoir's writings systematically challenge liberal individualism, bourgeois fantasies of authority and dominance, and white superiority. She says, for example, in an interview in 1980, speaking of Margaret Thatcher, Prime Minister of England, and Françoise Giroud, former Secretary of State for Women's Questions in France, that, "a woman in a position of power comes to resemble a man" (Schwarzer 1984, 97). In *Memoirs of a Dutiful Daughter* (1958), she links her own freedom, a freedom to study and pursue her path as an intellectual, to the death of her best friend, Zaza, a woman who died, as Beauvoir sees it, due to the suffocating strictures of bourgeois and Catholic beliefs about gender. In her public intervention into the case of Djamila Boupacha, a young Algerian woman tortured and raped by French soldiers during the Algerian War of Resistance, she theorizes the intersections of gender, class, race, colonial encounters, and state violence all at the same time. Beauvoir consistently made clear that she considered emancipation for women to be a collective, rather than an individual, effort. In the introduction to the 2015 collection, *Simone de Beauvoir: Feminist Writings*, Margaret Simons cites the documents within as evidence of "Beauvoir's decades-long feminist engagement" (2015, 10), and draws attention to the fact that Beauvoir argued that women "must fight together for their rights" (2015, 11).

Beauvoir became a writer to record her awakening to the world and its experiences, and to advocate on behalf of the oppressed. As she explains in "My Experience as a Writer":

> I got the desire to write very young, at fourteen or fifteen years of age … I endured the world which was given to me sometimes with joy, often with revolt or boredom; I wanted to make it mine in order to justify it in some way. So I thought I had everything to say: the whole world, life, everything. In my youthful, adolescent diaries, at eighteen, nineteen years old, this leitmotif appears over and over: I will say everything, I have everything to say.
>
> (Simons and Timmerman 2015, 282–83)

The Second Sex began from this need to give expression to her experience of being a woman. As she recalls in her autobiographical *Force of Circumstance*: "Wanting to talk about myself, I became aware that to do so I should first have to describe the condition of woman in general" (1968, 195). When she began to document what she calls, in phenomenological terms, women's "lived experiences," she started to see that young girls, although not biologically destined to have a diminished grasp on freedom, are culturally, politically, psychologically, and sociologically shaped to "become women," the second and inferior sex.

In writing *The Second Sex*, Beauvoir makes an appeal to readers to undo the process of becoming women. In Volume I, she interrupts the male interlocutors who shape (but cannot determine) women's lives. She features the voices of male authority figures—scientists, historians, psychoanalysts, philosophers, playwrights, theologians, and novelists—declaiming on the roots, legitimacy, and meanings of sexual difference. This rhetorical strategy of the first volume, inviting men to speak to each other while undermining their right to control conversation, has confused some readers. Beauvoir warns us: "It is noteworthy that physiologists and biologists all use a more or less finalistic language merely because they ascribe meaning [in this case, gendered hierarchical meaning] to vital phenomena; we will use their language" (2011, 26). From the perspective of the later French feminist work on *l'écriture féminine*, this strategy—"we will use their language"—may seem retrograde. But the two strategies together—using their language and developing our own—are what make up feminist resistance and imagination. Beauvoir does both.

What we learn in Volume II when Beauvoir includes women in the conversation to talk about their own bodies and experiences, is no surprise: women are too often drawn into the web of male dominance by the demand to "*be* women, *stay* women, *become* women" (2011, 3, my emphasis). But as readers, when we meet famous and minor characters from fiction, authors of autobiographies, Beauvoir's friends and acquaintances, actresses, prostitutes, wives, mothers, girlfriends, girls and friends—sharing their stories of becoming women, we are invited to see the world in a new way, and to take up the project(s) of unbecoming women.

Note

1 Simone de Beauvoir's writings and the way she lived her life have inspired countless women. See the documentary, *Daughters of de Beauvoir*, produced by Penny Foster (Filmmaker's Library, 1990) for an excellent introduction to the themes of *The Second Sex*, a synopsis of important events in

Beauvoir's life as narrated in her autobiography, video images of Beauvoir's funeral in 1986, and stories of the impact that Beauvoir's life and work have had on ordinary women and famous feminist writers such as Marge Piercy, Kate Millett, Ann Oakley, and Eva Figes. See also Beauvoir's conversation with Alice Schwarzer, "*The Second Sex*: Thirty Years On," in Schwarzer (1984) for Beauvoir's comments on the letters she has received from women who see themselves in the book, and are transformed.

Beauvoir's major writings

[1943] 1984. *She Came to Stay*. London: Fontana.

[1948] 2000. *America Day By Day*. Trans. Carol Cosman. Berkeley: University of California Press.

1948. *The Ethics of Ambiguity*. New York: Citadel.

[1949] 2011. *The Second Sex*. Trans. Constance Borde and Sheila Malovany-Chevallier. New York: Vintage.

[1949]. 2004. "An Eye for an Eye." In Margaret A. Simons (ed.), *Philosophical Writings*. Urbana: University of Illinois Press: 245–260.

[1952] 2012. "Must We Burn Sade?" In Margaret A. Simons (ed.), *Political Writings*. Urbana: University of Illinois Press: 44–101.

[1954] 1999. *The Mandarins: A Novel*. New York: W. W. Norton.

[1958] 2005. *Memoirs of a Dutiful Daughter*. New York: Harper Perennial.

1959. *Brigitte Bardot and the Lolita Syndrome*. London: The New English Library.

[1960] 1965. *Prime of Life: The Autobiography of Simone de Beauvoir*. New York: Penguin.

1962. *Djamila Boupacha*. New York: Macmillan Company.

[1963] 1968. *Force of Circumstance, II: Hard Times 1952–1962*. New York: Penguin.

[1966] 2011. "My Experience as a Writer." In Margaret A. Simons (ed.), *The Useless Mouths and Other Literary Writings*. Urbana: University of Illinois Press: 282–301.

[1967] 1969. *The Woman Destroyed*. New York: Pantheon.

[1970] 1972. *Old Age* (translated as *The Coming of Age*). Trans. Patrick O'Brian. New York: Putnam.

[1981] 1984. *Adieux: A Farewell to Sartre*. New York: Pantheon.

Further reading

Bair, Deidre. 1990. *Simone de Beauvoir: A Biography*. New York: Summit.
Bauer, Nancy. 2001. *Simone de Beauvoir, Philosophy, and Feminism*. New York: Columbia University Press.

— 2015. "Introduction to Femininity: The Trap." In Margaret A. Simons (ed.), *Simone de Beauvoir: Feminist Writings.* Urbana: University of Illinois Press: 37–41.

Kruks, Sonia. 2012. *Simone de Beauvoir and the Politics of Ambiguity.* Oxford: Oxford University Press.

Marso, Lori. 2012. "Thinking Politically with Simone de Beauvoir in *The Second Sex." theory&event* 15(2).

Marso, Lori and Patricia Moynagh (eds.). 2006. *Simone de Beauvoir's Political Thinking.* Urbana: University of Illinois Press.

Moi, Toril. 2000. *What is a Woman? And Other Essays.* Oxford: Oxford University Press.

Schwarzer, Alice. 1984. *After* The Second Sex: *Conversations with Simone de Beauvoir.* New York: Pantheon.

Simons, Margaret A. and Marybeth Timmerman (eds.). 2015. *Simone de Beauvoir: Feminist Writings.* Urbana: University of Illinois Press.

JUDITH BUTLER (1956–)

Birgit Schippers

One might wonder what use 'opening up possibilities' finally is, but no one who has understood what it is to live in the social world as what is 'impossible', illegible, unrealizable, unreal, and illegitimate is likely to pose that question.

Judith Butler

If feminism's key concern lies with 'opening up possibilities' that make life liveable, then scholars and students of feminist theory must engage with the work of the American philosopher Judith Butler. Her ideas have influenced the direction of feminist theorizing over the last twenty-five years, and the conceptual apparatus associated with her oeuvre, especially her assertion of gender as performative, permeates the vocabulary of contemporary feminist discourse, and continues to shape the agenda of feminist scholarship. Butler's significance as a feminist thinker is underpinned by a distinguished academic career: she is Maxine Elliot Professor in the Department of Rhetoric and Comparative Literature and Co-Director of the Program of Critical Theory at the University of California, Berkeley, and she holds the Hannah Arendt Chair of Philosophy at the European Graduate School in Switzerland. Previous academic appointments include two short periods at Wesleyan and Johns Hopkins universities. Butler is the recipient of many prizes and honours, including the Adorno Prize, awarded by the City of Frankfurt, Germany, for outstanding performances in the fields of philosophy, music, theatre and film, and the French Chevalier in the Order of Arts and Letters. A regular contributor to public debates, Butler served as Chair of the International Gay and Lesbian Human Rights Commission; she is an outspoken critic of Israeli policies in the occupied territories, and of US foreign policy in the Middle East.

Trained in the continental tradition of modern and contemporary philosophy, Butler's work draws on a broad range of poststructuralist and phenomenological thought. Hegel and Foucault are key interlocutors for her writings, while significant feminist influences include Simone de Beauvoir, Monique Wittig, and Gayle Rubin. She also engages with the works of Jacques Derrida and Sigmund Freud, and more recently, with Theodor Adorno (see Butler 2005), Spinoza (Butler 2004b), as well as Hannah Arendt, Walter Benjamin, Emmanuel Levinas, and Edward Said (see Butler 2012). Butler's interventions into post-9/11 political discourse (2004a, 2009), her engagement with the idea of cohabitation regarding Israel/Palestine (2012), and her attention to questions of ethical responsibility (2005), are beginning to make an impact on international political theory and global ethics (Schippers 2014). While this focus constitutes a reorientation in terms of her themes, it should not be read as a departure from her work as a feminist thinker. In fact, notwithstanding her impact on some of the key debates in contemporary critical theory beyond feminism, it is important to acknowledge that this impact draws on a set of philosophical ideas that also justify her significance to feminism.

What connects these diverse elements of her work is her commitment to a conception of the subject anchored in corporeal and affective experiences, as well as her assertion of the subject's ontological condition of vulnerability and susceptibility to dispossession, derived from a foundational relationality, or exposure, to others. Further, her work is driven by a concern for liveability that seeks to transcend the differential experiences of gendered, racialized or otherwise stratified subjectivities (2004a, 2004b, 2009). If anything, Butler's persistent attention to questions of embodied and affective life aims beyond the boundaries of feminist scholarship, and it points to the significance of feminist theorizing for wider critical theory.

To consider Butler's key contribution to feminism requires us to examine her critical engagement with, and reworking of, some of feminism's long-held assumptions about the nature and purpose of feminist politics and its key category, gender. In *Gender Trouble: Feminism and the Subversion of Identity* (1990), Butler's most famous book to date, she presents a systematic exposition of her critique of feminism, together with an account of gender that draws on the concept of performativity. *Gender Trouble's* impact on contemporary feminist theory cannot be overestimated, and it is prudent to identify the main threads that run through this book: these are (1) feminism's role in the discursive constitution of the female subject; (2) the relationship between sexed body, gender identity, and desire; and (3) the prospect for articulating a subversive gender politics (see Lloyd 2007). To begin with, *Gender Trouble* queries feminism's representational claims, specifically the idea that feminism can speak on behalf of women, when, according to Butler, the very category it seeks to represent, 'woman', is a contested concept. What she regards as particularly problematic are the heterosexist assumptions that inform feminism's representational claims as well as its wider assumptions about gender. Hence, one of *Gender Trouble's* aims is to unsettle the idea that (biological) sex constitutes a natural basis of one's gender identity, which in turn is said to inform the gendered subject's desire. At the heart of Butler's argument lies her claim that gender identity is shaped and stabilized by heterosexist assumptions about desire; according to her reading of feminism's sex-gender-desire analogy, gender identity is, by definition, heterosexual. That is, femininity and masculinity become intelligible categories only in relation to their heterosexist connotations. Offering an alternative reading, Butler advocates instead a rupture between sex, gender, and desire.

What, then, are the implications of Butler's critique of feminism for her rethinking of gender? *Gender Trouble's* challenge to feminism's representational claims advances her effort to free the concept of gender from its metaphysical moorings and ontological foundations. In contradistinction to expressive theories, which portend gender as the expression of an inner truth that is anchored in one's biology, Butler puts forward an idea with which her contribution to feminism is mostly associated: this is the notion of gender as performative, which she develops from her reading of Jacques Derrida, and from the speech act theory of the language philosopher J. L. Austin. In brief, to understand gender as performative suggests that gender is a practice, or a doing. Put differently, gender is not the logical or chronological consequence of an inner truth of one's identity, one that is anchored in one's sexed body. Rather, gender develops in a complex relationship to the body, and to understand gender as performative sheds light on the way that ontological effects generate gendered realities; in fact, performativity generates the social realities that make gendered lives possible in the first place, and that, by extension, produce those realms of abjection populated by gendered and sexual minorities (Butler 2004b, 2010). As she argues in a recent article, the assertion of gender as performative denotes

> a certain kind of enactment, which means that one is not first one's gender and then one decides how and when to enact it. The enactment is … a way of rethinking the ontological mode of gender, and so it matters how and when and with what consequences that enactment takes place, because all that changes the very gender that one 'is'.
>
> (2011, 14)

To acknowledge Butler's significance for feminism also requires consideration of the substantial anxiety that her theory of gender performativity has caused among some of her feminist critics. Two aspects in particular have dominated the critical reception of her work: these are the claim that the theory of performativity champions a radical voluntarism, and the concern that performativity forecloses the agency of the female subject and of the prospects for feminist politics (see Benhabib 1995; Nussbaum 1999). As Butler is at pains to stress, it would be wrong to suggest that gender is the outcome of voluntaristic acts performed by autonomous subjects. In fact, the practices associated with gender are always conducted under constraint, policed by gender norms that operate as part of a generative framework that she refers to as the heterosexual matrix, and that construes gender identity in accordance with the norms of heterosexuality. It would be equally misleading to read the theory of gender performativity as radically deterministic. Thus, to understand gender as performative also opens up possibilities of doing one's gender against, or outside, the norms of gendered intelligibility. In *Gender Trouble* and subsequent work, Butler ponders the prospect of practices of gender subversion, of the resignification of identity categories, and, increasingly, of challenging binary conceptions of gender (see also Butler 1993, 1997b, 2004b).

Despite Butler's robust defence of performativity against some of its more vocal critics, she has also utilized the occasion of this critique to consider more thoroughly the possible limitations to performativity, which she undertakes in publications following *Gender Trouble*. For example, *Bodies that Matter: On the Discursive Limits of 'Sex'* (1993) reflects on those discursive limits to gender's performative possibilities that are anchored in the body's materiality. In *The Psychic Life of Power: Theories in Subjection* (1997a), Butler develops an account of the psychic limitations imposed upon possible resignificatory practices open to the subject, an account that continues to influence her work to date. *Undoing Gender* (2004b) considers the possibilities for a 'new gender politics', a term that articulates the prospect of progressive sexual alliances unshackled by the boundaries of identity politics, and able to encompass the spectrum of feminist and LGBTI formations.

Central to these developments in her writings is Butler's re-engagement with phenomenological ideas, especially with the concept of liveability, and her recent turn to ethics, a topic that is attracting substantial attention in the critical scholarship on her work. Judging by the feminist reception of her ideas, the notion of performativity remains her key contribution to feminism, but it is also judicious to acknowledge performativity's wider significance to Butler's work, informing her reflections on hate speech and injurious language (1997b), some of her most recent writings on global alliances (2013), and her discussion of liveability. It is because of her concern for liveability and for opening up possibilities, sustained by a politics of the performative, that Butler can be described as the most significant feminist thinker of our era.

Butler's major writings

[1987] 1999. *Subjects of Desire: Hegelian Reflections in Twentieth-Century France*. New York: Columbia University Press.

1990. *Gender Trouble: Feminism and the Subversion of Identity*. New York and London: Routledge.

1993. *Bodies that Matter: On the Discursive Limits of 'Sex'*. New York and London: Routledge.

1997a. *The Psychic Life of Power: Theories in Subjection*. Stanford: Stanford University Press.

1997b. *Excitable Speech: A Politics of the Performative*. New York and London: Routledge.

2000. *Antigone's Claim: Kinship between Life and Death*. New York: Columbia University Press.

2004a. *Precarious Life: The Powers of Mourning and Violence*. London and New York: Verso.

2004b. *Undoing Gender*. London and New York: Routledge.

2005. *Giving an Account of Oneself*. New York: Fordham University Press.

2009. *Frames of War: When is Life Grievable?* London and New York: Verso.

2010. 'Performative Agency', *Journal of Cultural Economy* 3(2): 147–61.

2011. 'Bodies in Alliance and the Politics of the Street', *Transversal: #occupy and assemble* 10, http://eipcp.net/transversal/1011/butler/en (accessed 20 October 2011).

2012. *Parting Ways: Jewishness and the Critique of Zionism.* New York: Columbia University Press.

2013. *Dispossession: The Performative in the Political.* With Athena Athanasiou. Cambridge: Polity Press.

Further reading

Benhabib, S. (1995) 'Feminism and Postmodernism'. In S. Benhabib, J. Butler, D. Cornell, and N. Fraser, *Feminist Contentions: A Philosophical Exchange*, 17–34. New York and London: Routledge.

Carver, T. and S. A. Chambers (eds) (2008) *Judith Butler's Precarious Politics: Critical Encounters.* London and New York: Routledge.

Chambers, S. A. and T. Carver (2008) *Judith Butler and Political Theory: Troubling Politics.* London and New York: Routledge.

Lloyd, M. (2007) *Judith Butler: From Norms to Politics.* Cambridge: Polity Press.

Nussbaum, M. C. (1999) 'The Professor of Parody: The Hip Defeatism of Judith Butler', *The New Republic* 22: 37–45.

Schippers, B. (2014) *The Political Philosophy of Judith Butler.* London and New York: Routledge.

OCTAVIA E. BUTLER (1947–2006)

adrienne maree brown and Ayana A. H. Jamieson

Octavia Butler is an award-winning speculative fiction writer whose feminism is rooted in her working class origins. Butler redefined what feminism and heroism look like through her characters. She created dynamic female characters based in part on her mother and grandmother, domestics who migrated from Louisiana to California in 1930 with several children. A little black girl in Jim Crow America, Butler survived her lonely childhood and teen years by telling stories. Butler's future writing career began after watching the 1954 film, *Devil Girl from Mars*, at the age of twelve when she turned off the television and thought to herself that she could write a better story than that. She was told that little Negro girls couldn't grow up to be writers, but she sent out her stories for publication anyway.

Butler is regarded as the mother of Afrofuturism, and the most wide-ly recognized and honored black female science fiction writer in his-tory, a distinction that remains nearly a decade after her sudden death in 2006. She was awarded the Hugo and Nebula awards, the highest honors in the genre of science fiction, and was the only science fic-tion writer to win a MacArthur "Genius" Fellowship. In 1970, she attended the Clarion Science Fiction, and Fantasy Writing Workshop, where she eventually became an instructor, and later had a scholarship awarded in her name for participants of the workshop. In the four short pieces Butler produced over the course of six weeks at Clarion, the sociopolitical themes that make her one of the most important think-ers of our time were just beginning to sharpen. In one of those early, unpublished pieces, she deconstructs organized religion through the eyes of a deacon who has witnessed his pastor engaging in sexual rela-tions with a fifteen-year-old girl. In another, she drags readers through a domestic fight where a black woman is claiming her strength after years of codependence.

Throughout Butler's twelve published novels, and her collection of short stories and her essays, Butler steadily deconstructs each of the interlocking structures that uphold patriarchy and the status quo. She referred to herself as a "news junky" that used the news, local, state, and global events combined with meticulous research to extrapolate alternate realities in her fiction.

Butler's work is especially compelling since it addresses itself to subjects often neglected, excluded, or abused in the science fiction universe. Very often, Butler's protagonists are on the margins of the societies she creates for them, as they try to navigate harsh realities and form interdependent communities. In Butler's alternative worlds, we see black women birthing new belief systems, negotiating the future of humanity with aliens, unifying a network of telepaths and so much more.

In the late 1970s and 1980s, when mainstream feminism was focused on workplace equality, Butler reached down into a broader founda-tional place, showing that equality will only emerge from our evo-lution beyond the fatal combination of intelligence and hierarchy. In the *Xenogenesis/Lilith's Brood* trilogy, Butler invented the three-gendered Oankali, a complex alien species of gene-traders who res-cue the remaining members of the human race from the decimated, post-nuclear Earth (1989). The trilogy is named for Lilith Iyapo, a black woman chosen by the aliens to lead the first group of awak-ened humans to repopulate Earth and get used to the idea of the gene trade. Oankali can be male, female, or a third gender "ooloi," which are neither male nor female. (Butler was incited to write the novels after hearing President Reagan talk about a winnable nuclear war.) Humanity will survive, but only if it agrees to trade genes or breed with the aliens. The genetic mixing will aid humanity in weeding out what the Oankali call their Human Contradiction—the fatal combination of hierarchical behavior and intelligence (1989b, 476). Men in particular have a difficult time accepting that they must now reproduce with not only a human woman, but also one Oankali of each of the three genders. The ooloi represent Butler's thematic penchant for rejecting binary oppositions generally while specifically rejecting the male/female, heterosexual/homosexual binaries, problematizing the primacy of hetero-patriarchal masculinity.

In the first series of books Butler wrote, the five-novel *Patternist/Seed to Harvest* series, she traces the development of a human evolution into a race of super telepaths. Each book in this series does major work, examining the practices of self-healing, body snatching, shapeshifting, alien-enhancement, and telepathic rule, all presented as survival strategies and models for existence that are damaging and soul-destroying. Here she introduces readers to Anyanwu, a 400-year-old shapeshifting healer that can transform into the physical shape of any animal or person she comes in contact with and controls her own fertility and bodily integrity down to the cellular level.

Butler has bequeathed us stories in which women are destroying old worlds and paradigms, and creating new ones. In *Parable of the Sower*, Butler offers readers the life of a visionary leader living in California in the midst of cultural and economic collapse. Gasoline, water, and middle class services such as garbage collection, public education, and fire fighters are no longer guaranteed. In this near future coming-of-age novel, teenage protagonist Lauren Oya Olamina observes the fraught, chaotic world around her and articulates the tenets of a new religion, Earthseed, where God is Change (1993, 3). The only lasting truth, to accept, shape, and be shaped by, is archetypal Change. Olamina is forced to leave her home, a walled cul-de-sac in the suburbs based on Butler's native Pasadena, and walk to California highways north converting and gathering followers of Earthseed along the way. In *Fledgling*, Butler's amnesiac, adolescent black American human-vampire hybrid has to uncover the truth about her family's murders while learning what it means to be a member of the matriarchal Ina vampire species.

In the short story "The Evening and the Morning and the Night," Butler practices in her writing one of her central feminist contributions: shifting away from competition into cooperation and mentorship. The characters in this story are the second generation to suffer from a genetic disorder in which they deteriorate to self-mutilation, murder, and suicide—they dissociate from reality and dig at themselves and others. The genetic disorder is a side effect of a life-saving cancer treatment. The lead character is a woman who comes in contact with a black woman with whom she must navigate and negotiate power because they both have a calming, assuaging effect on the condition, and thus can create enclaves of healing and creativity for those with the genetic predisposition for the disease. The same quality that makes them comforting to the afflicted makes it nearly unbearable for them to be around each other on a visceral, physical response level via the pheromones they excrete. Like much of Butler's work, the story is open-ended, but it is implied that rather than tear each other apart, these women offer each other respect and space to do their work. There is also an explicit exchange of wisdom and mentoring, based in the belief that one leader, one healer, is not enough to support and uplift the community. Even if these two women can't be friends, they are both needed, and they can be allies.

After the time-travelling neo-slave narrative, *Kindred*, the Parables duology, *Parable of the Sower* and *Parable of the Talents*, are Butler's best-known works. Butler complicates the story of Lauren Oya Olamina by afflicting her with hyperempathy syndrome, a condition that scrambles the mirror neurons of the brain so that one feels the pain, and less often the pleasure, one witnesses in another living thing. Butler calls this biological conscience better than the one-upmanship and selfishness people typically exhibit. This selfishness has led to the deteriorated state the world is in via global warming, human trafficking, drug abuse, and religious fanaticism—all contributing factors to present conditions. "We are Earthseed," writes Olamina in her *Books of the Living*, "The Destiny of Earthseed is to take root amongst the stars" (1993, 84).

There is a womanist, black feminist or feminist of color reading of these beautiful stories—Earth as womb, as generative space, creating us to cast us out amongst the galaxies. It is a thrilling and dangerous conceit; Earthseed gives us the abundance of the universe and the potential to survive the unknown space exploration, with the understanding that should not render our next home uninhabitable through global warming, but doesn't show us how to avoid colonial patterns.

Young feminists, especially women of color, needed these stories as she was writing them, and perhaps need them even more today in order to imagine a world where they can heal themselves, reclaim lost parts of themselves, and have autonomy, agency, and control over their reproductive choices. Her work offers many perspectives that inspire her readers and would-be writers to speculate about the futures and realities we wish to see. A diverse community of readers—including academics, doulas, physicians, educators, artists, culture workers, and social justice activists—are drawn to Butler's work. In particular, members of social justice movements can look to Butler's work as models for sustainable communities rather than exhausting individual health and emotional resources in the process of advocating for a better world. Butler's work features leadership based on strengths of individuals within community.

Like Lilith Iyapo, Mary the Patternmaster, Lauren Oya Olamina, and Butler's other characters, readers witness the ways to go about adapting and adjusting to changing realities as a vital survival strategy that emerges from Butler's work. The praxes and approaches to change that arise from Butler's work can be categorized as emergent strategy. This means working with the emergent processes of this universe, adapting and relating a way into a future that works for all living beings and the planet(s) we call home. Now, slowly, more organizers, leaders, and organizations are integrating these practices into their daily lives. Butler was far ahead of her time. Her feminism was a future feminism, a way of seeing beyond binaries to offer new ways forward. To honor these emergent, relational, collaborative, and adaptive ways of being human is to honor both Butler's work and our own best selves.

Butler's major writings

Patternist series

1976. *Patternmaster*, Doubleday, New York.
1977. *Mind of My Mind*, Doubleday, New York.
1978. *Survivor*, Doubleday, New York.
1980. *Wild Seed*, Doubleday, New York.
1984. *Clay's Ark*, St. Martin, New York.
2007. *Seed to Harvest*, Grand Central Publishing, New York (omnibus excluding *Survivor*).

Xenogenesis series

1987. *Dawn*, Warner, New York.
1988. *Adulthood Rites*, Warner, New York.
1989a. *Imago*, Warner, New York.
1989b. *Xenogenesis*, Guild America Books, New York (omnibus).
2000. *Lilith's Brood*, Warner, New York (omnibus).

Parable series

1988. *Parable of the Talents*, Seven Stories Press, New York.
1993. *Parable of the Sower*, Four Walls, Eight Windows, New York.

Standalone novels

1979. *Kindred*, Doubleday, New York.
2005. *Fledgling*, Seven Stories Press, New York.

Short story collections

1995. *Bloodchild and Other Stories*, Four Walls, Eight Windows, New York; 1996, 2005, Seven Stories Press, New York (second edition includes "Amnesty" and "The Book of Martha").
2014. *Unexpected Stories*, Open Road Media, New York (includes "A Necessary Being" and "Childfinder").

Selected essays and speeches

1993. "Free Libraries: Are They Becoming Extinct?" *Omni* 15.10 (Aug.): 4.
2000. "Brave New Worlds: A Few Rules for Predicting the Future." *Essence* 31.1 (May): 164.
2002. "Eye Witness: 'Butler's Aha! Moment.'" *O: The Oprah Magazine* 3.5 (May): 79–80.

RACHEL CARSON (1907–1964)

Lynda Walsh

Rachel Carson is more famous today for her environmental activism than for her feminism. However, a closer examination of her life and work reveals a profound, sustained feminist mission. Carson is credited with popularizing ecology, with raising public awareness about the risks of indiscriminate pesticide use, and with fostering political action that led to the foundation of the Environmental Protection Agency in 1970 and the banning of dichlorodiphenyltrichloroethane (DDT) in 1972. Yet she did not achieve this influence via traditional channels. Instead, Carson leveraged her outsider stance, plus an array of feminist techniques, to project the voices of women and other marginalized populations into the halls of power.

Rachel Carson was born to a farming family in Springdale, Pennsylvania, in 1907. She won a scholarship to study English literature at the Pennsylvania College for Women, but she changed her major in 1928 after taking biology courses from Mary Scott Skinker. As Carson struggled to reconcile her new love of biology with her passion for writing and literature, she experienced a quasi-religious conversion. She was reading Tennyson's "Locksley Hall" for class while a violent storm rattled the windows in her dorm room; just then, she came to the line, "For the mighty wind arises, roaring seaward, and I go," and she had the epiphany that her future lay in writing about the sea.[1]

She went on to achieve a Master's degree in zoology from Johns Hopkins in 1932, one of two women in a class of 70. She pursued her dreams of the sea by doing fieldwork in the Florida Everglades and at the Woods Hole Oceanographic Institute. After graduation, she was hired as a technician for the United States Fish and Wildlife Service (USFWS) but was quickly promoted on the strength of her writing skills. By 1949, she was Editor-in-Chief for the USFWS publications bureau.

During this time, Carson was also publishing her own essays about her fieldwork and the emergent science of ecology in the *Atlantic* and the Baltimore *Sun*. Her first collection of essays, *Under the Sea-Wind*, appeared in 1941, and in 1951 *The Sea around Us* spent 86 weeks on the *New York Times* best-seller list and was serialized by the *New Yorker*. After this success, Carson was able to retire from the USFWS and devote her career to her popular writings on ecology.

Carson's work as a government scientist had acquainted her with the widespread and complex effects of pesticides. She was particularly troubled by the effects on fish and waterfowl of DDT, with which wetlands were being carpet-bombed to control mosquitoes. Toward the end of the 1950s, Carson found herself flooded with letters from readers begging her to investigate similar spraying campaigns against insects such as the elm bark beetle, mosquito, and gypsy moth. Though the scientific establishment and the chemical industry claimed insecticides were safe, Carson's correspondents believed the poisons were killing small animals and sickening children. These letters motivated Carson to write the series of investigative *New Yorker* essays that would become *Silent Spring* in 1962.

Much has been written on the impact of *Silent Spring*, but Carson herself admitted that her book was lifted to fame by a wave of public anxiety about the toxic effects of chemicals and radiation produced by the military–industrial complex.[2] This anxiety was fomented by events such as the Great Cranberry Scare of 1959, which exposed contamination of a food crop by pesticides; the Lucky Dragon incident, in which fallout from an H-bomb test sickened the crew of a Japanese fishing boat; and the detection of strontium-90, a by-product of atomic weapon tests, in cow's milk and baby's teeth.

Carson's rhetorical strategies worked synergistically with this public anxiety to drive toward policy change. They are still evident in the text of *Silent Spring*, in the talks she gave in support of the book, in the CBS program "The Silent Spring of Rachel Carson," and in her subsequent testimony before government committees—a media complex that I will call "Silent Spring." These strategies included a methodology of listening, prophetic ethos, narrative scholarship, and a rhetoric of uncertainty.

First and perhaps most crucially, Carson took seriously the reports of housewives, pediatricians, and birdwatchers that the scientific establishment discounted. Like a radio telescope, "Silent Spring" focused the voices of thousands of citizens—mostly women—into an intense indictment of the military–industrial complex that could not be ignored by policymakers. In a speech to the National Parks Association in October 1962, Carson explained her strategy:

> I came to realize that scattered throughout the country were thousands of people who were concerned—who were trying, as individuals or as small groups, to do what they could, in the face of great odds. Now, simply because I happen to have brought together the basic facts—because I have written a book that seems to be serving as a rallying point for an awakened public—both the strength and the needs of these people are flowing to me in a vast and wonderful way.
>
> (Murphy 2005, 39)

In the wake of the CBS program, letters calling for pesticide reform flooded the United States Department of Agriculture. In response, President Kennedy expedited a long-stalled federal report on the issue, which repeated many of the concerns articulated in *Silent Spring*; and, the Senate's Ribicoff Commission interviewed Carson as part of its own investigation.

This ability to channel the needs of silenced people and creatures contributed to the second feminist strategy in "Silent Spring"—prophetic ethos. Ethos is the public role or stance a speaker/writer inhabits. Prophetic ethos is the traditional stance that calls a community back to its core values in the face of crisis. Prophets can stand inside or outside centers of power; those who stand outside are most often from marginalized groups—women, children, foreigners, or the disabled. Carson clearly stood outside the scientific establishment during "Silent Spring." Using footage of her speaking and walking in the Maine woods, the CBS program depicted her quite literally as a "voice of one calling from the wilderness" (Is. 40:3). From this outside vantage-point, Carson could expose the corruption of the military–industrial complex and appeal to core American values like fairness and stewardship as she advocated for pesticide control. Prophets also have special vision—the primary reason we call on them when we have exhausted our usual political resources for solving problems. Carson demonstrated her special vision by being able to visualize not only invisible people groups but also ecosystems. An ecosystem is a network of being that frequently operates either above or below the limits of human experience. Carson made ecosystems visible to her readers by several means: by the engravings of soil microbes and exploded cells that headed the chapters of *Silent Spring*, by arguments locating the American dinner table within the "web of life" affected by pesticides (Chapter 11), and by passages such as the following:

> We poison the caddis flies in a stream and the salmon runs dwindle and die. We poison the gnats in a lake, and the poison travels from link to link of the food chain, and soon the birds of the lake margins become its victims. We spray our elms and the following springs are silent of robin song, not because we sprayed the robins directly, but because the poison traveled step by step, through the now familiar elm-leaf–earthworm–robin cycle.
>
> (2002, 19)

That Carson's readers recognized her performances of prophetic ethos is clear from multiple references to her as a "priestess," "prophet," or "true believer," both by her detractors and champions; the Ribicoff Commission chair even compared her to Harriet Beecher Stowe, the prophetic slavery reformer.

Carson's third feminist strategy was narrative scholarship, which has long been recognized as an effective strategy of resistance to the totalizing, patriarchal discourse of techno-science. *Silent Spring* didn't launch an academic critique, which Carson was certainly capable of producing given her training. Rather, she told stories—vivid, poetic illustrations of pesticides' damaging effects. The "Fable for Tomorrow" that opens the book presents an idyllic small town "in the heart of America where all life seemed to live in harmony" (2002, 1). Following a dusting with insecticides, spring brings no new wildflowers, no birds, no bees to the town—just silence: "No witchcraft, no enemy action had silenced the rebirth of new life in this stricken world. The people had done it themselves" (2002, 3). The rest of the book elaborates on this theme both with stories of the dystopia that awaited America if pesticide use continued unabated, and with elegies mourning lost ecosystems. The CBS special brought these apocalyptic tales to life using footage of planes engulfing fields in poisonous fog, chemical plants belching black smoke, and rivers choked with dead fish. The verbal and visual narratives of "Silent Spring" were designed to move readers to action through empathy and a sense of urgency, reactions unlikely to be sparked by highly technical arguments.

A final and powerful feminist strategy evident in "Silent Spring" was Carson's rhetoric of uncertainty. Expressions of uncertainty both open up debate and resist authoritative efforts to close it down. Against the scientific establishment's guarantees of the safety of pesticides, Carson consistently stressed the incompleteness of the research, the risks of pesticides, and scientists' ignorance of these risks. The CBS program amplified this strategy, repeatedly goading industrial and federal scientists into admitting "we don't know," "we can't say," or "we just don't have that information." This strategy had two aims. First, it opened a rhetorical gap into which the public could step. Carson wrote,

> We urgently need an end to these false assurances, to the sugar coating of unpalatable facts. It is the public that is being asked to assume the risks that the insect controllers calculate. The public must decide whether it wishes to continue on the present road, and it can do so only when in full possession of the facts.
>
> (2002, 13)

Second, on the basis of these uncertainties, Carson could call for preemptive action to limit pesticides, a political strategy often called the "precautionary principle."

Carson's status as a woman working outside the scientific establishment in post-war America was perceived by many as an insurmountable obstacle to her goals of limiting pesticide use and of preserving fragile ecosystems that included human beings. However, Carson was able to leverage the very elements her opponents interpreted as signs of weakness—dialogue with marginalized populations, prophetic language, storytelling, and uncertainty—to mount an effective rhetorical campaign. Carson was not singlehandedly responsible for the achievements with which she is credited. But her rhetoric shaped those events, and feminist techniques substantially shaped her rhetoric.

Notes

1 Lear 1988, 39. Other biographical notes about Carson are taken from this source.

2 Murphy 2005, 9. Other claims about the reception of *Silent Spring* are either from this source or from Walsh 2013.

Carson's major works

1955, 1998. *Edge of the Sea.* Reprint ed. New York: Mariner Books.
1951, 1991. *The Sea around Us.* Special ed. New York: Oxford University Press.
1965, 1998. *The Sense of Wonder.* Revised ed. New York: Harper.
1962, 2002. *Silent Spring.* Fortieth Anniversary ed. New York: Houghton Mifflin.
1941, 2007. *Under the Sea-Wind.* New ed. New York: Penguin Classics.

Further reading

Lear, Linda. *Rachel Carson: Witness for Nature.* New York: Henry Holt, 1988.
Murphy, Priscilla Coit. *What a Book Can Do: The Publication and Reception of Silent Spring.* Cambridge, MA: University of Massachusetts Press, 2005.
Waddell, Craig (ed.). *And No Birds Sing: Rhetorical Analyses of Rachel Carson's Silent Spring.* Carbondale: Southern Illinois University Press, 2000.
Walsh, Lynda. "Rachel Carson: Kairotic Prophet." In *Scientists as Prophets: A Rhetorical Genealogy,* 119–35. New York: Oxford University Press, 2013.

ANNA JULIA COOPER (1858–1964)

Penny Weiss

Anna Julia Cooper was an educator and an activist, an historian and a linguist, a writer on subjects from racism and sexism to literature and education. Her first book, *A Voice from the South,* was written in 1892, a time, she emphasizes, when "The race is just twenty-one years removed from the conception and experience of a chattel";[1] her dissertation was defended in 1925, and she lived to see the Civil Rights Movement. Her vision is of a world where it is safe for everyone to be weak and peaceful and caring, but where the internal and external resources to be fully developed are readily available. This ideal invigorates the writings of the young and the old Cooper, in multiple genres.

Cooper can be read as a feminist theorist of voice, as images of speech and silence are woven into everything she wrote. She starts with the fact that certain people and perspectives are more easily and accurately conveyed and heard than others, always with a host of consequences, for knowable reasons, and not absent solutions. Looked at from the other side, "across her body of work she exposes how power conspires to erase dissent, silence the marginalized, and render alternative views unthinkable" (May 2009, 17). The primary case for this is put in terms of race, but she speaks in similar terms of gender and indeed any "weaker" group (105). Her mission in her writing is to motivate and enable us to listen harder and better. At stake are truth, justice, and progress, for the individual, social groups, and society at large.

Cooper is a believer in the "individual soul, capable of eternal growth and unlimited development" (53), a "soul with unquenchable longings and inexhaustible possibilities" (80). Seeing in *everyone* this "cultivable soul" (105), she becomes an advocate of lifelong education and a believer in social progress. She is utterly committed to the fact, and urges us to join her in the knowledge, that no matter the circumstances, "the divine Spark is capable of awakening at the most unexpected moment and it never is wholly smothered or stamped out" (*Equality* 293). It is *never* wholly smothered, which we would know if we listened more sympathetically. But despite this optimism, and despite Cooper's deep connection to the oft-cited principles of the Declaration of Independence, her treatment of America always includes—indeed begins with—the introduction of slavery into the colonies: "a fact, silent and unforeseen which was destined nevertheless to embroil the entire future" (*Legislative* 3). She is knowledgeable, from her life (she was born into slavery) and her studies (her dissertation was on attitudes toward slavery around the French Revolution), about the institution of slavery, characterized as "founded solely on the abuse of power ... and only in the name of the right of the strongest" (2009, 31). She is also deeply acquainted with the everyday reinforcement of prejudice and "caste spirit" (103). It is within this broad constellation of the possible and the actual, historical, present, and future, that her ideas travel in her long life.

At the beginning of *A Voice from the South* the scene is of "an already full chorus": the images are "clash and clatter," "noisy controversy," and "ceaseless harangues"; the tone is one of argument and "busy objectivity" (51). One feels oneself alternatively listening to a heavily percussive piece of music, in an overheated courtroom, on a too-busy city street. And yet Cooper senses something missing despite the turbulence, notices those in the corners whose mouths are barely moving, hears those from whom but a cry or a moan escapes.

Focusing on muted strains is a notoriously difficult task. What Cooper sees most obviously blocking out others are the individual and political versions of the obnoxious know-it-all and the blustering bully. But just as overwhelming are many of the voices of legitimacy and authority; indeed, she asks, how readily distinguishable are these? While we are used to the form a courtroom drama takes, with its evidentiary rules and parliamentary procedures, Cooper recasts this as oppressive noise. She similarly puts down the "dry-as-dust abstractions and mental gymnastics" (*Humor* 233) of certain classrooms. Also accused are white novelists who fail at "the art of 'thinking one's self imaginatively into the experiences of others'" (139). What do they have in common? Each confidently mistakes their partial findings and admitted technical skill for conversation and inclusive knowledge. They are guilty, in literature, in the classroom, of the larger social vices: egotism, over-generalizing, and seeing "at long range or only in certain capacities" (149). So used are we to the din that it is the muffled strain that seems "jarring," not the "vociferous disputation" (51).

Near-silences and less than fully articulated voices make Cooper tune in harder, and bring her focus to outsiders. She teaches us that a liberatory theory of voice must comprehend more than imagined poles of free speech and oppressive silence. The most silent figure Cooper portrays is "open-eyed" (51), while the most outspoken is rude, silencing, and arrogant. Also, what we have only seems to resemble a continuum; because the voices are in the same chorus none can be taken out of context, and the speech of one always affects that of others. Further, because we exist in multiple roles and relationships, our silence or voice in one situation may differ dramatically from that in another. She turns from the imagined poles of silenced and silencing to a portrayal instead of interacting voices in varied circumstances with different degrees of education and credibility unevenly backed by social structures. Cooper's focus shifts from silencing to how we interact, where her thoughts on civil discourse and public manners become central.

It seems from a cursory glance that we *have* listened—every word has been "analyzed and dissected, theorized and synthesized" (51). Each attorney thoroughly presents a side. The well-reviewed novel reaches its conclusion. Yet somehow still there is "sublime ignorance or pathetic misapprehension" (51). There has not been a fair trial after all. Not all of the fictional characters are equally well developed. We have evaluated the French Revolution from almost every conceivable viewpoint—except that of those on the bottom, the enslaved in the colonies. This hushed scream is what we keep missing in the din, despite the fact that it colors everything, her dissertation informs us, and that our understanding is dangerously shortsighted without it. Larger systems of extreme prejudice infiltrate through various institutions and practices all the way down to our very imaginations.

We seem to miss or resist, Cooper thinks, the fact that there are truths "from *each* standpoint" and that we can alone have only partial knowledge. The power we possess by virtue of our race, sex, and class influences what we see, what we have been taught, what we can easily understand. There is an epistemology in Cooper, a standpoint epistemology that demands of us many great *dialogic virtues*, such as sympathy, modesty, compassion, appreciation, imagination, and humility.

One needs others in standpoint epistemology, which is why Cooper's theory of voice ultimately makes her a communitarian, someone who is inspired and required to relate to others civilly and open-mindedly, aware always that one needs "radically corrective" (52) perspectives from others. We cannot *quite*, Cooper tells us, put ourselves in one another's shoes, and even "broken utterances" (51) from another can help. We must be "delicately sensitive." What an exquisite social virtue: delicate sensitivity. Noise must be hemmed in or blocked out to exercise such skill. It takes something profound like a commitment to be one another's keeper to "purify and exalt the narrow, selfish and petty personal aims of life into a noble and sacred purpose" (64). "Wondrous whisperings" await the seekers of divergent perspectives (158) who can get past "preconceived notions" (*Ethics* 209). But there is not one tonic, because the problems come in many forms and moments allow of different resolution.

The work to be done is on all parties. The most oppressed need to recover "self-assertion" (143), "tongue," and "nerve" (173), and cannot allow themselves only to be spoken for. "Speak out and speak honestly" (159), she demands. One must challenge rules that function to silence, whether in the courtroom, in literature, even in what we think is conversation. We must all seek other voices, and make room for softer tones. Those same skillful ears that can make concordance out of noise can make a voice out of a cry. We will be rewarded with richer theories of theology, science, justice, and economics (76–77). We will be rewarded with friendships and expanded horizons—with cultivated souls.

There is better and worse "speaking for" others. Some of Cooper's most poignant negative examples come from literature, where she shows how white authors fail at "the art of 'thinking one's self imaginatively into the experiences of others'" (139). The better example is Cooper, who proclaims "I speak for the colored women of the South" (202). She does her homework and she cares, as both intellect and feeling are required (147). In speaking for others she testifies to the ideals of womanhood they maintained and acknowledges their "heroic struggle" (202). She celebrates their ignored accomplishments. To speak well for another one "vocalizes and inspires its better self" (142).

Most important, we have to cease our worship of the White, the male, the self, the bully, and the warmonger, in ourselves and each other. Cooper seems to believe that if we experience ourselves and one another through the fullness of community we would never give it up, for the gains—the gifts of a developed self, human friendship, and democratic society—would be so compelling. Through individual and group agency (62), and in the "flower of modern civilization" (54), people can come to true democratic relationships, where the humanity of each is respected. They require a culture to support this, and that culture is something to which everyone, especially women in gendered societies, can contribute. The set of civil manners they spread is capable of effecting a genuine revolution (97).

Throughout her work Cooper integrates theory, commentary, and biography. In the end, all direct her to civil conversation that nourishes every soul. Cooper has the same foes as do all the better enlightenment philosophers—"tradition and superstition," which have "manacled and muzzled" rationality and freedom (106) and undermined equality. "All prejudices, whether of race, sect or sex, class pride and caste distinctions are the belittling inheritance and badge of snobs and prigs" (105). Mere manners (105), she suggests, go a long way, giving us the means to listen and learn. Cooper's graphic portrayals of multiple forms and degrees of silence, in persons real and fictional, stay with the reader long after her works are read. She complicates every position. It is, after all, only "said that the South remains Silent" (51). Not being invited to participate, or having one's words "uncomprehended" (51), should not be mistaken for someone either having said nothing or having nothing to say. It is ultimately "subversive of every human interest" that the voices of certain groups be "stifled" (107).

Note

1 Lemert and Bhan 1998, 61. References to essays in *A Voice from the South* are placed in the text with pagination only.

Cooper's major writings

[1902] 1998. "The Ethics of the Negro Question." In Charles Lemert and Esme Bhan, *The Voice of Anna Julia Cooper*. Lanham, MD: Rowman & Littlefield: 206–15.

N.d. "A Personal Foreword." *Decennial Catalogue of Frelinghuysen University*. Box 23-2, Folder 16. Moorland-Spingarn Library, Howard University.

[1925] 1998. "Equality of Races and the Democratic Movement." In Charles Lemert and Esme Bhan, *The Voice of Anna Julia Cooper*. Lanham, MD: Rowman & Littlefield: 291–98.

1942. "Legislative Measures Concerning Slavery in the United States." Box 23-5, Folder 66. Moorland-Spingarn Library, Howard University.

[1923] 1998. "Sketches from a Teacher's Notebook: Loss of Speech Through Isolation." In Charles Lemert and Esme Bhan, *The Voice of Anna Julia Cooper*. Lanham, MD: Rowman & Littlefield: 224–29.

[1925] 2006. *Slavery and the French and Haitian Revolutionists*. Ed. and trans. Frances Richardson Keller. Lanham, MD: Rowman & Littlefield.

[1930] 1998. "The Humor of Teaching." In Charles Lemert and Esme Bhan, *The Voice of Anna Julia Cooper*. Lanham, MD: Rowman & Littlefield: 232–35.

[1892] 1998. *A Voice from the South by a Black Woman of the South*. In Charles Lemert and Esme Bhan, *The Voice of Anna Julia Cooper*. Lanham, MD: Rowman & Littlefield: 49–196.

1998. Lemert, Charles and Esme Bhan. *The Voice of Anna Julia Cooper*. Lanham, MD: Rowman & Littlefield.

Further reading

May, Vivian M. 2004. "Thinking from the Margins, Acting at the Intersections: Anna Julia Cooper's *A Voice from the South*." *Hypatia* 19(2): 74–91.

—. 2009. "Writing the Self into Being: Anna Julia Cooper's Textual Politics." *African American Review* 43(1): 17–34.

MARY DALY (1928–2010)

Krista Ratcliffe

Mary Daly, a prominent philosopher-activist of U.S. second-wave feminism, challenged mainstream religions for oppressing women and conceptualized a wildly original Radical Feminist metaethics. In her writings, Daly advocated language play (playing with etymologies, capitalization, spelling, puns, homonyms, etc.) as a deadly serious means through which women may expose patriarchal socialization and discover not only Radical Feminist Truths but also their authentic Selves. Born in Schenectady, New York, Daly earned a Ph.D. from St. Mary's College/Notre Dame University in 1954 and then two Ph.D.s from the University of Fribourg, Switzerland, one in theology in 1963 and one in philosophy in 1965. In 1967, she began teaching theology and ethics at Boston College. At this Jesuit institution, she gained a national and international reputation for her feminist scholarship in religion and philosophy and also for her pedagogical practices. Daly refused to admit men into her upper-division courses although she would agree to tutor them privately. This pedagogical choice was grounded in her principle of Radical Feminist Separatism, the idea that women should separate themselves from "all that is alienating and confining" in order to engage "deep questions" and "par[e] away the layers of false selves from the Self" (*Gyn/Ecology* 381). In sum, she believed women students talked more, and more honestly, when men were not in the room. In 1999, Daly's Separatist pedagogy was legally challenged by a male student at Boston College and resulted in her termination; she counter-filed and settled out of court, which resulted not in her admitting men into her classes but, rather, in her retiring in 2001. Throughout her life, Daly remained committed to writing and living a Radical Feminist philosophy that not only represents physical and metaphysical Truths of women but also provides women a method for dis-covering their Selves and, in the process, discovering and creating "a world other than patriarchy" (1).

Daly's Radical Feminist philosophy posits concepts and truths as actions, not abstractions. In *Gyn/Ecology* she defines *Radical Feminism* as "the journey of women becoming" (1), a journey made possible by Spooking (getting rid of old ghosts), Sparking (being fired up by foremothers), and Spinning (using generative, creative powers to change themselves and their worlds); this journey moves women's thinking and be-ing from the mystifications of patriarchal foreground knowledge into the realm of Radical Feminist Background Truths (34, 2–3). For years, this book was as popular in women's shelters as in feminist classrooms. In *Pure Lust*, Daly extends her definition of *Radical Feminism* by conceptualizing three more moves: Be-Longing or "experiencing our ontological connectedness with all that is Elemental" (354), Be-Friending or creating "a context/atmosphere in which acts/leaps of Metamorphosis can take place" (373), and Be-Witching or "the actual leaping/hopping/flying that is Metamorphosis" (388). Metamorphosis may be experienced by any Spinster and may result in her be-coming a thrice-born Athena: born not just of her mother's (Metis') womb, not just of her father's (Zeus') mind, but of her own Spinning herself into a "new be-ing" (*Gyn/Ecology* 14).

Daly's scholarship grows progressively more radical. Her early books, *The Church and the Second Sex* and *Beyond God the Father*, refute Judeo-Christian theology and condemn its institutions for their patriarchal theories, methods, and practices, all of which suppress women's consciousness and spirituality as well as their social, cultural, and legal potential. *In the Church and the Second Sex*, Daly does not conceive the Church as the sole cause of women's oppression, but she does deem it a major player (222). In this book Daly systematically explains how patriarchy became a controlling figure in history and theology, and she concludes with "Some Modest Proposals" intended to help readers exorcise patriarchal socialization and, thus, cultivate equality for men and women within the Church, an idea she later rejects in her "Autobiographical Preface to 1975 Edition" (6). These Modest Proposals include recognizing patriarchy's obsessions with self-fulfilling prophecies, self-destruction, inhibition of individual's potential, and disintegration/dissociation (192–94). Such recognitions, she argues, demand "confrontation, dialogue, and cooperation" (195). In her second book, *Beyond God the Father*, confrontation comes to the fore. Her introductory paragraphs state and then challenge the following assumption: "If God in 'his' heaven is a father ruling 'his' people, then it is in the 'nature' of things and according to divine plan and the order of the universe that society be male-dominated" (13). A few pages later, Daly restates this idea in one of her more famous lines: "If God is male, then the male is God" (19). To correct this patriarchal mystification, Daly encourages the women's movement to move beyond God the father and conceptualize a new deity. What is needed for this endeavor, according to Daly, is a "new language of transcendence" (21). Creating such a lexicon becomes her life's work.

Daly creates this new language of transcendence by "writing/ speaking New Words," a tactic with myriad manifestations (*The Church* 14). For instance, this tactic may entail reimagining Biblical representations of women not as an "'eternal feminine'" (149) but, rather, as characters embodying the cultural mores and power structures of their times (75). Writing/speaking New Words may consist of reimagining terms, such as *sin*, which Daly resuscitates from its connotations of evil and imbues with its etymological root (*es*) meaning "to be" (*Pure Lust* 151), hence her injunction to women to Sin Big, or to Be. Daly's writing/speaking New Words may involve redefining Biblical concepts, such as Daly's translating the seven deadly sins into New Words of Radical Feminism: pride becomes Professions, avarice becomes Possession, anger becomes Aggression, lust becomes Obsession, gluttony becomes Assimilation, envy becomes Elimination, and sloth becomes Fragmentation (*Gyn/Ecology* 30–31; *Pure Lust* x). Daly's writing/speaking New Words may necessitate embellishing upon established Judeo-Christian concepts: e.g., riffing off the traditional seven deadly sins, Daly conceptualizes an eighth one, Deception, which she argues is "the most crucial one, which the fathers … omit" because they must employ it to sustain patriarchal institutions (*Pure Lust* x). For Daly, then, the project of Radical Feminism is two-fold: first, to uncover any Deception that suppresses women's true Selves and, second, to encourage women to develop the "Courage to Leave" any institution that promulgates such Deceptions (*The Church* xiii). And finally, although Daly's tactic of writing/speaking New Words rejects Biblical hermeneutics grounded in the word (*logos*), it embraces a Radical Feminist hermeneutics grounded in active listening: for as she concludes in *Gyn/Ecology*, "In the beginning was not the word. In the beginning is the hearing…. Spinning is celebration/cerebration. Spinsters Spin all ways, always. Gyn/Ecology is Un-Creation; Gyn/Ecology is Creation" (424).

With *Gyn/Ecology* and her subsequent books, Daly shifts from critiquing patriarchal religions to writing her own Otherwor(l)dly Radical Feminist metaethics, whose precepts/practices are capitalized to distinguish them from lower-case patriarchal abstractions. Merging poetic wordplay with a philosophical impulse to define and classify, Daly's metaethics offers women methods for recognizing and re-cognizing patriarchal foreground truths and Spinning into Radical Feminist Background Truths, culminating in each woman's Be-ing (a verb) (*Beyond* xvii). One method for moving from foreground to Background is recognizing the "Sado-Ritual Syndrome" (*Gyn/Ecology* 130), which Daly posits as a universal structure of patriarchal oppression that emerges transculturally via Chinese footbinding, African genital mutilation, Indian widow burning, European witch burning, and American gynecology. The Sado-Ritual Syndrome encompasses the following moves: (1) obsessing about purity; (2) erasing responsibility for atrocious rituals performed in the name of transcendent truths; (3) encouraging rituals to spread quickly; (4) using women as "scapegoats and token torturers" in these rituals; (5) obsessing on order, repetition, and minute details as diversions; (6) accepting behavior as normal that otherwise would be unacceptable; and (7) legitimizing rituals through "objective" academic scholarship (*Gyn/Ecology* 130–3). Because of her universalizing impulse, Daly garnered criticism from other feminists, such as Audre Lorde, who in her "Open Letter to Mary Daly" accuses Daly of (perhaps inadvertently) erasing differences among women.

While *Pure Lust* extends *Gyn/Ecology*'s project of naming and defining moves of Radical Feminist Be-ing, Daly's *Wickedary* is a feisty feminist dictionary full of deadly serious yet wickedly humorous coined terms and phrases from her previous books and from her imaginings of what a Webster (a woman who weaves a web of Radical Feminism) might need. *Outercourse*, her autobiography, offers her life as an example of "Metapatriarchal Time/Space Travel, which takes the shape of quadruple Spiraling. Its parts (Spirals) describe clusters of Moments, each involving/requiring gigantic qualitative leaps into Other dimensions of the Background," a journey that she claims has rendered her "Crone-logical" (1). To exemplify what it means to become Crone-logical, Daly narrates her early fascination with Thomas Aquinas who, she claims, "became my teacher" and taught her "to use my mind in an intensively systematic way" while she studied "the 'Blessed Trinity'" (51):

> I clearly remember one particular sunny day when I stood on a street corner in South Bend, Indiana, watching the crowds of shoppers go by, thinking how sad it was that they were missing out on such rewarding knowledge. Years later, when I recalled that day and described the experience to friends, we almost rolled on the floor, cackling and whooping in convulsions of mirth. Still ... since the christian trinity is a sort of "house of fun" mirror image of the Triple Goddess—a reversal that can be reversed and decoded—it is not so strange that the study of that dogma made me happy.
>
> (51)

With her next book, *Quintessence*, Daly returns to articulating her Elemental Radical Feminist Philosophy and posits the concept of *Quintessence* as "a Name for what Wild Woman have always been seeking.... It means throwing one's life as far as it will go" in order to become "multidimensionally Present"; this multidimensional Presence, in turn, enables women to "move into further dimensions and yet ... fight for life on Earth" (4). *Amazon Grace*, Daly's final foray into the evils of patriarchy, forcefully argues that rejecting the concept of patriarchy and linking it only to 1970s (or earlier) feminism is a dangerous proposition in that such a linkage mystifies the power and presence of patriarchy in the twenty-first century. While making this argument,

Daly claims the future for Radical Feminism by invoking an intersection of women's power, ecology, and anti–George W. Bush politics; she also claims that working toward this future may afford determined and playful Amazons the Grace they all desire.

Poet-philosopher Mary Daly was and is an important twentieth- and twenty-first-century radical feminist thinker. She will be remembered for her facility with language in the service of naming and questioning patriarchy, that is, for her ability to expose ironies of language use (why are bras that bind branded Free Spirit?), for her ability to cull etymologies and definitions of words (what is significant that *paradise* also means *pleasure park*?), and for her ability to coin new terms that expand women's ways of Be-ing in the world (why not accept the passing of years and celebrate becoming *Crone-logical*?). But what is most remarkable about Daly's writings is that, taken collectively, they construct a systematic metaethics of Radical Feminism, which, whether one agrees with all of its particulars or not, must be recognized for its Be-dazzling brilliance, a brilliance Sparked by the mind/body/soul of a Webster named Mary Daly who lived a life dedicated to Spinning herself and many other women into Be-ing via her edict, and her example, to Sin Big.

Daly's major writings

[1968] 1975. *The Church and the Second Sex*. Boston: Beacon Press.

1973. *Beyond God the Father: Toward a Philosophy of Women's Liberation*. Boston: Beacon Press.

[1978] 1990. *Gyn/Ecology: The Metaethics of Radical Feminism*. Boston: Beacon Press.

1984. *Pure Lust: Elemental Feminist Philosophy*. New York: Harper Collins.

1992. *Outercourse: The Be-Dazzling Voyage*. San Francisco: Harper Collins.

1996. "Sin Big." *The New Yorker*. 26 February. p. 76. www.newyorker.com/magazine/1996/02/26/sin-big

1999. *Quintessence … Realizing the Archaic Future: A Radical Elemental Feminist Manifesto*. New York: Beacon Press.

2006. *Amazon Grace: Re-Calling the Courage to Sin Big*. New York: Palgrave Macmillan.

1987. Daly, M. and J. Caputi. *Websters' First New Intergalactic Wickedary of the English Language*. Boston: Beacon Press.

ANGELA DAVIS (1944–)

Lisa Guenther

Angela Davis is a scholar, activist, and former political prisoner. She is a leading figure in movements for prison abolition, racial and economic justice, intersectional feminism, queer and trans liberation, decolonization, and food justice.

From a very young age, Davis felt the impact of racial terrorism in the United States. She grew up in Birmingham, Alabama during the Jim Crow era, in a neighborhood called "Dynamite Hill," named in reference to the regular bombing of Black homes by white supremacists. She lost friends in the racist attack on the Sixteenth Street Baptist Church, which killed four girls in 1963. As a high school student on an exchange program at the "Little Red Schoolhouse" in New York City, Davis encountered a communist youth group, and she eventually became a member of the Communist Party USA, running for Vice-President twice (in 1980 and 1984). As an undergraduate at Brandeis University, she immersed herself in the work of Marx and Sartre, and she attended lectures by James Baldwin, Malcolm X, and others. Davis studied with Herbert Marcuse, first at Brandeis and later as a graduate student at the University of Frankfurt and the University of California, San Diego.

In 1968, Davis became involved in the Che Lumumba Club, the Black collective of the Communist Party, as well as the Black Panther Party for Self-Defense, and the Student Nonviolent Coordinating Committee (SNCC). Her first academic appointment was a two-year position in the philosophy department at UCLA, beginning in 1969, but when her involvement in the Communist Party was publicized, then-Governor Ronald Reagan convinced the Board of Regents to fire her. Undaunted, Davis showed up for the first day of classes and delivered her "Lectures on Liberation" to audiences of over 1,500 students and faculty members (Ruggiero 2010).

In 1970, Angela Davis joined a campaign to defend the Soledad brothers: three prisoners who were accused of killing a guard in retaliation for the shooting of Black prisoners. On August 7, 1970, Jonathan Jackson, the younger brother of Soledad Brother George Jackson, staged an armed attack on a courtroom in Marin County, California, which left four people dead, including a judge who had been taken hostage. The guns used in the attack were registered in Angela Davis' name, and since California law allows for the prosecution of anyone who is directly or indirectly involved in a crime, a warrant was issued for her arrest. She was charged with aggravated kidnapping and first degree murder in the death of the judge; if found guilty, she could have faced the death penalty.

Davis went into hiding for two months, becoming the third woman ever to appear on the FBI's Ten Most Wanted Fugitive List. She was apprehended in New York City and held for several months in the Women's House of Detention before being extradited to California. After eighteen months in jail, during which a global campaign was launched for her release, Angela Davis stood trial and was acquitted of all charges. Davis returned to academia as a professor in the History of Consciousness program at the University of California, Santa Cruz, from 1991 to 2008, where she is currently Distinguished Professor Emerita.

Angela Davis' life and work is often singled out as an example of engaged scholarship. But in her autobiography, Davis challenges the fetish of the heroic individual:

> I was reluctant to write this book because concentration on my personal history might detract from the movement which brought my case to the people in the first place. I was also unwilling to render my life as a personal "adventure"—as though there were a 'real" person separate and apart from the political person … When I decided to write the book after all, it was because I had come to envision it as a *political* autobiography that emphasized the people, the events and the forces in my life that propelled me to my present commitment. Such a book might serve a very important and practical purpose.
>
> (Davis 1988, xvi)

As a political autobiography, Davis' book serves an important theoretical purpose: to resist the individualist ontology of capitalism and, more broadly, of liberal political theory by accounting for the *bios* of the subject in terms of the relationships, histories, and structures that constitute the meaning of her life, while also resisting a reductivist account of structure as univocally determining the direction of that life. Davis' political autobiography is both the contingent story of a person caught in the dangerous intersection of race, class, and gender at a particular historical moment, and also the collective history of a movement to analyze and dismantle those intersectional forms of domination. There is no Angela Davis without the movement, and at the same time, there is no movement without Angela Davis, George Jackson, Kathleen Cleaver, Huey Newton, Ericka Huggins, and countless others who have found the meaning and materiality of their lives in collective theory and praxis.

In particular, Davis' life connects with her contribution to feminist thought in her articulation of what has come to be called "intersectional" feminism, her activism on behalf of prison abolition, and her investment in the politics of solidarity. *Women, Race and Class* (1981), for example, is an important work of intersectional feminism *avant la lettre*. The book tracks both the possibilities and the stumbling-blocks for solidarity across lines of gender, race, and class, from first wave movements for women's suffrage and the abolition of slavery, to second wave movements to end rape, reproductive injustice, and the patriarchal structure of housework. Throughout the book, Davis tracks the erasure and resistance of black women in relation to single-issue politics centered predominantly around the interests of white women or black men. She shows how feminist, anti-racist, and socialist movements to dismantle oppressive structures of gender, race, and class, are undermined by their own marginalization of impoverished black women, arguing that the liberation of any given group depends on the liberation of all. This is only possible when the perspectives of those who are directly impacted by multiple forms of oppression are located at the center of both our theoretical analysis and our political movement-building.

The chapters of *Women, Race and Class* on sexual violence and reproductive politics are especially relevant for feminism and anti-racism today. In "Rape, Racism, and the Myth of the Black Rapist," Davis anticipates contemporary critiques of carceral feminism by scholars such as Beth Richie and Victoria Law, showing how white radical feminists such as Susan Brownmiller re-inscribe racist tropes of black male sexuality as a threat to (white) women through their own narrowly-focused and ahistorical critique of sexual violence. Davis situates Brownmiller's account of rape in relation to white supremacist justifications for lynching, which both relied on the myth of the black rapist and also effaced the systemic rape of black women by white men. In so doing, she not only points out the shortcomings of Brownmiller's analysis, but she also develops a more powerful intersectional critique of racist sexual violence through an engagement with the theory and practice of Black scholar-activists such as Ida B. Wells and Frederick Douglass. Here, as throughout her life's work, Davis affirms the importance of historical memory and collective movement-building, not only for the sake of political integrity and effective organizing, but also for the sake of epistemic justice and a fuller understanding of who we are and how we came to be.

Davis' chapter on "Racism, Birth Control and Reproductive Rights" is also strikingly relevant to contemporary discussions of reproductive politics. While the political terrain has shifted since the essay was written in 1981, from legal challenges to women's access to abortion to constitutional battles over fetal personhood and the administrative micro-management of abortion clinics, Davis' intersectional account of reproductive justice, and her historical account of the early birth control movement's complicity with eugenic discourses and practices, is vital for navigating the dangerous intersections of reproductive politics today.

Today, Angela Davis is probably best known for her account of prison abolition. In *Are Prisons Obsolete?* (2003), she develops a powerful critique of mass incarceration and the hyper-incarceration of poor people of color in the United States, calling for readers to "imagine a world without prisons" (8). Beginning with the Thirteenth Amendment, which abolishes slavery "except as a punishment for crime whereof the party shall have been duly convicted," Davis situates the current situation of mass incarceration in an historical context of slavery, its partial abolition, the Black Codes, the convict leasing system, Jim Crow, and the continued existence of plantation prisons, some of which are literally built on former slave plantations. In addition to this genealogical account of mass incarceration as an instrument of white supremacy, Davis also develops a structural analysis of "how gender structures the prison system" (60–83) by reproducing norms of femininity and masculinity; by disciplining prisoners with the threat and practice of sexual violence, including routine strip searches and cavity searches; and by normalizing and enforcing a binary gender system that exposes transgender and gender-nonconforming prisoners to multiple forms of violence. Her account of the prison industrial complex adds another dimension to this intersectional analysis by showing how mass incarceration generates profits, both for private prison corporations like Corrections Corporation of America, and also in more indirect, insidious ways through military contracts, medical experiments and for-profit health care, manufacturing plants, pre-paid phone cards, and so on.

Building on this intersectional critique, Davis calls for a radical transformation, not just of the U.S. prison system, but also of the community that supports and profits from this system. This is what prison abolition means for Angela Davis: both a critical movement to dismantle the oppressive structures that (re)produce mass incarceration, and also a creative movement to build a constellation of strategies, institutions, structures, and practices that would make prisons obsolete. Drawing on DuBois' notion of an "abolition democracy" founded on the abolition of slavery, lynching, racial segregation, prisons, and the death penalty, she calls for a movement of radical reconstruction to uproot and transform the intersecting forms of domination that prison slavery both presupposes and intensifies. This constellation of alternatives to prison includes restorative and transformative justice, as well as a meaningful investment in public education and free health care (including mental health care and respectful, effective forms of treatment for addictions).

A movement for abolition democracy calls for solidarity in response to intersecting forms of oppression. This solidarity may take many forms. In her political autobiography, Davis recalls several moments—big and small—of solidarity in resistance to the prison industrial complex. On the first night after she is moved out of solitary confinement at the House of Detention in New York, Davis is introduced to a "good night ritual" in which the women call out to each other by name from the isolation of their cells. When someone calls, "Good night, Angela!" she feels like an "outsider to this ritual" and, not knowing anyone's name yet, can only answer with a lonely, unsupported, though no less vigorous, "good night" (Davis 1988, 49). Later, when supporters gather outside the jail shouting "Free Angela," she responds by "shout[ing] one by one the names of all the sisters on the floor participating in the demonstration. 'Free Vernell! Free Helen! Free Joan! Free Laura! Free Minnie!' I was hoarse for the next week" (65). These two moments, humble as they may seem in the face of interlocking systems of oppression and state violence, constitute powerful acts of community-building and world-making, even in spaces that are designed to (re)produce isolation and alienation. It is on the strength of this solidarity, and in resistance to the narrow interests of single-issue politics, that abolition democracy is founded.

Davis's major writings

[1969/71] 2010. "Lectures on Liberation." In Frederick Douglass, *Narrative of the Life of Frederick Douglass, an American Slave, Written by Himself.* Ed. Angela Davis. San Francisco: City Lights Open Media.

[1974] 1988. *Angela Davis: An Autobiography.* New York: International Publishers.

1981. *Women, Race and Class.* New York: Vintage.

2003. *Are Prisons Obsolete?* New York: Seven Stories Press.

2005. *Abolition Democracy: Beyond Empire, Prisons and Torture.* New York: Seven Stories Press.

Further reading

Ruggiero, Greg. 2010. "Editor's Note." In Frederick Douglass, *Narrative of the Life of Frederick Douglass, An American Slave, Written by Himself.* Ed. Angela Davis. San Francisco: City Lights Open Media: 9–20.

CHRISTINE DELPHY (1941–)

Lisa Disch

Christine Delphy is a rarity. She is a French activist-scholar whose work has done as much to spark movement politics as to shift theoretical paradigms. An architect of French "materialist" feminism, Delphy is best known for a proposition that many would take to render her an anachronism, the claim that women are a social class. To appreciate her originality and that of materialist feminism more generally, it is important to read that proposition in conjunction with Delphy's (1981, 1993, 1991, 2001b) critique of sex/gender. That critique, which she developed in conjunction with her feminist colleagues, defines what I call a "constructivist materialism": a materialist analysis of gender hierarchy premised on the conviction that sex difference is not the "physical substrate" of gender but its *effect* (Delphy 2013b, 27).

Delphy trained as a sociologist in the early 1960s, first in Paris at the Sorbonne and then in the US in the Committee on Social Thought at the University of Chicago and in the Department of Sociology at the University of California, Berkeley (Jackson 1996, 2). Inspired by the Civil Rights Movement, she took a break from her studies to work for the Urban League supported by a fellowship from the Eleanor Roosevelt Foundation for Human Relations. By the time she returned to Paris in the mid-1960s, to take up a research position at the Centre Nationale de Recherche Scientifique (CNRS), women's liberation groups were beginning to form in France as in the US. In 1968, Delphy joined "Féminin-Masculin-Avenir" (FMA, Feminine-Masculine-Future), one of the many decentralized groups that came together two years later to form the "Mouvement de Libération des Femmes" (MLF, Women's Liberation Movement). A leading radical feminist, Delphy was one among a handful of activists who participated in the inaugural protest of the MLF in August 1970, placing a large wreath on the tomb of the Unknown Soldier at the Arc de Triomphe in commemoration of legions of unknown women (Tristan and Pisan 1987). Despite being arrested before they could get close to the monument, this dramatic gesture and the media attention it inspired gave women's liberation a public presence in France (Jackson 1996, 7). Delphy took a leading role in organizing the next major public campaign, the abortion manifesto signed by over 300 French women and published in two of France's leading newspapers in April 1971, that drew mass support and catalyzed the legalization of abortion in 1975.

In 1977, Delphy, several of her MLF comrades and Simone de Beauvoir founded the radical feminist journal *Questions Féministes* (QF, Feminist Questions). In its pages, they developed the principal tenets of "materialist" feminism.[1] Theirs was not, as in the "new materialism" of today, a materialism focused on the agency of things (cf. Bennett 2010; Harman 2010; Latour 1999). Nor was it focused on the mode of production in the traditional Marxist sense. Instead, the materialist feminists—and Delphy in particular—extended the concept of production to the household and seeked to analyze the specific exploitation of women in their subjection to both normative heterosexuality and the domestic mode of production.

Politically, the materialists identified as "radical" feminists, by the distinctive meaning accorded to that term in the context of the women's movement in France. There were socialist feminists, who prioritized class struggle over the struggle against patriarchy, and there was the "ideology of neo-femininity" that characterized such groups as Psych et Po, which sought to liberate women by emphasizing sexual difference through revaluing femininity and inventing women's language (QF Collective 1980, 216). *Radical* feminism was defined, first, by its insistence on theorizing the "patriarchal social system" as at once distinct from the capitalist social system and uniquely oppressive to women, and, second, by the "effort to deconstruct the notion of 'sex differences' which gives a shape and a base to the concept of 'woman' and is an integral part of naturalist ideology" (QF Collective 1980, 214–15).

To the French materialists, materialist analysis of sex difference (and later, gender) centers neither on women, nor their "difference", nor "interests", nor "ethic". Rather, as Delphy (2013b, 25) maintained, they held that "subjection should be put at the heart of the analysis of the situation of subjugated persons and categories." The materialists rejected the focus on "characteristics, physical characteristics that do not explain subjection, or other characteristics that are generally the result of subjection," to underscore that "emphasis should be placed *on the opposition* and not on each of the terms" (Delphy 2013b,

25–6, emphasis added). A peculiar materialism indeed! These French feminists began not by affirming the "reality" of sex differences that expressed themselves in women's different labor and experience but by doubting that those differences "are *there*, anterior to their social use" (Delphy 2013b, 13). They set themselves against the very things that United States feminists' focus on personal "experience" often encouraged: romanticizing (straight middle-class) womanhood, resurrecting empiricism, and feeding a fundamentalist attachment to sexual difference in feminism's name (Grant 1993).

This was their brilliance: to premise materialist analysis on the conviction that difference is not the "substrate" of hierarchy but its *effect* (Delphy 1993, 27). This is why I term theirs a "constructivist materialism." They *deny* the materiality of sex in order to effect a materialist analysis of gender oppression. In short, it is constructivist by virtue of its "anti-naturalism" and materialist by virtue of theorizing the production of sex and, hence, women's oppression by the institution of patriarchy: the sex-differentiated division of labor that *constructs* wives through normative heterosexuality and *exploits* them through the institution of "compulsory [unpaid] housework" in marriage (QF Collective 1980, 217).

Exemplary of this approach was Delphy's pamphlet, "The Main Enemy. A Materialist Analysis of Women's Oppression." The most influential statement of the materialist position during the movement era, the pamphlet was published in France in 1970 in the journal *Partisans*, and was the first materialist text to be translated into English and circulated in Britain in 1974 (Leonard 1984, 57). Its core argument, derived from sociological and ethnographic data on women's work, is that patriarchal exploitation, not the class position of their husbands, determines women's social class. This was an important— and infamous—departure from Marxism. Put simply, for Delphy (QF Collective 1980, 216) and the materialists, "gender" is a "social class" to which "all women belong."

Critics have denounced this claim as an overgeneralization that makes actual materialist analysis all the more difficult to do by virtue of glossing over the "very real class divisions between women" (Barrett and McIntosh 1979, 101, 102, 97). This reading overlooks the constructivist strand in Delphy and her colleagues' materialism. She emphasizes that she has always understood class as a constructivist concept, "insofar as it privileges history, what is socially constructed, the arbitrariness of culture over nature" (Delphy 2013b, 27). Delphy (1984b, 25) emphasizes that she took up the "term 'class' to refer to the division between men and women" not to emphasize the homogeneity of those groups but to problematize the very notion that they are groups. Delphy (1984b, 26) observes that to simply invoke "men and women as being 'groups'" is to say "nothing about their mode of constitution," as if the already given differences "between" those groups account for the domination of one by the other (Delphy 1984b, 26). By conceptualizing gender on the model of class, Delphy (2013b, 27) shifts the analysis from relations of oppression *between* groups to a concern with grouping *per se*.

The radical potential of this move becomes evident in Delphy's (1993, 3) potentially pathbreaking—but overlooked—theorization of gender as, in her words, the "principle of partition itself." Rather than the social meaning that attaches, more or less arbitrarily, to the two "sexes," Delphy conceived of gender as what divides them into two in the first place, making sex consequential as a marker of group difference and justification for social hierarchy. Gender, then, is not something an individual has by virtue of his or her sex; it is the agency by means of which sexed groups and individuals come into being in the first place.

To Delphy, feminist critique does not go far enough if it merely criticizes the *arbitrariness* of the sex roles that are assigned on the basis of the two sexes. It must also consider whether gender is at work in partitioning people *by* sex, constructing sex as the basis for such categorizations in the first place. Delphy recognized that this was more radical than the way most feminists were thinking of sex/gender—as she wryly put it—imagining gender "set on anatomical sex like the beret on the head of the legendary Frenchman" (Delphy 1984b, 24). Such feminists would never think to ask "why sex should give rise to any sort of social classification" in the first place (Delphy 1984b, 24; 1993, 4). Delphy argued that the critical power of gender is not that to parse the nature/social divide but to enable feminists to ask "*why* sex is more prominent than other physical traits, which are equally distinguishable, but which do not give birth to classifications which are (i) dichotomous and (ii) imply social roles which are not just distinct but hierarchical" (Delphy 1993, 4). In short, with the concept "partitioning," Delphy argued that gender works not only by naturalizing social hierarchy but also by imbuing a particular difference (sex) with the capacity to signify systematic variation. Sex, then, is more than simply one way (among others) of differing; it is that on the basis of which such other differences as aptitude for math or disposition toward empathy are distributed.

Christine Delphy is a leading feminist theorist of sex/gender. She is also a principal intellectual architect of a materialist feminism that defies contemporary discourses in which materialism appears as a corrective to constructivism. Her major works are not only of interest in their own historical and political context but in pivotal feminist conversations today.

Note

1 The original QF editorial collective was Delphy, Emmanuelle de Lesseps, Collette Guillaumin, Nicole Mathieu, and Monique Plaza. The collective split in 1980 over separatism, provoked by Monique Wittig's "The Straight Mind," which was published in tandem with Emmanuelle de Lesseps' "Heterosexuality and Feminism." Delphy and Emmanuelle de Lesseps launched *Nouvelles Questions Féministes* in protest against the radical lesbian position. Simone de Beauvoir supported both of them (Jackson 1999, 127).

Delphy's major writings

1980. "The Main Enemy." *Feminist Issues* 1(1): 23–40.

1984a. *Close to Home*, translated by Diana Leonard. Amherst: University of Massachusetts Press.

[1981] 1984b. "Patriarchy, Feminism and their Intellectuals." In *Close to Home*, translated by Diana Leonard, 138–53. Amherst: University of Massachusetts Press.

1984c. "Introduction to the Collection." In *Close to Home*, translated by Diana Leonard, 15–27. Amherst: University of Massachusetts Press.

1991. "Penser le Genre: Quels Problèmes?" In *Sexe et Genre: De la Hiérarchie entre les Sexes*, edited by Marie-Claude Hurtig, Michèle Kail and Hélène Rouch, 89–101. Paris: Éditions du Centre National de la Recherche Scientifique.

[1991] 1993. "Rethinking Sex and Gender." *Women's Studies International Forum* 16(1): 1–9 (English translation of "Penser le Genre: Quels Problèmes?").

[2001a]. 2013a. *L'Ennemi Principal, Tome 2. Penser le Genre*. Third Edition. Paris: Éditions Syllepse.

[2001b] 2013b. "Préface: Critique de la Raison Naturelle." In *L'Ennemi Principal, Tome 2. Penser le Genre*, 7–49. Third Edition. Paris: Éditions Syllepse.

2008. *Classer, Dominer: Qui Sont les 'Autres'?* Paris: La Fabrique.

Further reading

Barrett, Michèle and Mary McIntosh. 1979. "Christine Delphy: Towards a Materialist Feminism?" *Feminist Review* 1: 95–106.

Bennett, Jane. 2010. *Vibrant Matter: A Political Ecology of Things.* Durham, NC: Duke University Press.

Grant, Judith. 1993. *Fundamental Feminism: Contesting the Core Concepts of Feminist Theory.* New York: Routledge.

Harman, Graham. 2010. *Prince of Networks: Bruno Latour and Metaphysics.* Victoria, Australia: re.Press.

Jackson, Stevi. 1996. *Christine Delphy.* New York: Sage.

—. 1999. *Heterosexuality in Question.* London, Thousand Oaks and New Delhi: Sage.

Latour, Bruno. 1999. *Pandora's Hope: Essays on the Reality of Science Studies.* Cambridge, MA: Harvard University Press.

Leonard, Diana. 1984. "Preface." In *Close to Home,* Christine Delphy, 7–13. Amherst: University of Massachusetts Press.

Questions Féministes Collective. [1977] 1980. "Variations on Common Themes." In *New French Feminisms: An Anthology*, edited by Elaine Marks and Isabelle de Courtivron, 212–230. New York: Schocken Books.

Tristan, Anne and Annie de Pisan. 1987. "Tales from the Women's Movement." In *French Feminist Thought,* edited by Toril Moi, 33–69. Oxford and New York: Blackwell.

Acknowledgements

I am grateful to Julia Masters for compiling the bibliography and to Lori Marso for spearheading this project.

ANNE FAUSTO-STERLING (1944–)

Evelynn Hammonds

Anne Fausto-Sterling's careful, detailed, and groundbreaking critiques of the biological basis of sex and gender have made her one of the most influential feminist scientists of her generation. She is the Nancy Duke Lewis Professor of Biology and Gender Studies Emerita at Brown University. She earned her undergraduate degree in zoology from the University of Wisconsin (1965) and her Ph.D. from Brown in developmental genetics (1970). She has spent her entire academic career teaching and writing at Brown University.

Her most influential books and articles include her first book, *Myths of Gender: Biological Theories about Women and Men* published in 1985, and a second edition published in 1992; *Sexing the Body: Gender Politics and the Construction of Sexuality* in 2000; and the provocative article, "The Five Sexes," first published in 1993.

In *Myths of Gender*, Fausto-Sterling took up the vexed question of the ways in which ideas about sex and gender difference have been constructed through biological studies. She writes:

> Male and female babies may be born. But those complex, gender-loaded individuals we call men and women are produced. The complex assembly line includes all of our socialization processes, of which the acquisition of scientific knowledge is but one. Since our culture offers a privileged place to science, however, it is an especially important one.
>
> (1992, 270)

Scientific explanations have led to pernicious political justifications for why women should not be educated or work outside of the home or why men desire multiple sex partners, for example. Saying that the "acquisition of scientific knowledge" is itself a "socialization process," Fausto-Sterling questions "nature" all the way down, and shows how biological explanations, themselves political, are privileged over social, cultural and political practices. Fausto-Sterling's book takes up the following ordinary questions: Are men really smarter than women? Do genes dictate male and female behavior and how? What role do hormones play in male and female behavior especially aggressive behavior? Do men and women have fundamentally different brains? Can biology explain all social behavior?

Through the meticulous analysis of the most prominent scientific articles on these questions Fausto-Sterling teases apart the methodological and interpretive biases present in such works. In one sense she is calling into question the limitations of the scientific work, not dismissing science altogether. However she is deeply committed as a feminist to making it clear that biologizing societies' understanding of sex and gender does not serve science or society. She writes as a scientist who does not disavow her own political alliances. Indeed she insists that scientists should not and cannot deny their own embeddedness in society organized around sex, gender and race. As one critic noted, she wants to "warn us of the problems that rise when the question of difference becomes a question of the biological basis of difference" (Keller 1986, 37).

Myths of Gender had a huge influence on the field of feminist science studies in part because sex differences research is so pervasive in U.S. science and because Fausto-Sterling did not offer any neat solutions to the problem of difference. Her work served as a critical jumping off point for many other feminists from philosophy to political science (to name just two) to take up these questions.

In her second book, *Sexing the Body: Gender Politics and the Construction of Sexuality*, Fausto-Sterling turned her attention to gender and sex with respect to the body and the construction of sexuality itself. She argued that a body's sex is complex, and most importantly it is not either male or female. In this book she makes the claim that "labeling someone a man or a woman is a social decision. We may use scientific knowledge to help us make the decision, but only our beliefs about gender—not science—can define our sex" (2000, 3). The book examines the 'sexing' of the body by examining several case studies that start with physical structures of the body and move to behaviors, i.e. from the physical body to the psyche.

Again this book employs her now standard method of carefully exposing the bias in the scientific studies of sexuality, which include the problematic use of mice/rodents in studies of the hormonal basis of human sexual behaviors and the history of the role of hormones in human sexual development. Finally, she begins the move away from identifying bias in existing studies of human sexuality to positing a different way we might think about sex/gender. Her major contribution in this book is to argue that we must take a developmental systems approach to understanding gender embodiment and human sexuality. She posits that to understand sex and gender we need to focus on development of the self—that is the ways in which "behavior, experience, and identifications, including sexual desire and object choice … are a basic or primary 'core' of identity" (2000, 245). Drawing on the work of developmental psychologists, sociologists, historians of science, medicine and technology, she asked if there was some way to "envision the double-sided process that connects the production of gendered knowledge about the body on the one surface to materialization of gender within the body on the other?" (2000, 255). She concludes that sexuality and gender have many-sided meanings, not one-to-one identifications; thus only a multi-disciplinary systems approach can give scholars a more contextual and complete understanding of human sexuality.

Fausto-Sterling takes up this last point in one of her most provocative articles, "The Five Sexes," that questions the meaning of gender when we challenge the stability of sex. She argues that the two-sex model, that of a male and female, is far too limiting to explain the range of human sexes. There are many gradations running from male to female and along this spectrum she posits that there are at least five sexes. In contemporary western societies all gradations between the two poles of male and female are collapsed into the vague category called intersex—those individuals with both indeterminate genitalia and thus indeterminate sex. Using the example of the 'intersex' Fausto-Sterling questions both the rationales and the technologies employed by surgeons to fix such individuals in a context where what is thought of as ambiguous sex is policed and surveilled. Might we, she suggests, embrace the intersex as just one example of human sexuality rather than a deviant one?

Throughout her work as a practicing scientist and feminist, Fausto-Sterling has addressed "three major thematic dichotomies: male/female, 'real'/constructed, nature/nurture" (Kenen 2002, 532). Through the exploration of these canonical dichotomies she has raised fundamental questions about science, identity, politics, and sexuality in the twenty-first century—questions with no easy or simple answers but ones that must be addressed to build the more equitable world she so deeply envisions.

Fausto-Sterling's major writings

Books

1985. *Myths of Gender: Biological Theories about Women and Men.* New York: Basic Books.
1992. *Myths of Gender: Biological Theories about Women and Men.* Second Edition (with two new chapters). New York: Basic Books.
2000. *Sexing the Body: Gender Politics and the Construction of Sexuality.* New York: Basic Books.
2012. *Sex/Gender: Biology in a Social World.* New York: Routledge.

Articles

1993. "The Five Sexes: Why Male and Female Are Not Enough." *The Sciences* 33(2): 20–4.
1995. "Gender, Race and Nation: The Comparative Anatomy of Hottentot Women in Europe I: 1815–1817." In *Deviant Bodies*, eds. Jennifer Terry and Jacqueline Urla, 19–48. Indianapolis: Indiana University Press.
1995. "Animal Models for the Development of Human Sexuality: A Critical Evaluation." *Journal of Homosexuality* 28(3–4): 217–36.

1997. "Beyond Difference: A Biologist's Perspective." *Journal of Social Issues* 53(2): 233–58.
1999. "Is Gender Essential?" In *Sissies and Tomboys: Gender Nonconformity and Homosexual Childhood*, ed. Matthew Rottnek, 52–7. New York: New York University Press.
2000. "The Five Sexes, Revisited." *The Sciences* 40(4): 18–23.
2003. "Science Matters, Culture Matters." *Perspectives in Biology and Medicine* 46(1): 109–24.
2003. "The Problem with Sex/Gender and Nature/Nurture." In *Debating Biology: Reflections on Health, Medicine and Society*, eds. Williams Simon, J., Birke, L. and G. Bendelow, 123–32. London: Routledge.
2004. "Refashioning Race: DNA and the Politics of Health Care." *differences: A Journal of Feminist Cultural Studies* 15(3): 1–37.
2005. "The Bare Bones of Sex: Part 1—Sex and Gender." *Signs: Journal of Women in Culture and Society* 30(2): 1491–527.
2008. "Race and Bones (The Bare Bones of Sex Part 2)." *Social Studies of Science* 38(5): 657–94.
2010. With Cynthia Garcia Cool, Meghan Lamarre. "Sexing the Baby: Part 1—What Do We Really Know about Sex Differentiation in the First Three Years of Life?" *Social Science & Medicine* 74(11): 1684–92.
2012. With Cynthia Garcia Cool, Meghan Lamarre. "Sexing the Baby: Part 2—Applying Dynamic Systems Theory to the Mergences of Sex-Related Differences in Infants and Toddlers." *Social Science & Medicine* 74(11): 1693–702.
2014. "Nature." In *Critical Terms for the Study of Gender*, eds. C. Stimpson and G. Herdt, 294–319. Chicago: University of Chicago Press.
2015. "How Else Can We Study Sex Differences in Early Infancy?" *Developmental Psychobiology* 08/2015; doi: 10.1002/dev.21345.

Further reading

Keller, Evelyn Fox. 1986. "The Bounds of Biology." *The New Republic* (Feb. 3): 37–39.
Kenen, Stephanie. 2002. "Review of *Sexing the Body: Gender Politics and the Construction of Sexuality* (2000)." *Isis: Journal of the History of Science Society* 93(3): 532–34.

SHULAMITH FIRESTONE (1945–2012)

Kathi Weeks

"If there were another word more all-embracing than *revolution* we would use it" (2003, 3). This line from the opening paragraph of Shulamith Firestone's tour de force, *The Dialectic of Sex: The Case for Feminist Revolution*, captures something of the political ambitions of both the analysis and the historical moment of its emergence. The book was designed to serve the project of feminist revolution by mapping the structures of women's oppression, unmasking their ideological and subjective supports, and sketching an inspiring vision of a possible future. Drawing on inventive readings of both Freud and Marx/Engels, Firestone develops a powerful critique of the systems of production and reproduction and a provocative outline of a post-gender, post-family model of cybernetic communism. Fittingly characterized by Ann Snitow as one of feminism's infamous "demon texts" (1991, 34), *The Dialectic of Sex* has managed to variously—and more often, all at once—surprise, edify, and infuriate generations of feminists.

Firestone was one of the leading organizers and theoreticians of the U.S. women's liberation movement of the late 1960s. Born in 1945 and raised in Missouri, shortly after receiving a BFA in painting from the Art Institute of Chicago she moved in 1967 to New York City where she co-founded three of the period's most influential feminist groups: New York Radical Women, Redstockings, and New York Radical Feminists. By the time *The Dialectic of Sex* was published in 1970, Firestone had retired from the movement, and not long after that, began a long struggle with mental illness. Her second and final monograph, *Airless Spaces*, published in 1998, is composed of a series of harrowingly beautiful vignettes about her own and other people's experiences with psychiatric problems and the conditions and aftereffects of their institutionalization. Firestone died in her New York City apartment of natural causes in 2012 at the age of 67.

Besides offering a still potent critique of, and alternative to, patriarchal capitalism, each of which I will go on to discuss, Firestone's *Dialectic of Sex* remains an essential feminist text in at least two respects. The book continues to be noteworthy first of all because it is at once representative of an epochal moment in U.S. feminist history and the exceptional product of a unique thinker. So on the one hand, it offers a crash course in the fundamentals of early second wave radical feminism. Most of the topics of analysis are drawn from the politicization of "private" life pioneered under the radical feminist slogan that "the personal is political," and many of its insights are informed by the small-group consciousness-raising practice that flourished at the time. In addition, not only the subject matter, but the tone of the writing too, is exemplary of the excitement, seriousness of purpose, and spirit of experimentation that was characteristic of the historical moment. On the other hand, the work also defies categorization. This is not only because the version of radical feminism she articulates bears little resemblance to the feminisms that later come to assume the label, but also because there is something so distinctive about her thinking, so inimitable about her voice, that it is difficult to pigeon-hole Firestone as a writer. Despite her membership in various activist groups, Firestone was also ready and willing to go against the grain; towards her fellow feminists she was at once accommodating and utterly uncompromising. In this sense the text is remarkable for being equally representative of radical feminist common sense and the singular vision of an individual theorist.

The second source of the text's iconicity has to do with the way it serves to illustrate—in such dramatic fashion—both the very best and very worst of early second wave feminist theory. Indeed, in some instances, the same elements are responsible for the best and worst features of the analysis. One of these is its singular focus on gender as an axis of oppression. By concentrating so intently on women as a sex-class, radical feminists like Firestone taught us how to recognize gender as a legitimate theoretical category and viable locus of political struggle. The problem was that, as a way to insist on its validity, gender was presented as more fundamental than, and indeed, as the model for, the secondary hierarchies of class, race, and sexuality. The most disturbing example of this over-privileging of gender as an isolated category can be found in the fifth chapter where she offers an argument about racism as merely an outgrowth of and support system for sexism together with a particularly repellant account of the psychodynamics of U.S. racism as analogous to the model of the patriarchal nuclear family, an account that relies on stereotypes and caricatures for depictions of psychological types on both sides of the analogy.[1]

The *Dialectic of Sex* is written in the style of a manifesto—which is also one of its best or worst qualities, depending on one's opinion of the genre. It is a spectacle of a text, written in theatrical manner and performing its passions with frequent italics, occasionally outrageous assertions, and hilarious asides. Written in a bold, self-assured voice, the prose vibrates with equal parts rage and joy, hard-hitting critique and biting sarcasm. She makes no effort to speak to the delicate sensibilities of a skeptical audience; her goal is not to convince those in power to understand women's plight or to seduce them with a polite willingness to be reasonable. Most of all, she refuses to indulge the usual "benefit-of-the-doubtism towards men" from which she claims most women suffer (2003, 99). Instead, the text is addressed to would-be fellow travelers: to the radical feminist audience she wanted to arm with empowering knowledge and infectious emotion. Speaking in a tone of aggressive truth-telling, Firestone offers few concessions to the uninitiated, let alone hostile, reader.

Firestone's most controversial move was then, and remains today, her unapologetic assertion that the oppression of women is grounded in their reproductive biology. Women's lot may be natural in origin, but it is not for that reason either normative or immutable; we are now on the brink of a new historical stage, she claims, when technological developments, including extra-uterine childbirth, could fundamentally alter the "natural" order of things. It would be an interesting project to catalog the various reactions to this argument about the natural basis of gender hierarchy in relation to feminism's contested and evolving theoretical conceptions of, and political claims about, the status of sexual difference. Many have, for example, read Firestone's position as a conceptual mistake that replicates antifeminism's biological essentialism. But it could also be read, from another angle, as an effort to grasp in phenomenological terms the cultural force of that difference. One could approach the assertion as a shrewd political move that concedes the anti-feminist argument only to then reveal its historical obsolescence. Or it could be treated as a utopian exercise in cognitive estrangement designed to thrust the reader into a future scenario where she can then access new horizons of possibility.[2] In any case, it remains a certainly troubling, but perhaps still potentially generative element of Firestone's theoretical intervention.

Perhaps the strongest, and today most relevant, legacy of the *Dialectic of Sex* is Firestone's critique of the family. The central claim of her argument is that the institution of the family, together with its various ideological reinforcements, serves as the lynchpin of the larger socioeconomic system and constitutes the locus of women's economic, psychological, and political oppression. Anchored in the gender division of reproductive labor, the patriarchal nuclear family—her primary target—is sustained by various cultural formations, including gendered subjectivities, modes of sexual repression, and popular platitudes about heterosexual love and romance. The critique of the family and its supports offers some brilliant examples of the demystificatory power of ideology critique. Key to these ideologies is what she usefully names the sex privatization of women. Women are sex privatized, for example, when their sense of themselves as individuals becomes sutured to standard codes of femininity or when they approach the privatized institution of marriage with "a defiant 'We're different' brand of optimism" about the authenticity of the relationship and its prospects for securing their happiness (2003, 200). More controversially, as part of the critique of the structures and socialities of the family, she also takes on what she sees as the cultural mystification of childbirth, the non-technologically mediated form of which she declares "barbaric" (180); the sentimentalization of childhood, which, she claims, veils at once our envy and contempt for children; and the gender division of parenting that persists, she claims, regardless of whether women are "granted a new [waged] job to add to their old one" (196). There remains much that feminists could still glean, certainly from the systematic scope, and possibly from certain of the specifics of Firestone's all-out assault on the structures and cultural conventions of heterosexual intimacy, marriage, and family.

Whereas Firestone's critique of the family as a fundamental component of patriarchal capitalism has often been treated respectfully, if not always enthusiastically, by feminist readers over the years, the admittedly "sketchy" (203) model of a feminist future she offers at the end of the book has not been met with as generous a reception. Yet, it may be that history has finally caught up with Firestone's utopian vision, rendering what was typically considered a naïve bit of eccentricity into a credible exercise of the political imagination. The utopia she outlines revolutionizes the systems of production and reproduction and eliminates all gendered divisions of labor. Automation leads to an ecologically sustainable economy predicated on a massive reduction of work and a guaranteed basic income. Women and children are liberated from the institution of the family, which is replaced by a wide variety of associational opportunities and relations of care and cooperation. Polymorphous sexuality is released, eroticism expanded, and gender itself withers away once sex distinctions no longer carry cultural significance. Although her goal was not to prescribe a future so much as to demonstrate utopian thinking, it is not only the form of the exercise but also some of the contents of the vision that merit reconsidering. Today, when it is becoming increasingly clear that neither the employment system nor the privatized family function adequately as mechanisms of income distribution, labor organization, care delivery, or social incorporation, Firestone's alternative vision of economic organization and household formation offers what might function as a timely political imaginary; when the binary gender order is becoming ever more untenable, Firestone's provocation to speculate about a world beyond gender might now be worth once again seriously entertaining.

Notes

1 For a critique focused on Chapter 5, see Spillers 1984.
2 I develop this argument in Weeks 2015.

Firestone's major works

[1970] 2003. *The Dialectic of Sex: The Case for Feminist Revolution*. New York: Farrar, Straus and Giroux.
1998. *Airless Spaces*. New York: Semiotext(e).

Further reading

Atkinson, Ti-Grace, et al. 2013. "In Memoriam: On Shulamith Firestone." *n + 1* 15 (Winter). www.nplusonemag.com/issue-15/in-memoriam/on-shulamith-firestone/
Echols, Alice. 2002. "Totally Ready to Go: Shulamith Firestone and *The Dialectic of Sex*." In *Shaky Ground: The Sixties and Its Aftershocks*, 103–08. New York: Columbia University Press.
Faludi, Susan. 2013. "Death of a Revolutionary." *The New Yorker*, April 15. www.newyorker.com/magazine/2013/04/15/death-of-a-revolutionary
Merck, Mandy and Stella Sandford, eds. 2010. *Further Adventures of* The Dialectic of Sex: *Critical Essays on Shulamith Firestone*. New York: Palgrave Macmillan.
Snitow, Ann. 1991. "Motherhood—Reclaiming the Demon Texts," *Ms.* 1(6): 34–37.
—. 1994. "Returning to the Well." *Dissent* Fall: 557–58. www.dissentmagazine.org/online_articles/returning-to-the-well-fall-1994
Spillers, Hortense J. 1984. "Interstices: A Small Drama of Words." In *Pleasure and Danger: Exploring Female Sexuality*, ed. Carole S. Vance, 73–100. Boston: Routledge and Kegan Paul.
Weeks, Kathi. 2015. "The Vanishing *Dialectic*: Shulamith Firestone and the Future of the Feminist 1970s." *South Atlantic Quarterly* 114(4): 735–54.

BETTY FRIEDAN (1921–2006)

Rebecca Jo Plant

One of the most famous American feminists of the twentieth century, Betty Friedan first attracted national attention as the author of the 1963 bestseller, *The Feminine Mystique*. A scorching indictment of the post-World War II domestic ideal and its narrow conception of womanhood, the book is widely credited with inaugurating a new wave of feminist activism. Friedan went on to play a key role in founding several influential feminist organizations that remain active to the present day, including the National Organization of Women (NOW), the National Association for the Repeal of Abortion Laws (NARAL), and the National Women's Political Caucus. Often described by scholars as a "liberal" feminist to differentiate her from her more radical counterparts, Friedan believed in fostering a broad-based movement that focused primarily on securing economic and political equality for women.

Born on February 4, 1921, in Peoria, Illinois, Bettye Goldstein (she would later drop the "e") was the oldest child of Harry Goldstein, a Jewish immigrant from Kiev, and his much younger, American-born wife, Miriam Horowitz. When Betty and her two younger siblings were children, Harry's successful jewelry business afforded the family an affluent lifestyle, complete with a nursemaid, cook, and a butler/chauffeur. Yet despite their wealth, the family experienced anti-Semitism in the form of social exclusions and sleights. They were barred from joining the town's most exclusive country club, and Friedan was rejected from a high school sorority due primarily to "being Jewish"—an experience that reinforced her identification as an "outsider" and fueled her passion for social justice.

A strained relationship with her mother also cast a shadow over Friedan's formative years. According to her first-born, Miriam badgered her children, belittled her husband, and suffered from bouts of colitis that left her bedridden and "screaming in pain." Friedan later came to believe that much of her mother's unhappiness and even her physical ailments stemmed from the lack of a meaningful outlet for her immense energy. These convictions regarding her mother's thwarted ambition and its negative effects on her family would strongly inform Friedan's critical depiction of suburban womanhood in *The Feminine Mystique*.

In 1938, Friedan entered Smith College, where she came into her own. She excelled academically, revamped and edited the school newspaper, and grew increasingly interested in radical politics. In 1941, she attended a summer course at Highlander Folk School in Tennessee—which served as a training ground for labor and civil rights activists—and supported a strike by Smith College's domestic workers. After graduating *summa cum laude* with a degree in psychology in 1942, she began a graduate program in psychology at University of California, Berkeley, where she studied with Erik Erikson, among others. After a year, however, she declined a prestigious graduate fellowship and moved back to New York, taking a job as a journalist for the United Federated News, a labor syndicate. In 1946 she was hired to write for the *UE News*, the official organ of the United Electrical, Radio and Machine Workers of America, one of the nation's most radical unions. Historian David Horowitz has argued that her work during this period "placed her in the most progressive and controversial reaches of the American left" (1998, 102).

In 1947, Friedan entered into what would prove to be a tempestuous and at times even violent twenty-two-year marriage with Carl Friedan, a theater producer who later became an advertising executive. Between 1948 and 1956 she gave birth to three children. As a mother, Friedan was in some ways typical of highly educated, middle-class women of the time. She avidly read Dr. Spock and insisted on breastfeeding, despite a lack of support from hospital personnel. But unlike most of her peers, Friedan also worked outside the home, even when her children were quite young—a fact that she later obscured when describing the origins of *The Feminine Mystique*. When she became pregnant for the second time, the *UE News* fired her. In her memoir, Friedan recalled feeling angry but also relieved, "because all those negative books and magazine articles about 'career women' were beginning to get to me." Yet soon after she had "dispensed with the nursemaid," she grew depressed and suffered a recurrence of severe asthma, an ailment that had plagued her since childhood.

Friedan's profound unhappiness eventually led her to enter therapy with the psychoanalyst William Menaker. Although she condemned popularized Freudianism in *The Feminine Mystique*, her own experiences with psychoanalytic therapy in the 1950s actually proved quite liberating. Rather than pathologizing her ambitions, Menaker asked her why she confined herself to "'playing the role' of suburban housewife." Before her second child had reached his first birthday, Friedan had hired a maid to come three days a week, allowing her to begin a new career as a freelance journalist. Her experience with Menaker proved so positive, in fact, that she approached him several years later, after receiving the contract for what would become *The Feminine Mystique*.

Believing that his expertise would lend her work "more authority," Friedan proposed that they collaborate. Had her editor not nixed the idea, the name of an authorizing "eminent male psychoanalyst" might therefore have graced the cover of *The Feminine Mystique*—a mind-boggling notion, given the book's ultimate trajectory.

It took Friedan five years to research and write *The Feminine Mystique*. When published in 1963, its popular success was immediate and phenomenal: it spent six weeks on the *New York Times* bestseller list, and sales of the first paperback printing eventually reached 1.4 million. While today the book is associated with sparking a new phase of feminist activism, its appeal actually lay less in Friedan's somewhat blurry vision of the future than in her sharp assessment of the present and the recent past. With the end of World War II, she argued, a whole generation of American women, weary of economic hardship and war, had made a "mistaken choice" (153–72). Turning their backs on the hard-won achievements of an earlier generation of suffragists and feminists, they had abandoned educational and career ambitions and plunged headlong into early marriage and motherhood, producing an extraordinary baby boom. Social scientists and psychological experts, popular writers, and advertisers had fueled these trends by propagating the belief that well-adjusted women derived fulfillment only through motherhood and domesticity. This was the spurious ideology—the "feminine mystique"—that Friedan sought to demolish. Women caught in its throes, she argued, suffered from "the problem with no name"—a pervasive sense of purposelessness that manifested itself any number of ways, as crushing ennui, alcoholism, overbearing mothering, insatiable sexual desire, even mental illness and suicide.

Even as Friedan condemned certain experts, she also appropriated the theories of others to validate her findings; the book, which has numerous footnotes, reads like a cross between academic treatise and journalistic exposé. Her views are particularly indebted to the work of psychoanalysts Erik Erikson and Abraham Maslow, who respectively introduced the concepts of "identity crisis" and "self-actualization." "It is my thesis," she argued, "that the core of the problem for women today is ... a problem of identity—a stunting or evasion of growth that is perpetuated by the feminine mystique" (61). To become a "self-actualized" woman who attained fulfillment and growth as an individual, one had to break free of the culture's narrow definition of womanhood. By identifying "the problem with no name" and exposing its emotional toll, Friedan captured the attention of thousands of women, many of whom expressed profound relief to know that they were not alone in feeling trapped by domesticity.

In retrospect, it is easy to identify shortcomings in Friedan's work. By conflating "American women" with suburban wives and mothers, she implied that all the nation's women were white and middle class. As feminist theorist bell hooks later pointed out, she wrote as if working-class women and women of color "did not exist." Given Friedan's prior work on labor issues, this myopia is hard is explain. Her analysis is also marred by Cold War homophobia and mother-blaming; she blamed insufficiently occupied and overbearing mothers for "the homosexuality that is spreading like a murky fog over the American scene" (267). Finally, she portrayed the suburban housewives she hoped to liberate in strikingly harsh terms that offended and alienated many readers. Indeed, just as one can see intimations of a new feminist movement in the letters from Friedan's fans, so can one see the sentiments that would give rise to the New Right in the letters from her critics, who viewed her work as belittling the contributions of American mothers and wives.

Surprisingly, *The Feminine Mystique* offered little in the way of a policy-oriented agenda. Friedan looked forward to a time when women would demand "maternity leaves or even maternity sabbaticals, professionally run nurseries, and other changes ... that may be necessary"; she also called for a government program similar to the GI Bill to help homemakers who want to return to school (370–78). But the final chapter of *The Feminine Mystique* mainly featured stories of remarkable women who had managed to pursue fulfilling careers without forgoing marriage and motherhood. Entitled "A New Life Plan," it appeared to suggest that women could simply reject society's definition of femininity and forge a more rewarding path for themselves through individual choice and willpower alone.

Within three years of publishing *The Feminine Mystique*, Friedan had moved in a decidedly more political direction. In 1966, she became the first president of NOW, formed to serve as an "NAACP for women." Along with lawyer Pauli Murray, Friedan coauthored the organization's Statement of Purpose—a powerful manifesto that in some ways echoes *The Feminine Mystique*. But it also signaled a departure with its use of the new term "sex discrimination" and its explicit rejection of the notion that the problems women experienced combining work and domestic responsibilities were "the unique responsibility of each individual" to resolve.

By the late 1970s, however, Friedan had distanced herself from the feminist movement, frustrated with those who sought to emphasize issues related to sexuality and violence, such as rape, pornography, sexual harassment, and domestic abuse. In 1981, soon after the election of

Ronald Reagan, she published *The Second Stage*, written in part as a last-ditch attempt to rally support for the Equal Rights Amendment. Here, Friedan argued that the "first stage" of feminist movement—the fight for equal opportunities in the workplace—had basically been won. Yet as many women had discovered, "The equality we fought for isn't livable, isn't workable, isn't comfortable in the terms that structured our battle" (29). Because Friedan declared victory prematurely while continuing to employ a universalizing "we," most feminists dismissed the book as a disappointing retreat. It was prescient in some respects, however, for the concerns she raised about the difficulties of combining work and motherhood have only grown more pronounced over time.

In the decades that followed, Friedan published *The Fountain of Age*, a book about aging and age discrimination, as well as her memoir, *Life So Far*. She died on February 4, 2006, her eighty-fifth birthday. Given the remarkable timing, it is tempting to imagine that, even in death, she managed to exert her indomitable will, departing on her own terms.

Friedan's major writings

[1963] 2012. *The Feminine Mystique: A Norton Critical Edition*, eds. Kirsten Fermaglich and Lisa M. Fine. New York: W. W. Norton.

[1976] 1998. *It Changed My Life*. Cambridge, MA: Harvard University Press.

[1981] 1998. *The Second Stage*. Cambridge, MA: Harvard University Press.

1993. *The Fountain of Age*. New York: Simon and Schuster.

2000. *Life So Far: A Memoir*. New York: Simon and Schuster.

Further reading

Coontz, Stephanie. 2011. *A Strange Stirring: The Feminine Mystique and American Women at the Dawn of the 1960s*. New York: Basic Books.

Hennessee, Judith. 1999. *Betty Friedan: Her Life*. New York: Random House.

Horowitz, Daniel. 1998. *Betty Friedan and the Making of "The Feminine Mystique": The American Left, the Cold War and Liberal Feminism*. Amherst: University of Massachusetts Press.

Meyerowitz, Joanne. 1993. "Beyond the Feminine Mystique: A Reassessment of Postwar Mass Culture, 1946–1958." *Journal of American History* 79(4): 1455–82.

Plant, Rebecca Jo. 2010. *Mom: The Transformation of Motherhood in Modern America*. Chicago: University of Chicago Press.

Shermann, Janann. 2003. *Interviews with Betty Friedan*. Jackson: University of Mississippi Press.

Weiss, Jessica. 2012. "'Fraud of Femininity': Domesticity, Selflessness, and Individualism in Responses to Betty Friedan." In *Liberty and Justice for All? Rethinking Politics in Cold War America*, Kathleen G. Donohue (ed.). Amherst: University of Massachusetts Press: 124–56.

MARGARET FULLER (1810–1850)

Jeffrey Steele

Born in Cambridgeport, Massachusetts, Margaret Fuller came of age during a key period of U.S. political and intellectual awakening. Unlike friends such as Ralph Waldo Emerson and Henry David Thoreau, she did not enjoy the direct benefit of being educated at nearby Harvard University. But as the eldest child of an influential father, Timothy Fuller (who served both as a state representative and congressman), Fuller received the kind of intellectual training that was usually reserved for boys. Fluent in multiple languages, she was able to rely upon her wide reading of the world's classics to teach in multiple venues and to gain entry into the foremost literary circles of her time. Fuller is remembered as one of the leaders of the Transcendentalist circle and the first editor of its journal, *The Dial*. In her Conversations for Boston women, she pioneered one of the country's first consciousness-raising groups. She was the foremost literary critic of her generation and a leading public intellectual who published *Woman in the Nineteenth Century*, the most important feminist treatise of the first half of the century. In the last five years of her life, she was a widely-read columnist and correspondent for the *New-York Tribune*, publishing a wide range of cultural reviews, reform essays, and—near the end of her life—dispatches from war-torn Italy. Fuller helped to redefine the position of women, often by creating exalted images of what women might achieve if the barriers to their development were removed. When she died tragically in a shipwreck, off the coast of Fire Island in 1850, the woman's movement in America lost one its most eloquent and visionary leaders. In their monumental *History of Woman Suffrage*, Elizabeth Cady Stanton and Susan B. Anthony declared that she "possessed more influence on the thought of American women than any woman previous to her time" (Flexnor 1973, 342).

Fuller's first important step in articulating this feminist vision occurred in her unpublished "Autobiographical Romance" (1840)—a critique of the patriarchal, "Roman" values that she absorbed while studying and translating Latin classics in her father's study. The young Fuller discovered that her father's emphasis upon intellectual "precision," masculine command, and "the power of will" left little room for the imagination and emotional fluidity that she located in "the enchanted gardens of Greek mythology" and in her mother's garden. His rigid sense of literary decorum led to a deep split in her character: "My own world sank deep within, away from the surface of my life," while her "true life" was "secluded and veiled over by ... Common Sense" (1992a, 28–30). In the ensuing drama of self-recovery, Fuller pursued a lost self that she came to associate with mythic images of female greatness. This pursuit accelerated as she expanded her study of mythology for her Boston Conversations and when she assumed the editorship of the Transcendentalist journal *The Dial*, where she began publishing mythical explorations of the divine feminine. In "The Magnolia of Lake Pontchartrain" (1841), an enigmatic female figure describes her discovery of a hidden region of maternal deity. Dedicating herself to the "goddess" that she discovered within, she learned how to "[t]ake a step inward" and "retire" into her "own heart" (1992b, 48–49). The mystical essay "Leila" (1841) depicts the meditative pursuit of a divine figure, who takes on the lineaments of Isis, Diana, and even Jesus. Feminizing Emerson's model of self-reliance (which depended upon the intuition of "god within"), Fuller demonstrated that goddess images might embody an equivalent imaginative energy.

In Fuller's feminist masterpiece, *Woman in the Nineteenth Century* (1845), figures such as Leila became part of a larger pantheon of exalted female images. The position of women in America, Fuller discerned, was shifting. Her goal was to combine an overview of the contemporary social conditions with a prophetic and often visionary portrait of "the coming age" (1992d, 313) that she saw crystallizing around her. As a roadmap to the "New individualities" (318) that are appearing, Fuller turns to literature, mythology, and women's history. Rather than allowing her society to maintain the either/or dichotomy of "true women" and "fallen women," she vastly expands the repertoire of female subject positions, providing a plethora of role models, each embodying what she terms the "idea of woman" (269). These figures range from Queen Elizabeth I and Joan of Arc to Isis, Diana, and the Christian Madonna. But what each potential avatar embodies is "a standard within herself"

(258), manifesting "the power of self-poise" (311). Fuller's goal is to facilitate her readers in nurturing a corresponding development of female independence. Only when women achieve personal dignity and strength will they be able to take their place as part of a harmonious union of male and female qualities both in the psyche and society. Since, in Fuller's eyes, "man and woman ... are the two halves of one thought, ... the development of the one cannot be effected without that of the other" (245). Thus, the social suppression of women and the psychological repression of female qualities damages both men and women, who lose a sense of equilibrium and "harmony." In her most ecstatic moments, Fuller imagines a mystical Sacred Marriage of male and female principles—a union in which "king" and "queen" balance each other. But, at the present, man "has found himself a king without a queen" and is trapped in an "unequal union" (343).

Fuller challenged the prevailing gender roles in American society. Women, she observes, "are so overloaded with precepts by guardians ... that their minds are impeded by doubts" (262). This captivity is perpetuated by "treatises, intended to mark out with precision the limits of woman's sphere, and woman's mission, to prevent other than the rightful shepherd from climbing the wall" (257). The dominant ideology of female submission, she suggests, was supported by appeals to scripture. But in the Bible, thieves—not shepherds—climb walls. In Fuller's striking Biblical revision, it is the male shepherd (for example, the husband) whose proprietary control of his wife amounts to an act of theft. Elsewhere, Fuller brings into visibility the dominant gender ideology by staging a dialogue between her narrator and a slave-trader, who defends male supremacy. Granting greater freedom to women, he asserts, will "break up the national union, ... break up the family union," and "take my wife away from the cradle and the kitchen hearth to vote at polls, and preach from a pulpit" (255). Challenging this ideology of separate spheres, Fuller asserts that: "We would have every arbitrary barrier thrown down. We would have every path laid open to woman as freely as to man" (260). At the heart of Fuller's plea for gender equality is her perception that men and women possess both masculine and feminine qualities in different proportions. "There is no wholly masculine man," she affirms, "no purely feminine woman" (310). But the great flaw in American society is that it lacks images of female strength and agency. Thus, one of her primary goals is to supplement the social imaginary by providing these missing images of womanhood. Initially, Fuller supplies such images in her many examples of "the idea of woman." But, then, she moves closer to home by examining the group of individuals "contemptuously designated as old maids" (298). Since they are "undistracted by other relationships" (299), such persons exemplify a spiritual and intellectual independence that expresses the suppressed side of female character.

Fuller's defense of independent, single women was one of the most controversial aspects of her book, since some male reviewers believed that sexually inexperienced, unmarried women lacked the authority to be giving advice about gender roles. Countering such arguments, Fuller provides numerous examples of noble, female independence. She reminds her readers of prominent religious leaders (such as St.Teresa of Avila and the Shaker Mother Anne Lee), who exemplify the 'marriage' to divine power that she also locates in depictions of the Annunciation of the Virgin Mary and an American Indian narrative of a woman who lived apart, "betrothed to the Sun" (301). All these figures exemplify the Transcendentalist ideal of self-reliance, since they represent "the soul which is poised upon itself ... in harmony with the central soul" (312). In order to stabilize her vision of female independence, Fuller— like Sigmund Freud and Carl Jung—maps the psyche through the use of myth. "There are two aspects of woman's nature," she asserts, "represented by the ancients as Muse and Minerva [a.k.a. Athena]" (309). Overlapping with popular images of female beauty and influence, the Muse is the more accessible figure, but—for Fuller—she also exemplifies spiritual intensity, "the unimpeded clearness of the intuitive powers" (310). However, "in the present crisis," Fuller gives "preference ... to Minerva," the warrior goddess who personifies female strength and independence and provides a model of how women might use "the armor and the javelin" (311, 313).

In addition to remapping society's image of female character, Fuller also makes a number of strategic interventions in contemporary social conditions. She includes a controversial discussion of prostitution and the sexual exploitation of women. Condemning "slavery to the body" (321) and its "brute passions" (330), she argues for male sexual control during a period when urban centers were marked by hundreds of brothels. Turning to the smug complacency of many middle and upper-class women, she argues that their reinforcement of superficial and materialistic values—"love of dress, love of flattery, love of excitement"—has contributed to the corruption of fallen women. In rejection of sexual ostracism and a powerful appeal to sisterhood, she implores them to: "Seek out these degraded women, give them tender sympathy, counsel, employment. Take the place of mothers, such as might have saved them originally" (329). Turning to the proposed Annexation of Texas (a key topic in the Presidential campaign of 1844), she calls on American women to use their "moral power"

(341) to the point of gender non-compliance in order to stop the spread of slave-holding territory. Countering the widespread "ennui" of underemployed women, she argues for "a much greater range of occupations," even the role of "sea-captains" (345–46).

As a whole, Fuller's feminist treatise aims to release women from ideological and social captivity. Instead of being constrained, woman needs "as a nature to grow, as an intellect to discern, as a soul to live freely and unimpeded, to unfold such powers as were given her when we left our common home" (261). Ultimately, Fuller attempts to inspire her readers to an exalted vision of female potential. Realigning self-expectation, she models a transformation of consciousness that might change the contours of being. Citing Matthew 7, she focuses on the way preconception shapes awareness: "Whatever the soul knows how to seek, it cannot fail to obtain" (249). Social and psychological change, in other words, is facilitated by a change of preconception. As Fuller's friend Henry David Thoreau later asserted: "The universe answers to our conceptions." Realigning one's viewpoint, Fuller's essay thus creates a new structure of consciousness, in which ideal forms of female being can take root and flourish. Her exalted images of classical goddesses, literary heroines, and great female leaders exist for a while in the reader's awareness and summon, in their wake, new more expansive forms of self-expectation and being.

Fuller's major writings

[1840] 1992a. "Autobiographical Romance." In *The Essential Margaret Fuller*. Ed. Jeffrey Steele. New Brunswick: Rutgers University Press: 24–43.

[1841] 1992b. "The Magnolia of Lake Pontchartrain." In *The Essential Margaret Fuller*. Ed. Jeffrey Steele. New Brunswick: Rutgers University Press: 44–49.

[1841] 1992c. "Leila." In *The Essential Margaret Fuller*. Ed. Jeffrey Steele. New Brunswick: Rutgers University Press: 53–58.

[1845] 1992d. *Woman in the Nineteenth Century.* In *The Essential Margaret Fuller*. Ed. Jeffrey Steele. New Brunswick: Rutgers University Press: 243–378.

Further reading

Bean, Judith Mattson and Joel Myerson. 2000. *Margaret Fuller, Critic: Writings from the* New-York Tribune, *1844–1846.* New York: Columbia University Press.

Capper, Charles. 1992. *Margaret Fuller: An American Romantic Life, Vol. 1: The Private Years*. New York and Oxford: Oxford University Press.

—. 2010. *Margaret Fuller: An American Romantic Life, Vol. 2: The Public Years*. New York and Oxford: Oxford University Press.

Flexnor, Eleanor. [1959] 1973. *Century of Struggle: The Woman's Rights Movement in the United States*. New York: Atheneum.

Marshall, Megan. 2013. *Margaret Fuller: A New American Life*. Boston and New York: Houghton Mifflin Harcourt.

Reynolds, Larry J. and Susan Belasco Smith. 1991. *"These Sad but Glorious Days": Dispatches from Europe, 1846–1850*. New Haven and London: Yale University Press.

Steele, Jeffrey. 2001. *Transfiguring American: Myth, Ideology, and Mourning in Margaret Fuller's Writing*. Columbia: University of Missouri Press.

CHARLOTTE PERKINS GILMAN (1860–1935)

Cynthia J. Davis

"The personal is political" was an important motto of the second wave of the U.S. women's movement, but in numerous ways it also motivated one of the key thinkers of the first wave: Charlotte Perkins Gilman. The challenges of her personal life deeply informed her efforts to reform conventional understandings of femininity, masculinity, domesticity, marriage, work, religion, literature, and society.

Gilman remains intriguing for both modern-day feminism and modern thought more generally for her advocacy of an impersonal mode of living, where interests beyond the self are consistently prioritized, against a mounting tide of individualism and a burgeoning cult of personality. Her life story is all the more interesting due to her understandable personal difficulties maintaining the unswervingly selfless course she set for herself and others. She remains relevant today for her persistent attention to the varied issues that continue to vex modern women, including employment and economic viability, equitable relationships, the work-family balance, domestic responsibilities, child-rearing difficulties, and the pursuit of a meaningful life. Her personal challenges with all of these issues lent heft and urgency to her theories about them, a connection between the personal and the political that she rarely acknowledged publicly but that nonetheless helps to explain her staying power.

Her personal troubles date at least from her infancy when her father, the librarian, editor and author Frederic Beecher Perkins, first left his wife and two surviving children; the couple eventually divorced in 1873. Charlotte and her older brother Thomas were raised in penurious circumstances as their mother, Mary A. Fitch (Westcott) Perkins, moved them around New England nineteen times in eighteen years in search of financial or familial support. Charlotte's mother withheld affection on principle and her father kept in touch sporadically. Charlotte grew up resenting maternal expectations and enforced domesticity and pining for the personal and intellectual freedom she associated with her father's side of the family; his mother was a Beecher, a family of renowned ministers and reformers who symbolized for the young girl the possibility of a life devoted to public service.

Charlotte demonstrated considerable talent as an artist but eventually scorned art as a possible career due to its limited social utility. As a teenager in Providence, Rhode Island, she immersed herself in the physical culture movement even though her reform ambitions already extended beyond the self. Periodically and especially in her twenties and thirties, she formed intense attachments to other women and mourned these relationships as each unraveled or frayed. Her career aspirations help to explain her preference for these supportive, intimate, same-sex relationships uncomplicated by the conventional expectations of marriage and husband. Although raised during an era that exalted the private sphere and especially the home, she resisted this cultural tendency and instead consistently romanticized the public sphere and rewarding work as essential sites of human fulfillment.

She had already vowed to embark on a life of social service when in 1882 she met a significant obstacle in the shape of Charles Walter Stetson, a brooding, romantic artist with fairly traditional understandings of women's roles. After two years spent anguishing over whether she could combine marriage and career, she finally resolved to marry Walter; some ten months after their wedding, the couple's first and only child, a daughter, was born. During the ensuing months Charlotte experienced bouts of debilitating mental and physical illness. By 1887 her health had grown so dire that concerned friends sent her to Dr. S. Weir Mitchell's sanitarium to undergo a "rest cure," which proscribed all mental and physical activity. The cure for this patient proved worse than the disease. She would dramatize her postpartum, post-treatment breakdown in her haunting short story, "The Yellow Wall-Paper" (1892), for which she remains best known. While the story with its thematic and formal complexity testifies to her literary talents, it remains one of the few exceptions to her didactic rule. She came to view literature as simply another tool in her reform arsenal. Travel and work eventually helped her to recover from this severe nervous collapse, but she continued to experience depression and nervous exhaustion intermittently throughout her remaining years.

Resolving to serve mankind versus just one man, in 1888 she left her husband behind and moved with her young daughter to the west coast. During her California years she published a volume of poetry and immersed herself in numerous social causes including the woman's suffrage movement, which was regaining momentum in the late century as a series of western states granted women the vote. Through her involvement in local women's causes in the Bay Area, she met a number of influential female activists including Susan B. Anthony and Jane Addams. In 1894, a month after her divorce was finalized, she sent her daughter Katharine back east to live with Walter, who would soon marry Charlotte's dear friend Grace Channing, with Charlotte's blessing. Insisting she was acting in her daughter's best interests, she defended her controversial actions by invoking her intention to devote herself fully to her career as a lecturer, social philosopher, and self-described "world-servant." Her career aspirations and feminism, cited as grounds for her divorce, along with her supposed child abandonment produced an intense backlash that inspired, however indirectly, a number of her subsequent works. For example, in *Concerning Children* (1900), she calls for a nation of trained mothers and "baby gardens" as a means of improving the haphazard, isolated method of childrearing so prevalent in America and that had proven so hazardous to her own health.

At the midpoint of five itinerant years (1895–1900) on the lecture circuit, she drafted *Women and Economics* (1898). The book made her fame and saw her celebrated as the foremost theorist of the U.S. woman's movement. In this treatise, the first she published, she argues (universalizing the experience of most middle-class women at the time) that women's economic dependence on men is both unnatural and deforming, accentuating feminine characteristics over human ones. She encourages women to find financial independence through fulfilling work unrestricted to a traditionally gendered sphere or role. She sought to practice what she preached, having learned the book's lessons at great personal cost. Ironically, although she claimed to be happiest whenever she could lose herself in work and service, she rarely found her calling to be remunerative, and she often suffered from loneliness on the road. Her itinerant years included several stays of varying lengths at Hull House, the famous Chicago settlement house run by Addams. She soon grew restless, however, even in a community of mostly female reformers where she might have been expected to feel at home. In part this can be attributed to her abiding discomfort with domesticity and its persistent conflation with femininity, a conflation she sought to unravel in her witty treatise, *The Home* (1903).

On a visit to New York City in 1897, she was reunited with her first cousin, George Houghton Gilman, who was seven years her junior. After a lengthy courtship, the couple married in 1900. The marriage, which lasted until Houghton's sudden death from a stroke in 1934, was entirely amicable, largely unaffected by the health issues and career anxieties that had doomed her first marriage. Houghton's easygoing personality and support of his wife's ambitions help to explain the difference, but Charlotte was also feeling more confident at this stage of her career. Soon after their wedding the couple settled in New York City. The woman now known as Charlotte Perkins Gilman continued to write and lecture on behalf of various social causes. She also traveled and lectured internationally on several occasions, beginning with a trip to a socialist convention in Great Britain in 1896 and ending with a trip through Europe in 1913 to speak on women's issues.

Although hailed in our day as an influential feminist, Gilman's relationship with feminism as it was defined in her day remained uneasy. She considered the movement too narrowly focused, not only on suffrage versus other women's causes but also on women versus the larger human race. Frustrated by decreasing opportunities to broadcast her message of social service, she decided to publish and write her own monthly magazine, *The Forerunner*, which ran from 1909 until 1916. The pressure to produce enough material to fill an entire magazine every month made this a tremendously prolific period: in addition to numerous poems, stories, and commentaries, during *The Forerunner's* run she produced seven treatises and seven novels—one of each appeared in each annual run of the journal. Included among these serialized works were her female Western, *The Crux* (1911), her well-received critique of the "Man-Made World" (1911), which she serialized under the title *Our Androcentric Culture*, and her aptly-named utopian novel, *Herland* (1915).

The Forerunner years coincide with the intensification of Gilman's xenophobic tendencies and her embrace of eugenics. She joined other reformers in viewing the latter as a means of improving the world by ridding it of those deemed "undesirable." During this period, her vision of the "human race" she hoped to serve narrowed considerably. *The Forerunner* folded in 1916 as subscriptions dwindled, the war fever mounted, and its sole author and editor ran out of enough original and noteworthy things to say. She continued to write and lecture during her remaining years in New York City, often on behalf of woman's suffrage (the suffrage amendment passed in 1919 and was ratified by 1920). In 1922, the Gilmans fled the polyglot city for Norwich, Connecticut, to a house that Houghton and his brother had recently inherited and that the brothers, each with his wife, planned to share.

In her sixties, Gilman continued her often unsuccessful attempts to reach a wider audience through her lectures and publications even as she frequently turned her attention to gardening and games. Her increasingly strained relationship with her in-laws tested her patience along with her resolve to live above personal concerns. In 1923 she published her last treatise, entitled *His Religion and Hers*. It denounces masculine religious traditions for emphasizing sin, death, and the afterlife and endorses instead a woman-made faith—resembling her personal creed—dedicated to selfless service, the possibilities of birth and growth, and this world versus the next. In the 1920s she fruitlessly revisited the book she considered her masterpiece, *Human Work* (1904), hoping that yet another take and title would secure it a new publisher and a wider readership. The book advances an ethics grounded in social rather than personal interests along with a case for useful work as the highest human calling, messages that were out of step with the increasingly individualistic, pleasure-seeking times. She also began drafting the autobiography that appeared posthumously as *The Living of Charlotte Perkins Gilman*. (She had long insisted that life was a verb rather than a noun—hence the gerund in the title.)

After Houghton's death in 1934, she acted on her long-postponed desire to spend her remaining days in beautiful Pasadena, California, her initial destination when she had fled to California years earlier and the city where her daughter now lived. There, while battling breast cancer diagnosed in 1932, she struggled to write and lecture in an effort to help support Katharine's family during the Great Depression. She also sought to secure her legacy by ensuring that her autobiography would see print. When the pain grew too intense, she took her own life; as she wrote in her suicide note, she preferred chloroform to cancer. Even in her death she sought to make a difference: her article defending euthanasia as a benevolent social practice, mercifully ending lives she considered no longer useful, was published posthumously.

Gilman's major writings

1892. "The Yellow Wall-Paper." *New England Magazine.*
1893. *In This Our World*. Oakland, CA: McCombs & Vaughn.

1898. *Women and Economics: A Study of the Economic Relation between Men and Women as a Factor in Social Evolution.* Boston: Small, Maynard & Co.

1900. *Concerning Children.* Boston: Small, Maynard & Co.

1903. *The Home: Its Work and Influence.* New York: McClure, Phillips & Co.

1904. *Human Work.* New York: McClure, Phillips & Co.

1911. *The Man-Made World; or, Our Androcentric Culture.* New York: Charlton Co.

1911. *The Crux.* New York: Charlton Co.

[1915] 1979. *Herland.* New York: Pantheon.

1923. *His Religion and Hers: A Study of the Faith of Our Fathers and the Work of Our Mothers.* New York and London: Century Co.

1935. *The Living of Charlotte Perkins Gilman: An Autobiography.* New York and London: D. Appleton–Century Co.

Further reading

Davis, Cynthia J. 2010. *Charlotte Perkins Gilman: A Biography.* Stanford: Stanford University Press.

Knight, Denise, ed. 1998. *The Abridged Diaries of Charlotte Perkins Gilman.* 2 vols. Charlottesville: Virginia University Press.

Knight, Denise, and Jennifer Tuttle, eds. 2009. *The Selected Letters of Charlotte Perkins Gilman.* Tuscaloosa: University of Alabama Press.

Scharnhorst, Gary. 1985. *Charlotte Perkins Gilman: A Bibliography.* Metuchen, NJ: Scarecrow Press.

EMMA GOLDMAN (1869–1940)

Kathy E. Ferguson

"Emma said it in 1910; now we're going to say it again" (McDonald and Derrida 1982, 68). So went the chant offered by the women of the Emma Goldman Brigade at a rally entitled "Women's Strike for Equality" on August 26, 1970, in New York City. Emma Goldman's anarchist feminism has been commemorated in plays, operas, graphic novels, and films; her name graces health clinics, preschools, cafés, punk bands, and bookstores; her life and her ideas continue to attract attention from scholars and activists.

Goldman was born in Kovno, Lithuania, on June 27, 1869, and first exposed to radical politics through her brush with the nihilist student movement in Russia. She immigrated to the U.S. in 1885, part of the first mass wave of immigration of Russian Jews. She made her living first with her sewing machine, and later as a nurse and midwife. Her indignation over the execution of anarchists who were framed for the Haymarket bombing in Chicago in 1886 brought her into the anarchist movement. While her formal schooling terminated at about eighth grade, she received a lifetime of education from the movement's intellectuals and activists. She became one of anarchism's leading orators; her annual cross-country lecture tours drew many thousands of attendees and made her name a virtual household word in the U.S. She also founded and edited *Mother Earth*, the most influential anarchist journal in the country, from 1906 to 1918. She was a prodigious correspondent and developed an epistolary style that combined the analytic power of an essay with the intimate address of a letter. She published four books: a collection called *Anarchism and Other Essays*; an assessment of anti-establishment plays in *The Social Significance of Modern Drama*; an incisive critique of the Bolshevik revolution, *My Disillusionment in Russia*; and her momentous two volume autobiography *Living My Life*. A fifth manuscript on Russian theater was unpublished, but provided material for her drama lectures. She was active in the Modern School movement, helping to set up several free schools, and through the radical gathering place called the Ferrer Center in New York City she supported rebellions in the art world. After she and her life-long comrade Alexander Berkman were deported from the U.S. in 1919, she participated in revolutions in Russia in the 1920s and Spain in the 1930s. She also conducted lecture tours in England, Canada, parts of Europe, and, during one brief ninety-day return in 1934, in the U.S. Goldman died in Toronto, Canada on May 14, 1940, while fighting the extradition of young anarchists who would have been executed had they been forced to return to their native Italy under fascist rule.

Goldman's lasting impact has been her insistence on a relentlessly radical feminism, one that situates women's liberation firmly within the larger struggle for all people's freedom from the intertwining power structures of capitalism, government, militarism, patriarchy, religion, and empire. She came to feminism primarily through direct contact, through her work as a garment worker, nurse, and midwife, with women engaged in domestic labor, paid labor, birth, death, marriage, prostitution, and love. She started with the basic anarchist insight that systems of power produce the things they claim to oppose: the requirements of traditional marriage, along with the insecurities of low-paid labor, produce prostitution; husbands' sexual entitlement to their wives' bodies, along with suppression of information on preventing conception, leads to the underground provision of dangerous and illegal abortions; promises that marriage will protect women and children are a smokescreen to obfuscate their dependency on their "protector."

Goldman invented an early version of intersectionality to address the mutually constitutive interactions among vectors of power as well as the needed interconnections among struggles for freedom. The feminism Goldman advocated connected macro-level arrangements of capitalism and militarism with micro-level practices of family life:

> The defenders of authority dread the advent of a free motherhood, lest it will rob them of their prey. Who would fight wars? Who would create wealth? Who would make the policeman, the jailer, if women were to refuse the indiscriminate breeding of children?
>
> (1969d, 237)

Women should be able to make their own decisions about their own minds and bodies because *everyone* should make their own decisions about their own minds and bodies: women should control their wombs; workers, their labor; students, their education; soldiers, their fighting. The people most affected by decisions should have the power to make those decisions.

Goldman condemned all arrangements of hierarchy and exploitation in the name of an alternative future in which free and self-creating individuals voluntarily organize self-governing communities. Goldman was a critic of the movement for women's emancipation of her time because it aimed for too little: a chance to vote (within a governmental system hopelessly skewed to the interests of the rich) and to enter previously all-male careers (without a critique of the class structure and the personal sacrifices such work entails). She recognized that her dissatisfaction with the suffrage movement would probably lead to being "put down as an opponent of woman" (1969c, 209). Yet she insisted,

> I … have been more interested in the fate of woman and by far from a broader and deep[er] point of [view] than those who label themselves Feminists but have no interest whatever in the general social questions … My quarrel with the Feminists wasn't that they were too free, or demanded too much. It was that they are not free enough and that most of them see their slavery apart from the rest of the human family.
>
> (Goldman 1990)

While Goldman supported some legal reforms, such as the decriminalization of prostitution or the official recognition of political prisoners, she insisted that true change required revolution to overthrow both the "external tyrannies" of unjust institutions and the "internal tyrants" of "ethical and social conventions" (1969a, 220). Truly revolutionary politics, Goldman argued, required that the methods of change and the goals of change be mutually consistent: "The means employed become, through individual habit and social practice, part and parcel of the final purpose; they influence it, modify it, and presently the aims and means become identical" (1970b, 260). Revolution for Goldman meant a *"fundamental transvaluation of values"* in which people invent themselves anew (1970b, 258–59, italics in original).

Goldman was arrested so frequently for speaking on forbidden topics that she took a book with her to her own talks so she would have something to read in jail. She served three prison terms, each for violating the law with regard to an issue or injustice that was central to her anarchist feminism. First, in 1893 she was arrested for unlawful assembly and incitement to riot after speaking to a demonstration of the unemployed in Union Square in New York City, where she urged a large crowd to "become daring enough to demand your rights." She went on to encourage the unemployed to "demonstrate before the palaces of the rich; demand work. If they do not give you work, demand bread. If they deny you both, take bread. It is your sacred right" (1970a, 123). For this incendiary speech, she was sentenced to a year's imprisonment on Blackwell's Island, where she received training in nursing and a broad education in the lives of the poor outside of her familiar immigrant communities. Second, in 1916 she spoke on methods of contraception, was arrested for violating the laws regarding obscenity, and served fifteen days in Queens County Jail. Third, in 1917 she and Berkman were convicted of opposing conscription in World War I, in violation of the Selective Service Act, and sentenced to two years in prison, which Goldman served in the Jefferson City, Missouri, state penitentiary, and Berkman in the much harsher federal penitentiary in Atlanta, Georgia. Both anarchists created communities within the prison walls and became advocates for their fellow prisoners. Afterward, Goldman was illegally stripped of her citizenship and the two anarchists were deported to the nascent U.S.S.R.

Each of these prison terms is a window into the intertwined issues and ideas in Goldman's anarchist feminism. She urged the workers, including prisoners and the unemployed, to challenge the owning class and take control of the means of production. She encouraged women to challenge patriarchal authorities and take control of the means of reproduction as well as sexual desire. She called for all people to refuse to fight wars on behalf of governments and the wealthy. Her intersectional thinking about the relation of war, labor, reproduction, religion and the state produced the frame for thinking about each new situation she encountered. The Russian Revolution disappointed her bitterly because a new elite emerged through the Communist Party and became the new ruling class. The Spanish Revolution galvanized her enthusiasm because, for a time, anarchist communities organized themselves to work, to live, and to fight. The crushing of the anarchist revolution in Spain by the combined forces of the communists and fascists was one of the greatest tragedies of her life.

Freedom of speech was a central component of Goldman's political activities. Organizing workers, educating them about birth control, and opposing war required forms of public speech: the ability to speak, write and publish freely was the heart of anarchist activism. Yet the draconian Comstock laws governing obscenity (including birth control), and the severe restrictions on dissent of a whole host of federal and state laws, especially those passed during war time, resulted in ongoing censorship of anarchist events and publications. Goldman deliberately broke these laws in order to contest them. She could persist in these confrontations with authorities in part because she had a supportive network in the international anarchist movement to sustain her. Big public meetings and celebratory dinners were organized by her comrades to send Goldman off to prison and to welcome her home when she returned. Radical publications around the world printed and reprinted her statements. Other progressive individuals and groups allied with Goldman on specific issues, such as birth control and conscription. While Goldman is the best known (often the only known) anarchist feminist to those outside the movement, in fact, Goldman was surrounded by radical women and men who also sought social transformation, not just social reform. Goldman was not a lone anarchist feminist voice, but a potent, visible link in a vigorous radical global movement.

Goldman's major writings

[1906] 1969a. "The Tragedy of Women's Emancipation." In *Anarchism and Other Essays*, 219–33 (New York: Dover).

[1910] 1969b. *Anarchism and Other Essays* (New York: Dover). Originally published by Mother Earth Publishing Company.

[1911] 1969c. "Woman Suffrage." In *Anarchism and Other Essays*, 201–18 (New York: Dover).

[1911] 1969d. "Marriage and Love." In *Anarchism and Other Essays*, 233–46 (New York: Dover).

[1914] 1987. *The Social Significance of Modern Drama* (New York: Applause Theater Book Publishers). Originally published by Richard G. Badge.

[1919] 1990. Goldman, Emma, to Stella Ballantine, April 3. In *The Emma Goldman Papers: A Microfilm Edition*. Edited by Candace Falk with Ronald J. Zboray, et al. Alexandria, VA: Chadwyck-Healey. Reel 11.

[1922]. 1970b. *My Disillusionment in Russia* (New York: Apollo Editions). Originally published by Thomas Y. Crowell.

[1931] 1970a. *Living My Life* (New York: Dover). Originally published by Alfred A. Knopf.

1983. *Vision on Fire: Emma Goldman on the Spanish Revolution*. Edited by David Porter (New Paltz, NY: Commonground Press).

1996. *Red Emma Speaks: An Emma Goldman Reader*. Third Edition. Edited by Alix Kates Shulman (Amherst, NY: Humanity Books).

2001. *Anarchy! An Anthology of Emma Goldman's Mother Earth*. Edited by Peter Glassgold (Washington, DC: Counterpoint).

Further reading

Avrich, Paul and Karen Avrich. 2012. *Sasha and Emma: The Anarchist Odyssey of Alexander Berkman and Emma Goldman* (Cambridge, MA: Harvard University Press).

Falk, Candace, ed. 2003. *Emma Goldman: A Documentary History of the American Years, Volume 1—Made for America, 1890–1901* (Berkeley: University of California Press).

—. 2005. *Emma Goldman: A Documentary History of the American Years, Volume 2—Making Speech Free, 1902–1909* (Berkeley: University of California Press).

—. 2012. *Emma Goldman: A Documentary History of the American Years. Volume 3—Light and Shadows, 1910–1916* (Berkeley: University of California Press).

Ferguson, Kathy E. 2011. *Emma Goldman: Political Thinking in the Streets* (Lanham, MD: Rowman and Littlefield).

McDonald, Christie V. and Jacques Derrida. 1982. "Choreographies," *Diacritics* 12(2): 66–76.

OLYMPE DE GOUGES (1748–1793)

Ariella Azoulay

Through different genres—theatre plays, novels, essays, dreams, treaties and declarations—Olympe de Gouges unfolded her feminist and anti-imperial political philosophy. She is still one of the rare philosophers who dissociate sovereignty from the prerogative of taking life and one of the first to imagine sovereignty as emanating from a heterogeneous body politic consisting of the entire population—including women and people of colour. Several of her writings were re-published in French in the late 1980s, but are still inaccessible in other languages and almost never discussed by political philosophers. Her *Declaration of the Rights of Woman and Female Citizens* (also known as the *Declaration of the Rights of Woman*), composed in 1791 and offered by her to Marie Antoinette as an invitation to engage with her feminist political initiatives, is a feminist performative act of reiteration. Not only are women assumed to be full citizens, but their citizenship is inseparable from the way they are engaged in the marriage contract, and the social contract ceases to be limited to the public sphere and is necessarily constitutive of the private one.

Criticism of white male political supremacy is at the heart of de Gouges' writings. Her texts bear traces of another competing conception of citizenship—an inclusive one—that soon after would be buried in the archive for more than a century until women would be granted citizenship as a sign of progress. "Man, are you capable of being just?" de Gouges asks and makes clear that this is not an abstract question since "it is a woman who poses the question; you will not deprive her of that right at least" (de Gouges 2007, 176). The political vocabulary that was consolidated in the late eighteenth century with women's exclusion was instrumental in rendering differential rule into the political principle of democratic regime.

In "The Three Ballot Boxes," written in 1793, she questions the form of governance that was sanctified and calls for a referendum. She presents three options of rule based on the political experience in different French communities during the *ancien régime*. This was the text that cost her her life, sending her to the guillotine. When she argued in her *Declaration* that since "woman has the right to mount the scaffold, she must equally have the right to mount the rostrum," she could not predict that she would be the first woman during the French Revolution executed for what she had written, nor that her other prophecies stating that the oppression of particular groups (women or colored people) could not be incidental to the political rule but rather, necessarily, its essence.

De Gouges' play *Black Slavery*, written in 1782, seven years before the outbreak of the French Revolution, deals with the authority of the king—vested in his deputy, governor of the island—to take lives. The plot unfolds against the background of a governed population that gradually negates the sovereign's authority to take life through their common struggle against being governed unequally. The play makes it clear that the sovereign's authority to take life is disabled once the dividing lines of differential rule are not respected and citizens partner with slaves and men with women. A black slave, Zamor, had killed his master's white guard when the latter demanded him to attack his beloved Mirza—a slave like himself—for having refused the guard's overtures. After murdering the white guard, the two escape. On their way they rescue a French couple whose boat has sunk. The grateful French white couple propose to defend them. For the most part, the play deals with the question whether the runaways would be executed or spared. Sophie (the French woman), the governor's wife, other slaves, servants and apprentices, men and women, and even a military officer, all gradually come together to save Zamor and Mirza from a band of armed men who, led by a judge, hunt them down to execute them for their crime. The governor wavers between the two newly polarized factions created in the play—the men demanding execution and the non-citizens—women, blacks and deserters who cross the lines and join the demand to free the two slaves. The judge calls upon the governor to restore the order and reach a decision: "They must be put to death at once, more especially as two Europeans have incited a general revolt among the slaves [...] all have promised not to execute the orders that they were given" (Act II, Scene 6).

The play explicitly justifies disobedience of obviously violent laws and, rather than discussing Zamor's act from the perspective of the law under which he should be judged, calls for a reconsideration of the regime that outlawed him in the first place, and abandoned him to injuries that would not be inflicted upon white citizens. When the entire population stands for the body politic, an assumed agreement to take slaves' lives cannot be achieved and rather emerges as an unacceptable measure. The governor's decision will hence impact not solely the life of Zamor, but the preservation or dismantling of differential body politic as a principle of rule. A decision *not to take* their lives would undermine previous agreement about whose life may be taken. The play ends not only with the governor's preventing the execution of the slaves: he also calls upon the residents of the island to come out and celebrate the opening of a new political pact as the different governed parties associate with each other and refuse to be ruled differentially. Even though de Gouges revised this play several times, including after the outbreak of the French Revolution, the play preserved an anticipation of a revolution that did *not* take place yet: the joining together of a heterogeneous corpus of the governed—women, slaves and men who refuse to recognize any law or authority that abandons their lives or enlists them to take others' lives.

Unlike interpretations of the play that draw an analogy between the governor and the king, the fictional setting and France, a straightforward reading of the depicted situation enables us to elaborate different meanings of revolution and sovereignty other than those consolidated through the French Revolution. The governor addresses an absent king whose absence obliges him to refrain from taking Zamor's life, to pardon Zamor for his crime, and to change the law creating the hothouse that actually nurtured this crime. As the judge in the play demands, Zamor's execution would have been an example to the people of what would happen to anyone who ever dared to challenge the ruling power, its laws and its single, unified, irrefutable sovereignty. In this play, as in her political pamphlet "The Three Ballot Boxes," de Gouges attempts to turn the people's uprising against injustices into a lesson for tyrants, "that to win their revolution will be a lesson to tyrants and not to the people" (1993, 246).

De Gouges does not think of sovereign political rule as a means towards overcoming an imagined catastrophe of a war of all against all, or as a means of justifying a project of sovereign power under whose auspices political existence is considered a trait of men—not of every one, only of those considered worthy by the powers that be. Unlike most of the revolutionaries of her generation, de Gouges did not propose to transfer sovereignty from the king to the people. With de Gouges, sovereignty is a form of contract between the sovereign and the governed people and is shaped by both, and hence can differ from one place to another. Her novel *The Philosopher King* can be read as a treaty on sovereignty. The novel tells of a journey through the kingdom of reason, imagination and power. It is an adventurous and brilliant novel, full of humor and philosophical insights comparable to Voltaire's *Candide*, published four decades earlier.

Almoladin, the philosopher king, travels through several kingdoms in order to study how political relations between human beings and sovereigns are managed in each, and how relations between the sovereign and his subjects are conducted. Having achieved glory through the counsel he offers and the deeds he performs, he returns to his own country, Siam, and rules it for fourteen years. He is renowned as a beloved king and a caring father to his children. After grooming his son to rule after him, Almoladin chooses to leave, to give up his throne and live as a commoner in a village with Palmire, the woman with whom he had fallen in love some fifteen years earlier and whose love he was forced to forfeit for marriage with Queen Idamée, to whom he had already been betrothed at the time. Before leaving his kingdom, Almoladin assembles his people and, donning his royal robes, appears before them in his full authority:

> My children, for fourteen years now you have been subject to my laws, they have not been a burden to you and your gentleness has proved to me, thousands of times over, that you were satisfied with your sovereign. I have not ruled you at all as a tyrant, I have always loved you gently and ruled you like a father; but if fate had allowed me to choose my avocation, my heart would not have led me to kingship. I will never forget the sacred words uttered by he who brought me into this world, in his very last moments, "My son", he told me, "a good king who has done everything for his people has not done enough if he hasn't given them a worthy successor to replace him."
>
> (1993, 70)

Almoladin relinquishes the throne as soon as he feels able to trust his son to take his place in a worthy manner and to trust the people to resist his son's rule should it exceed appropriate limits. The coronation at which he passes his crown to his son is then not a ceremony that continues the royal dynasty as in the past but, rather, a ceremony that constitutes a new covenant in the framework of which a new type of sovereign rule is founded. Almoladin imposes two conditions that shake up the structure of sovereignty: "Here is the condition that I have decided to impose upon my son," he says, turning to the people before he goes on, "I do not know how many years I will be absent from my kingdom. I request and demand that without my express instructions not a single death sentence against a single offender will be carried out" (ibid.).

It may seem as if Almoladin remains the sovereign, he who is authorized to declare an exception, while his son, the acting sovereign, is his father's subject, thus leaving the structure of sovereignty as it was. However, two significant details undermine this interpretation and reveal the complexity of the proposed scheme of sovereignty. First, Almoladin is physically abandoning the territory and retreats from the political space in which he will, in fact, remain only as an absent authority—one that could be termed nature, philosopher-king, invisible entity, godhead or even international tribunal—which the people or the (acting) sovereign can mobilize should either of them dare to disobey Almoladin's commandment not to take anyone's life. This commandment was intended to protect both the people from the king and the king from the people. The second condition placed by Almoladin at the coronation concerns the structure of the relations between these three poles: the invisible absent authority, the acting sovereign and the people. During the coronation a covenant is established between them, articulating a new structure of sovereignty. In the course of the ceremony and in the presence of the people, Almoladin warns his son, forbidding him not only the localized use of the death sentence, but also not to found his regime on a mechanism of exception whose meaning is the taking of lives. From here on, Almoladin will become an invisible entity, an absent presence, through the condition he leaves behind for the continuation of power. As he is about to disappear, his consent will be forever unobtainable. In so doing, he accordingly renders the taking of life—still one of the constitutive elements of democratic sovereignties—patently illegal.

De Gouges' major writings

[1791] 2007. "The Declaration of the Rights of Woman." In *The Human Rights Reader: Major Political Essays, Speeches, and Documents from Ancient Times to the Present.* Second edition, 175–180. Micheline Ishay (ed.). New York: Routledge.

[1792] 1995. *Le Prince philosophe: conte oriental.* Paris: Indigo & Coté-Femmes.

[1793] 1993. "The Three Ballot Boxes." In *Ecrits Politiques 1792–1793.* Paris: Coté-Femmes.

[1782] 1994. "Black Slavery," trans. Maryann DeJulio. In *Translating Slavery: Gender and Race in French Women's Writing, 1783–1823,* 87–118. Doris K. Kadish and Françoise Massardier-Kenney (eds.). Kent, OH and London: Kent State University Press.

DONNA HARAWAY (1944–)

Jana Sawicki

Born in Denver, Colorado in 1944, to a middle-class Irish Roman Catholic family, Donna Haraway describes herself as "an *organism* shaped by a post-World War II biology that is saturated with information sciences and technologies, a *biologist* schooled in those discourses, and a *practitioner* of the humanities and ethnographic social sciences" (2008, 13). After spending a year studying philosophy of evolution at the University of Paris, Haraway completed an interdisciplinary Ph.D. from Yale University in Biology in cooperation with the departments of Philosophy and History of Science and Medicine. Since 1984 she has been a professor in the History of Consciousness Program at the University of California, Santa Cruz. For her lifetime contributions to the field, the Society for Social Studies of Science awarded her the J. Bernal award in 2000.

The language Haraway uses in her self-description captures abiding features of her thought: the centrality of location and situation, her emphasis on thinking as a practice—a hybrid fusion of the scientific and the literary, and her sense of herself as merely one organism within a multispecies world. Haraway urges her readers to move beyond human exceptionalism and its myriad entanglements with "technoscience," sexism, racism, colonialism, and imperialism, as well as massive and accelerating reductions in biodiversity across the planet.

Haraway's forty-year career resists any definitive description, partly because she is always responding to, learning from, and changing her point of view in the wake of her encounters with the different worlds with which she has come in contact: the world of technoscience, the world of non-human primates, the worlds of science fiction, and the different worlds in which women, but also men, animals, and other life forms live and die under conditions of domination and exploitation.

Borrowing a metaphor associated with the work of French post-structuralist Michel Foucault, one might describe Haraway's theories as "tool kits"—technologies designed to do things: to remap and redescribe worlds, and to create the conditions for building new ones. Her thinking is speculative yet firmly situated in these worlds—worlds that cannot be grasped independently of the stories, tropes and figures we use to grasp them. She refers to them as "material-semiotic." One astute commentator, Joseph Schneider, aptly captures both the materialist and fantastic elements characteristic of her work when he describes it as "always grounded in the details of lived reality or embodied material … inviting us to think, act and relate in hopeful ways that point" to new possibilities for living and being (2005, 5). Hers is, indeed a "queer" sort of feminist thinking.

Haraway's path-breaking essay "A Manifesto for Cyborgs" (1985), nothing less than an "event" or "happening" in feminist thought, "queered" Second Wave feminism by pushing it beyond itself—particularly its disciplinary allegiances, but also its wariness toward science, and its sense of its subject. By appropriating the figure of the cyborg, a disorienting and monstrous hybrid of human and machine, human and animal, it attempted to draw Western feminist attention to women both at "home" and across the globe working within transnational corporate ventures in industries such as microelectronics, biomedicine, and information science. At a more philosophical level, it also represented a challenge to the dualistic ontologies and dominant meta-narratives in the Western patriarchal tradition upon which much feminist thought depended.

It is easy to imagine a genealogical narrative of queer feminist thought originating in Haraway's writing and thinking practices. Like many of the concepts and figures that populate her subsequent writing, i.e., FemaleMan, material-semiotic, natureculture, the cyborg symbolized her willingness to embrace queerness and contradiction. Both an insider and an outsider, Haraway engages science from within the humanities, feminism within science, and both poststructuralism and science studies within feminism. Her relationship to her disciplinary influences is eccentric, and her work is more *trans-* than interdisciplinary. As she admits, hers is a risky venture. Indeed, her willingness to fuse disciplinary boundaries, and to focus not only on the dangers of technoscientific culture, but also its pleasures and possibilities, has led at times to hostile receptions of her work within both feminist and the social and biological communities.

Haraway's intellectual strategy is "opportunistic" (to borrow a microbiological metaphor to which she appeals in later writings). Among her intellectual resources are poststructuralism, science studies, Marxism, Darwinism, microbiology, anthropology, and feminist science fiction, to name the most salient. Her method draws upon Derridean deconstruction to "implode" oppositional concepts (e.g., nature/culture, human/animal, mind/body, sex/gender, male/female, self/other, subject/object, material/semiotic, fabrication/real). From her perspective, binary thinking limits our sense of the possible, erasing differences within categories and the ways in which they depend upon but exceed them. Her delight in fusing contradictory terms transgresses the boundaries of thought, queers the terms, in an effort to make visible patterns of difference that otherwise remain unseen. Ever attentive to radical otherness—to the alien, Haraway exhibits her concern for myriad life forms—the hidden, the misfit, the monster, the unthinkable and impossible. Among the panoply of promising queer figures that she introduces is the genetically engineered research animal OncoMouse™, the feminist technoscientist, ModestWitness@Second Millennium, the Navajo coyote, the dog, and companion species—each represented as a hybrid assemblage of natureculture.

To be sure, the cyborg is not an innocent figure, connected as it is to the history of militarism, the Cold War, the space race, and the rise of the Internet. Hence, some leftist and feminist readers challenged Haraway's view as naively technophilic. Still, millennial feminists interested in science studies, information technologies, and animal studies as well as queer theory have been very receptive to the possibilities of continuing to work with the cyborg figure in new ways. Furthermore, Haraway's willingness to redeploy this compromised figure belies her conviction that the search for pure critical, epistemological, ethical or political standpoints is futile. In the end there are no pure identities or locations. The resources available for critique must inevitably originate in the worlds we inhabit. Human, machine, animal—each can co-constitute another in the numerous intra-actions that make up material-semiotic worlds. Each responds, or reacts, to the other; each is implicated in the other. Rather than rely upon progressive, messianic, or apocalyptic narratives and tropes that have governed Western thinking for two millennia, Haraway subverts them. Her approach to theorizing could be characterized as a performative gesture resembling Judith Butler's strategy of "repetition with a difference," or perhaps, even better, one might describe it as a form of "recycling."

As we have seen, Haraway understands knowledge as "situated." If no location is innocent, then the idea of an emancipatory feminist standpoint, or of "objective" grounding, might also be queered. While Haraway shares standpoint theory's project to enhance freedom, her own project is neither universalist nor emancipatory. The standpoint of the oppressed, even when understood as a historical achievement, she observes, does not represent the interests of all. In her texts, time and space are queered as well. Situations, locations, concepts, practices, serve as nodes within many networks, transfer points for multiple genealogies, and multiple and crisscrossing patterns of relationship. Neither nature nor culture are reducible to one another, neither determines the other, both are in constant intra-action, co-constitutively related.

Haraway's model of critique differs from that found in traditional critical theories. Although she does adopt an oppositional relationship to capitalist technoscience, her project is more constructive and activist than it is critical. She joins ("articulates") knowledge producing and world building in order to "regenerate"—to generate something different, and to produce multiple worlds, that is, multiple pockets of "finite flourishing." She hopes to open "lines of flight"—new modes of thinking and being that break through present limits on our sense of what is possible or intelligible. Thus, Haraway's ethico-political practice involves rethinking and re-experiencing our sense of the boundaries between self and other, and our understanding of change. She does not envision a holistic and harmonious reconciliation of contradictions. Indeed she is remarkably comfortable with suspending ethical and political judgment at times in order to allow contradictory points of view to co-exist, and to enable the potential of both to unfold. As she puts it, everything is not connected to everything, but everything is connected to something.

For Haraway, "freedom" means both freedom *from* the dominant tropes of filial relations, teleological narratives, hierarchical structures and reproductive logics, and freedom *to* invent new stories, tropes and figures that stimulate new imaginings: images of regeneration (not reproduction), non-filial kin relations, and lateral connections or relation between myriad species rather than generational ones. Her re-descriptions of natureculture borrow microbiology for their inspiration. Drawing on the regenerative processes found in microbiological life processes, she envisions a world where entities connect through processes of "attraction, merger, fusion, incorporation, cohabitation, [and] recombination" (2008, 31).

In Haraway's project, thinking and practice are intertwined—thinking is an ethico-political practice offering the possibility of recreating both our worlds and ourselves. Curiosity, "responsibility," and a suspicious generosity represent the core virtues that she exemplifies and advocates for companion species, a world in which human and non-human forms "intra-act" and "become with" in order that they might build viable forms of life. Curiosity facilitates a capacity to recognize the

> creative force of the prosaic, the propinquity of things in many registers, the concatenation of specific empirical circumstances, the misrecognition of experience by holding to an idea of the experience before having had it, and how different orders of things hold together coevally.
>
> (2008, 313, footnote 32)

Generous suspicion is in order insofar as there is often more happening than what is visible from within our habitual frames of mind, and our involvement in the world. Yet, since things are not only what they seem, openness to fresh experiences of our everyday being in the world, to taking another look, and to seeing things differently must be tempered with suspicion since the human capacities for reflexivity are limited. To paraphrase another queer thinker, French philosopher and historian of science Michel Foucault, an important resource in Haraway's theoretical tool kit, not everything is bad, but everything can be dangerous.

Finally, Haraway stresses the value of cultivating capacities for responsiveness and communication, rather than habitual reactions to other forms of life—to live with the discomfort, even the anxiety, of holding open space for other types of relationship, different responses, to the myriad, if radically other, forms of life (e.g., animals, plants, microbiological entities) with which we cohabitate. The goal of Haraway's ethico-political practice is not simply to reduce suffering, the dominant concern of utilitarians, but to "become with"—to experiment with possibilities for relating, and to explore connections beyond those associated with the "familiar." In a particularly poignant passage Haraway laments:

> I am sick to death of bonding through kinship and "the family," and I long for models of solidarity and human unity and difference rooted in friendship, work, partially shared purposes, intractable collective pain, inescapable mortality, and persistent hope … Ties through blood … have been bloody enough already.
>
> (2003c, 285)

Haraway's major writings

[1985] 2003a. "A Manifesto for Cyborgs: Science, Technology, and Socialist Feminism in the 1980s." In *The Haraway Reader*. New York and London: Routledge.

1989. *Primate Visions: Gender, Race, and Nature in the World of Modern Science*. New York: Routledge.

1991. *Simians, Cyborgs, and Women: The Reinvention of Nature*. New York: Routledge.

1996. *Modest_Witness@Second_Millennium.FemaleMan©_Meets_Oncomouse™*. New York: Routledge.

1999. *How Like a Leaf, Donna J. Haraway: An interview with Thyrza Nichols Goodeve*. New York: Routledge.

2003b. *The Companion Species Manifesto: Dogs, People, and Significant Otherness*. Cambridge: Prickly Paradigm Press.

2003c. *The Haraway Reader.* New York and London: Routledge.
2003d. "Cyborgs to Companion Species: Reconfiguring Kinship in Technoscience." In Don Ihde and Evan Selinger (Eds.), *Chasing Technoscience: Matrix for Materiality,* 58–82. Bloomington: Indiana University Press.
2004. *Crystals, Fabrics and Fields: Metaphors that Shape Embryos.* Berkeley, CA: North Atlantic Books.
2008. *When Species Meet.* Minneapolis and London: University of Minnesota Press.
2012. *SF, Speculative Fabulation and String Figures: 100 Notes, 100 Thoughts.* Ostfildern, Germany: Hatje Cantz.
2007. Haraway, Donna J. and Irene Reti (Eds.) *Edges and Ecotones: Donna Haraway's Worlds at UCSC: An Oral History.* Santa Cruz: University of California.

Further reading

Grebewicz, Margret and Helen Merrick. 2013. *Beyond the Cyborg: Adventures with Donna Haraway.* New York: Columbia University Press.
Schneider, Joseph. 2005. *Donna Haraway: Live Theory.* London: Bloomsbury Academic.

bell hooks (1952–)

Namulundah Florence

Born Gloria Jean Watkins in 1952, bell hooks was raised in the tobacco-growing southwest Kentucky town of Hopkinsville. hooks' home-life, as well as her schooling and professional experiences in predominantly white institutions, illustrate what she terms the impact of a pervasive interlocking system of imperialistic-capitalistic, white-supremacist patriarchy or dominator culture on both black men and black women. Family and social dysfunction, including impoverished communities, represent for hooks the everyday brutality of a dominant culture's control and oppression; a reality further complicated by mass media's reductive, stereotypical, and sensational imagery. Her key contribution to feminist thought lies in her incisive ability to explain the dynamics of patriarchal culture, and the ways gender, race, and class structure black experience in the United States.

hooks draws from personal experience and the mass media to illustrate the endemic nature of sexism and racism in the United States. From an early age, hooks (2003b; hooks & Mesa-Bains 2006) defined herself in resistance to patriarchy, although her parents and teachers tried to socialize her differently. In *Bone Black: Memories of Childhood* (1996a), hooks contrasts her mother's demeanor in the presence and absence of her husband: "how she became energetic, noisy, silly, funny, fussy, strong, capable, tender, everything that she was not when he was around. When he was around she became silent" (98). Not unlike her mother, in many patriarchal families complicit females cover up for husbands and sons. Many black women attribute black male anger, irritability, and violence to pressures in a racist society and forgive their men for this behavior (hooks 1990). Older now, hooks' mother resents her investment in patriarchy. Meanwhile, her father remains "committed to patriarchal thought … even though it keeps him isolated emotionally from loved ones, even though his sexism, and its concomitant violence and abuse has ruined a marriage of more than fifty years" (hooks 2004b, xv). For many black males, violence becomes a legitimate way to "exert power, to influence a situation, to maintain control" (63). However, hooks contrasts her father with her maternal grandfather Daddy Gus who repudiated the patriarchal norm in his embrace of affectivity and connectedness.

Describing patriarchal culture, hooks writes:

> Patriarchy is a political-social system that insists that males are inherently dominating, superior to everything and everyone deemed weak, especially females, and endowed with the right to dominate and rule over the weak and to maintain that dominance through various forms of psychological terrorism and violence.
>
> (hooks 2004a, 18)

She claims that patriarchal masculinity teaches males to be pathologically narcissistic, infantile, and psychologically dependent for self-definition on the privileges (however relative) that they receive from having been born male (hooks 2004a, 116).

Patriarchal domination and control supports, promotes, and condones sexist violence. Religion, school, family, and corporate systems in most societies reinforce this superordination of males. Male visibility as household heads or political representatives, coupled with society's devaluation of female-related tasks and characteristics, further reinforce gender hierarchy. Gender stereotyping and role expectations sanction differences in the socialization of children. Boys learn to be tough, mask feelings, stand their ground, and fight, while girls acquire habits of obedience, service, and subservience (hooks 1992, 2003b; hooks & Mesa-Bains 2006). As children grow older, parents, peers, and community reward or shame youth that uphold or transgress these gender roles.

hooks has criticized mass media and popular culture in several of her writings. She insists, for example, that mass media indoctrinates boys into patriarchal thinking by glorifying war and violence (as examples, she cites *Saving Private Ryan*, *Independence Day*, *Men in Black*, *Blackhawk Down*, *Pearl Harbor*, etc.). Even progressive novels such as *Jagged Edge* and *The Analysand* promote patriarchal violence. Even J. K. Rowling's Harry Potter movie series, hooks says, glorifies "the use of violence to maintain control over others" (hooks 2004a, 52). And in contrast with hooks' *Be Boy Buzz*, most children's literature reinscribes patriarchal attitudes and behaviors.

Homemaking men are viewed as chivalrous for sacrificing corporate power and privileges to do "women's work." hooks attributes the Dr. Jekyll and Mr. Hyde split in males to disparities between the harsh reality of most men's lives and an idealized manhood. Rising standards of living—rent, mortgages, child support—sometimes rebellious children and incompliant partners, in no particular order, belie the myth of male control. hooks asserts that,

> if you cannot prove that you are "much of a man" by becoming president, or becoming rich, or becoming a public leader, or becoming a boss, then violence is your ticket in to the patriarchal manhood context, your ability to do violence levels the playing field. On that field, the field of violence, any man can win.
>
> (hooks 2004a, 72)

Rarely does society acknowledge the price men pay to uphold the debilitating manhood ideal. Men learn early to deny their feelings and shun dependence on others, particularly mothers. Feeling disenfranchised in the work place, many men feel pressured to conform to patriarchal roles—the tough, detached, principled executive. Ironically, the public expresses shock at increasing male violence, particularly among teenage boys against parents, peers, or even strangers, despite the conventional link of manhood to violence and domination that is reinforced by the mass media (hooks 2004a). hooks views patriarchy as the "single most life-threatening social disease assaulting the male body and spirit in our nation" (17). She goes on to say that,

> As a product, this rage can be garnered to further imperialism, hatred, and oppression of women and men globally. This rage is

needed if boys are to become men willing to travel around the world to fight wars without ever demanding that other ways of solving conflict be found.

(hooks 2004a, 51)

In *We Real Cool: Black Men and Masculinity* (2004b) as well as *The Will to Change: Men, Masculinity, and Love* (2004a), hooks specifically addresses the plight of black men in the United States. Objectified since slavery, much of society still views black men as violent or potentially dangerous despite their touted "uniqueness" as an endangered species. In black communities, despite reality to the contrary, children learn that their father's love and presence is more central to their survival and well-being than their mother's love and presence. However, society depicts many black men preferring to be playboys than home providers. Socially eroticized and vilified, black men, as the life of hooks' brother Kenneth exemplifies, receive contradictory messages of who and what they can be. Like most African-Americans, he faced assaults on his self-esteem in public arenas as well as the peril of a dysfunctional family. His parents pampered him for being the boy of the family, but he was also subjected to "verbal abusive shaming or violent beatings" from his patriarchal father for failing to meet the standards of patriarchal maleness. He was expected to be obedient and quiet yet assertive and aggressive, too. He could only show feelings when adults demanded it. For many black boys, the "bewilderment at the inconsistency of these demands leads to overwhelming feelings of powerlessness" (hooks 2004b, 90).

Such depictions run the danger of an essentialism hooks herself consistently discounts, i.e., not all blacks are academically disconnected, violent and misogynist, unreliable, etc. Herein lies the challenge: staying open to the complexity of human identity and experience, always with the context of the larger society that denies humanity to either one (hooks 1990). Hence, the popularity of youth gangs and adult clubs offer black males a sense of belonging that traditional family networks appear to lack. Regardless, the ambivalence lures black young men to obtain quick money and other transient pleasures at the expense of ongoing accountability as Julius Lester's *Look Out, Whitey! Black Power's Gon' Get Your Mama* illustrates (hooks 2004b). Because the consumerism among youth reflects wider patterns, the claim to a macho identity comes at a high price. hooks writes that,

thriving on sadomasochistic bonds, cultures of domination make desire for what is despised take on the appearance of care, of love.

If Black males were loved they could hope for more than a life locked down, caged, confined; they could imagine themselves beyond containment. … Whether in an actual prison or not, practically every Black male in the United States has been forced at some point in his life to hold back the self he wants to express and contain for fear of being attacked, slaughtered, destroyed.

(hooks 2004b, xii)

Forging a black community requires the redefinition of prevailing gender roles and stereotypes. Nineteenth-century black leaders like Martin Delaney, Frederick Douglass, and W.E.B. Du Bois recognized the importance of gender equality for racial uplift. Dr. Martin Luther King, Jr., in *Where Do We Go from Here*, and Malcolm X challenged the capitalistic-based materialism and resultant "false consciousness" perpetuated by unchecked television, movies, as well as state-sponsored lotteries (hooks 2004b).

In contrast, Daniel Patrick Moynihan's report, "The Negro Family" (1965), accused black women of emasculating black men, sanctioning a need for subjugating black women. Similarly, Shahrazad Ali's book, *The Black Man's Guide to Understanding the Black Woman*, calls black men to put women in their place. Furthermore there was a series of *Newsweek* articles in 2003 that cited the dominance of black women in education and work (hooks 2004b). Views like these have led to an unnecessary jockeying for positions between black men and women along with envy and jealousy that undermine solidarity (hooks & West 1991). In reality, in the late nineteenth and early twentieth century, economic pressures compelled families to educate girls while boys took on jobs. White racist society viewed black men as more of a threat than women. And yet, in *Sisters of the Yam: Black Women and Self-Recovery*, hooks identifies Angela Davis, June Jordan, Fannie Lou Hammer, Joycelyn Elders, Shirley Chisholm, Maya Angelou, among others, as females campaigning for black liberation and the love of blackness (hooks 2001).

Females have been said to sanction sexism in their complicity. Their focus on looks, clothing, and their relationship to men reinforces their objectification. hooks attributes sexist attitudes and practices in males as well as females to socialization patterns that promote gender roles and expectations—passivity in females and aggressiveness in males. In a patriarchal culture, females tend to define themselves relative to men as blacks have relative to white society and privilege. Mass media further reinforces these roles by glorifying male violence and control, while emphasizing the sexual lure in females. But the image of dominating males in homes, workplaces, and on imperialistic quests contrasts with the harsh reality many men confront in a capitalist and racist society. Females become a safe target for this ambivalent macho identity.

hooks' major writings

1984. *Feminist Theory: From Margin to Center*. Boston: South End Press.
1990. *Yearning: Race, Gender and Cultural Politics*. Boston: South End Press.
1992. *Black Looks: Race and Representation*. Boston: South End Press.
1993. *Sisters of the Yam: Black Women and Self-recovery*. Boston: South End Press.
1994a. *Outlaw Culture: Resisting Representation*. New York: Routledge.
1994b. *Teaching to Transgress: Education as the Practice of Freedom*. New York: Routledge.
1995. *Killing Rage: Ending Racism*. New York: Henry Holt.
1996a. *Bone Black: Memories of Childhood*. New York: Henry Holt.
1996b. *Reel to Real: Race, Sex, and Class at the Movies*. New York: Routledge.
2000. *Where We Stand: Class Matters*. New York: Routledge.
2001. *Salvation: Black People and Love*. New York: William Murrow.
2003a. *Rock My Soul: Black People and Self-esteem*. New York: Atria Books.
2003b. *Teaching Community: A Pedagogy of Hope*. New York: Routledge.
2004a. *The Will to Change: Men, Masculinity, and Love*. New York: Atria Books.
2004b. *We Real Cool: Black Men and Masculinity*. New York: Routledge.
2006. hooks, bell and Mesa-Bains, Amalia. *Homegrown: Engaged Cultural Criticism*. Boston: South End Press.
1991. hooks, bell and West, Cornel. *Breaking Bread: Insurgent Black Intellectual Life*. Boston: South End Press.

Further reading

Florence, N. 2009. "Reflections on bell hooks' Social Theory and Pedagogy: Practices of Freedom." *American Philosophical Association Newsletter on Philosophy and the Black Experience* 8(2): 11–20. Parts of this essay were adapted from this source.

ZORA NEALE HURSTON (1891–1960)

Deborah G. Plant

For three days she lay naked on a couch, her navel pressed against a snakeskin coverlet. Red and yellow paint zigzagged her back, from right shoulder to left hip. The lightening symbol was to be her sign forever, and she was to commune with the Great One through storms. "She shall be called the Rain-Bringer." A pair of eyes was painted on her cheeks and the sun on her forehead ([1935] 1978, 208–10).

Zora Neale Hurston, "the Rain-Bringer," was initiated as a Hoodoo priestess in New Orleans by Luke Turner, nephew of legendary Hoodoo Queen Marie Leveau. By the time Hurston met Turner, she had undergone initiation ceremonies with five other "two-headed" doctors. Her investigation into Hoodoo was integral to the folklore collecting expedition she undertook between 1928 and 1931. Her fieldwork took her from the work camps and phosphate mines of Florida, to Alabama and Louisiana where she collected narratives, songs, and games, and conducted a systematic study of Hoodoo, conjure practices, and religious expressions. With the lore collected in the Bahamas, she began comparative studies of African Diaspora folk communities. Hurston's experiences and observations emboldened her to declare African American folklore as "the greatest cultural wealth on the continent" ([1935] 1978, 164).

Collecting and documenting this wealth of material was neither easy nor without danger. The 1896 *Plessy vs. Ferguson* decision sanctioned racial segregation in public facilities and complicated travel for black people. Jim Crow accommodations were separate and never equal—when they existed at all. Black, female, and alone, Hurston was vulnerable to rape, as well as lynching. And in the lawless environs of the work camps, she "shivered at the thought of dying with a knife in [her] back, or having [her] face mutilated" ([1935] 1978, 164). Dangers notwithstanding, Hurston coursed the highways and Southern backwoods by car and packed a chrome-plated pistol.

An anthropologist, folklorist, ethnographer, dramatist, and writer, Hurston was born in Notasulga, Alabama, on January 7, 1891. Her parents, John and Lucy Hurston, moved the family to Eatonville, Florida, when she was about three years old. Eatonville was an all-black town, incorporated by and run by its black citizens. Hurston grew up observing the genius of black folk on a daily basis. In the aftermath of her mother's death in 1904, she struggled to support herself and to complete her high school education. In 1917 she attended night school

in Baltimore, Maryland, then enrolled in Morgan College's preparatory academy. The following year she transferred to Howard University's preparatory school, in Washington, D.C. Earning her diploma in
May of 1919, she began taking courses for college credit. She joined
the Zeta Phi Beta Sorority, became a member of the Howard Players
theater troupe, and a member of the Stylus literary club.

With the publication of "John Redding Goes to Sea," in the May
1921 issue of *The Stylus*, the club's literary journal, Hurston came to
the attention of Howard University professor Alain Locke and Charles
Spurgeon Johnson, director of research for the National Urban League
and founding editor of *Opportunity: A Journal of Negro Life.* "John Redding" is set in a rural village in Florida that recalls the author's home-
town of Eatonville. The characters speak in the rhythms of southern
black dialect, and their beliefs, behaviors, humor, and interactions with
one another and with nature reflect a black folk ethos and sensibility,
features that would become signature aspects of Hurston's writing.

"John Redding" and "Drenched in Light," published in the December 1924 issue of *Opportunity*, ushered Hurston into the fold of the
New Negro writers of the Harlem Renaissance, the African American cultural movement that flourished from the 1920s to the early
1930s. Whereas Renaissance artists and pundits saw the significance of
folk culture as the bases for the development of a distinctively *African*
American artistic expression, Hurston was one of few writers who
saw the intrinsic value of the folk and folklore, and she was the only
one among the Harlem literati who was formally trained as a cultural
anthropologist.

While she majored in English at Barnard College, in New York,
earning her degree in 1928, she took courses in Anthropology at
Columbia University, studying with Ruth Benedict, Gladys Reichard,
and Franz Boas, the father of American Anthropology. With a 1927
Fellowship funded by Carter G. Woodson's Association for the Study of
Negro Life and History and the American Folk-Lore Society, she conducted fieldwork for both Woodson and Boas. The patronage of Charlotte Osgood Mason supported the fieldwork she initiated in 1928.
Hurston's course work and fieldwork merited her membership in the
American Folk-Lore Society, the American Ethnological Society, and
the American Anthropology Society.

From her collection of lore, Hurston drew material to produce
several theatrical productions. She considered drama to be the most
prominent characteristic of Negro expression and deduced that the
best way to introduce this cultural wealth to the nation was through
the performance arts. In June 1932, she produced *The Great Day*, an

original black folk concert, at the John Golden Theater in New York. Lavishly praised, the production was restaged at various New York venues. Versions of the play were performed in several Florida cities, at the National Folk Festival in St. Louis, Missouri, in 1933, and in Chicago, Illinois, in 1934.

In the meantime *Jonah's Gourd Vine* was published in 1934. John Pearson is the novel's anti-hero, a preacher whose poetic folk sermons gain him an admiring congregation and status, but whose marital infidelities contribute to his downfall and eventual death. *Mules and Men* was published a year later. The volume makes accessible folk materials Hurston collected from the work camps and from her investigations into Hoodoo. The critical acclaim of the folk concerts, the popularity of *Jonah's Gourd Vine*, and the publication of *Mules and Men* gained Hurston renown as the foremost national authority on African American folk culture. She was awarded a Guggenheim Fellowship in 1936 and 1937 in support of her study of Maroon society in Jamaica and a systematic exploration and documentation of Voodoo religion in Haiti. True to her participant-observer approach to the study and collection of folklore, Hurston immersed herself into Haitian communities and was initiated several times as a Voodoo priestess. Her findings in Jamaica and Haiti were published in *Tell My Horse* in 1938. In honor of her collective achievement, Morgan College awarded Hurston an honorary Doctor of Letters degree in 1939.

Hurston's fieldwork was continuous. She collected songs and stories in 1939 for the Library of Congress and the Folk Arts Committee of the Work Projects Administration in North Carolina, Georgia, and Florida. In 1940, she worked with anthropologist Jane Belo among the Gullah people of South Carolina. Hurston's work as a social scientist was nothing short of masterful, heroic, and revolutionary. Scholars are mindful of the importance of Hurston's anthropological work, yet there is still a depth and breadth to her efforts that require more penetrating investigation.

It might be useful to regard Hurston's anthropological work as social activism. In the face of late nineteenth- and early twentieth-century theories of social evolution, biological determinism, and the pseudo-science of eugenics, Hurston courageously and boldly insisted on the authentic representation of African American folks and folk culture. In spite of criticism from the Black Intelligentsia, who accused her of perpetuating "darky" stereotypes, popularized by black-faced white minstrels, Hurston continued to celebrate folk life and dared to insist on a cultural relativist perspective that equated black folk culture with white American culture. She perceived the lore of the folk as externalized interpretations and formulations of the unutterable and the ineffable, emanations of "that which the soul lives by" ([1935] 1978, 4).

With the endeavors of scholars like Lillie Howard, Robert Hemenway, and Alice Walker, Hurston's recognition as a literary foremother is well established. Even so, the case remains that much of Hurston's literary acclaim is based on a few short stories and her novel *Their Eyes Were Watching God* (1937). Revered as a literary masterpiece, the novel follows the journey of Janie Crawford through three marriages, from a child bride to a mature, introspective woman. Like the widely anthologized stories "Sweat" (1926) and "The Gilded Six-Bits (1933), and the novel *Jonah's Gourd Vine, Their Eyes* questions the institution of marriage and the unequal power dynamic in male-female relationships. Hurston personally experienced marriage as a problematic affair, as she married and divorced three times. She married Herbert Sheen in 1927, Albert Price III in 1939, and James Howell Pitts in 1944. Marriage and relationships would be constant themes in her fiction.

Moses, Man of the Mountain (1939), a lesser-known masterpiece, is an allegorical rendering of the biblical story of Moses. The novel critiques black leadership and the black masses, while it explores the nature of freedom and autonomy. *Seraph on the Suwannee* (1948), like *Moses*, is a novel that awaits fuller critical attention. Largely ignored because it doesn't fit easily into a feminist-womanist framework, *Seraph* is a psychoanalytic examination of white and southern Arvay Henson, who, like Janie, struggles to find her voice and her path in life.

Hurston was not a one-book wonder as the unevenness in the assessment of her novels suggests. Hurston scholarship must expand to include the full body of Hurston's literary work as a writer and the full breadth of her genius as a social scientist. Hurston's short stories, novels, plays, and essays are the leaves of a tree whose roots are deeply embedded in the African-enriched soil of black southern folk culture.

A hero in life, Hurston's heroic deeds transcend her physical death. Hurston died on January 28, 1960, in Fort Pierce, Florida. Her lifework is a mirror reflecting black life as "undiminished." It is a path to the inside life of each of us, beckoning us to find our own genius, our own unique voice, and that by which our own soul lives.

Hurston's major writings

[1934] 1990. *Jonah's Gourd Vine*. Reprint. New York: Harper.
[1935] 1978. *Mules and Men*. Reprint. Bloomington: Indiana University Press.

[1937] 1978. *Their Eyes Were Watching God*. Reprint. Urbana: University of Illinois Press.

[1938] 1990. *Tell My Horse*. Reprint. New York: Harper.

[1939] 1987. *Moses, Man of the Mountain*. Reprint. Urbana: University of Illinois Press.

[1942] 2006. *Dust Tracks on a Road*. Reprint. New York: Harper.

[1948] 1991. *Seraph on the Suwannee*. Reprint. New York: Harper.

1983. *The Sanctified Church*. Edited by Toni Cade Bambara. Berkeley: Turtle Island.

1995. *The Complete Stories*. New York: Harper.

1999. *Go Gator and Muddy the Water: Writings by Zora Neale Hurston from the Federal Writers' Project*. Edited by Pamela Bordelon. New York: Norton.

2001. *Every Tongue Got to Confess: Negro Folk-Tales from the Gulf States*. Edited by Carla Kaplan. New York: Harper.

2002. *Zora Neale Hurston: A Life in Letters*. Edited by Carla Kaplan. New York: Doubleday.

2004. *Speak So You Can Speak Again: The Life of Zora Neale Hurston*. Compiled by Lucy Ann Hurston and the Estate of Zora Neale Hurston. New York: Doubleday.

2008. *Zora Neale Hurston: Collected Plays*. Edited by Jean Lee Cole and Charles Mitchell. New Brunswick, NJ: Rutgers University Press.

1991. Hurston, Zora Neale with Langston Hughes. *Mule Bone: A Comedy of Negro Life*. Edited by George Houston Bass and Henry Louis Gates, Jr. New York: Harper.

Further reading

Boyd, Valerie. 2003. *Wrapped in Rainbows: The Life of Zora Neale Hurston*. New York: Scribner.

Glassman, Steve and Kathryn Lee Seidel, eds. 1991. *Zora in Florida*. Orlando: University of Central Florida Press.

Hemenway, Robert E. 1977. *Zora Neale Hurston: A Literary Biography*. Urbana: University of Illinois Press.

Howard, Lillie P. 1980. *Zora Neale Hurston*. Boston: Twayne.

Lewis, David L. 1979. *When Harlem Was in Vogue*. New York: Vintage.

Moylan, Virginia. 2011. *Zora Neale Hurston's Final Decade*. Gainesville: University of Florida Press.

Nathiri, N. Y., ed. 1991. *Zora! Zora Neale Hurston: A Woman and Her Community*. Orlando: Sentinel Communications.

Plant, Deborah G., ed. 2010. *The Inside Light: New Critical Essays on Zora Neale Hurston*. Santa Barbara: ABC-CLIO.

—. 2007. *Zora Neale Hurston: A Biography of the Spirit.* Westport, CT: Praeger.

Walker, Alice. 1983. *In Search of Our Mother's Gardens.* New York: Harcourt, Brace, and Jovanovich.

LUCE IRIGARAY (1930–)

Lynne Huffer

Luce Irigaray is a contemporary French philosopher, psychoanalyst, and feminist theorist. Best known for her conception of sexual difference as the occlusion of difference, her work challenges the sameness of a Western sexual order that reflects only the perspectives and interests of men. Irigaray's goals are both critical and constructive: her work aims to dismantle *sexual* difference (*différence sexuelle*) and, positively, to reconstruct *sexuate* difference (*différence sexuée*) as a culture of two sexed subjects within a new ontological order she calls "being-two" (*être-deux*). The stakes of her work are both conceptual and political: to "jam the theoretical machinery" (1985b, 78) of Western thought by exposing its exclusionary structures, and to bring attention to the limits of a liberal feminist politics of inclusion that leaves sexual difference itself unaltered.

Irigaray's antifoundationalist approach to sexual difference is exemplified in her first major book, *Speculum of the Other Woman*, published in French in 1974. In *Speculum*, Irigaray repeats, disrupts, and mimetically inverts the story of Western philosophy, beginning with Freud and ending with Plato. For Irigaray, the speculum represents both the medieval *speculum mundi*, or mirror of the world, and the mimetic symbolic system that reduces woman to the status of man's inferior copy, or what Irigaray calls the other of the same. Irigaray builds on Simone de Beauvoir's description in *The Second Sex* (1949) of woman as a relational being who, asymmetrically, reflects man back to himself: the negation of his position as both positive and neutral, as universal man. Drawing on Lacan's psychoanalytic conception of woman as void, Irigaray shows how feminine difference can only be conceived as the unrepresentable, or what she calls the other's other. Irigaray calls this system of the same *hommo-sexual*, with a double m. In her rendering, *hommo-sexuality* links men (*hommes*) to one another through the bonds of sameness (the *homo*) that undergird Western culture. To appear or to be heard in such a homosocial system, woman must participate as the derivative, defective other of man, either by repeating his actions and replicating his interests, or by taking on her traditional roles as wife and mother. Any place outside these positions is literally unthinkable: the place of the other's other.

Since *Speculum*, Irigaray has achieved the status of one of the most important feminist thinkers of our age. Looking back over four decades of her work, Irigaray describes her trajectory as comprising three periods: first, an early period where she critiques the "monosubjective character of our Western tradition"; second, a middle period where she seeks "to define the necessary mediations to develop a culture in the feminine" and to construct a feminine subject; and third, a later project that aims to develop the conditions for "making possible a coexistence between masculine and feminine subjects without subjection to one another" (2008a, 160). And while some have bemoaned Irigaray's shift away from the irreverence of her antifoundationalist beginnings, she insists that her project has been consistent over the three phases of her work: to critique the monosexual economy of the same and to create a true hetero-difference of "the two."

To be sure, Irigaray's *hommo-sexuality*, her "feminine" subject, and her culture of "being-two" have all been criticized as essentialist and heterosexist. Eve Kosofsky Sedgwick (1993), for example, regards Irigaray's denunciation of *hommo-sexuality* as homophobic. Shannon Winnubst (2006) reads Irigaray's privileging of sexual difference as an essentialist "cannibalism" of other forms of difference such as race, class, religion, and ethnicity. And in *Split Decisions* (2006), Janet Halley aligns Irigaray with the pastoral, redemptive sexuality of a moralistic cultural feminism.

Others have come to Irigaray's defense, explicating her notion of the feminine as non-essentialist and her "being-two" as a queering of heterosexuality. Reading Irigaray in such antifoundationalist terms requires an understanding of her philosophical methods as well as a sensitivity to her style, from *Speculum*'s ironies to the lyrical rhythms, poetic imagery, and clever neologisms that mark almost all her writing. Irigaray's most well-known stylistic trick, most prominent in *Speculum*, is her use of mimicry as a linguistic strategy for subverting the logic of the same. If woman must speak as man's puppet in order to be heard at all, she can strategically choose to repeat man's language to the point of nonsense or rupture.

Some interpreters of Irigaray link her mimetic style to her later articulations of a feminine voice and an ethics of sexuate difference. Rachel Jones, for example, hears in "La Mystérique" (in *Speculum*) not only a description of female mystics (and hysterics), but also someone

115

speaking "*as* a mystic, making language twist and turn until it begins to stammer in a voice that defies the logic of the subject" (Jones 2011, 155). To hear such speech requires a different mode of ethical attunement: as Irigaray puts it in *This Sex*, "one must know how to listen otherwise than in good form(s) to hear what it says" (1985b, 111). Thus, as Jones insists, Irigaray

> risks taking up the supposedly illogical voice of the female hysteric and mystic so as to disrupt the subject's discourse, not as an end in itself, but to try and make space for a different kind of language, a different logic, and different circuits of desire.
>
> (2011, 155)

Through the "silent plasticity" of the hysteric's body, material "divergencies" begin to emerge, "snipping the wires, cutting the current, breaking the circuits, switching the connections," making way for "the irruption of other circuits" (Irigaray 1985a, 142). Calling for new modes of listening, the Irigarayan mimic not only interrupts but also stammers "until the ear tunes into another music" and "the voice starts to sing again" (143). This early "double syntax" of a speech that undoes language even as it recreates language anew remains a crucial condition for the "being-two" of Irigaray's later work.

Ultimately Irigaray's sexuate difference aims to transform otherness into a new ethics and a new relational ontology. Such an ethics and ontology requires a new conception of eros as the "sensible transcendental," or "being-two" of lovers. With the "sensible transcendental" Irigaray reworks the opposition between immanence and transcendence which, as Beauvoir shows, consigns women to the subordinated immediacy of matter, nature, or the given. Irigaray's paradoxical concept of the "sensible transcendental" defies the logic of noncontradiction and, as Jones argues, allows her to rethink "the conditions of experience in ways that no longer depend[] on opposing concepts and intuitions" (2011, 126). Locating the "being" of "being-two" in the "in-between," Irigaray transforms the meaning of love and erotic relations, reworking eros to give "new life to lovers" (Chanter 1995, 220) and to reconstruct love as nonprocreative, both auto-affectional and reciprocal.

This relational ontology of love brings us full circle to Irigaray's beginnings in *Speculum*, to the place of the mother as the forgotten other of Western metaphysics. Irigaray shows how the patrilineal system of the same is founded on the always prior murder of a maternal other who remains unthinkable within the phallic structures of

Freudian psychoanalysis or the transcendent truth of Platonic Forms. Irigaray shows how the killing of the mother names a pre-originary violence that has itself been forgotten, masked by our culture's founding myth about the killing of the father by the primal horde. Importantly, Western culture's forgotten pre-origin in matricide produces what Irigaray calls the absence of a maternal genealogy at the level of the symbolic. As Margaret Whitford puts it, "there is no maternal genealogy" (1991, 76).

This metaphysical securing of patrilineal descent through a forgetting of sexual differentiation in an act of violence that is itself forgotten consigns woman-as-wife-and-mother to symbolic non-existence, except as man's false copy, as object of exchange between father and son, or as the procreative womb that gives birth to transcendent man. Consequently, the mother-daughter relation and relations among women generally remain unsymbolized. This analysis opens a lens onto the repeated failures of female solidarity that mark feminism's diverse histories. On a symbolic level, female sociality fails because relations among women cannot appear, except as derivative of relations among men. Thus feminists must repeatedly confront what Whitford describes as the gap between "the idealization of women's nature found in some early feminist writings and the actual hostilities and dissensions engendered within the women's movement itself" (1991, 78). Irigaray's diagnosis of the occluded production of absence through matricidal violence helps to explain the invisible symbolic conditions for the ethical failures, aggressions, hostilities, and betrayals that plague relations among women. She allows us to see that these failures are not simply the result of tactical mistakes or blindspots, but rather the consequence of idealizing, Platonic modes of thinking that repeatedly construct feminist fantasies of female harmony without exclusion to be repaired by inclusive political gestures. Irigaray's analysis helps us to reimagine solidarity among women in less idealizing ways and to regard exclusion and betrayal as constitutive of sociality. Only by facing up to the agonistic violence that attends the forging of social bonds can feminists take on the constructive work of building an alternative ethics and relational ontology.

The work of that construction is, of necessity, catachrestic: that is, it requires the figuration of relations through an abuse of trope, the necessary naming of something as that which it is not. Irigaray's best image for such relations is the figure of the lips, made famous in "When Our Lips Speak Together" (in *This Sex*). Both singular and multiple, both oral and genital, and yet, catachrestically, neither, the lips articulate the in-between, auto-affectional, projective announcement that Irigaray describes as an incalculable difference-to-come. As Jones demonstrates, unlike the matrix or mathematical *matriciel* that calculates difference within a logic of the same, Irigaray's erotic *matriciel* combines the womb or matrix (*la matrice*) with sky or heavens (*le ciel*) to invoke an image of generation that is neither purely corporeal nor "fathered by the Forms" (2011, 81). Rather, Irigaray invites us to approach what Jones calls "a different horizon" (81), a maternal body, or *mater* as matter, that is "active and generative" and that acknowledges matter's "capacity to engender form" (92). This rethinking of phallogocentrism in Irigaray's work not only challenges the current linguistic, ethical, and political order; more radically, it aims to reconfigure the form–matter relation at the heart of Western metaphysics.

Irigaray's major works

[1974] 1985a. *Speculum of the Other Woman.* Trans. G. C. Gill. Ithaca, NY: Cornell University Press.
[1977] 1985b. *This Sex Which Is Not One.* Trans. C. Porter with C. Burke. Ithaca, NY: Cornell University Press.
[1984] 1993. *An Ethics of Sexual Difference.* Trans. C. Burke and G. C. Gill. Ithaca, NY: Cornell University Press.
2002. *The Way of Love.* Trans. H. Bostic and S. Pluháček. London: Continuum.
2008a. *Conversations.* London: Continuum.
2008b. *Sharing the World.* London: Continuum.

Further reading

Beauvoir, S. de. [1949] 2010. *The Second Sex.* Trans. C. Borde and S. Malovany-Chevallier. New York: Knopf.
Chanter, T. 1995. *Ethics of Eros: Irigaray's Rewriting of the Philosophers.* New York: Routledge.
Deutscher, P. 2002. *A Politics of Impossible Difference: The Later Work of Luce Irigaray.* Ithaca, NY: Cornell University Press.
Grosz, E. 2011. "Irigaray and the Ontology of Sexual Difference." In *Becoming Undone: Darwinian Reflections on Life, Politics, and Art*, 99–112. Durham, NC: Duke University Press.
Halley, J. 2006. *Split Decisions: How and Why to Take a Break from Feminism.* Princeton, NJ: Princeton University Press.
Huffer, L. 2013. *Are the Lips a Grave? A Queer Feminist on the Ethics of Sex.* New York: Columbia University Press.
Jones, R. 2011. *Irigaray: Toward a Sexuate Philosophy.* Cambridge: Polity.

Sedgwick, E. 1993. *Tendencies*. Durham, NC: Duke University Press.

Whitford, M. 1991. *Luce Irigaray: Philosophy in the Feminine*. London: Routledge.

Winnubst, S. 2006. *Queering Freedom*. Bloomington: Indiana University Press.

BARBARA E. JOHNSON (1947–2009)

Deborah Jenson

Barbara E. Johnson was a feminist literary critic and translator who used gender difference as a starting point for the critical theorization of language and personhood. She taught at Yale and Harvard, in disciplines ranging from French, Comparative Literature, and African-American Studies, to Law, and Psychiatry. A student of the theorist of deconstruction Paul de Man, Johnson was a key interlocutor in post-structuralist debates from the late 1970s to the early 1990s through monographs such as *The Critical Difference* and *The Wake of Deconstruction*, as well as her translations of work by Jacques Derrida. Unlike many of her critical contemporaries, Johnson segued effortlessly from the "linguistic turn" of literary theory to social issues of race, sexuality, reproduction, psychology, and human rights. In Johnson's work, social issues are processed through a rhetorical and philosophical engagement with learning, integrating, translating, disseminating, and legislating the boundaries of the other. One of the most celebrated essayists on gender, femininity, maternity, and women's writing of her era, Johnson made contestation of "the unequivocal domination of one mode of signifying over another" (Derrida 1981, xv) into a feminist art.

Johnson had, in the words of Christopher L. Miller, a "gift for lapidary phrases and ironic turns,"[1] amounting over time to a singular poetics, most palpable in the use of incongruity in the titles of her publications, such as "Using People: Kant with Winnicott" ([2000] 2014) or "Apostrophe, Animation, and Abortion" ([1986] 2014). Language was not a tool like any other tool in Johnson's outlook and praxis: it involved what she called "the throwing of voice, the giving of animation" ([1986] 2014, 221), whether in the sense of a proverbial sleight of hand, or the animating *fiat lux* ("Let there be light") of Genesis. What could be a more basic human preoccupation, a more basic linguistic labor, Johnson in effect asked, than the rhetorical personification of the world, in which we struggle to control the stakes and parameters of our personification as social and civil beings?

In *Persons and Things* she wrote, "After all, according to Marx, human beings become historical the moment they start to work, and the first 'thing' they produce is—the concept of 'human beings'" (2008, 3). This Marxian allusion to the work of human being parallels Johnson's observation that we tend to fetishize a freestanding notion of self much as the commodity is fetishized:

> emphasis on the isolated self as a locus of value (positive and negative) risks duplicating, in the psychological realm, the structures Marx identified as the "fetishism of the commodity"—the belief that the commodity, abstracted from both labor and use, "contains" value in and of itself.
>
> (2008, 3)

The self as abstracted from labor and use is particularly prey to what Johnson called "orthopedic" shaping, like the orthopedic shoes meant to support and even shape proper development of the foot: "Femininity has always been an orthopedic notion (orthopedic: from *ortho*, straight, and *paideia*, education). Including but not restricted to notions of Beauty, the concept of femininity acts as a mold for shaping and controlling women's behavior" (1998, 101).

Johnson explored the desiring dialectics of voice and animation, silence and stillness, in many common places and commonplaces. These loci included childhood development, sexual desire, puppets and prostheses, translation, legal status, gaming, artificial life, doing time, construction work, alphabetization—virtually the whole intelligent and intelligible world that she had time to encounter in words.

For Johnson, ironically, "The ego ideal of the poetic voice" would seem "to reside in the muteness of things" ([1985] 1996, 131) (poetic things like Keats' Grecian urn), such that the vaunted condition of human being is articulated at moments of slippage from person to non-person. Johnson described Percy Bysshe Shelley's "Ode to the West Wind" as follows:

> In saying "be thou me," he is attempting to restore metaphorical exchange and equality. If apostrophe is the giving of voice, the throwing of voice, the giving of animation, then a poet using it is always in a sense saying to the addressee "Be thou me."
>
> ([1986] 2014, 221)

The pathos of the formula "be thou me," almost obscures the fact that the addressee is not necessarily a human being, not necessarily the Laura to the Petrarchean poet or the Elvire to Lamartine. In saying, "Be thou me" to the West Wind, the poet is literally throwing voice to the wind. The commodified self, which seems to "contain" an inherent value—meaning an identity that gives it a value—can be emptied like an urn. Scholars of literature, Johnson puns, *urn* ("earn") a living by filling and emptying that container, as if they were filling a funereal urn with ashes, or a symbolic electoral urn with crucial ballots.

The lyric, far from an erudite genre of a dying high culture of print, was for Johnson a model, a template, a tool, for the basic construction of cognitive and communicative selves and worlds through echo, like bats. "Is there any *inherent* connection between figurative language and questions of life and death, of who will wield and who will receive violence in any given society?" she asked in "Apostrophe, Animation, and Abortion" ([1986] 2014, 218). (The answer, as to an inherent connection, is *no*, but as to a practical connection, *yes*.) This is the profound redundancy of the Heideggerean phrases "The thing things" and "The world worlds." As Johnson notes in "They Urn It" in *Persons and Things*, here

> the verb says exactly the same thing as the subject. … And to transform the nouns "thing" and "world" into verbs may be precisely what Heidegger is after. … the 'doing' of thing and world tells us no more than we learned from the noun—*except that the thing has now become an act.*
>
> (2008, 62–64)

The lyric is implicated in Hannah Arendt's notion that "company is chosen by thinking in examples" (2005, 146).

There may also be few better ways than reflection on personification to think our way out of epistemological ghettos. In "Metaphor, Metonymy, and Voice in *Their Eyes Were Watching God*," Johnson first pondered the phenomenon through which "metaphor and metonymy had burst into prominence as the salt and pepper, the Laurel and Hardy, the yin and yang, and often the Scylla and Charybdis of literary theory" ([1984] 2014, 108). Johnson was tapping into the psychoanalytic notion of transference as it applies to social groups, such as the humanities in academia, in the presence not of the compelling psycho-analyst, like Sigmund Freud, but the compelling literary-analyst. For Johnson's students and colleagues, to read that metaphor and metonymy "had acquired the brief but powerful privilege of dividing and naming the whole of human reality, from Mommy and Daddy ... to God and Country" ([1984] 2014, 108) was to wish to be adopted into that metaphor and metonymy family, where "arcane rhetorical figures" suddenly read like old photographs, making a world of meaning intimate and conflicted. Those in Barbara Johnson's orbit yearned after apostrophe and chiasmus like middle-aged analysands suddenly giving a startled young Freud a soon to be familiar "come hither" look. But she used this transferential journey through language to powerful political effect. In metaphor, the operation of substitution is based on condensation of meaning, as in the application of the word "Camelot" to John Kennedy's Washington, but in metaphor, it is based on an association of contiguity, as in the use of the word "Camelot" to refer to King Arthur's world. Contiguity, however, has "a tendency to become overlaid by similarity, and vice versa" ([1984] 2014, 111) as in the proverb, "'Birds of a feather flock together: qui se ressemble s'assemble'" ([1984] 2014, 111). For Johnson, "One has only to think of the applicability of this proverb to the composition of neighborhoods in America," to consider the way that contiguous associations may segue into a symbolic branding, just as the metonymy of color, "the White House," becomes "somehow metaphorically connected to the whiteness of its inhabitant" ([1984] 2014, 111). From this rhetorical analysis, Johnson leads the reader to bond with the African-American writer Zora Neale Hurston's "joyous liberation from the rigidities of status, image, and property" ([1984] 2014, 113). Through her own writing, Johnson nurtures the reader's transference to the emancipatory potential for the black woman to become *visible* in Hurston's *Their Eyes Were Watching God*.

Because so many readers and students of Barbara Johnson had experienced these scholarly journeys through transference, their feminist engagement was typically a very personal self-emancipation from unconscious hegemonic logics embedded in the workings of meaning.

Although Barbara Johnson became disabled in her fifties by cerebellar degeneration, encountering the "muteness" she had theorized in "Muteness Envy" ([1985] 1996) through obstacles to fluent speech including a tracheotomy, she managed to use a computer keyboard and sometimes to write by hand until the very end of her life, completing many of the projects she had been too busy to finalize in the midst of her intensive educational and administrative commitments. Some of her most important work was published during the period of her diagnosed illness, including *Mother Tongues*

122

in 2003, *Persons and Things* in 2008, and her eloquent translation of Mallarmé's *Divagations*, the multiform poetic prose collection of which Mallarmé had said "'This is a book just the way I don't like them'" (2009, 10). Johnson's posthumous work included *Moses and Multiculturalism* and *A Life with Mary Shelley*, as well as the *Barbara Johnson Reader* edited by former students. At Johnson's memorial service at Harvard, Judith Butler commented that Johnson's thematization of voice had made her expert in the meaningfulness of her illness:

> Perhaps this is why she could finally approach her own demise with such uncanny composure, since she had been thinking about what is inaudible in language, what is crucial about death in any piece of writing, how dependent and intertwined the human and object worlds must be.[2]

Johnson's poetics will continue to reanimate the familial and romantic valences of words in their beautiful collectivities on the page, with reader and text, person and world, ventriloquizing and animating each other, "Be thou me."

Notes

1 Christopher L. Miller wrote for the Yale French Department newsletter, "To be a graduate student in the Yale French Department in the late 1970's was to be in awe of Barbara Johnson. Her critical acuity, her intellectual originality, her gift for lapidary phrases and ironic turns were all astonishing and great fun to behold. Sadly for Yale, she went to Harvard as (in her phrase) a 'missionary.'"
2 Judith Butler, eulogy, Barbara Johnson memorial service. Cited with permission of the author.

Johnson's major writings

1979. *Défigurations du langage poétique: La seconde révolution baudelairienne.* Paris: Flammarion.
1980. *The Critical Difference: Essays in the Contemporary Rhetoric of Reading.* Baltimore, MD: Johns Hopkins University Press.
[1984] 2014. "Metaphor, Metonymy, and Voice in *Their Eyes Were Watching God.*" In *The Barbara Johnson Reader: The Surprise of Otherness*, 108–25. Edited by Melissa Feuerstein, Bill Johnson González, Lili Porten, and Keja Velans. Durham, NC: Duke University Press.

[1985] 1996. "Muteness Envy." In *Human, All Too Human*, 131–48. Edited by Diana Fuss. New York and London: Routledge.

[1986] 2014. "Apostrophe, Animation, and Abortion." In *The Barbara Johnson Reader: The Surprise of Otherness*, 217–35. Edited by Melissa Feuerstein, Bill Johnson González, Lili Porten, and Keja Velans. Durham, NC: Duke University Press.

1987. *A World of Difference*. Baltimore, MD: Johns Hopkins University Press.

1994. *The Wake of Deconstruction*. Oxford: Blackwell.

1998. *The Feminist Difference: Literature, Psychoanalysis, Race, and Gender*. Cambridge, MA: Harvard University Press.

[2000] 2014. "Using People: Kant with Winnicott." In *The Barbara Johnson Reader: The Surprise of Otherness*, 262–74. Edited by Melissa Feuerstein, Bill Johnson González, Lili Porten, and Keja Velans. Durham, NC: Duke University Press.

2003. *Mother Tongues: Sexuality, Trials, Motherhood, Translation*. Cambridge, MA: Harvard University Press.

2008. *Persons and Things*. Cambridge, MA: Harvard University Press.

2010. *Moses and Multiculturalism*. Berkeley: California University Press.

2014a. *A Life with Mary Shelley*. Redwood City, CA: Stanford University Press.

2014b. *The Barbara Johnson Reader: The Surprise of Otherness*. Edited by Melissa Feuerstein, Bill Johnson González, Lili Porten, and Keja Velans. Durham, NC: Duke University Press.

Translations

Derrida, Jacques. 1981. *Dissemination*. Chicago: Chicago University Press.

Mallarmé, Stéphane. 2009. *Divagations*. Cambridge, MA: Harvard University Press.

Further reading

Arendt, Hannah. 2005. "Some Questions of Moral Philosophy." In *Responsibility and Judgment*, 49–146. New York: Schocken.

Berlant, Lauren, et al. 2006. "Difference: Reading with Barbara Johnson." Special issue of *Differences: A Journal of Feminist Cultural Studies* 17(3).

JAMAICA KINCAID (1949–)

Marla Brettschneider

Understanding Jamaica Kincaid's contribution as a feminist thinker requires theorizing the interstices and the gendered dimensions of diaspora. Kincaid's life and themes in her writing speak to the experiences of myriad exiled women and communities as she transforms diaspora thinking from a feminist perspective. She does this by deepening the capacity to appreciate both homes and diasporas and their varied relationships, central for feminist theory, without essentializing them.

Raised in Antigua, Kincaid was born Elaine Cynthia Potter Richardson in 1949. An excellent student who loved literature, she had the fraught experience of having the best of a British colonial education. As a gendered manifestation of her situation as a poor and female colonial subject, she was sent to the US to work as an au pair in 1965 at age sixteen, before earning her high school diploma. She published her first article in 1973, at that time taking the name Jamaica Kincaid. She is also active in her Jewish community. Central themes in Kincaid's work are the devastation of colonialism and imperialism, migration and diaspora, exile and loss, global inequalities, self-exploration and family. These feminist and broader themes in Kincaid's work are also perennial Jewish themes.

Kincaid's work assists us in seeing beyond binaries that have been instrumental in much of patriarchal thinking about experiences in diaspora. She challenges dichotomous notions of power and powerlessness, homeland and exile, leaving and returning, continuity and disruption, assimilation and isolation. Doing so, she affirms other complex possibilities. These dialectics of the diasporic are core to the experience of so many women across the globe as well as mutually constitutive gender, raced, anti-Semitic, and classed analysis of the histories of micro and macro migrations key to masses of the human population. Yet, there remains a tendency to revive a static binary of home/exile in diaspora theory more broadly. Kincaid's feminist telling of her life challenges these tendencies. She situates herself in relationship to multiple homes (African, Caribbean, Vermont), multiple conquests (Taino, Carib, European, US), multiple dislocations (from Israel to other parts of Africa, to the Caribbean, to the US), and multiple efforts to be at home in the world as a diasporic subject. Her work is firmly situated within feminist accountings of home, yet leaves space for feminist namings of what aspects of home/homeland might be continued and/ or reclaimed across communal diasporic transformations.

The term "diaspora" in its current usage began with the Greek translation of the Hebrew bible. Previously, the term "diaspora" referred to those sent by a conquering empire to live in the acquired lands to govern the new subjects. Introduced in the context of the Israelite's Babylonian exile, the term "diaspora" was used in a new way in reference to the victims of an imperialist takeover who are then scattered from their homeland. While not all those in diaspora experience themselves in exile, much of diaspora theorizing struggles between binary notions of home/ exile, grounded in the Jewish experience of Zion/outside of Israel.

In literary studies that are not explicitly Jewish or feminist, Kincaid's work is usually discussed in terms of a "prior"-pre-Babylonian-exile. Kincaid was taught and often required to memorize long passages (often as punishment) of Milton's *Paradise Lost*. Kincaid's early work (*At the Bottom of the River* and *Annie John*) is often analyzed as recasting a paradise lost, an Edenic rather than Babylonian exile. However, noting Kincaid's feminist approach in a Jewish context helps to complicate this reading in productive ways.

As a girl, Kincaid was close with her mother. As she grew to puberty, with the potential for independence and autonomous sexuality, she describes her mother's rejection. This dynamic is a female-gendered parallel, personalized, of a common power dynamic of colonialism. Kincaid's feminist analysis demonstrates that while a colonized population remains perceived as "simple" and easily directed, colonizers can think of themselves as civilizers. When colonized populations begin to clarify a sense of themselves as oppressed, demand redress for grievances, and/or rebel, the dynamics tend to shift.

By her third book, *Lucy*, the feminist home/diaspora scenario shifts as the teenage female protagonist is sent by her parents to the US to work. Seen again in *Autobiography of My Mother*, Antigua and the Caribbean, instead of private home and mother, become locations for the metaphor of a paradise lost. Like the biblical Abram and Sarai, Kincaid is sent off to a land she does not know. Kincaid's destination represents a promised land in gendered neocolonial global relations. In this re-gendered telling, however, she is a young woman on her own, abandoned by her family in the context of global colonialism.

Moving beyond an essentialist center-periphery binary frees up feminist diasporic theorizing not only to embrace many possible homes of diaspora but also to choose to stay in relation to plural communal centers and plural homes. Kincaid helps us see that both homes and exiles are not clear cut phenomena, existing outside of history and politics. In contrast, in the biblical telling, the Hebrews have to make a long arduous journey to the place that will be then called home. Then they become exiled (the origin of the term now used as diaspora). The ancient Hebrews went to the land of Canaan. And the Canaanites might have conquered another people before the biblical telling.

Kincaid's work, however, creates a feminist parallel to this ancient story. Kincaid's notions of home(s)/exile(s) stem from creation of the African diaspora formed through patriarchy and other modes of devaluing humans, most significantly here, the slave trade. The Caribbean thus becomes a diaspora. Due to the de-valuation of her as a daughter, Kincaid then leaves the Caribbean and becomes also part of the Caribbean diaspora. But the Caribs were not the "first" inhabitants of the islands in the region known as home in Kincaid's work. In various forms of militarism historically important to feminist critique, the Carib peoples overtook the Tainos. In the creation of the Afro-Caribbean experience, the Caribs are largely genocided.

Further, patriarchal elites often create and refer to imagined stable traditions in efforts to control their communities. In Kincaid's feminist approach, however, with a deeper Jewish biblical exegesis not stopping at Eden, there are numerous expulsions, devastations of the home place, and setting up new homes. She repositions women and feminist possibilities of voice and agency in her tellings. For example, echoed in *Mr. Potter*, about Kincaid's biological father, the biblical story does not dwell on Noah's experience of the loss of the world as he knows it—but we do know that he turns to drink and that sexual improprieties follow surviving his voyage to a new home. Kincaid's discussion in *My Brother* resonates with the tower of Babel story in which the people have their city destroyed and become among those scattered across the earth speaking different languages. Lot does not easily leave Sodom and Gomora when the most powerful ruling authority he recognizes wipes out these home cities—but he does not technically look back. Alternatively, in *Autobiography of My Mother*, Kincaid portrays Lot's wife, the woman who will look back. As seen in *At the Bottom of the River, Annie John, Lucy, My Brother*, and *See Now Then*, through many migrations and large scale loss, a Jewish read of the biblical text recounts who is who and related to whom, reminding us of relationship and community across time and physical wandering necessary in/for feminist politics. Kincaid's feminist work becomes more subversive in this Jewish context than only in relation to the Christian analytic context of reclaiming Milton's *Paradise Lost*.

These narratives resonate strongly with the phenomena of contemporary diasporic conditions that feminist scholars highlight. By the exile into Babylon, the story is of a people with much experience of expulsion, chosen and forced wanderings, creation of new homes understood as temporary or hoped to be permanent.

Another instantiation of complex diaspora theorizing brought into relief by Kincaid's work as a feminist thinker is the way barrenness is linked to diaspora. The first usages for the Hebrew word *akara* (as opposed to the Greek work *diaspora*)—referring to Israel after the Babylonian exile—are in the story of Sarah's barrenness (followed by similar stories). A common association of diaspora is alienation from a fount of fertile collective culture. Kincaid interestingly presents a feminist portrayal of the evils of colonialism in the barren winter of northern climes—what Kincaid calls in *See Now Then* "the horrid something called Winter" (2013, 11). Of exile, Kincaid refers to the "hollow space inside" (1985, 144). This feminist reading makes room for the complex, flawed, strong, conflicted, and beautiful women of Kincaid's life and work as a way to grapple with the concreteness of the dialectic of alienation and renewal in exile. The yearning of the biblical barren women is for sons, Kincaid's expulsion from the paradise of her mother's adoration comes in her life with the birth of her younger brothers.

Kincaid's feminist work moves within the constant interaction of seeking life and beauty in multiple locations, homes and homelands, exiles, oppressive powers, resistive gestures. Interestingly, compared to her writings, when Kincaid herself is in the picture in her lived life, something happens to the lifeless barrenness of these gray winter neocolonial climes. In her life, as discussed in *See Now Then* and *Among Flowers: A Walk in the Himalayas*, while living in New England, Kincaid becomes a gardener and is surrounded by beauty and bounty in nature. While the place of her recent exile, Antigua, is the primary landscape of her fiction, the Caribbean does not serve as a simplistic, primal, positively valenced home (characteristic of patriarchal tropes). Kincaid is able to write in her exile, and so she is able to survive a life of deadness she understands would have been fated for her had she remained in Antigua. The isolation of the alienation of diaspora is turned on its head in the context of Kincaid's feminism with a lived life in exile. In her feminist thinking, she employs tropes of loss, longing, and melancholy to support agency, to survive and to thrive through the creation of beautiful works of art, scathing political analysis, and a life well lived in a nexus of individual and communal relationships.

Kincaid's major writings

1983. *At the Bottom of the River.* New York: Farrar, Straus, Giroux.
1985. *Annie John.* New York: Farrar, Straus, Giroux.

1988. *A Small Place*. New York: Farrar, Straus, Giroux.

1990. *Lucy*. New York: Farrar, Straus, Giroux.

1996. *Autobiography of My Mother*. New York: Farrar, Straus, Giroux.

1997. *My Brother*. New York: Farrar, Straus, Giroux.

2001. *Talk Stories*. New York: Farrar, Straus, Giroux.

2002. *Mr. Potter*. New York: Farrar, Straus, Giroux.

2005. *Among Flowers: A Walk in the Himalayas*. Washington, DC: National Geographic.

2013. *See Now Then*. New York: Farrar, Straus, Giroux.

JULIA KRISTEVA (1941–)

Fanny Söderbäck

There looms, within abjection, one of those violent, dark revolts of being, directed against a threat that seems to emanate from an exorbitant outside or inside, ejected beyond the scope of the possible, the tolerable, the thinkable.

Kristeva, *Powers of Horror: An Essay on Abjection*

Few thinkers—feminist or not—have ventured as deep into the muddy waters of *disgust* as has Bulgarian-French linguist, psychoanalyst, philosopher, and novelist Julia Kristeva. And few thinkers have provided as rich a theoretical toolbox for those of us who are interested in examining that which is met with varying degrees of disgust in our culture: the fleshy, the fluid, the messy, the non-binary, the feminine, the sexually devious, the disabled, the rejected, the racially other, the exiled, that which defies systems and borders…

In *Powers of Horror*, Kristeva introduced the idea of the abject: that which is neither subject nor object; which "draws me toward the place where meaning collapses" (1982, 2); and which "disturbs identity, system, order" (4). Kristeva's discussion of abjection is her contribution to one of the most important debates of psychoanalytic theory, namely how a subject—an "I"—comes into being as someone distinct from others. Kristeva's discussion of this process begins at the brink of subjectivity, in the symbiotic relationship between mother and infant. This early relationship is described as marked by an oceanic feeling of plenitude and wholeness on the part of an infant who has yet to distinguish inside from outside, self from other, me from mother. As the process of separation begins, it is far from clear-cut, indeed marked by

ambivalence, loathing, and continuously diffuse boundaries. Since the infant feels like it is 'one' with its mother, the very process of separating from her inevitably involves a sort of self-separation. As Noëlle McAfee puts it, the infant "must renounce a part of itself … in order to become a self" (2005, 48). This process can be violent, painful, and messy: "During that course in which 'I' become," Kristeva writes, "I give birth to myself amid the violence of sobs, of vomit" (1982, 3).

Kristeva brings attention not only to the experience of the infant in the midst of separating from its mother. Her work also often turns to the experience of motherhood—from pregnancy to birth and that early symbiotic bond. The essay "Stabat Mater" (published in English in *Tales of Love*) provides a deeply personal and poetic account of the fleshy, messy, and ambivalent experience of entering motherhood, juxtaposing it with a much more formal discussion of idealized motherhood represented by the figure of the Virgin Mother. This relationship between the embodied and the formal—or what she calls the 'semiotic' and the 'symbolic'—takes center stage in much of her early writings, such as *Revolution in Poetic Language*, and is one of the most distinct contributions of her work.

Kristeva's theory of the subject is premised on the idea that "the subject is an effect of linguistic processes" (McAfee 2005, 29). As such, it can never be defined once and for all—Kristeva's *sujet en procès* is, precisely, a subject in process, an evolving being, someone who is continuously shaped and reshaped by signifying processes. Kristeva is particularly attuned to those dimensions of language that escape the symbolic order of grammar and syntax. Language, for her, is always necessarily rooted in the embodied and affective, it becomes meaningful through its rhythm and melody, its irregularities and flow. That early relationship between mother and infant is one that may lack language proper, but certainly not meaningful exchanges. And the blabber of the infant lives on in poetic language, and other forms of artistic expression that push beyond the boundaries of structure and order. When language sings. And when meaning remains embodied. I dare say this attention and attunement to the embodied and desirous registers of language—and, as an extension, subjectivity—is feminist in kind. It is no coincidence that Kristeva returns to the mother-infant-dyad (even to her own personal experience of it) as she gives articulation to the semiotic dimensions of language. Her philosophy of language, and her theory of subjectivity, offer a challenge to a philosophical discourse that by and large has ignored, indeed repressed, anything that threatens (patriarchal) order. Again, the fleshy, the fluid, the messy, the non-binary, the feminine…

Feminist thinkers as well as others who are attuned to structures of exclusion have often borrowed Kristeva's notion of abjection, or the abject, to make sense of such structures. Whether it be 'illegal' immigrants crammed together in cargo ships, cultural minorities threatened by genocide, or women and girls who are being trafficked for sex work, the 'abject' has been a useful category for framing the conditions under which these people live. And while Kristeva's own work rarely touches on the most extreme forms of exclusion, she has always been fascinated with the role and place of the foreigner, the outsider, the other. In the vein of Simone de Beauvoir, this other is, for Kristeva, often a female subject. But throughout her work, she has been concerned with otherness in ways that extend far beyond female subjectivity. In her book *Strangers to Ourselves*—which provides a sort of genealogy of the category of the foreigner from Ancient Greece to modern cosmopolitanism—she ultimately speaks of the stranger that inhabits each of us. In the final chapter of that book, Kristeva draws from the psychoanalytic insight of the unconscious and the fact that human subjects, in the wake of Sigmund Freud, are opaque and internally divided, insofar as the unconscious—or the Id in Freud's later language—remains largely hidden yet formative of who we are.

The book opens with the claim that "the foreigner lives within us: he is the hidden face of our identity, the space that wrecks our abode, the time in which understanding and affinity founder" (Kristeva 1991, 1). Kristeva goes on to emphasize the ethical implications of becoming aware of our own strangeness: "Henceforth, we know that we are foreigners to ourselves, and it is with the help of that sole support that we can attempt to live with others" (170). Such ethics has political implications. By recognizing the foreigner within ourselves, "we are spared detesting him in himself," Kristeva claims (1). Conversely, it is only in relation to the other that we can come to know ourselves in our fundamental strangeness. What is at stake for Kristeva is something other than simply 'acceptance of' or 'respect for' those who are different from us. "Living with the other, with the foreigner," she writes, "confronts us with the possibility or not of *being an other*" (13). It forces us to imagine and confront our very own strangeness.

Kristeva herself was born in 1941 in Bulgaria. She grew up in an Eastern bloc that celebrated homogeneity and that would not allow her to enter public school since her father worked as an accountant for the Church. She received a French education at a school run by Dominican nuns, and went on to study at the University of Sofia. In December 1965, she was awarded a scholarship to spend time as a student in France, and while the scholarship money would not reach her until late January, she left her native Bulgaria without delay, worrying that the communist director of her university might prevent her from going. She arrived in Paris on Christmas Eve, with only five dollars in her pocket, and soon joined the circles of literary theorist Roland Barthes, anthropologist Claude Lévi-Strauss, linguist Émile Benveniste, psychoanalyst Jacques Lacan, philosopher Michel Foucault, and others. Kristeva gained immediate respect and became an active member of *Tel Quel*—a group of politically engaged intellectuals who published a journal by the same name (McAfee 2005, 4–6).

Much of Kristeva's work since her arrival in France has been a critical response to the call for homogeneity that so characterized the world in which she had grown up. Her work celebrates pluralism, singularity, and difference. And while she has always joined with the Left in political matters, her philosophy is distinctly grounded in the individual first and foremost—not in the collective. Indeed, time and again, she has been wary to identify even with feminism, precisely because she worries that as a 'movement' focusing on the struggles of 'women' it runs the risk of grouping together and homogenizing women under one banner without attention to the particularity and individuality of each woman, in her difference.

In the essay "Women's Time" (published in English in *New Maladies of the Soul*), she addresses these issues explicitly. Women in the Eastern bloc, she notes, undeniably achieved equal positions in society and in the State. But at what cost? Besides the many lives that had been lost, the very specificity of female experience was also under threat: "In the spirit of the egalitarian and universalist context of Enlightenment humanism, the only idea that socialism has held to is the notion that identity between the sexes is the only way to liberate the 'second sex'" (Kristeva 1995, 209). Note that her critique here is of socialism *as well as* liberal humanism. Both are guilty of a kind of egalitarian universalism that ultimately runs the risk of erasing female specificity as well as the uniqueness of each individual (woman or man). Her own universalism is therefore firmly grounded in an affirmation of difference, indeed her claim is that if there is anything we all have in common, universally, it is that we are all other, all in a certain sense foreign: "The foreigner is within me, hence we are all foreigners," as she puts it in *Strangers to Ourselves* (1991, 192).

In her later work, Kristeva has persisted to emphasize this human uniqueness and singularity. She has done so in terms of the 'intimate revolt' that so marks her political project as one that begins on an individual and psychic level so as to reverberate culturally, more as a side-effect of individual transformation and change (in books like *The Sense and Non-Sense of Revolt* and *Intimate Revolt*). She has done so in terms of her examination of 'female genius' through comprehensive studies of the life and work of German philosopher Hannah Arendt, British psychoanalyst Melanie Klein, and French author Colette, respectively (*Female Genius: Life, Madness, Words*). Finally, she has done so through a journey into the mystical in her portrait of Teresa of Avila (*Teresa, My Love: An Imagined Life of the Saint of Avila*) as well as her examination of our human need to believe (*This Incredible Need to Believe*).

Kristeva's feminist revolution is fought neither in the courtrooms nor in the streets. It unfolds in singular intersubjective encounters, in artistic practice as well as philosophical reflection, through personal transformation, and sometimes in mystical revelations. For Kristeva, the personal is inevitably political, yet feminism can never be reduced to a slogan of that kind. On her account, it must remain heterogeneous in nature, and always in touch with that which might bring us unease: the fleshy, the fluid, the messy, the non-binary, the feminine, the sexually devious, the disabled, the rejected, the racially other, the exiled, that which defies systems and borders…

Kristeva's major writings

[1974] 1984. *Revolution in Poetic Language.* Trans. Margaret Waller. New York: Columbia University Press.

[1980] 1982. *Powers of Horror: An Essay on Abjection.* Trans. Leon S. Roudiez. New York: Columbia University Press.

[1984] 1987. *Tales of Love.* Trans. Leon S. Roudiez. New York: Columbia University Press.

[1987] 1989. *Black Sun: Depression and Melancholia.* Trans. Leon S. Roudiez. New York: Columbia University Press.

[1988] 1991. *Strangers to Ourselves.* Trans. Leon S. Roudiez. New York: Columbia University Press.

[1993] 1995. *New Maladies of the Soul.* Trans. Ross Guberman. New York: Columbia University Press.

[1996] 2000. *The Sense and Non-Sense of Revolt.* Trans. Jeanine Herman. New York: Columbia University Press.

[1997] 2002. *Intimate Revolt.* Trans. Jeanine Herman. New York: Columbia University Press.

[1999–2002] 2001–2004. *Female Genius: Life, Madness, Words—Hannah Arendt, Melanie Klein, Colette.* 3 vols. Trans. Ross Guberman and Jane Marie Todd. New York: Columbia University Press.

[2007] 2009. *This Incredible Need to Believe.* Trans. Beverley Bie Brahic. New York: Columbia University Press.

[2008] 2015. *Teresa, My Love: An Imagined Life of the Saint of Avila.* Trans. Lorna Scott Fox. New York: Columbia University Press.

Further reading

Beardsworth, Sara. 2004. *Julia Kristeva: Psychoanalysis and Modernity.* Albany: SUNY Press.

Becker-Leckrone, Megan. 2005. *Julia Kristeva and Literary Theory.* New York: Palgrave.

Bove, Carol Mastrangelo. 2006. *Language and Politics in Julia Kristeva: Literature, Art, Therapy.* Albany: SUNY Press.

Keltner, Stacey. 2011. *Kristeva: Thresholds.* Cambridge: Polity Press.

Lechte, John and Maria Margaroni. 2004. *Julia Kristeva: Live Theory.* London: Continuum.

McAfee, Noëlle. 2005. *Julia Kristeva.* New York: Routledge.

Miller, Elaine. 2014. *Head Cases: Julia Kristeva on Philosophy and Art in Depressed Times.* New York: Columbia University Press.

Oliver, Kelly. 1983. *Reading Kristeva: Unraveling the Double-Bind.* Bloomington: Indiana University Press.

—. 1993. *Ethics, Politics and Difference in Julia Kristeva's Writing.* New York: Routledge.

Schippers, Birgit. 2010. *Julia Kristeva and Feminist Thought.* Edinburgh: Edinburgh University Press.

Sjöholm, Cecilia. 2005. *Kristeva and the Political.* London: Routledge.

Websites

www.kristeva.fr/ (Kristeva's own website)
www.kristevacircle.org/ (The Kristeva Circle)
http://hvolat.netai.net/Kristeva/kristeva.htm (exhaustive bibliography)

DORIS LESSING (1919–2013)

Alice Ridout

Born in 1919 to parents who met as a nurse and soldier in the First World War, Doris Lessing has repeatedly identified her generation as the "Children of Violence," the title of her semi-autobiographical series of five novels about her fictional alter ego, Martha Quest. Born Doris May Tayler in Persia (now Iran) where her father was a clerk in the Imperial Bank of Persia and then brought up from 1925 in Southern Rhodesia (now Zimbabwe), Lessing was also a child of the British Empire, albeit a highly critical one. She would go on to decline an OBE (Officer of the British Empire) in 1977 and a DBE (Dame Commander of the British Empire) in 1992 before finally accepting an appointment as a Companion of Honour in 2000. By moving to London in 1949, Lessing was joining an influx of immigrants to the war-scarred city. Lessing left behind her first marriage to Frank Wisdom and their two children, and travelled to London with her son from her second marriage to Gottfried Lessing. Lessing's first novel, *The Grass is Singing*, was published in 1950 and her final novel, *Alfred and Emily*, appeared in 2008. Between these two publications, Lessing achieved a remarkably productive career as a writer mainly, but not exclusively, of fiction. Lessing received the Nobel Prize for Literature in 2007. This occasion, followed by her death on November 17, 2013, initiated a period of re-evaluation of Lessing's work as scholars embark upon the project of identifying the enduring aspects of Lessing's literary contributions.

Despite appearing as the final author in Elaine Showalter's influential study *A Literature of Their Own: From Charlotte Brontë to Doris Lessing* in 1977, Lessing's place in the feminist canon is not entirely free from dispute; as Susan Watkins puts it, "the association between Lessing's work and feminism has been a close but not always a happy one" (2010, 22). Central to Lessing's identification as a feminist writer is her most famous publication, *The Golden Notebook* (1962). In 1971, Lessing intervened in the reception of her novel by adding a Preface that stated "this novel was not a trumpet for Women's Liberation" (xiii). As Barbara Ellen comments in her 2001 interview with Lessing, "[t]he interesting thing about Doris Lessing is not that she's not a feminist, but how insistent she is that she's not a feminist." Feminist critics have tended to respond to Lessing's rejection of the feminist label as Gayle Greene does in *Doris Lessing:The Poetics of Change*: "she is not a feminist writer in any simple way, yet I persist in believing that she is deeply feminist" (1994, 28). In her personal essay "Timing is All: *The Golden Notebook* Then and Now," Florence Howe, herself a fellow involuntary architect of second wave feminism through her editorial work with the Feminist Press, asks directly whether the novel is a "feminist book" (2015, 203). In the closing paragraph of her essay, Howe finds herself undermining her own argument that "if one expects a feminist book to challenge male power, then *The Golden Notebook* is not a feminist book" (207) by quoting a clearly feminist passage from the novel itself. Howe's focus on historicity in thinking about this question of Lessing's feminism is crucial.

As I note in "Rereading *The Golden Notebook* After Chick Lit," "[a]n important similarity between *The Golden Notebook* and Helen Fielding's *Bridget Jones's Diary* is that both can be positioned outside the moment of feminism by being respectively too early and too late" (2015, 156). The question of whether Lessing belongs in this list of fifty-one key feminist thinkers could easily become the determining framework for this entry. Instead, I will identify three aspects of Lessing's work that have made enduring contributions to feminist thinking and writing.

The first is Lessing's explicit explorations of women's embodied experiences—"the first tampax in world literature" (DuPlessis 1986, 279–80) as Rachel Blau DuPlessis so famously pointed out with regards to Lessing's description of menstruation in *The Golden Notebook*. This is only one of a number of silences regarding the female body that Lessing breaks. In *A Proper Marriage* (1954), Lessing describes her pregnant protagonist, Martha Quest, abandoning herself to "the warm rocking of the water" in a "pothole" of "heavy mud" on the African veld (177). Martha notices that "in the jelly spawn were tiny dark dots of life," her attention to that unborn life heightened because "she felt the crouching infant, still moving tentatively" in her own stomach (178). Lying in her bath afterwards, Martha "traced the purple stretch marks with one finger, and felt something like satisfaction mingled with half-humorous appreciation of the ironies of her position" (180). *The Diaries of Jane Somers* (1985), published previously under the pseudonym of Jane Somers as *The Diary of a Good Neighbour* (1983) and *If the Old Could* (1984), has, as Watkins notes, "been celebrated for its provocative treatment of aging, gender and the body, a subject which has until recently received little serious treatment in fiction, despite growing concerns about an aging population at the close of the twentieth century" (2010, 96). Lessing's many explicit depictions of women's bodies have broken barriers of silence about women's embodied experiences in ways that have made enduring contributions to feminism.

Edith Frampton's study of the "revulsion that Mary [Turner] experiences in relation to the lactating bodies of African women" (2009, 19) in Lessing's *The Grass is Singing* offers another example of Lessing writing the female body. It also points to Lessing's second significant contribution to feminist thought and that is her insistence on intersectionality. Florence Howe admits that when she interviewed Lessing in the summer of 1966, "I too did not want to talk about feminism" (2015, 200) but rather she was "more interested in questions of racial freedom and the political rights of organized protest" (201). As Frampton's essay on *The Grass is Singing* makes clear, in Lessing's work race and gender always intersect. *The Golden Notebook* offers a perfect example of this when the protagonist, Anna, is attempting to negotiate her desire for George Hounslow—"this man, George, the trapped one, the man who had put that unfortunate woman, his wife, in a cage, also represented for me, and I knew it, a powerful sexuality from which I fled inwardly, but then inevitably turned towards" (2008, 122). Anna experiences "the most extraordinary tumult of emotion" when she learns that George's mistress is the Boothbys' black cook's wife, Marie: "First, I was jealous of the woman … And then, … I was surprised to find I resented the fact the woman was black … I had imagined myself free of any such emotion, but it seemed I was not, and I was ashamed and angry— … I suffered, like so many 'emancipated' girls, from a terror of being trapped and tamed by domesticity" (ibid.). The complex interplay here between race, gender, class, and desire in limiting individual freedom predicts the focus on intersectionality evident in contemporary identity politics. It is also pertinent to note that Lessing's description of the "ultimate horror" "of being trapped and tamed by domesticity" pre-dates Betty Friedan's *The Feminine Mystique* by a year.

In her 1971 Preface to *The Golden Notebook*, Lessing emphasized that her novel pre-dated second wave feminism: "This book was written as if the attitudes that have been created by the Women's Liberation movements already existed" (xiv). I would argue that, in fact, *The Golden Notebook* itself helped to create "the attitudes" of second wave feminism. Central to that contribution is Lessing's assumption from her very first novel, *The Grass is Singing*, to her very last, *Alfred and Emily*, that "the personal is political," to quote that second wave feminist mantra. As I argue in a more detailed reading of *The Grass is Singing* in "Doris Lessing: 'Political in the Most Basic Sense,'" Lessing's belief that "the personal is political" is central to her ethical and political view of the world. Repeatedly in her fiction we find individual characters inside private spaces and within personal relationships coming to a realization of their relatedness to broader politics and history. A recurrent trope in Lessing's fiction is that of protagonists trying to reconstruct in their imagination the details of the room they lie in while simultaneously holding the world as a whole in their minds. Anna in *The Golden Notebook* calls this "the game." It is a game that Lessing's whole *oeuvre* participates in and that feminist thinkers constantly challenge themselves to play.

Lessing's major works

[1950] 1994. *The Grass is Singing*. London: Flamingo-Harper.
[1952] 1966. *Martha Quest*. Children of Violence 1. London: Panther-Granada.

[1954] 1990. *A Proper Marriage*. Children of Violence 2. London: Paladin-Collins.

[1962] 2008. *The Golden Notebook*. New York: HarperPerennial Modern Classics.

[1969] 1972. *The Four-Gated City*. Children of Violence 5. London: Panther-Granada.

1985. *The Diaries of Jane Somers*. Harmondsworth: Penguin.

1987. *Prisons We Choose to Live Inside*. New York: Harper & Row.

1994. *A Small Personal Voice: Essays, Reviews, Interviews*. Ed. Paul Schlueter. London: Flamingo-Harper.

2008. *Alfred and Emily*. London: Fourth Estate.

Further reading

DuPlessis, Rachel Blau. 1986. "For the Etruscans." In *The New Feminist Criticism: Essays on Women, Literature and Theory*. Ed. Elaine Showalter. London: Virago: 271–91.

Ellen, Barbara. 2001. "'I Have Nothing in Common with Feminists. They Never Seem to Think that One Might Enjoy Men.'" *The Observer*, 9 Sept. www.theguardian.com/books/2001/sep/09/fiction.dorislessing

Fielding, Helen. 1996. *Bridget Jones's Diary*. London: Picador.

Frampton, Edith. 2009. "Horrors of the Breast: Cultural Boundaries and the Abject in *The Grass is Singing*." In *Doris Lessing: Border Crossings*. Eds. Alice Ridout and Susan Watkins. London: Continuum: 15–25.

Friedan, Betty. [1973] 2010. *The Feminist Mystique*. Harmondsworth: Penguin.

Greene, Gayle. 1994. *Doris Lessing: The Poetics of Change*. Ann Arbor: University of Michigan Press.

Howe, Florence. 2015. "Timing is All: *The Golden Notebook* Then and Now." In *Doris Lessing's* The Golden Notebook *After Fifty*. Eds. Alice Ridout, Roberta Rubenstein and Sandra Singer. New York: Palgrave-Macmillan: 195–208.

Ridout, Alice. 2014. "Doris Lessing: 'Political in the Most Basic Sense.'" In *Political Fiction: Critical Insights*. Ed. Mark Levene. Hackensack, NJ: Salem Press: 171–86.

—. 2015. "Rereading *The Golden Notebook* After Chick Lit." In *Doris Lessing's* The Golden Notebook *After Fifty*. Eds. Alice Ridout, Roberta Rubenstein and Sandra Singer. New York: Palgrave-Macmillan: 153–69.

Ridout, Alice, Roberta Rubenstein and Sandra Singer, eds. 2015. *Doris Lessing's* The Golden Notebook *After Fifty*. New York: Palgrave-Macmillan.

Ridout, Alice and Susan Watkins, eds. 2009. *Doris Lessing: Border Crossings*. London: Continuum.

Rubenstein, Roberta. 1979. *The Novelistic Vision of Doris Lessing: Breaking the Forms of Consciousness*. Urbana: University of Illinois Press.

—. 2014. *Literary Half-Lives: Doris Lessing, Clancy Sigal, and Roman á Clef*. New York: Palgrave.

Sage, Lorna. 1983. *Doris Lessing*. Contemporary Writers. London: Methuen.

Showalter, Elaine. [1977] 1982. *A Literature of Their Own: From Charlotte Brontë to Doris Lessing*. Rev. ed. London: Virago.

Watkins, Susan. 2010. *Doris Lessing: Contemporary World Writers*. Manchester: Manchester University Press.

AUDRE LORDE (1934–1992)

M. Jacqui Alexander

Can we meet Audre Lorde at the junction of the poetic, the primordial, and the sacred? In "Call" she says "my whole life has been an altar" (*Our Dead Behind Us*, 1986, 74). Life as an altar, not confined to a designated space, the imagined restrictions of time or fictive geography. A praying ground so awesome that only the most "ancient [of] goddesses … fire-tongued" Oya, Seboulisa, Mawu, Afrekete can bear the cosmic weight of the declaration from this Black woman stripped down: "I have offered up the safety of separations." Fierce, naked, stark, this declaration is Audre Lorde's, ensconced in her sung poem "Call," published first in 1986 (*Our Dead Behind Us*, 1986, 73), a mere six years before she "slipped anchor and wander[ed] to the end of the jetty" (*The Marvelous Arithmetics of Distance*, 1993, 59).

By this time, we were no strangers to Lorde's insistence on a vocabulary of difference that yearned for the "me-ness in you," but in "Call," after more than four decades of political aesthetic work at the junction of civil rights, queer and feminist liberation movements across the globe, Lorde feels compelled to renew her covenant by reissuing an urgent "call" for interdependence and intersubjectivity—this time within the medicine gourd of an ancient African metaphysic.

Who but Audre Lorde could summon "the strength and courage, to see, to feel, to speak and to dare" (*Sister Outsider*, 1984, 39)? In the face of capitalism's racialized, heterosexist penchant for othering, who but Audre Lorde could undertake that immense task of insinuating metaphor into the mundane by surrendering in the form of an offering? Only the echo of a poet, whom sister/friend/comrade Adrienne Rich described as "a voice of oceans, of city concrete of honey of fracture" (quoted in *The Marvelous Arithmetics of Distance*, 1993, back cover) could put the transformative power of fire to work on melding those elements of our being, our living, our transgressive loving so violently torn apart. She is the one for whom the architecture of "the master's house" could only be dismantled with a set of tools forged in the smithy of difference. Only the labor of the poet could seduce silence into speech and action enough to turn what appears to be an act of vulnerability—offering up the safety of separations—into a source of power, intimate and real.

To touch the animating pulse underlying Lorde's pervasive engagement with African cosmology is to unearth something fundamental about the sacred dimensions of our existence. Conjuring Mawu, the androgynous creation goddess of the Fon peoples, establishes and seals that sacred connection. Lorde consistently placed herself "In the hands of Afrekete," in autographs and in closing almost all of her correspondence, signaling a mnemonic of utter surrender and sacred trust, which in no way resembles the closing sentiment 'Sincerely,' or its more passive counterpart, 'Regards.' A reflection, which Lorde provides on the mechanics of revising a poem, is instructive here.

> In order to revise effectively … one must establish the world of the poem—that constellation within emotional time and space from which the poem draws power and life. A molten hot light shines up through the poem from the core of those experiences. This is the human truth that illuminates the poem … surrounding it in light that makes it come alive.
>
> (*Undersong*, 1992, ii, iii)

Her prophetic collapse of emotional time and space comes in the midst of the devastation wrought by Hurricane Hugo in St. Croix (1989), so much so that the revision (of a poem) is made to mirror the storm, both of which assume seismic proportions. That storm *is* Oya, who bears witness to Lorde's offering, one among those she says in "Call" are the "ancient goddesses … fire-tongued," the (Yorùbà) West African Òrìsà, who was masculinized and renamed 'Hugo.' Lorde's elegant invitation to touch that molten hot light, that catalyst for the cataclysmic, helps to nudge the necessary collapse of time and space, a primordial re-ordering, from where fundamental change derives. Thus the demands of revising a poem are simultaneously the demands of the constant re-visioning of a life. And it is this constancy, this permanent impermanence, which brings us squarely within Oya's cyclonic domain, the metaphysical domain of persistent, turbulent change. Is there a time when Wind is ever absent? Who can catch Her? Or match the lightning speed with which She re-orders or reassembles by turning things upside down?

This synchrony between re-visioning a poem and re-visioning a life marks one moment in Lorde's work where we find that aesthetic sacred junction of the poetic and the primordial. We need not fear the word primordial if we jettison its normative definition—the 'primitive,' or prehistoric—and pair it with the core elements of two of Lorde's path-breaking essays: "The Uses of the Erotic, the Erotic as Power," and "Poetry is not a Luxury" (both in *Sister Outsider*). In these poetics, the primordial becomes the deepest and most fundamental dimensions of our existence, the feminine ancient, that "dark place within, where hidden and growing our true spirit rises, 'beautiful/and tough as chestnut/stanchions against (y)our nightmare of weakness' and of impotence" (*Ibid.*, 1984, 36). When in the closing lines of the poem "Coal" Lorde states, "I am Black because I come from the Earth's insides," the statement is less about skin color and more about our elemental affinity to the energetics of the Earth's bowels where jewels abound (*The Collected Poems of Audre Lorde*, 1997, 163). We share Earth's pulsing life force. The rhythm at Her center is the same as the heart rhythm that keeps us alive. Inside Earth sound comes into words comes into poetry because mystery and mysticism live there, forming a poetic arc encompassing that which is dark, light, ancient, phantasmic, and everything in between and around. Earth's jewels mirror ours: "Good Mirrors are not Cheap" (*Ibid.*, 1997, 67). And each living thing carries its particular set of instructions. "The myrtle tree," Lorde notes "[is] unconcerned with not being a birch" (*The Black Unicorn*, 1978, 73). Both are *seemingly* contradictory existential truths.

If Lorde's work is about anything, it is most certainly about consciousness, that consistent cultivation and application of scrutiny and (self) reflexivity with which we compose our very existence. Alongside her self-description: "I am a Black, lesbian, warrior, poet, mother doing her work," came a provocation: "And I'm here to ask you: Are you doing yours?" Barbara Smith (co-founder with Lorde, Cherríe Moraga, Hattie Gossett, Helena Byard, Susan Yung, Ana Oliveira, Rosie

Alvarez, Alma Gomez, and Leota Lone Dog of Kitchen Table Women of Color Press) was fond of recounting how many a woman stopped in her tracks when Audre posed that question, expectant. This very idea, then, of knowing who you are, why you came, and living that commitment to purpose, is fundamental to consciousness—as fundamental to Audre's work as it is to the idea of *Ori* (the inner head/consciousness that aligns our destiny—within the Yorúbà metaphysical universe where Oya breathes life). In the closing lines of the poem "Sacrifice" (in *The Collected Poems of Audre Lorde*) Lorde underscores the sacred dimensions of an agreement we made *prior* to coming to Earth, which in turn fuels the urgent terms of our daily living.

For Lorde, this interweave between the poetic and the sacred is indispensable nourishment.

> lend[ing] strength and insight to *all* of my endeavors … The bread of art and the water of my spiritual life … remind me always to reach for what is highest within my capacities and in my demands of myself and others.
>
> (Byrd et al. 2009, 142)

As indispensable as bread and water are, however, they would be worthless without labor, self-reflexivity, revision, reconstruction, and attention to that molten light. We can't make bread out of stone. We need water to nurture, to feed, our spiritual and aesthetic selves, the full dimension of our being. All would be impossible without consciousness—the deepest dimensions of who we are, an alignment with that which is dark and ancient. If we are to honor that agreement and live that alignment, Lorde suggests that the 'I' who made that agreement to come and to do what she was meant to do in the first place *is* the primordial 'I,' not because she is essentialist, prehistoric or primitive, but because that 'I' wrote "[their] names on [her] cheekbones" (*Our Dead Behind Us*, 1986, 74); she has remembered, and therefore chosen, out of that remembering, to live that agreement so as to reach for all that is highest within. These are among the fundamental spiritual technologies we develop by living in community, without which "there is certainly no liberation, no future, only the most vulnerable and temporary armistice between me and my oppression" (*The Cancer Journals*, 1980, 12–13). It is the alignment with the highest parts of who we are that seals the agreement as sacred. It is chronicling/writing with bloody hands that makes for the poetic.

In that hyphen between February 18, 1934–17 November 17, 1992, Audre Lorde, who later took the name Gamba Adisa (she who makes her meaning known), was engaged in a long, complex and fierce conversation with freedom—a freedom project across inherited boundaries of "age, race, sex, class," living a lesbian, feminist, transnational feminism long before we gave name to it by catalyzing Afro descendant, women of color, feminist and queer movements in the United States of North America, the Caribbean, Amsterdam, Berlin, Hawai'i, New Zealand and South Africa; wrestling with the innards of that precious, necessary, fragile thing, with "a promise [she] made [her] pen never to leave it lying in someone else's blood" (*The Collected Poems of Audre Lorde*, 1997, 359). The evidence: fifteen books, crisscrossing genres, including the legendary *Zami: A New Spelling of My Name* (1982), where she bridges the void of biography and myth as a way of reinventing herself. Creating a praying ground, a capacious meeting ground of things 'sacred' and 'secular,' Gamba Adisa turned poetry into philosophy, joy into desire, the erotic into living theory, the political into the spiritual as she refused to confuse or conflate the sacred with the patriarchal and the oppressive, choosing instead to utilize it as a liberatory force. Without her genius, the queer scapes of twentieth century feminism would have been sadly scarred. Now among *Our Dead Behind Us*, she has completed her piece of the bargain, daring to speak posthumously beyond the artificial limits of an absent body in *The Marvelous Arithmetics of Distance*.

Lorde's major writings

1968. *The First Cities*. New York: Poets Press.

[1970] 1973a. *Cables to Rage*. London: Paul Bremen Press.

1973b. *From a Land Where Other People Live*. Detroit: Broad Street Press.

[1974] 1975. *New York Head Shop and Museum*. Detroit: Broad Side Press.

1976a. *Coal*. New York: W. W. Norton.

1976b. *Between Our Selves*. Point Reyes, CA: Eidolon Editions.

1978. *The Black Unicorn*. New York: W. W. Norton.

1980. *The Cancer Journals*. San Francisco: Aunt Lute Books.

[1982] 1992. *Undersong: Chosen Poems: Old and New*. New York: W. W. Norton.

1982. *Zami—A New Spelling of My Name*. New York: Crossing Press.

[1984] 2007. *Sister Outsider: Essays and Speeches*. New York: Crossing Press.

[1986] 1994. *Our Dead Behind Us: Poems*. New York: W. W. Norton.

[1988] 1996. *A Burst of Light*. Ann Arbor, MI: Firebrand Books.

1993. *The Marvelous Arithmetics of Distance: Poems 1987–1992.* New York: W. W. Norton.

[1997] 2000. *The Collected Poems of Audre Lorde.* New York: W. W. Norton.

Further reading and documentaries

Abod, Jennifer (dir.). 2002. *The Edge of Each Other's Battles: The Vision of Audre Lorde.* Profile Productions.

Bolaki, Stella and Sabine Broeck (eds.). 2015. *Audre Lorde's Transnational Legacies.* Amherst and Boston: University of Massachusetts Press.

Bowen, Angela. 1997. "Who Said It Was Simple: Audre Lorde's Complex Connection to 3 U.S. Liberation Movements, 1952–1992." Ph.D. dissertation. Worcester, MA: Clark University.

Byrd, Rudolph P., Johnnetta Betsch Cole, and Beverly Guy-Sheftall (eds.) 2009. *I AM YOUR SISTER: Collected and Unpublished Writings by Audre Lorde.* New York: Oxford University Press.

Griffin, Ada Gay and Michelle Parkerson (dirs.). 1995. *A Litany for Survival: The Life and Work of Audre Lorde.*

Joseph, Gloria I. (ed.). Forthcoming 2016. *The Wind is Spirit: The Life, Love and Legacy of Audre Lorde: A Bio/Anthology.* New York: Villarosa Media.

Opitz, May, Katharina Oguntoye, and Dagmar Schultz. (eds.). 1992. *Showing Our Colors: Afro-German Women Speak Out.* Amherst: University of Massachusetts Press.

Schultz, Dagmar (dir.). 2012. *Audre Lorde: The Berlin Years 1984–1992.*

Simmons, Aishah Shahidah. 2014. Commemorative On-Line Forum on Audre Lorde. www.thefeministwire.com/2014/11/black-lesbian-feminist-mother-warrior-poet-audre-lorde/

ROSA LUXEMBURG (1871–1919)

Jodi Dean

Rosa Luxemburg was a communist revolutionary during the heyday of proletarian struggle in Europe. An organizer, speaker, propagandist, and theorist for the Polish Socialist Party, the Social Democratic Party of the Kingdom of Poland and Lithuania, the German Social Democratic Party, and the German Communist Party, Luxemburg was murdered together with Karl Liebknecht by *Freikorps* soldiers in January 1919.

She and Liebknecht were blamed for instigating the failed Spartacist uprising, a moment in the German 1918–1919 revolution. Newspaper headlines announced that Liebknecht "was shot while trying to escape" and that Luxemburg was "beaten to death by the multitude." Both were actually struck by rifle-butts and then shot. Luxemburg's body was thrown from the Liechtenstein Bridge into a canal. It washed up five months later.

Excoriated as "Red Rosa" while alive, Luxemburg became enormously popular after her death. Beginning with the funeral march of tens of thousands of Berlin workers to bury Liebknecht and an empty coffin for Luxemburg, annual commemorations continued until the end of the German Democratic Republic (Weitz 1994). These were known as the Lenin-Liebknecht-Luxemburg (LLL) festivals. Led by Communist Party officials, the marches regularly attracted over 200,000 people. In the late 1950s, the Soviet Union featured Luxemburg on a stamp.

Even as evocations of Luxemburg figured in practices of political legitimation in the USSR and GDR, they also appeared in the language of political dissidents. Communist state power and those resisting it both positioned themselves as followers of Rosa Luxemburg. In the 1980s, the West German anti-nuclear movement and East German dissidents cited Luxemburg as a political-theoretical resource. The latter took their slogan from Luxemburg: "freedom is always the freedom of the dissenters." In 1986, Luxemburg was the subject of an important film directed by Margarethe von Trotta, *Die Geduld der Rosa Luxemburg*. Barbara Sukowa, who plays Luxemburg, would later go on to star in the title role of von Trotta's film, *Hannah Arendt* (2013).

After the collapse of state socialism, Luxemburg, unique among communist leaders, remained a respected figure. Leftists claimed her for radical democracy. In 2006, a publicly funded memorial designed by artist Hans Haacke was unveiled on the Rosa-Luxemburg-Platz in Berlin, following a decade of debate and a competition for the commission. In 2015, Luxemburg won the internet competition, "Marx Madness." Modeled after the US collegiate basketball tournament, "Marx Madness" positioned sixty-four influential Marxist political and intellectual leaders in thirty-two brackets. Voters chose favorites in each round. Luxemburg defeated such luminaries as Engels, Lenin, Mao, and Che Guevera, as well as post-Marxists like Stuart Hall.

As the divergent politics of Luxemburg's admirers attest, her legacy is disputed. Competing factions claim her for their side. Interpretations of Luxemburg's work do not simply disagree with each other. They contradict each other on the most basic points of Luxemburg's personality, views, and position.

These contradictions arise in part from the popularity of Luxemburg's letters. Luxemburg's feminist biographers generally prefer her letters to her polemical writing, which is deeply embedded in the revolutionary milieu of the Second International. In contrast to her excoriation of German Social Democrat Edward Bernstein for the opportunism of his advocacy of reform over revolution, to her nuanced critique of Lenin for his centralist model of the revolutionary party (itself a response to opportunism), and to her detailed mathematical explanation of the way that intrinsic limits to capital accumulation compel the capitalist system to draw its resources from outside the system itself, to mention but a few of Luxemburg's political-theoretical concerns, her letters are personal, even sentimental. For example, in her April 19, 1917 letter to Sophie Liebknecht, Luxemburg writes, "We have to take everything as it comes, and to find beauty in everything. That's what I manage to do" (Luxemburg 1923). Luxemburg's letters to Liebknecht are filled with nature writing, observations of weather and seasons, detailed descriptions of birds. Interpreters looking to separate Luxemburg from her revolutionary communism find in these letters evidence of the true, feminine, and emotional Luxemburg. They suggest that she was a woman who desired romance and babies, directing us away from the fact of her life as a militant communist who wanted to die in prison or in battle, doing the work of the revolution.

Those who engage her theoretical and polemical work also take it in divergent directions. This divergence involves the most fundamental elements of her legacy, such as her commitment to Marxism. Bolshevik leaders Lenin and Trotsky commend Luxemburg's Marxism. Lenin refers to Luxemburg as an "outstanding representative of the revolutionary proletariat and of unfalsified Marxism" (Lenin 1965). Trotsky observes that Luxemburg "had such perfect command of the Marxist method that it almost seemed a physical part of her. One could truly say that Marxism has entered into her very blood" (Trotsky 1977, 18). In contrast, Hannah Arendt questions Luxemburg's Marxism: "she was not an orthodox Marxist, so little orthodox indeed that it might be doubted that she was a Marxist at all" (Arendt 1968, 38).

The divergent treatments of Luxemburg's Marxism continue in efforts to separate Luxemburg from Lenin. But where Arendt is virtually alone in doubting Luxemburg's Marxism, many commentators contrast Luxemburg and Lenin. These commentators accentuate her disagreement with Lenin on matters of party organization, national self-determination, and the theorization of imperialism. At times, they move beyond the critical disputes characteristic of the revolutionary circles of the Second International to present Luxemburg as a kind of anti-Lenin. He is narrow and authoritarian. She is broad and demo-cratic. He is the theorist of the centralized party. She is the defender of spontaneity and the mass strike. He is rigid and uncompromising. She is a real, human, emotional person. He is calculating. She is "tempes-tuous and enigmatic," capable of scaling "the heights of revolutionary ecstasy only to plunge the next moment into revolutionary despair" (Rousseas 1979). Luxemburg as anti-Lenin opens a path to a humanist Marxism not taken by the Bolsheviks, perhaps because of the personal-ity of their leader.

The soft humanist view of Luxemburg is not without its critics. Trotsky describes Luxemburg as "an unyielding revolutionary woman." He writes: "By the force of her logic and the power of her sarcasm she silenced her most inveterate enemies. Rosa knew how to hate the enemies of the proletariat and for that very reason she could arouse their hatred of her" (Trotsky 1977, 18–19). Others similarly note her intransigence, combativeness, and unwillingness to compromise.

Further disagreement with regard to Luxemburg's legacy involves her position in German Social Democracy. Again, Arendt de-radicalizes Luxemburg. Using a term with which she herself would be identified, Arendt characterizes Luxemburg as a pariah, as an outsider because she was Polish, Jewish, and a woman. Later feminists repeat this characteri-zation. The problem with this view is that Luxemburg was a prominent speaker and publicist at the heart of the German Socialist Party. She wrote for the major party papers and taught in the party school.

The (mistaken) view of Luxemburg as a pariah because of her nationality, religion, and gender is carried further in feminist treat-ments of Luxemburg, which highlight Luxemburg's difference. Such treatments read Luxemburg as a site of intersecting identities. Luxem-burg's pronounced limp (mentioned in every description of her) sug-gests her availability as a resource for disability studies. There are also elements in her letters that hint as further openings for queer and trans theory. In her April 19, 1917 letter, Luxemburg tells Sophie Liebknecht that she loves her "as a housewife." Luxemburg also referred to herself and Clara Zetkin as the last two great men of German Socialism.

Intersectional and identitarian treatments of Luxemburg stand in stark contrast to her commitment to proletarian internationalism, her resolute rejection of nationalism in any form. Although Polish, she opposed Polish independence, disagreeing with Lenin on the question of national self-determination. Further, Luxemburg famously said that she had no special place in her heart for the Jewish ghetto. She was just as concerned with "the Blacks in Africa with whose corpses the Europeans play catch" (Luxemburg 2011, 375). And, with respect to the matter of women's suffrage, Luxemburg placed it in the context of class struggle, highlighting the importance of the vote for proletarian women rather than women as such.

A final conflict in interpretations of Luxemburg's legacy centers on democracy. A slew of commentators treat Luxemburg as a defender of rights, freedom, and democracy. Others point out that she never argued for extending rights to the bourgeoisie. Luxemburg explained, "Social-ism does not mean sitting together in a parliament and passing laws. Socialism signifies the suppression of the ruling class with all of the brutality that the proletariat can bring to bear in its struggle" (Weitz 1994). So again there is a tension between the reading of Luxemburg as on the side of proletarian dictatorship (understood in terms of coun-cil communism with suffrage restricted to workers and soldiers) over and against a reading of Luxemburg as a defender of civil liberties and participatory democracy.

To sum up, Rosa Luxemburg's legacy is contested: revolutionary or private self, leader or pariah, proletarian internationalist or site of inter-secting identities, communist or democrat. Yet while other revolution-ary communists have been largely disavowed by leftists and democrats, Luxemburg continues to be celebrated. She remains a martyr for the left, a symbol of aspirations for equality and justice. Even for those who eschew revolution, Luxemburg signifies zeal, commitment, the willing-ness to die for the struggle. That she was murdered by proto-fascists allows her to function as a screen onto which the left can project fanta-sies of what might have been. In this respect, Luxemburg is a symptom of the failure of left politics since 1968 when the left began to cham-pion society, private life, and spontaneity and rejected militancy, the state, and the party. The reduction of Rosa Luxemburg to her identity as a Polish, Jewish, woman tries to make her exceptional, a unique indi-vidual rather than the personification of proletarian revolution. These reductions enable her to function like a remainder of revolutionary communism that would-be radicals can carry with them even as they embrace the capitalist system Luxemburg gave her life to overthrowing.

Luxemburg's major writings

The Marxist Internet Archive (MIA) has an extensive archive of Lux-emburg's letters and essays available for free online access.

1900. "Reform or Revolution." MIA.

1904. "Organizational Questions of the Russian Social Democracy." MIA.

1906. "The Mass Strike." MIA.
1909. "The National Question." MIA.
1910. "Theory and Practice." MIA.
1912. "Women's Suffrage and Class Struggle." MIA.
1913. *The Accumulation of Capital*. MIA.
1915. *The Junius Pamphlet*. MIA.
[1916–18] 1923. *Letters from Prison to Sophie Liebknecht*. MIA.
1918. "The Russian Revolution." MIA.
2011. *The Letters of Rosa Luxemburg*, eds. Georg Adler, Peter Hudis, and Annelies Laschitza. London:Verso.

Further reading

Arendt, Hannah. 1968. *Men in Dark Times*. New York: Harcourt, Brace and World.

Bronner, Stephen Eric. [1981] 1997. *Rosa Luxemburg: A Revolutionary for Our Times*. University Park: Pennsylvania State University Press.

Dunayevskaya, Raya. [1981] 1991. *Rosa Luxemburg, Women's Liberation, and Marx's Philosophy of Revolution*. Urbana: University of Illinois Press.

Ettinger, Elżbieta. 1986. *Rosa Luxemburg: A Life*. Boston: Beacon Press.

Frölich, Paul. [1939] 1972. *Rosa Luxemburg*. London: Pluto Press.

Geras, Norman. 1976. *The Legacy of Rosa Luxemburg*. London: New Left Books.

Lenin, V. I. [1920] 1965. "A Contribution to the History of the Question of the Dictatorship." In *Collected Works*. Moscow: Progress: 340–61.

Nettl, J. P. 1966. *Rosa Luxemburg*. London: Oxford University Press.

Nye, Andrea. 1994. *Philosophia: The Thought of Rosa Luxemburg, Simone Weil, and Hannah Arendt*. New York: Routledge.

Rose, Jacqueline. 2014. *Women in Dark Times*. London: Bloomsbury.

Rousseas, Stephen. 1979. "Rosa Luxemburg and the Origins of Capitalist Catastrophe Theory." *Journal of Post Keynesian Economics* 1(4): 3–23.

Trotsky, Leon. 1977. *Portraits: Political and Personal*. New York: Pathfinder Press.

Weitz, Eric D. 1994. "'Rosa Luxemburg Belongs to Us!' German Communism and the Luxemburg Legacy." *Central European History* 27(1): 27–64.

CATHARINE A. MACKINNON (1946–)

Judith Grant

Catharine MacKinnon became a controversial figure within feminism largely due to her role in the "sexuality debates" of the 1980s. Born in Minneapolis, Minnesota in 1946, MacKinnon received her B.A. from Smith College, and went on to earn a J.D. and Ph.D. in Political Science from Yale University. Currently, she is the Elizabeth A. Long professor of Law at the University of Michigan Law School, and the James Barr Visiting Professor of Law at Harvard University.

MacKinnon's work has made important contributions to feminist understandings of the role of sexuality in the maintenance of gender inequality. Her creative approaches to sexual harassment, pornography and the law have been taken up in important debates within feminist theory on questions of sexuality, gender and the meaning of "woman" under conditions of patriarchy on a global scale. Though MacKinnon is sometimes read as an essentialist, her work is more productively read as feminist structuralism in that it posits gender as a universal structure of power wherein the male and masculine are systematically hierarchicalized over the female and feminine. For her, male and female are subject positions that are not reducible to embodiment. MacKinnon's three most significant contributions to feminist theory are: her use of Marxism, the concept of sexual harassment, and her analysis of pornography.

MacKinnon is interested in Marxism only insofar as she is interested in the problems of ideology, consciousness and political action. Her work on the utility of the Marxian method (published in a two-part article in *Signs*—MacKinnon 1982 and 1983) should be read as a discussion of just one point in Marx—consciousness. Borrowing from Marx's articulation of consciousness, MacKinnon generates a theory about the gendered nature of consciousness formation under the structural conditions of patriarchy. She begins by arguing that sexuality holds a position in feminism similar to the one held by labor in Marxism in that both are transformative subject-forming activities. Just as workers with false-consciousness misunderstand their roles in the labor process, Woman misunderstands her own sexual agency when she conceptualizes her desire as synonymous with the sexual affect she is mandated to have in order to maintain her status as sexual object under conditions of patriarchy. That is, women (and here Woman becomes all women) can no longer tell their own sexual desires apart from the feeling of being desired by an Other. At present, "Woman" is defined as "being who identifies and is identified as one whose sexuality exists for someone else, who is socially male" (1989, p. 118). Thus, being dominated by men does not appear as a political problem to women, but is experienced as the reality of one's own feelings and desires.

MacKinnon argues that women's collusion in the system of male domination is the central epistemological and political problem for feminism. MacKinnon turns to what she calls the true feminist method: "consciousness raising." Consciousness raising, MacKinnon argues, is "the collective reconstitution of the meaning of women's social experience as women live through it" (1989, p. 83). It seeks to create a new social meaning of "woman" that is forged from her own point of view. Pornography emerges as that artifact that most clearly expresses the sexualized hierarchy that is truth from the male point of view. MacKinnon calls for the development of a feminist jurisprudence that begins from the standpoint of a raised consciousness wherein women have begun to construct themselves as concrete subjects. Women's own political and material interests lie in a social transformation of the meaning of "woman." Feminism, she argues, has its own voice, and is not just liberalism applied to women. The central issue of feminism is not the "gender difference, but the difference gender makes" (1987, p. 23).

Another central component of MacKinnon's feminism is her analysis of sexual harassment as sex discrimination developed in her book *Sexual Harassment of Working Women*, and later, in some of the essays in *Feminism Unmodified: Discourses on Life and Law*. MacKinnon differentiates her view from two prevailing doctrines concerning sex discrimination: the "difference" approach, and the "inequality" (or, "sameness" approach). The difference approach, which requires that women show they are treated differently than men, means that sex discrimination cannot be proven unless the sexes can be compared. The inequality approach recognizes social inequality and seeks to give women equal rights to men. MacKinnon points out that in reality both are "difference approaches" since they both use men as the standard against which women are judged to be different. Neither recognizes gender itself as a hierarchy. In place of these, MacKinnon advocates what she terms the "dominance approach." The dominance approach begins from the axiom that men always have power over women and that gender is in and of itself a hierarchy. She writes, "If you follow my shift in perspective from gender as difference to gender as dominance, gender changes from a distinction that is presumptively valid to a detriment that is presumptively suspect" (quoted in Strebeigh 1991, p. 44).

For MacKinnon, women are socially defined as existing sexually for men, thus both sexual harassment and pornography are ultimately about making women sexually accessible as a fundamental condition of their existence as women. MacKinnon argues that the issue is not whether one is treated fairly or neutrally with regard to one's sex, but whether a certain policy or practice acknowledges that gender is dominance rather than neutral or nature, and whether it contributes to the maintenance of the gender hierarchy as such or attempts to dismantle it. The harassment of one woman is not just about the harassed woman alone; harassment is an ideological practice that supports the domination of all women by supporting a naturalized gender hierarchy.

MacKinnon's theories about words and actions re-emerge in her work on pornography in the book, *Only Words*. Here, MacKinnon takes aim at arguments that distinguish between speech and action regarding pornography. Pornography should not be protected as free speech, because it is not speech. Rather, "To say it is to do it, and to do it is to say it" (1993, p. 33). To the extent that men are aroused and achieve orgasm by watching it in pornography, they are engaging in a sex act that goes beyond mere words, pictures or communication. Pornography communicates a way of thinking about women that affects all women by perpetuating the male ideology that women want to be dominated, and that domination is erotic. This teaches men, who still continue to be the vast majority of customers, the experience of purchased sex. The similarities between her argument here and the "dominance approach" elaborated upon above in the section on sexual harassment should be noted. MacKinnon's viewpoint that gender is a power structure characterized by a hierarchicalized male-over-female dominance (and not merely difference), means that women cannot really consent to pornography, because they cannot really be certain that their desires are their own. In fact, the more closely their desires relate to sex (which she believes is the lynchpin of the gender hierarchy), the less likely their desires are to be "authentic," and the more likely they are to be products of male domination on the level of consciousness itself.

Subsequent to the publication of *Only Words* MacKinnon has continued to point to the relationship between representation and reality with regard to the sexual abuse of women internationally, particularly with regard to war. In *Mass Rape: The War Against Women in Bosnia-Herzegovina* (Stiglmayer 1993), MacKinnon analyzed reports that Serbian soldiers raped Croatian and Bosnian women during the Bosnian conflict, videotaped the rapes, and then used the videotapes as pornography. MacKinnon argues that those rapes under conditions of war in concentration camps are merely a more specialized version of what happens to women on a daily basis. An important difference is that the

Serbians engaged in "ethnic rape." However, rape has long been associated with soldiers, and it has been a common practice for nation states to set up camps of prostitutes near battlegrounds for male soldiers. MacKinnon's analysis of the rapes in Bosnia and Rwanda parallels those she makes concerning sexual harassment and pornography. MacKinnon made the case that to prove discrimination, women had to show that what was done to them was not done to men in similar situations, but was uniquely done to women. This meant that men were the standard of "human" to which women were compared as specific objects of discriminatory actions. MacKinnon suggests a dominance model in which one would have to engage in no such comparison, as gender would be acknowledged as a hierarchy. Sexual crimes against women should be seen as always taking place in a coercive context. This is the main principle of the current gender arrangement.

In an essay against postmodernism, MacKinnon argues as she did in her two-part *Signs* article: that ideas are connected to the body through sexuality, which is the lived practice of a gender arrangement that is by definition an experience of hierarchy. While postmodernism and multiculturalism assume the speaker takes their own values and critiques everything from that point of view as if it were reality, feminism, "questions the cultural validity of subordinating women to men anywhere. Feminism does not assume that 'other' cultures are to be measured against the validity of their own, because feminism does not assume that anyone's culture, including their own is valid" (2000, p. 699). And even more significantly, "Male power virtually always appears in local guises; one might hazard that there are *nothing but* local guises for male power" (2000, p. 699). This is a particularly excellent statement of MacKinnon's feminist structuralism, arguing that universality is highly contingent on the particular. MacKinnon's structuralism roots universalism in the local, material practices of gender.

MacKinnon is well known for her work on pornography with Andrea Dworkin. The Dworkin/MacKinnon approach attempted to regulate pornography as a manifestation of violence against women rather than as obscenity, departing from the prevailing obscenity jurisprudence developed by the United States Supreme Court in *Miller v. U.S.* The so-called *Miller* test offered a regulatory scheme wherein communities could regulate pornography according to their own moral standards. Of this "contemporary community standards" test, Dworkin and MacKinnon wrote, they

> have meant almost nothing, being (actually) dependent upon the viewpoint of the observer. This makes obscenity law less useful the

more pornography is a problem, because the more pornography is consumed, the more observer's views are shaped by it, and the more the world it makes confirms that view.

(1988, p. 27)

Thus, they argued, contemporary community standards cannot serve as benchmarks for obscenity, since a community that is very tolerant of pornography is only indicative of how great the harm to women is in that community due to its high tolerance for pornography. For Dworkin and MacKinnon, viewing pornography as a harm to women rather than obscenity shifts the decision in two ways. It ignores the moralistic arguments often rooted in religious beliefs, and it changes who gets to define what constitutes pornography. In the Dworkin/Mackinnon scheme, pornography is defined by the women who feel harmed by it, not by the men who are the consumers of it. A series of ordinances written by MacKinnon and Dworkin were first introduced in Minneapolis in 1983 and purported to define pornography according to what it is in practice (1988, p. 37). The ordinances define pornography as the graphic sexually explicit subordination of women through pictures and/or words. They also included a wide array of other characteristics that Dworkin and MacKinnon argued was the true definition of pornography; something designed for sexual excitement that showed women as sexual and subordinate at the same time (1988, p. 38).

MacKinnon's major writings

1979. *Sexual Harassment of Working Women: A Case of Sex Discrimination* (New Haven, CT and London: Yale University Press).

1982. "Feminism, Marxism, Method and the State: An Agenda for Theory." *Signs: Journal of Women in Culture and Society* 7(3): 515–44.

1983. "Feminism, Marxism, Method and the State: Toward a Feminist Jurisprudence." *Signs: Journal of Women in Culture and Society* 8(4): 635–58.

1987. *Feminism Unmodified: Discourses on Life and Law* (Cambridge, MA: Harvard University Press).

1989. *Toward a Feminist Theory of the State* (Cambridge, MA: Harvard University Press).

1993. *Only Words* (Cambridge, MA: Harvard University Press).

2000. "Points Against Postmodernism." *Chicago-Kent Law Review* 75(3): 689–700.

2004. "Of Mice and Men: A Feminist Fragment on Animal Rights." In Cass R. Sunstein and Martha C. Nussbaum (eds.), *Animal Rights: Current Debates and New Directions* (New York: Oxford University Press): 263–76.

2006. *Are Women Human? And Other International Dialogues* (Cambridge, MA: Belknap of Harvard University Press).

1997. MacKinnon, Catharine A., and Andrea Dworkin. *In Harm's Way: The Pornography Civil Rights Hearings* (Cambridge, MA: Harvard University Press).

Further reading

Brown, Wendy. 1995. *States of Injury: Power and Freedom in Late Modernity* (Princeton, NJ: Princeton University Press).

Cornell, Drucill. 1999. *Beyond Accommodation* (Lanham, MD: Rowman and Littlefield).

Dworkin, Andrea and Catharine MacKinnon. 1988. *Pornography and Civil Rights: A New Day for Women's Equality* (Minneapolis, MN: Organizing Against Pornography).

Nussbaum, Martha C. 1999. *Sex and Social Justice* (Oxford and New York: Oxford University Press).

Rorty, Richard. 1991. "Feminism and Pragmatism." *Michigan Quarterly Review* 30(2): 231–58.

Rubin, Gayle S. 2011. "Thinking Sex." In *Deviations: A Gayle Rubin Reader* (Durham, NC: Duke University Press): 137–81.

Stiglmayer, Alexandra, ed. 1993. *Mass Rape: The War Against Women in Bosnia-Herzegovina*. Translated by Marion Faber, foreword by Roy Gutman (Lincoln, NE and London: University of Nebraska Press).

Strebeigh, Fred. 1991. "Defining Law on the Feminist Frontier." *The New York Times*, October 6.

MARGARET MEAD (1901–1978)

Nancy Lutkehaus

We may say that many, if not all, of the personality traits which we have called masculine or feminine are as lightly linked to sex as are the clothing, the manners, and the form of headdress that a society at a given period assigns to either sex.

Mead, *Sex and Temperament in Three Primitive Societies*

The American anthropologist, Margaret Mead, made this statement in her provocative book *Sex and Temperament in Three Primitive Societies* (1935) based on her ethnographic research among three New Guinea tribes that Mead and her second husband, New Zealand anthropologist Reo Fortune, studied between 1931 and 1933. Mead's words proved prescient as they introduced what has become a foundational idea in feminist thought: that there is a distinction between an individual's sex (the biological sexual attributes a person is born with) versus his or her gender (an individual's sexual identity as either "male" or "female"). As scientists now acknowledge, it is not biologically "abnormal" that one's sex might be different from one's gender identity—there is a continuum in the fit, or lack thereof, between one's physical sex and one's gender identity and their conformity with a given society's gender norms (Rosenberg 2004). Mead based her findings on the contrasts she observed among the Mundugumor, Tchambuli, and Arapesh peoples of the Sepik region of New Guinea. Each culture, Mead argued, exhibited different combinations of culturally normative gender roles for men and women (Mead did not use the term "gender" or "gender roles"; this terminology came later). Each was as different from the other as they all were from the types of masculine and feminine behavior assumed to be "natural" in the west. In Mundugumor society both men and women were aggressive and exhibited other traits that in the west would be considered masculine. In particular, both sexes eschewed maternal behavior and disliked children. In nearby Arapesh society, the opposite was true. Here both women and men were overtly maternal in their gendered behavior, with men taking as great an interest in childcare and nurturance as the Arapesh women. Finally, the Tchambuli were in stark contrast to both of the other two societies, as well as our own, in that Tchambuli women took a dominant role in economic activities. They were fisher folk who both caught and marketed their fish at distant markets, while the men stayed at home with the children and focused their attention on producing dramatic sculptures and elaborate rituals, replete with dancing, music, feathered headdresses, and dogs' teeth finery.

When published in 1935 Mead's findings provoked comment and controversy among scientists, scholars, intellectuals, and the media. At that time most westerners still believed that one's biological sex and one's gender identity were uniform and innate, the result of natural endowment and not amenable to change. In reviewing *Sex and Temperament in Three Primitive Societies*, the British feminist and author Rebecca West associated it with the work of anthropologist Ruth Benedict, Mead's professor and mentor at Columbia University: "It is even more startling than anything in *Patterns of Culture* [Benedict's ground-breaking 1934 book that argued that human nature was more malleable than we commonly think] because it concerns the differentiation in the characters of men and women which we are most apt to take as inherent in human structure" (West 1936). Indeed, despite many other topics that Mead wrote about, such as culture change, childhood and socialization, the family, education, and psychology, her name was associated most frequently with the topic of sexuality. Some detractors and fans alike even went so far as to attribute America's "sexual revolution" of the 1960s to her.

Despite being labeled a feminist (a label she initially rejected) and "radical-thinker" by the media, Margaret Mead's background was solidly middle-class and conventional. She was born in Philadelphia in 1901, the eldest of five children. Her father was a professor of business at the University of Pennsylvania's Wharton School. Her mother, educated at Wellesley College, was a graduate student in sociology when she met Margaret's father at the University of Chicago. Additionally, her paternal grandmother, who lived with the family, had been a schoolteacher who homeschooled Mead for a number of years. As a child Mead recalled being taken to suffragette rallies with her mother, an ardent feminist. Mead also accompanied her mother on her dissertation research, a study of Italian immigrants in New Jersey. Initially her father did not support Mead's desire to attend college until she agreed to go to his alma mater, DePauw University (Indiana). Extremely unhappy at a school that emphasized fraternity life over the life of the mind, Mead transferred to Barnard College in New York City. Initially an English major who aspired to be a poet or novelist, at Barnard she met Ruth Benedict and Franz Boas, the founder of the Department of Anthropology at Columbia University. They convinced Mead to pursue a Ph.D. in anthropology, impressing upon her the urgency of conducting ethnographic research on the "disappearing" cultures of so-called "primitive people." After completing her first fieldwork, in American Samoa, Mead retuned to New York to work as a curator at the American Museum of Natural History. She maintained an office there until her death in November 1978.

All three of Mead's husbands were anthropologists (Luther Cressman, Reo Fortune, and Gregory Bateson) (Mead 1972), as were the two women she was romantically involved with (Ruth Benedict, when Mead was in her twenties, and Rhoda Metraux, with whom Mead lived for the last twenty years of her life) (Bateson 1984). Although Mead kept her private life just that—private—she did write a seemingly autobiographical statement about her own bisexuality in one of her monthly columns for the popular women's magazine, *Redbook*. In an article titled "Bisexuality: What's It All About?" she noted that it was not unusual for a woman to be attracted to other women in her teens and twenties, to then marry a man and have children during her childbearing years, and to resume her intimacy with women after she had reached menopause (Mead 1975). Once again she stressed the idea of the malleability of an individual's sexuality, depending upon one's social context and life course.

The results of Mead's first fieldwork, an ethnographic study of adolescent girls in American Samoa, were published in 1928 as *Coming of Age in Samoa*. Subtitled "A Psychological Study of Primitive Youth for Western Civilization," the book became a best-seller. Mead's descriptions of Samoan girls' stress-free adolescence, including pre-marital sex with both men and women, fueled the imaginations of 1920s American youth. While exuberantly enjoying the jazz age, prohibition-era bootleg liquor, and women's achievement of the vote, they were intent on challenging what they felt to be outmoded sexual mores and gender roles, especially for women. Mead had the uncanny ability to articulate and *shape* changing norms and values in her own society, often by alluding to alternative ways of life that she had observed in the non-western societies she studied in Samoa, New Guinea and Bali. She developed this ability, and mode of communication—the use of insights from other cultures as a means of illuminating the malleability of human behavior and the impact of culture on an individual's actions and beliefs—to suggest that western society, especially American society, could also change behaviors that most people had believed to be innate. She used her Samoan research to challenge the then dominant notion that the stresses that accompanied adolescence in American society were innate and thus the result of psychological and biological changes experienced during adolescence. Instead, she argued, they were due to conflict between the generations, especially in times of social change, such as post-World War I America.

Mead's work was not without critics—both liberal and conservative. Perhaps most surprising was feminist Betty Friedan who criticized Mead in *The Feminine Mystique* (1963). It is important to note however that Friedan spoke highly of Mead's early work and her findings about sex and gender in *Coming of Age in Samoa* and *Sex and Temperament in Three Primitive Societies*. It was Mead's later book, *Male and Female: A Study of the Sexes in a Changing World* (1949), that Friedan found problematic. She thought that Mead had abandoned her earlier stance regarding the malleability of gender roles and that she had reverted to advocating that American women accept "traditional" feminine gender roles of domesticity and maternalism rather than following Mead's own example as a career woman and working mother (Lutkehaus 2008: 70–72).

Fifty-five years after *Coming of Age in Samoa* had been published, and after Mead had died, Australian anthropologist Derek Freeman published a critique of Mead's Samoan findings (Freeman 1983). Freeman had done ethnographic research in another part of Samoa decades after Mead's work. He argued that her findings about Samoan adolescent girls were wrong. Although Mead was not able to defend her work, American anthropologists did, vindicating her conclusions, if not all of her assertions, in *Coming of Age in Samoa* (Shankman 2009). However, the media had picked up the controversy and Mead's posthumous reputation was damaged, especially among the general public who were not interested in following the technical arguments that ensued between Freeman and other anthropologists about the minutiae of Samoan culture.

These controversies reveal two important points about Mead's career and her contributions to feminist thought. First is the contentious nature of issues concerning the interactions between nature and nurture in human behavior, especially with regard to sex and gender. Second is the important role that the media played in the development of Mead's career and the transmission of her ideas (Lutkehaus 2008). Mead benefited greatly from her ability to speak and write in an engaging and clear manner that the public enjoyed listening to and reading. She also had a delicious sense of humor and quick wit, traits that endeared her to television talk show hosts and audiences alike. However, male academics often criticized her for her popular writing style, suggesting that it was not scientifically rigorous (Lutkehaus 1995). Mead's life spanned much of the twentieth century and she witnessed the development of new modes of mass communication. She was the most media-savvy of her generation of academics, quickly adopting first radio and then television as means of communicating her research findings and ideas. She even wrote a monthly column for *Redbook* magazine, soliciting topics of interest from her readership. She always used her anthropological training in cross-cultural comparison as the basis for her comments and suggestions on a plethora of topics, from female priests and trial marriages to atomic energy and the environment.

Despite her tarnished legacy, Mead's early findings about alternative models of adolescent behavior, the malleability of sexuality, and the culture-bound nature of notions of masculinity and femininity have had a profound impact on the twentieth century's understanding of the relationship between nature and nurture and its effect on behavior, especially regarding sex and gender—and continue to do so.

Mead's major writings

1928. *Coming of Age in Samoa*. New York: William Morrow.
1935. *Sex and Temperament in Three Primitive Societies*. New York: William Morrow.

1949. *Male and Female: A Study of the Sexes in a Changing World.* New York: William Morrow.
1972. *Blackberry Winter: My Earlier Years.* New York: William Morrow.
1975. "Bisexuality: What's It All About?" *Redbook* 144(3): 29–31.

Further reading

Bateson, M. C. 1984 *With a Daughter's Eye: A Memoir of Margaret Mead and Gregory Bateson.* New York: William Morrow.
Benedict, R. 1934. *Patterns of Culture.* Boston: Houghton Mifflin.
Freeman, D. 1983. *Margaret Mead and Samoa: The Making and Unmaking of an Anthropological Myth.* Cambridge, MA: Harvard University Press.
Friedan, B. 1963. *The Feminine Mystique.* New York: W. W. Norton.
Lutkehaus, N. 1995. "Margaret Mead and the 'Rustling-of-the-Wind-in-the-Palm-Trees' School of Ethnographic Writing." In R. Behar and D. A. Gordon, eds. *Women Writing Culture.* Berkeley: University of California Press. 186–206.
—. 2008. *Margaret Mead: The Making of an American Icon.* Princeton, NJ: Princeton University Press.
Rosenberg, R. 2004. *Changing the Subject: How the Women of Columbia Shaped the Way We Think About Sex and Politics.* New York: Columbia University Press.
Shankman, P. 2009. *The Trashing of Margaret Mead: Anatomy of an Anthropological Controversy.* Madison: University of Wisconsin Press.
West, R. 1936. "Sex and Character among Primitive Societies." Review of *Sex and Temperament in Three Primitive Societies,* by M. Mead. *Sunday Times,* January 12.

KATE MILLETT (1934–)

Victoria Hesford

In 1970 Kate Millett became, for a moment, the most famous feminist in the United States. In July of that year she published *Sexual Politics,* originally her Ph.D. thesis, to widespread attention in the women's movement and the mainstream media. *Life* magazine called it the *Das Kapital* of women's liberation and *Time,* as part of its extensive analysis of the women's liberation movement in the summer of that year, called Millett the Mao Tse-tung of feminism and put her on the front cover (Wrenn 1970; *Time* 1970a). The media's attitude to both women's liberation and Millett, however, soon turned from bemused curiosity to outright condemnation: by December of 1970 various mainstream news outlets published highly critical articles on women's liberation, including *Time*, which in a vitriolic attack accused Millett of being bisexual and, therefore, of bringing into question the legitimacy of women's liberation as a political movement (*Time* 1970b). At the same time, some influential activists within women's liberation accused Millett of pretending straightness to the media while claiming lesbian sisterhood in private (Shelley 1970–71). In the short space of one year Millett had gone from radical feminist icon of the mainstream media to designated betrayer of an entire movement.

Kate Millett's notoriety in 1970 as both media-anointed leader and lesbian betrayer of a movement meant she became both a controversial and somewhat eccentric figure within women's liberation. As a result, her work—most obviously *Sexual Politics*, but also her subsequent writing, including *Flying*, her 1974 experimental autobiography of the years immediately following the publication of *Sexual Politics*, and *Going to Iran*, her controversial account of visiting Iranian feminists in the chaotic aftermath of the 1979 revolution—has either tended to be read retrospectively as emblematic of a certain kind of radical feminist thought that is now regarded as dated or simply wrong, or as an artifact of second wave feminism that signals its historical moment but does not say anything of interest to the present day concerns of feminists. In other words, Millett's infamy in 1970 has largely condemned her to that moment, despite the fact she has gone on to have a long and varied life as a writer, conceptual artist, filmmaker, teacher, and activist.[1] Indeed, what marks Millett out as one of the most interesting and original feminist thinkers of the last forty or so years is precisely her promiscuous engagement with various forms and genres of artistic and political expression. If Millett's reputation as a feminist thinker has largely been defined by *Sexual Politics* and its association with the emergence of women's liberation in the U.S., the improvisational, unorthodox, and multi-generic character of her writing and thinking since 1970 has to be read in conjunction with that moment, not against it.

An unconventional approach characterizes Millett's method in *Sexual Politics*. As she notes in the preface, the book is "composed" in "equal parts of literary and cultural criticism" and at that time therefore was "something of an anomaly" (Millett 1978, xx). Echoing in intention the broad historical sweep and universalizing argument of Simone de Beauvoir's *The Second Sex*, *Sexual Politics* set out to "formulate a systematic overview of patriarchy as a political institution" by attributing its historical and social constancy to the "political aspect" of sex (xi). To make this argument, Millett drew upon sociology, history, psychology, and literature in order to make bold claims about the centrality of sex to western and masculine forms of social and cultural domination. Part one offers a theory of sexual politics as a "social constant" running "through all other political, social, and economic forms" (31), while part two offers an historical overview of patriarchy as a social system that could ebb and flow with the fluctuations of the modern sexual revolution and counterrevolution. The book concludes with Millett's reading of the work of four male writers—Norman Mailer, Henry Miller, D. H. Lawrence, and Jean Genet—which she reads as offering exemplary instances of sexual politics in literature, or in the case of Genet, as offering an exposé of its ideological apparatus.

As Cora Kaplan notes in her essay on *Sexual Politics*, one of the book's most lasting contributions to feminist literary criticism is its reading of literature as both venue and source for the production of sexual norms and values. In the aftermath of Millett's interdisciplinary, if overly positivistic, critiques of high literary depictions of sex, it is now almost impossible to read the representation of sex in literature and film without addressing it as an ideological issue. And read within the context of the newly emergent gay and women's liberation movements, Millett's insistence on criticizing the sexual explicitness and presumed radicalism of writers like Mailer and Miller as both homophobic and misogynistic opened up the possibilities for a wide-ranging critique of heterosex in both movements. Indeed, the explosive appeal of *Sexual Politics* in 1970 can be attributed to the way in which it participated in a mainstream and countercultural fascination with the emancipatory possibilities of sex. From Hugh Hefner to Herbert Marcuse, sex was thought of as a potential practice of freedom from the instrumentalization of modern capitalist society or, as in Hefner's case, the disciplinary and financial burdens (for men) of middle-class family life.

Millett's intervention in this widespread fascination with the liberatory possibilities of sex, of course, significantly shifted the terms of the discussion by inserting a strong feminist critique of the inherent masculinist bias in the institutions and representations of sexual practice. Yet, despite this critique, Millett also located the future emancipation of women in a new sexual revolution:

> It may be that a second wave of the sexual revolution might at last accomplish its aim of freeing half the race from its immemorial subordination—and in the process bring us all a great deal closer to humanity. It may be that we shall even be able to retire sex from

the harsh realities of politics, but not until we have created a world we can bear out of the desert we inhabit.

(Millett 1978, 363)

In locating the source of women's subjugation in sex as well as their potential emancipation, Millett's thesis can be read as doing what Michel Foucault famously accuses the gay and women's liberation movements more generally of doing: of finding the truth of one's being in sex and, therefore, of extending rather than challenging the disciplinary regimes of the modern nation-state (Foucault 1990). Nevertheless, it is in Millett's notion of "sexual politics" that we find one of the more enduring and suggestive conceptual remainders of the second wave era. The term conjoins her definition of the political as "power-structured relationships, arrangements whereby one group of persons is controlled by another" through "techniques of control," with her equally succinct identification of "coitus" as a "charged microcosm" of psychological feelings, social relations, and cultural values (Millett 1978, 31). In her suggestion that sexual acts operate as a locus for the reproduction of social power, Millett's understanding of sexuality echoes, rather than contradicts, Foucault's near contemporaneous definition of sex as a "dense transfer point for relations of power" (Foucault 1990, 103).

To think of Millett's definition of "sexual politics" as an echo of Foucault's understanding of sexuality is not to make it the same, or to think of it as an immediate precursor to Foucault's perhaps more sophisticated theoretical and historical elaboration. Rather it is to think of it as another instantiation of what, at the time, was a widespread interest in the political meaning and implications of sex and sexuality for understanding the violent and exploitative operations of western economic and cultural domination of the colonized, people of color, and women. Millett's book can be read within this context as an attempt to map the historical relationship between the sexual and the political in order to understand the subjugation of women as something that happened through the reproduction of social institutions and ideologies like the family and heterosexuality, and through what the French sociologist, Pierre Bourdieu, would later call "family feelings," and what Millett herself referred to as psychological domination (Bourdieu 1998, 67–69). Millett, along with radical feminist contemporaries like Shulamith Firestone, Anne Koedt, and Ti-grace Atkinson, attempted to expand the doing of politics into an understanding of the family—often read, problematically, as synonymous with patriarchy— as an "instrument" of social reproduction, and they, along with other gay and women's liberationist thinkers like Laura X, Martha Shelley,

Allen Young, and Craig Rodman, also identified sex as a source and conduit of familial and social power. It is this effective dispersal of the political into the realm of social relations, conceived at the same time as also sexual and affective, that forms one of the key interventions of early women's and gay liberation problematizations of the "personal" in relation to the idea and practice of politics.

Much of the feminist criticism of *Sexual Politics* since its publication in 1970 has centered on Millett's reactionary critique of Freud and her tendency towards literal readings of sexual violence in literature (Mitchell 2000; Kaplan 1986). And yet, *Sexual Politics* must also be read as offering one of the first examples of a feminist criticism that attempted to theorize the subjugation of women as something endemic to the emergence of modern nation states and their societies of control—an approach to modern forms of power Millett continued to explore in her later writing on psychiatry and torture (Millett 1990b and 1994). Millett's interdisciplinary readings of literature in *Sexual Politics*, and her turn to Genet to provide an "oblique," what we might now call *queer*, reading of sex roles meant that heterosexuality and "women" became historical and cultural productions in need of analysis rather than, as in much feminist literary criticism of the 1970s and early 1980s, the assumed ground for feminist political claims. That is, *Sexual Politics* made heterosexuality a point of historical contention and investigation for feminism, not its raison d'etre, and for that reason it helped create the conditions of possibility for feminist and queer theory in the decades to come.

Note

1 For a pretty extensive list of Millett's creative and literary output, see her excellent Wikipedia page and personal website: www.katemillett.com.

Millett's major writings

Kate Millett Papers, 1912–2002, Sallie Bingham Center for Women's History and Culture, Rubenstein Library, Duke University, Durham NC.

[1970] 1978. *Sexual Politics*. New York: Ballantine Books.

[1974] 1990a. *Flying*. New York: Simon and Schuster.

1977. *Sita*. New York: Ballantine Books.

1982. *Going to Iran*. New York: Coward, McCann, and Geoghegan.

1990b. *The Loony-Bin Trip*. New York: Simon and Schuster.

1994. *The Politics of Cruelty: An Essay on the Literature of Political Imprisonment*. New York: W. W. Norton.

Further reading

Allen, Leah Claire. 2014. "Facts and Fictions: Feminist Literary Criticism and Cultural Critique, 1968–2012." Dissertation, Duke University, Durham, NC.

Bourdieu, Pierre. 1998. "The Family Spirit." In *Practical Reason: On the Theory of Action*, 64–74. Stanford, CA: Stanford University Press.

Foucault, Michel. 1990. *The History of Sexuality, Volume 1: An Introduction*. New York: Vintage Press.

Hesford, Victoria. 2013. *Feeling Women's Liberation*. Durham, NC: Duke University Press.

Juhasz, Suzanne. 1980. "Towards a Theory of Feminist Autobiography: Kate Millett's *Flying* and *Sita*; Maxine Hong Kingston's *The Woman Warrior*." In *Women's Autobiography: Essays in Criticism*, edited by Estelle Jelinek, 221–37. Bloomington: Indiana University Press.

Kaplan, Cora. 1986. "Radical Feminism and Literature: Rethinking Millett's *Sexual Politics*." In *Sea Changes: Essays on Culture and Feminism*, 15–30. London: Verso.

Kolodny, Annette. 1980. "The Lady's Not for Spurning: Kate Millett and the Critics." In *Women's Autobiography: Essays in Criticism*, edited by Estelle Jelinek, 238–59. Bloomington: Indiana University Press.

Mitchell, Juliet. 2000. *Psychoanalysis and Feminism: A Radical Reassessment of Freudian Psychoanalysis*. Second edition, 351–55. New York: Basic Books.

Shelley, Martha. 1970–71. "Women's Liberation Media Star." *Come Out*, n.p.

Time. 1970a. "Who's Come a Long Way Baby?" August 31.

—. 1970b. "Women's Lib: A Second Look." December 14.

Wrenn, Marie-Claude. 1970. "The Furious Young Philosopher Who Got It Down on Paper." *Life*, September 4.

TONI MORRISON (1931–)

Lawrie Balfour

Of all the signs that divided the Jim Crow landscape into black and white spaces, writes Toni Morrison, there was one that was *not* "malevolent": "The pair that said 'White Ladies' and 'Colored Women'" (2008b, 18). In "What the Black Woman Thinks About Women's Lib," Morrison declares herself satisfied with this distinction, despite the violence it underwrites. For it acknowledges the accomplishment of generations of black women who have lived and acted in defiance of norms of femininity that apply to white women only. "Out of the profound desolation of her reality," writes Morrison, "[the black woman] may very well have invented herself." If she celebrates a subjectivity grounded in the effort to take responsibility in the face of a hostile world, however, Morrison defies any tendency toward "lump thinking"—whether it is used to denigrate or to vindicate black women as a group. Instead, her career is defined by a series of intricate investigations of the historical contours and intimate experiences of African Americans in all of their variation and contradictions. Against confining stereotypes of race, gender, and class, Morrison's literary creations are faithful to the (often untold) historical record and consistently defy expectations.

When Morrison published "What the Black Woman Thinks About Women's Lib" in August 1971, the *New York Times* identified her as an editor at Random House and the author of *The Bluest Eye* (1970). Although she was just on the threshold of a career as a novelist that would earn her global acclaim, most notably the 1993 Nobel Prize for Literature, Morrison was already deeply enmeshed in the project of constituting and expanding the field of African American letters. Born Chloe Ardelia Wofford in Lorain, Ohio, in 1931, Morrison studied literature at Howard University and Cornell and began her career as a college teacher. As an editor in the 1970s and 1980s, she cultivated the work of black authors, insisting on seeing the world from vantages dismissed as narrow or particular and grasping the importance of canon formation in a culture where "in spite of its implicit and explicit acknowledgment, 'race' is still a virtually unspeakable thing" (1989, 3). Notably, Morrison's list includes landmark texts of twentieth-century feminist fiction, poetry, and theory by Gayl Jones, Toni Cade Bambara, Angela Davis, June Jordan, and others (Wall 2008).

Her own writing extends and deepens this aspiration to articulate the unspeakable and explore thoughts unspoken. The author of eleven novels, the most recent published in 2015, several books for children, a short story, work for the theater and opera, and a substantial body of social and literary criticism, Morrison crafts her words to model a form of care for individuals and communities that have been essential to the emergence of modern culture but sequestered from official history. Telling stories from the perspectives of "the persons no one inquired of," Morrison vivifies their complex interior lives and relationships (1989, 22). Telling these stories with fidelity, Morrison notes, is treacherous. Acutely attuned to the violence enacted by and through language,

Morrison moves carefully into the worlds inhabited by women and girls, boys and men, who are the victims of profound trauma and who are, nonetheless, far more than the sum of their injuries.

Morrison's work is replete with historical detail, stretching from the seventeenth century, when slavery and race were not yet fully hitched together, to the post-racial pretensions of the twenty-first century. The richness of her language and the tenderness of her description inspirit her characters even as her narratives disclose the brutal specificity of Americans' twinned commitment to freedom and white supremacy. Among the many reservoirs from which she draws, Morrison notes that she is particularly indebted to the heritage of slave narratives. While the political imperatives that constrained fugitive and former slaves to tell stories that would move white readers to act have changed, Morrison maintains that the impetus to oppose the devaluation of racialized lives is ongoing:

> For me—a writer in the last quarter of the twentieth century, not much more than a hundred years after Emancipation, a writer who is black and a woman—the exercise is very different. My job becomes how to rip that veil drawn over 'proceedings too terrible to relate.' The exercise is also critical for any person who is black, or who belongs to any marginalized category, for, historically, we were seldom invited to participate in the discourse even when we were its topic.
>
> (2008b, 70)

Such participation entails resurrecting the details that earlier generations of writers were required to "forget"—of the body as a site of sexual domination and of pleasure, of the dispossession of mothers, of possession by the past, and of the interior lives of the "disremembered and unaccounted for" (1987, 275).

One of the themes that connects all of Morrison's work and that makes a distinctive contribution to feminist thought—whether or not that is her explicit aim—is her interest in finding, in language and in life, "a merging of responsibility and liberty" (2004b, xiv). The recurrence of the word "responsibility" and Morrison's meditations on its several meanings rebut the thoughtless, yet devastating, deployment of the word to figure black people as less accountable to themselves and others. Against the cruelty of public discourses of "personal responsibility," Morrison details what it means to take action in the context of oppression and to do so without desiring the conquest of others. Responsibility, in this sense, abandons the illusion of control and the aspiration for mastery and seeks out unlikely spaces of freedom. Thus,

Morrison's characters steal themselves and their children from slavery, "extract choice from choicelessness" (1989, 25), and found communities apart from the strictures of racial purity (black or white), respectability, or patriarchy.

This is not to say that Morrison romanticizes oppression or the individuals who endure it. Her point, precisely, is to capture their human weight, the truth of lives disregarded by a racist and sexist society. One of her most vivid characters, Sula Peace, might stand as a feminist icon, insofar as she determines to create herself in defiance of the disapprobation of her black neighbors and the savage norms of Jim Crow. She refuses to accept the verdict rendered by her best friend, Nel: "You *can't* do it all. You a woman and a colored woman at that. You can't act like a man. You can't be walking around all independent-like, doing whatever you like, taking what you want, leaving what you don't" (2004b, 142). Yet Nel's admonition is less straightforward than it appears, revealing the intricate moral imagination of her creator's art. Morrison simultaneously limns as unjustified the constraints on black women and discredits the license that many men, and women like Sula, mistake for freedom. Sula's self-creation is not a model for anyone insofar as it is irresponsible and even cruel. As Hortense Spillers observes, however, "Sula's outlawry may not be the best kind, but that she has the will toward rebellion itself *is* the stunning idea" (2003, 118).

While Morrison insists on the significance of every human being, she is equally concerned with the conditions of collective life. Communities, too, can enact freedom in the face of oppression, can fulfill or disavow their responsibilities. Whether communities are familial or chosen, enforced by enslavement/segregation/conscription or produced through happenstance, all-black or multiracial, they provide the context in which individual action acquires its meaning. Morrison's interest in individual freedom, in other words, refutes the claims of rugged individualism. Instead, her imagination ranges across a variety of collectives, paying special attention to those formed by "unmastered women" (2008a, 58). Some of these communities are dangerous to their members, but through them Morrison offers glimpses of worlds not fully structured by patriarchal rules. At the same time, she demonstrates the degree to which such collectivities are perceived as threatening by those on the outside precisely because they lack such rules; and like all experiences of freedom, their accomplishment is exhilarating and fleeting.

One of the signal features of Morrison's writing is that, along with its persistent critique of patriarchal power and other forms of mastery, it is defined by a frank interest in the lives of men and the operations of gender broadly speaking. *Song of Solomon* (1977) is the first of her novels to focus on a male protagonist, but Morrison's fiction and non-fiction examine the racing of American masculinity with exceptional care. Several novels reflect on the waste of war and its costs to African American soldiers and veterans, thereby shattering heroic conceptions of martial manhood. By capturing the ways in which white suprema-cist power has emasculated African American men, furthermore, Mor-rison negotiates a treacherous course that affirms their thwarted desire to assert themselves and take care of their loved ones, on the one hand, without conceding that women should accept the bargain of "mascu-linist protection," on the other.[1]

While the novel is the genre for which Morrison is justly renowned, her commitment to exploring the liberatory possibilities of language extends well beyond fiction. Her contributions to public discussions include reflections on the entanglement of race, gender, and sex in the Anita Hill–Clarence Thomas hearings, the murder trial of O. J. Simpson, and the presidency of Bill Clinton and lectures on the public value of the university and of the arts. In *Playing in the Dark*, a study of the "Africanist presence" in American literature, Morrison does not focus centrally on gender; yet her insights into the white creativity that was made possible by the presence of slaves recalls *Beloved*'s devastating portrait of slavery as a regime of sexual violence. And Morrison's investigation of the tradition of white lit-erary masculinity that is predicated on the unacknowledged pres-ence of "enabling black nursemen" raises broad questions about the unowned operations of race in the constitution of gender in the U.S. (1992b, 82).

Fittingly, Morrison's meditation on Women's Lib concludes with an observation that is both affirmative and challenging. Even as she dis-sects the forms of entitlement and parochialism that define a woman's movement grounded in the experiences of "White Ladies" and their descendants, Morrison also relishes the possibility of generating some-thing new and politically powerful. For an example of such a prospect, she looks to the founding meeting of the National Women's Politi-cal Caucus in Washington and notes that U.S. Representative Shirley Chisholm, civil rights leader Fannie Lou Hamer, and welfare rights activist Beulah Sanders were all there. In their words and work and example, Morrison discerns the shape of women's empowerment that refuses "lump thinking." "They see, perhaps, something real," she remarks: "women talking about human rights rather than sexual rights—something other than a family quarrel, and the air is shivery with possibilities" (2008b, 30).

Note

1 Iris Marion Young (2003) uses this phrase to explicate the gendered character of Americans' embrace of a strong security state in the aftermath of September 11, but it can be extended to address the ways that the desire for security from terror has been associated with the assertion of (male) protective power on the part of the vulnerable (read as female and/or juvenile).

Morrison's major writings

1970. *The Bluest Eye.* New York: Washington Square Press.
1971. "What the Black Woman Thinks About Women's Lib; The Black Woman and Woman's Lib." *New York Times Magazine,* August 22.
[1973] 2004a. *Sula.* New York: Vintage.
[1977] 2004b. *Song of Solomon.* New York: Vintage.
1981. *Tar Baby.* New York: Knopf.
1987. *Beloved.* New York: Plume.
1989. "Unspeakable Things Unspoken: The Afro-American Presence in American Literature." *Michigan Quarterly Review* 28(1): 1–34.
1992a. *Jazz.* New York: Knopf.
1992b. *Playing in the Dark: Whiteness and the Literary Imagination.* Cambridge, MA: Harvard University Press.
1997. *Paradise.* New York: Knopf.
2003. *Love.* New York: Knopf.
2008a. *A Mercy.* New York: Knopf.
2008b. *What Moves at the Margin: Selected Nonfiction.* Edited by Carolyn C. Denard. Jackson: University Press of Mississippi.
2012. *Home.* New York: Knopf.
2015. *God Help the Child.* New York: Knopf.
1992. (ed.). *Race-ing Justice, En-gendering Power: Essays on Anita Hill, Clarence Thomas, and the Construction of Social Reality.* New York: Pantheon.

Further reading

Spillers, Hortense J. 2003. "A Hateful Passion, a Lost Love: Three Women's Fiction." In *Black, White, and in Color: Essays on American Literature and Culture.* Chicago: University of Chicago Press, 93–118.

Wall, Cheryl A. 2008. "Toni Morrison, Editor and Teacher." In Justine Tally (ed.), *The Cambridge Companion to Toni Morrison*. Cambridge: Cambridge University Press, 139–48.
Young, Iris M. 2003. "The Logic of Masculinist Protection: Reflections on the Current Security State." *Signs* 29(1): 1–25.

LAURA MULVEY (1941–)

Rosalind Galt

Laura Mulvey is undoubtedly the most cited feminist film theorist, possibly the most cited scholar in any area of film studies. The influence of her 1975 polemic "Visual Pleasure and Narrative Cinema" ("VPNC") can hardly be overstated not only in film studies itself but across art history, cultural studies, and critical theory. Mulvey studied history at St Hilda's College at the University of Oxford. In the 1970s she was a feminist activist and filmmaker, writing for politically-oriented magazines such as *Spare Rib*, and her early work was produced outside the academy. This background indicates how generative feminist praxis was for a theory that was often misunderstood as alienated from material conditions. It also signals the fact that there was little institutional space for feminist film scholarship at the time: Mulvey did not take up her first academic job until 1979. Writing outside the academy, Mulvey published what was to become an indispensable piece of feminist scholarship in the British film journal *Screen*, and her career thereafter maps the emergence and evolution of feminist film theory.

Why did this article become so influential? One of the key contributions of "VPNC" is its insistence on cinema as a social apparatus that constructs and maintains patriarchal ways of looking. This insight has several consequences. One is to effect a move away from an earlier feminist film criticism that analyzed gender in relation to the content of individual films ('images of women') toward a feminist film theory that understands cinema's role in reproducing patriarchal structures of subjectivity. Another consequence helps explain all those citations. "VPNC" demonstrates that gender in cinema is not simply one topic among many but that it is inscribed so closely into the cinematic apparatus that any film theory attentive to medium specificity must at once be feminist theory. This polemic has radically shaped the field: although it is certainly possible to find approaches to cinema that ignore feminism, most significant thought in film theory since the

1970s has understood the cinematic apparatus as a locus of gendered subjectivity and politically-mediated desire.

Mulvey uses psychoanalysis as the central method for feminist analysis of cinema. Along with scholars such as Juliet Mitchell and Jacqueline Rose, Mulvey sees psychoanalysis as a uniquely detailed map of patriarchal subjectivity. She asserts that "psychoanalytic theory is thus appropriated here as a political weapon, demonstrating the way the unconscious of patriarchal society has structured film form" (2009, 14). Mulvey argues that the spectator position constructed by mainstream cinema is male, and that cinema plays on the tensions between the spectator as ego (identifying with an ideal self onscreen) and as libido (looking desiringly at another). The figure of the woman mediates these contradictory impulses. Mulvey describes the classical cinema's system of identification and desire in terms of a patriarchal gaze:

> In a world ordered by sexual imbalance, pleasure in looking has been split between active/male and passive/female. The determining male gaze projects its fantasy onto the female figure, which is styled accordingly. In their traditional exhibitionist role women are simultaneously looked at and displayed, with their appearance coded for strong visual and erotic impact so that they can be said to connote *to-be-looked-at-ness*.
>
> (2009, 19)

The article goes on to outline the operations of classical film form in psychoanalytic terms, arguing that the patriarchal response to castration anxiety is ordered by voyeurism and fetishism. Voyeurism describes narrative drive to investigate the woman, to demystify, devalue and punish, while fetishism overvalues her, making the female star reassuring rather than threatening. This latter process results in spectacular images that take pleasure in the surface of the image. Fetishism and voyeurism describe the representation of gender difference in films but they also describe the patriarchal workings of the cinematic itself. For Mulvey, "cinematic codes create a gaze, a world, and an object, thereby producing an illusion cut to the measure of desire" (2009, 26).

Mandy Merck has emphasized the article's polemic qualities, reading it as a manifesto. She sees its programmatic rhetoric as an incitement; what Lynn Spiegel terms "a call to arms" and which Merck situates in a history of feminist manifestos from Mary Wollestonecraft to Shulamith Firestone (2007, 7). This approach usefully frames the critical responses to Mulvey, which themselves narrate a history of feminist film theory. Many feminist scholars have taken on her claims, seeking to prove that certain films evade patriarchal looking relations, or that certain types of spectator actively resist them. For instance, Mary Ann Doane considers the position of the female spectator, bell hooks specifies the gaze of black female spectators, and Carol-Ann Tyler revises feminist film theory from a queer perspective.

Mulvey herself revised her account of spectatorship in the 1981 article "Afterthoughts on 'Visual Pleasure and Narrative Cinema' Inspired by *Duel in the Sun* (1946)." Here she addresses the problem of the female spectator, who is expected to identify across gender lines and to fetishize images of women. Mulvey considers the complexity of this position: what happens when women take up the freedom, agency, and sexual subjectivity that cinema routes through male bodies and desires? These questions open important directions for thinking cinema, gender, and sexuality. Queer theory takes up (and takes on) the implications of what Mulvey calls women's "borrowed transvestite clothes" (2009, 33). One response is that we need to theorize lesbian spectatorship, critiquing Mulvey's theory as oriented to straight women. Women, after all, need not take on male positions to desire women on screen. But Mulvey's trans-sex identification equally offers an implicit account of cinema as always already queer; as an apparatus whose patriarchal and heteronormative structures are never as complete as they might seem, and whose most ideologically normalizing operations (having male agency, looking with desire at female figures) can destabilize both gendered identification and desire.

Mulvey's film theory is striking for the range of cinematic registers it encompasses, from popular genre to the avant-garde. She considers melodrama as uniquely able to reveal the ideological contradictions of gender. "There is a dizzy satisfaction," she writes, "in witnessing the way that sexual difference under patriarchy is fraught, explosive, and erupts dramatically into violence within its own private stamping ground, the family." Whereas most genres celebrate male experience, melodrama uniquely explores the "emotion, bitterness and disillusion" characteristic of women's lives in bourgeois patriarchy (Mulvey 2009, 42). Melodrama also intersects gender with class and race. On *Imitation of Life* (dir. Sirk, 1959), she writes that, "The tension between the artifice available to the white woman, an assumed sheen of protective glamour, and the unveiling of the black woman back to essence, creates a visual discourse on race that is only possible in the cinema" (1996, 31). This revelation is again, crucially, staged via cinematic form.

Experimental filmmaking is of formative importance for Mulvey as a feminist practice. Some of her key films include *Penthesilea: Queen of the Amazons* (1974), *Riddles of the Sphinx* (1977), and *Frida Kahlo and*

Tina Modotti (1982). Mulvey's films make an important contribution to feminist thought: their formal challenge to patriarchal vision enacts her manifesto in a different medium. What is cinema for Mulvey the filmmaker? *Riddles of the Sphinx* proposes a female temporality, rooted in the feminist critique of gendered labor time that we also see in the films of Chantal Akerman and Yvonne Rainer. *Penthesilea*'s response to male myths is in conversation with Mulvey's own writing on Oedipal narrative, but it equally engages the queerly feminist cinema of Ulrike Ottinger, and feminist revisions of masculinist narratives from Hélène Cixous and Teresa de Lauretis to Angela Carter and Catherine Breillat. In "Film, Feminism and the Avant Garde" (in *Visual and Other Pleasures*), Mulvey argues that experimental film makes spaces in which women can attack dominant language and culture.

In *Fetishism and Curiosity* (1996), Mulvey argues that cinema provides a place where Freudian and Marxist fetishisms merge, with commodity culture intertwining with sexualized disavowals. This approach allows for a culturally-specific account of the desiring subject and a nuancing of her earlier polemics. In "Close Ups and Commodities" she explores the affective power of the close up shot, and in particular the way that images of glamorous female stars create eroticized stasis (1996, 41). Mulvey reads this formal effect across histories of American cinema and modernity. The 1920s 'New Woman' centers attitudes to sexual liberation, consumer capitalism, and women as social and economic agents, while a postwar star fetish like Marilyn Monroe signifies both extreme whiteness and the artifice required to sustain this vision of femininity. Her work expands increasingly from the 1990s onward to address non-Western cinemas, especially those of the Middle East and Africa. In "The Carapace that Failed: Ousmane Sembene's *Xala*," she reads the fetishisms of European capitalism in a neocolonial context. Here the troublesome phallus of the impotent protagonist centers histories of colonial violence and economic exploitation in Senegal. Mulvey insists on the geopolitical location of the fetish: whereas psychoanalysis has often been accused of ahistoricism, Mulvey puts it to work in historical analysis.

Her 2006 book, *Death 24x a Second*, advances the centrality of film as a medium to feminist thought. She argues that the changes in spectatorship brought about by DVDs and other home-viewing technologies have reordered the inscription of gender, activity, and power described in her earlier work. What she terms 'delayed cinema' tends toward fetishistic scopophilia, in which spectators become fascinated with image rather than narrative, and with still compositions rather than the sadistic temporality of narrative movement. The classical binary of spectatorial identification with the active male protagonist and desiring gaze at the female object of the look is both reinforced and decomposed when the spectator controls the movement of the film. This argument demonstrates the plasticity of her psychoanalysis: Mulvey uses Freud's concepts of sadism, the death drive, repetition compulsion and the uncanny to rethink the psychic economy of cinema in the digital era. She draws out what's at stake for women in our obsessive return to cinema's ephemeral gestures and uncanny repetitions.

Merck reminds us that "the political stakes of feminist iconoclasm have always been high" (2007, 17), and yet Mulvey is an ambivalent iconoclast. Her own filmmaking reveals an investment in the political potentialities of the image, and even in "VPNC" she at once depends on histories of iconoclasm to describe the anxiety prompted by the image and reverses that iconophobia, exposing its patriarchal foundations. In an interview with Martine Beugnet, Mulvey rejects "a totalizing critique of the optical as such" (Mulvey and Rogers 2015, 197). Her analysis of patriarchal visuality has never been easily categorized as iconophobic precisely because iconophobia is itself a patriarchal logic. Both the image itself and the process of looking contain potentials for feminist inquiry, resistance and pleasure, and part of Mulvey's importance has been her eloquent insistence that we take the image seriously.

Mulvey's major writings

1975. "Visual Pleasure and Narrative Cinema." *Screen* 16(3): 6–18.
1977–1978. "Notes on Sirk and Melodrama." *Movie* 25: 56.
1981. "Afterthoughts on 'Visual Pleasure and Narrative Cinema' Inspired by *Duel in the Sun* (1946)." *Framework* 15–17: 12–15.
[1989] 2009. *Visual and Other Pleasures.* Second edition. London: Palgrave.
1996. *Fetishism and Curiosity.* London: BFI.
2006. *Death 24x a Second: Stillness and the Moving Image.* London: Reaktion Books.
2015. Mulvey, Laura and Anna Backman Rogers, eds. *Feminisms: Diversity, Difference and Multiplicity in Contemporary Film Cultures.* Amsterdam: Amsterdam University Press.

Further reading

Doane, Mary Ann. 1991. *Femmes Fatales: Feminism, Film Theory, Psychoanalysis.* New York: Routledge.

Merck, Mandy. 2007. "Mulvey's Manifesto." *Camera Obscura* 22(3 66): 1–23.

Rainer, Yvonne. 2006. "Mulvey's Legacy." *Camera Obscura* 21(3 63): 167–70.

Rose, Jacqueline. 1987. *Sexuality in the Field of Vision.* London:Verso.

SUSAN MOLLER OKIN (1946–2004)

Joan Tronto

Susan Moller Okin was the most steadfast liberal feminist political theorist of the late twentieth century. Originally from New Zealand, Okin was in graduate school when feminist movements revivified in the 1970s. The basic idea that motivated Okin's work was captured in *Justice, Gender, and the Family* (1989). She wrote, "A just future would be one without gender. In its social structures and practices, one's sex would have no more relevance than one's eye color or the length of one's toes" (171), and that, since "the family is the linchpin of gender, reproducing it from one generation to the next ... the family *needs* to be a just institution" (170).

Her first book, *Women in Western Political Thought* (1979), began as her doctoral dissertation at Harvard. After completing her PhD, she taught at several universities, spending most of her career at Stanford University. Okin's strong commitment to a universal concern for the fate of all women as women made her a lightning rod for criticisms of this approach later in her career. It is easy to overlook, then, some of her central contributions. Now that feminist critiques are a main-stream concern in the academy, it is difficult to recall how bold and path-breaking all of her work was. In the 1970s, some had pronounced political theory to be passé. John Rawls had published his magisterial *A Theory of Justice* (1971), and historians of political theory seemed to have exhausted the task of finding the central ideas in the works of canonical thinkers. Okin's life work pointed to a new direction for political theory: using the history of political thought and other tools of political theory to address real issues in the political world.

Women in Western Political Thought was a pioneering work. In it Okin examined traditional political theorists—Plato, Aristotle, Rousseau and John Stuart Mill—to examine how their theories understood the place of women in society. She argued that these thinkers conceived of men and women differently, thinking about men's natures but asking of women, "what are women good for?" This functionalist difference, deeply buried in the internal logic of Western thought (as demonstrated in another chapter that explored women's place in American law), was prima facie evidence for Okin that women were not conceived of as equals. Although Okin acknowledged that the text was not a comprehensive review of women's place in political theory, her work inspired generations of future thinkers to look more closely at the hidden dimensions of political theorists' thinking. This book not only brought feminist theorizing to the core of the historical study of political theory, but also raised a basic question about how to read and think about political theorists' works. At the end of the Introduction she compared her work to Tom Stoppard's play *Rosencrantz and Guildenstern Are Dead*, and noted how it transformed our understandings of Hamlet. "Similarly, when women, who have always been minor characters in the social and political theory of a patriarchal world, are transformed into major ones, the entire cast and the play in which it is acting look very different" (12). *Women in Western Political Thought* was not a comprehensive treatment of women in Western political thought, but it opened new avenues of thinking for political theory that are not yet exhausted.

In her second book, *Justice, Gender, and the Family*, Okin was motivated by her impatience and dismay with her contemporaries to take seriously questions of gender as they framed theories of justice. The book consists largely of a critique of the leading theorists of justice at the time (Rawls, Alan Bloom, Alasdair MacIntyre, Robert Nozick, Michael Walzer) for their failures to take gender seriously as a category of analysis. The persistence of the split between public and private life, Okin argued, allowed theorists of justice to continue to simply ignore the role of justice in an important sphere for women, the family. Following the thinking of John Stuart Mill, Okin argued that if families are not just, then there can be no way for citizens to become just later in their lives. In her chapter on "Vulnerability By Marriage," Okin brought theories of justice down to the ground by exploring the real experiences in marriage and families, experienced by real men, women, and children. Okin demonstrated that, rather than thinking of the household as a "haven in a heartless world," injustices that persist in employment, education, and other public opportunities continue to have consequences within the household itself.

Okin demonstrated these continuing injustices by ingeniously using a framework from the economist Albert O. Hirschmann: exit, voice, loyalty (Hirschman 1970). Liberals do not often see domination as a central feature of social life. If people have equal choices, then how can one say that some are more harmed by the choices that they have made than others? To do so interferes with people's liberties. As conservative critics of feminism argued in the 1980s, marriage was a "good deal" for women because they were protected in their households (see, e.g., Schlafly 1977). Okin's recognition of the different levels of "exit" and "voice" options available to men and women made women more vulnerable to being in, and exiting from, marriages. Okin's specific critiques and arguments may not be remembered, but her idea that one must apply standards of justice to what happens in households seems so obvious now that hardly anyone would challenge it.

In her third book, provocatively titled *Is Multiculturalism Bad for Women?* published ten years later in 1999, Okin made an argument that was challenged not only among mainstream theorists of justice, but feminist writers as well. Okin argued in this text that liberal thinkers taken with arguments for multicultural group rights had to be attentive to an ongoing concern. While groups deserve recognition, Okin argued, many cultures (and especially religions) did not believe in gender equity. Yet the reception of this work was largely critical. In the intervening decade, scholars had begun to raise this challenge: *who* is the subject of feminist thought? Is there a single framework of "woman" for which political claims can be made? Okin had continued to view gender as if it were the equivalent of sex, and to view sex as irrelevant in framing people's lives. But in the 1990s, thinkers from Judith Butler to Elizabeth Spelman had claimed that gender was a more complicated notion, and its intersection with other aspects of life—sexuality, group membership, culture, etc.—made it impossible to speak about a universal category "women." Okin had little sympathy for such arguments, which she frequently described as "anti-essentialist." At the same time that she argued that she was no essentialist, she also made what we might call an anti-anti-essentialist argument. Okin's concern was not to defend any group of women's experiences as universal, but to recall that sexism and forms of gender discrimination were found throughout the world. Focus on real discriminations that exist, Okin argued. Focus on the diversity of women's experience and ideas, her critics insisted. This is actually a fateful discussion that arose out of the ongoing and changing fortunes of feminist politics. Which is more feminist: trying to end discrimination or trying to faithfully present the views and lives of women? Okin's firm view was the first, and her impatience was palpable. This strong view made her a target for other feminists, whose critiques she often suggested distorted her views and unfairly cast her as only interested in white middle-class women's experiences (see, e.g., Putnam 1995; Okin 1995).

Okin's caution was clearly expressed in some additional essays that she published: she insisted that liberals interested in group rights also had to defend a right of exit (Okin 2002). Towards the end of her life, she was beginning to take the thrust of critics' points seriously and thinking about her claims for women's equality on a global level (Okin 2003). In one of her last essays, published after her death, Okin returned to offer a scathing critique of Rawls' *Political Liberalism*, arguing that he has still ignored the needs of justice in households (Okin 2005).

Okin criticized mainstream theorists of justice and feminist colleagues alike. She never understood the de-politicized directions in which feminist political thought began to move. Her former student Brooke Ackerly perhaps captured Okin's contributions best: "Susan Okin was a critic, not because she loved argument, rather because she loved justice" (2004, 448).

Okin's major writings

1979. *Women in Western Political Thought*. Princeton, NJ: Princeton University Press.

1989. *Justice, Gender, and the Family*. New York: Basic.

1995. "Inequalities Between the Sexes in Different Cultural Contexts." In *Women, Culture and Development: A Study of Human Capabilities*, edited by Martha C. Nussbaum and Jonathan Glover, 274–97. Oxford: Clarendon Press.

1999. *Is Multiculturalism Bad for Women?* Edited by Joshua Cohen, Matthew Howard, and Martha Craven Nussbaum. Princeton, NJ: Princeton University Press.

2002. "'Mistresses of Their Own Destiny': Group Rights, Gender, and Realistic Rights of Exit." *Ethics* 112(2): 205–30. doi: 10.1086/324645.

2003. "Poverty, Well-Being, and Gender: What Counts, Who's Heard?" *Philosophy and Public Affairs* 31(3): 280–316. doi: 10.2307/3558008.

2005. "'Forty Acres and a Mule' for Women: Rawls and Feminism." *Politics, Philosophy and Economics* 4(2): 233–48.

Further reading

Ackerly, Brooke A. 2004. "Susan Moller Okin (1946–2004)." *Political Theory* 32(4): 446–48.

Hirschman, Albert O. 1970. *Exit, Voice, and Loyalty: Responses to Decline in Firms, Organizations, and States*. Cambridge, MA: Harvard University Press.

Putnam, Ruth Anna. 1995. "Why Not a Feminist Theory of Justice?" In *Women, Culture and Development: A Study of Human Capabilities*, edited by Martha C. Nussbaum and Jonathan Glover, 298–331. Oxford: Clarendon Press.

Schlafly, P. 1977. *The Power of the Positive Woman*. New Rochelle, NY: Arlington House.

CHRISTINE DE PIZAN (c. 1364–1430)

Renate Blumenfeld-Kosinski

> But if women had written the books, I know for a fact that they would have been written differently, for women know well that they are wrongly condemned.
>
> de Pizan, *The God of Love's Letter*

With these words Christine de Pizan challenged the entire Western corpus of male writing. Christine was uniquely qualified not only to challenge but to revise a dominant misogynistic tradition. She was born around 1364 in Venice and at the age of four moved with her family to Paris where her father, Thomas de Pizan, became the court physician and astrologer of the French king Charles V (Margolis 2011). In several autobiographical passages she described the warm welcome the expatriate family received at court and the prosperity they experienced as a result of her father's high position.[1] In 1380 Christine married the notary Etienne de Castel with whom she had two sons and a daughter. But 1380 also marked the beginning of a more difficult period with the death of the family's benefactor Charles V. His son, Charles VI, aged eleven, acceded to the throne, and when twelve years later the young king began to experience more and more frequent bouts of madness the political situation in France began to deteriorate. In the midst of the Hundred Years War with England (1337–1453) and the papal schism that tore apart the Catholic Church (1378–1417), France was further destabilized by constant quarrels between the king's brother, uncles, and cousins that finally erupted into civil war. In 1387 Thomas de Pizan died, and just three years later Christine's husband perished in an epidemic, leaving her a twenty-five-year-old widow with three children, her mother, and a niece to provide for. He also left many debts. This was a key moment for Christine: she used the learning she had acquired from her father to begin a literary career of many decades during which she wrote some forty works of lyric poetry, political allegories, and didactic and devotional texts. By skill-fully courting patrons and producing her own manuscripts she managed to earn a living from her writing, making her the first professional woman writer in history. As a woman she could not have a university or ecclesiastical affiliation. These two areas were the major sources of income for her learned male contemporaries, who did not live from their writing. Through this professional activity alone Christine has become a key figure for feminist thought. But she is also an important key thinker for the feminist tradition. Throughout her works we find a passionate engagement with contemporary mores and politics. Indeed, her feminist ideas cannot be separated from the moral and political issues she addresses in her many works (Brown-Grant 1999).

Today, Christine de Pizan is best known for her *Book of the City of Ladies* (1404–1405), in which she constructed an allegorical city that protects women from a longstanding misogynist tradition and gives them back their rightful place in history (Blumenfeld-Kosinski 1990). The 1982 translation into English of this important text made Christine's ideas available to a wide public (de Pizan 1982).[2] But before the later part of the twentieth century Christine was more often cited as a political writer; in fact, the first book-length study devoted to her by Raymond Thomassy in 1838 was focused on her political writings (Thomassy 1838). The rediscovery of Christine as a feminist thinker in the 1980s was conditioned by the rapid development of feminist theory and women's studies programs that tried to unearth foremothers who had helped pave the way for modern efforts to give women true equality in society and to do justice to their important roles in history.

What then are the ideas that make Christine de Pizan a feminist *avant la lettre*? One of the most important is her utter confidence that women can do just about anything men can do, and sometimes better than men. A crucial point Christine made repeatedly was that women need to be given access to education:

If it were customary to send daughters to school like sons, and if they were then taught the natural sciences, they would learn as thoroughly and understand the subtleties of all the arts and sciences as well as sons. And by chance there happen to be such women, for just as women have more delicate bodies than men, weaker and less able to perform many tasks, so do they have minds that are freer and sharper whenever they apply themselves.

(1982, 63)

Thus Christine recognized women's physical limitations but did not see them as negative; rather their "lighter" bodies sharpen women's minds! Christine also put a personal reminiscence into the mouth of one of the allegorical ladies who helps her build the city:

> Your father, who was a great scientist and philosopher, did not believe that women were worth less by knowing science; rather, as you know, he took great pleasure from seeing your inclination to learning. The feminine opinion of your mother, however, who wanted to keep you busy with spinning and silly girlishness, following the common custom of women, was the major obstacle to your being more involved in the sciences.
>
> (1982, 154–55)

This is a loaded passage since she blamed her mother as well as the "common custom of women" for perpetuating female ignorance. Thus the struggle to have women progress and be recognized for their true worth faces multiple hurdles: a strong male political, social, and literary tradition that excludes women from positions of power, the professions and the universities; and the omnipresence of texts that malign and slander women. At the same time women have bought into these habits and prejudices, as the example of her mother shows. It is therefore on multiple fronts that Christine must wage her battle.

In the political realm women are just as capable as men, as Christine proved through the many examples of female rulers and military leaders that reside in the *City of Ladies*. In the sequel to that text, the didactic *Book of the Three Virtues* (1405), Christine fleshed out her historical examples with advice for contemporary women who, during their husbands' absences or because they were widowed, had to take over positions of leadership (de Pizan 2003). 1405 also marked the moment when Christine became more actively engaged in politics herself. In her *Letter to the Queen of France* Christine strove to shore up Isabeau of Bavaria's claim to become regent of France while her husband suffered from his fits of insanity (de Pizan 1984; Adams 2014, 113–18). Queen Isabeau occupied a special position in Christine's thoughts. Before her urgent appeal to the queen to work for peace in France in her 1405 letter, Christine had, three years earlier, offered her a manuscript in which she had collected documents relating to the famous quarrel over the *Roman de la Rose* (de Lorris and de Meun, 1995). This thirteenth-century love allegory, championed by some of Christine's male contemporaries, was condemned as immoral by her and by her important ally Jean Gerson (1363–1429), chancellor of the University of Paris (de Pizan 2010). The strategic move of including only some of these documents and framing them with a letter to the queen marked her public entry into the intellectual world of late medieval Paris. She consolidated her devotion to and support of Queen Isabeau with the famous manuscript Harley 4431 (1410), now in the British Library, whose arrangement of texts and gorgeous illustrations, all written and supervised by Christine herself, makes an argument for female leadership and piety (Walters 2016),[3] thus refuting two of the widespread misogynistic commonplaces that denied women's political abilities and accused them of a lack of morals and religious devotion.

The second front of her battle, women's education, was one of the major themes of the *City of Ladies* and of the *Book of the Three Virtues*. The third, a strong textual tradition of misogyny in the form of slander and defamation of women's moral character, was a theme wending its way through many of her works, from her early lyrical love poetry to later prose texts like the *City of Ladies* which ends with a cri de coeur: "My ladies, see how these men accuse you of so many vices in everything. Make liars of them all by showing forth your virtue, and prove their attacks wrong by acting well … Flee, flee the foolish love they urge on you" (1982, 256). Christine was aware of the connection between women's behavior, their reputation, and the roles they were allowed to play in society. To uncover the true nature of women, their virtue as well as their capacity for learning and leadership, was one of Christine's primary missions. Another major goal was to bring peace to the warring factions in France and thus her later works moved away from feminist concerns to political advice she offers to rulers in such texts as *The Book of the Body Politic* (1407) and *The Book of Peace* (1412–1414). Only at the end of her life did the two major concerns of Christine, a role for women in history and the fate of France, converge: her last poem of 1429, *Le ditié de Jehanne d'Arc*, is in praise of Joan of Arc who at that point seemed to have saved France from the English. Joan's tragic fate postdated Christine's death.

In her own time Christine was highly regarded by a number of contemporaries. The famous poet Eustache Deschamps (1346–1407) addressed her as the "most eloquent of the Nine Muses" (de Pizan 1997, 112) and Jean Gerson recognized her as a learned woman. She also was greatly praised together with Joan of Arc in the fifteenth-century poem of Martin le Franc, *Le champion des dames* (*The Champion of Ladies*) (1440–1442). In the Renaissance and the Enlightenment Christine was often mentioned positively, though not primarily as a feminist thinker (McLeod 1991). And, as mentioned above, the first book-length study in 1838 centered on Christine's political thought.

Some modern scholars have criticized Christine for not being radical enough, for not advocating a society of total equality (Delany 1997). This view misreads Christine's time and her situation. The fact is that no other thinker, for centuries before or after her, raised the issues that are central for a feminist agenda: women's education, intellectual and professional equality, and access to leadership positions.

Notes

1 See Parts 1 of *The Book of Fortune's Transformation* and of *Christine's Vision.* Both excerpts are translated in Blumenfeld-Kosinski 1997 at 88–109 and 173–201 respectively. See Pizan 2005 for a full translation of *The Vision.*

2 Since the early 1980s the critical literature on Christine de Pizan has exploded, with hundreds of articles, and dozens of books and essay collections. There is a Christine de Pizan Society and regular international conferences devoted to her many works.

3 The website www.pizan.lib.ed.ac.uk offers digitalization as well as studies and links concerning Harley 4431.

Christine de Pizan's major writings

Note: Only English translations of Christine de Pizan's works are listed.

[1399] 1997. "The God of Love's Letter," trans. Kevin Brownlee in Renate Blumenfeld-Kosinski (ed.), *The Selected Writings of Christine de Pizan*, 15–29. New York: W. W. Norton.

[1404–1405] 1982. *The Book of the City of Ladies*, trans. Earl Jeffrey Richards. New York: Persea.

[1405] 2005. *Christine's Vision*, trans. Glenda McLeod and Charity Cannon Willard. Cambridge: D. S. Brewer.

[1405] 2003. *The Treasure of the City of Ladies or The Book of the Three Virtues*, trans. Sarah Lawson. London: Penguin.

[1407] 1994. *The Book of the Body Politic*, trans. Kate Langdon Forhan. Cambridge: Cambridge University Press.

[1412–1414] 2008. *The Book of Peace*, ed. and trans. Karen Green, Constant J. Mews, and Janice Pinder. University Park: Penn State University Press.

[1418, 1405, 1410] 1984. *The Epistle of the Prison of Human Life with An Epistle to the Queen of France, and Lamentation on the Evils of Civil War*, ed. and trans. Josette A. Wisman. New York: Garland.

[1429] 1977. *Le ditié de Jehanne d'Arc*, ed. and trans. Angus J. Kennedy and Kenneth Varty. Oxford: Society for the Study of Medieval Languages and Literatures.

2010. *Debate of the "Romance of the Rose,"* ed. and trans. David F. Hult. Chicago: Chicago University Press.

Further reading

Adams, Tracy. 2014. *Christine de Pizan and the Fight for France.* University Park: Penn State University Press.

Altmann, Barbara K. and Deborah L. McGrady, eds. 2003. *Christine de Pizan: A Casebook.* New York: Routledge.

Blumenfeld-Kosinski, Renate. 1990. "Christine de Pizan and the Misogynistic Tradition." *Romanic Review* 81: 279–92.

—. (ed.) 1997. *The Selected Writings of Christine de Pizan,* trans. Renate Blumenfeld-Kosinski and Kevin Brownlee. New York: W. W. Norton.

—. 2003. "Christine de Pizan and the Political Life in Late Medieval France." In Barbara K. Altmann and Deborah L. McGrady (eds.), *Christine de Pizan: A Casebook,* 9–24. New York: Routledge.

Brown-Grant, Rosalind. 1999. *Christine de Pizan and the Moral Defence of Women: Reading beyond Gender.* Cambridge: Cambridge University Press.

Delany, Sheila. 1997. "'Mothers to think back through': Who Are They? The Ambiguous Example of Christine de Pizan." In Renate Blumenfeld-Kosinski (ed.), *The Selected Writings of Christine de Pizan,* 312–28. New York: W. W. Norton.

Le Franc, Martin. 1999. *Le champion des dames,* 5 vols., ed. Robert Deschaux. Paris: Champion.

Lorris, Guillaume de and Jean de Meun. 1995. *The Romance of the Rose,* trans. Charles Dahlberg. Third edition. Princeton, NJ: Princeton University Press.

Margolis, Nadia. 2011. *An Introduction to Christine de Pizan.* Gainesville: University Press of Florida. (On pp. 200–36 a bibliographical guide offers references to all editions and translations of Christine de Pizan's texts currently available as well as an extensive list of critical works.)

McLeod, Glenda (ed.). 1991. *The Reception of Christine de Pizan from the Fifteenth to the Nineteenth Centuries: Visitors to the City.* Lewiston, NY: Edwin Mellen Press.

Thomassy, Raymond. 1838. *Essai sur les écrits politiques de Christine de Pisan.* Paris: Debécourt.

Walters, Lori. Forthcoming 2016. "The Queen's Manuscript (London, BL, Harley 4431) as a Gift of Wisdom." *Digital Philology: A Journal of Medieval Cultures* 5.

ADRIENNE RICH (1929–2012)

Susan McCabe

Celebrated as one of the most influential poets of her generation, Adrienne Rich's almost century-long life made the slogan "the personal is political" into a sustaining mantra, emblematic of the way poetics and poetry connected to a wide social and political praxis. After winning the Yale Younger Series Award, judged by W. H. Auden, for *A Change of World* (1951) while finishing college at Radcliffe College, Rich was launched on a career that continuously challenged, centrally, patriarchy. She won many awards, including the Bollingen Prize in 2003, and the Griffin in 2010. She went on to publish twenty-five poetry collections (almost five a decade), while also setting the stage for feminist poetry through eight non-fiction volumes, seriously thinking through the repressive regime of male domination—a subject masked in prior poetry.

Although most well known and accomplished as a poet, her non-fiction, like her poetry, was relentless in its insistence on truth and demystifying gender inequalities. Some readers know Rich through her watershed study, *Of Woman Born: Motherhood as Experience and Institution* (1974), in which she dismantled patriarchy's omnipresent domination of women's reproductive life, addressing realities of rape, abortion, and an ambivalence about the very "institution" of motherhood; the book, she reflected, allowed her to birth herself. By using personal reflection with historical testimony and research, the book returned us all back to our mothers, to what she regarded as a threshold love experience. The Civil Rights Movement further shaped her writing and was shaped by it in the 1970s, a period when she widened her thinking, connecting feminist aims with a larger cultural awareness, one that highlighted local dynamics of oppression as they fed global expression.

Thus the scope of her career, like a widening eye, caught in its meshes the interdependency of race, class and gender, plunging further into the liberating human-scale aesthetic in *The Dream of a Common Language* (1978). *On Lies, Secrets, and Silence: Selected Prose 1966–1978* (1979) further elaborated ideas her poems fleshed out, calling for resistance to those forces that have diminished women's lives. This interchange between poetry and essays distinguished her as activist philosopher. By the 1990s, Rich was tapping into her Jewish roots, part of her sense of being an outsider. *An Atlas of the Difficult World* (1991) addressed the conflicts of post-Holocaust history as they haunt us as well as the wars that continue to be fought. In short, Rich's career embodied a legislator role: like the Romantic poet Percy Bysshe Shelley, her poetry acts as cultural conscience, foregrounding expression of what might otherwise be erased.

Rich's poems developed away from the "perfected" forms of her first book, such as the oft-anthologized poem, "Aunt Jennifer's Tigers": a dense impersonal conceit, it embodies a trapped marriage. Her subsequent poetry resisted this impersonality, inherited from the New Critics, who relied upon T. S. Eliot's near-fetishism for the Metaphysical poets, with his sense of their unity of intellect and emotion. Rich, however, managed to combine thought and emotion by exploring the sensual and difficult experiences women specifically faced, and continued to face. Inspired by the seventeenth century Metaphysical John Donne and his poem "Valediction Forbidding Mourning," converting its extended metaphor of a couple as two feet of a compass: while the male partner freely travels from the center (i.e. domesticity, "home"), the female partner makes it possible for him to complete his journey at the same centered point, her revisionary poem of the same title transforms the speaker's gender. She is bleeding on a bus—departing from Donne's symmetrical romance, the visceral, discordant image of "[a] red plant in a cemetery of plastic wreaths" upsets such power differentials, making "[a] last attempt: the language is a dialect called metaphor" ([1970] 1993, p. 44). In other words, c. 1970, when this poem appeared in *The Will to Change* (1971), Rich had begun to expose a metaphor's power to either destroy or to transform, leading to her masterpiece essay, "When We Dead Awaken," written as she puts it, while "the sleepwalkers are coming awake," an "exciting" time period that required "re-vision—the act of looking back, of seeing with fresh eyes, of entering an old text from a new critical direction" ([1971] 1993, p. 167). Such re-visioning, not an academic exercise, was "an act of survival," central to Rich's life-long project.

Rich's ideas gained more heat when paired with the embodied, subjective gambits of her poems; likewise, she altered the scope of women's non-fiction. We can think of pre-Rich poetry versus post-Rich—given her decisive impact on an entire generation emerging in her wake, through her words breaking the silence surrounding women's issues and sexuality so profoundly engulfing post-1950s America. In later essays, Rich described difficult beginnings: in search of a vocation, more than the technical poetic skill she had acquired. After all, she had herself followed convention, marrying in 1953 an economics professor at Harvard, Alfred Haskell Conrad, and with him, had three sons. As a wife and mother, she drew upon her experiences for

Snapshots of a Daughter-in-Law: Poems 1954–1962 (1963); met with dismissive reviews, it marked Rich as *the* exemplar feminist poet, a status consecrated in her critical writing. The title poem of *Snapshots* compiles a series of "snapshots," intercutting domestic frustrations ("Banging the coffee-pot into the sink / she hears the angels chiding," "her hand above the kettle's snout" in order to rout out lost sensation even through a burn) with assertions such as: "A thinking woman sleeps with monsters," an oft quoted line, a declarative that acknowledges women's subjectivity, its demons *and* angels ([1958] 1993, p. 9). The poem invokes Emily Dickinson's poem "My Life had stood—a Loaded Gun—"; she also quotes from male writers, excerpting for instance, from Samuel Johnson who, in positing women preachers as misguided, wrote *"Not that it is done well, but/that it is done at all?"* (1993, p. 12).

Whose voices are silenced? This question runs through Rich's writing. When she won the 1974 National Book Award (split with Allen Ginsberg) for *Diving into the Wreck* (1973), they accepted it with two other feminist nominees, Alice Walker and Audre Lorde, on behalf of voices that been repressed. During this tremendously volatile period for African Americans struggling to access civil rights, Rich held antiwar and Black Panther fundraisers, contributing to the breakdown of her marriage, and tragically, linked to her husband's suicide shortly after the pair's separation.

Given the vastness of Rich's ideas, it is helpful to track several major tenets in her "philosophy," regardless of timeline. First, her pledge was to "excavate" women's voices, hers an epic-scale resuscitation of lost historical figures (Marie Curie, Ethel Rosenberg, and numerous unknown housewives). In "Paula Becker to Clara Westhoff," an epistolary poem, Rich takes the voice of a posthumous Paula, who died in childbirth: "Marriage is lonelier than solitude" (1978, p. 42). Paula was married to Rainer Maria Rilke, who "feeds on" women: "His whole life, his art / is protected by women" (1978, p. 43). This last volume contained "Twenty-One Love Poems," honoring her new partner in love and politics, Jamaican-born novelist Michelle Cliff. Along with the female-to-female eroticism the sequence revealed, one section acknowledged how "[o]nce open the books, you have to face / the underside of everything you've loved—," where "we still have to reckon with Swift / loathing the woman's flesh while praising her mind, / Goethe's dread of the Mothers, Claudel vilifying Gide" (1978, p. 27). This "underside" of literary precedents offered a foundation for re-imagining a world not governed by violent misogynistic imagery.

"Diving into the Wreck," the title poem of a volume published in 1973, posed an androgyny of "merman" with "mermaid," yet her double-gendered diver discovers traces of a lost matriarchy; though fitted out like Jacques Cousteau, Rich's diver discovers a buried communal consciousness: "We are, I am, you are" returned "back to this scene" to discover "a book of myths / in which / our names do not appear" (1993, p. 55). This erasure spurs her debate over "power": her "Power," a poem pocked with spaces marking traces of digging up "the earth deposits of our history," spotlights Curie who "must have known she suffered from radiation sickness" though "she denied to the end" the paradox: "her wounds came from the same source as her power" (1978, p. 3). Ambivalent about Curie as heroic role model, Rich's version functions as incentive to find alternatives to male power, such as Lorde's same-named "Power" that rages over a white policeman shooting down an unarmed black boy.

Second to her tenet of excavation, Rich delineates a female sexuality that does it justice. She doesn't depart from lyricism, just switches its focus: instead of a male beloved, she addresses a same-sex beloved: "Your small hands, precisely equal to my own—"; in these hands, the lover "could trust the world, or in many hands like these" (1978, p. 28). Passionate *and* philosophical, Rich broke from the silence that shut down articulation of queer identities—and pioneered the first overtly *lesbian* same-sex suite of love poems (since Sappho!). "THE FLOATING POEM, UNNUMBERED" (among the "Twenty-One Love Poems" in *Dream*) boldly incants: "Your traveled, generous thighs / between which my whole face has come and come—" (1978, p. 32).

Rich's most classical essay, following "Re-Vision," remains "Compulsory Heterosexuality and Lesbian Existence," which undoes the clinical ring of "lesbian":

> as we deepen and broaden the range of what we define as lesbian existence, as we delineate a lesbian continuum, we begin to discover the erotic in female terms: as that which is unconfined to any single part of the body or solely to the body itself.
>
> ([1980] 1993, p. 217)

The essay posed the question that if women were the first sources of emotional caretaking, what motivated a deviation from this primal sustenance? In essence, Rich tackled psychoanalytic homilies of opposite-sex attraction as destined, opening up possibilities for multiple gender identifications. Eros, key to Rich's poetics, energizes the most vital "thinking." Further, for Rich, love was work and free choice, not a result of fate or destiny.

Building then on Rich's method of excavation and truth-telling eroticism, she sought an ethics of connectivity. *The Dream of a Common Language* linked her to a poetic past, following Wordsworth, Whitman, even Eliot, in their claims that poetry must remain tuned to the language of one's time. Yet Rich performs a miraculous doubling: she both enters the male canon through her lyricism, and rejects it through her insistent inclusion of the often maligned topics of same-sex affection, geopolitical fall-out, breast cancer (to name a few): a world-view, in other words, that announces itself as committed to the inadmissible "common." "Transcendental Etude," the last poem in *Dream of a Common Language*, invokes Wordsworth's "Ode to Immortality," for here, instead of the child begetting its father, a woman's singing evokes the pain of losing that primal contact: "Everything else is too soon, / too sudden, the wrenching–apart, that woman's heartbeat / heard ever after from a distance"; after generous white space, she announces "a whole new poetry beginning here," beyond the "striving for greatness, brilliance" (1978, pp. 76–77). This meditative piece conceives of poetry as constantly evolving, linked to an apparitional mother-muse who listens in the dark to the stories she *must* tell. Rich's poems are both radical and forgiving of the "human," knowing "that creatures must find each other for bodily comfort," stating unequivocally, "without tenderness, we are in hell" (1978, p. 30). This world-view of beauty and truth still functions as part of a "dream," one we seem closer to achieving, in part due to the poetic philosophy, philosophical poetry of Adrienne Rich.

Rich's major writings

1963. *Snapshots of a Daughter-in-Law*. New York: W. W. Norton.

1973. *Diving into the Wreck*. New York: W. W. Norton.

1974. *Of Woman Born: Motherhood as Experience and Institution*. New York: W. W. Norton.

1978. *The Dream of a Common Language 1974–1977*. New York: W. W. Norton.

1979. *On Lies, Secrets, and Silence: Selected Prose 1966–1978*. New York: W. W. Norton.

1993. *Adrienne Rich's Poetry and Prose: Poems, Prose, Reviews and Criticism*. New York: W. W. Norton.

1993b. *What is Found There: Notebooks on Poetry and Politics*. New York: W. W. Norton.

2013. *Later Poems: Selected and New*. New York: W. W. Norton.

Further reading

Dickie, Margaret. 1997. *Stein, Bishop and Rich: Lyrics of Love, War and Place*. Chapel Hill: University of North Carolina Press.

Gelpi, Albert. 2015. *American Poetry after Modernism: The Power of the Word*. Cambridge: Cambridge University Press.

Kalstone, David. 1977. *Five Temperaments: Elizabeth Bishop, Robert Lowell, James Merrill, Adrienne Rich, John Ashbery*. New York: Oxford University Press.

Templeton, Alice. 1994. *The Dream and the Dialogue: Adrienne Rich's Feminist Poetics*. Knoxville: University of Tennessee Press.

NAWAL EL SAADAWI (1931–)

Amal Amirah

Nawal El Saadawi has been the foremost Arab feminist thinker for the past fifty years. Her ideas have inspired generations of Arab women but have also provoked controversy and criticism. She has been prolific, publishing over fifty fiction and nonfiction books in Arabic, many of which have been translated into several languages and have received much attention, particularly in England and the United States where she has been called the "Simone de Beauvoir of Egypt" (2011). Focusing on sex, politics, and religion, El Saadawi articulates critiques of multiple systems of oppression. According to her, patriarchy, capitalism, and imperialism intertwine to exploit Arab women and to prevent them from reaching their full human potential. The trajectory of El Saadawi's intellectual life follows major developments in Arab society and culture from the 1940s to the present; to understand her contribution, it is important to see her in the context of the historical moment that made her work possible, necessary, and provocative.

El Saadawi was born in 1931, in the village of Kafr Tahla, near Cairo, into a middle-class family. The second of nine children, she came of age at the cusp of key changes, foremost among them the drive for girls' education pioneered in Egypt by an earlier generation of women activists. El Saadawi, in fact, attended a school established by Nabawyya Mousa, an activist for women's education. Supported by a father who believed in the importance of education for social mobility, El Saadawi later attended the British school. Her academic excellence allowed her to evade early marriage and to receive a scholarship to study medicine at the University of Cairo, graduating in 1955 with a specialization in psychiatry. During her tenure at university, she was exposed to nationalist, anti-colonialist politics. She participated in student demonstrations against the British and married a fellow activist who joined fighters defending Suez against colonial aggression. They had a daughter together but eventually divorced. However, anti-colonialism and anti-imperialism continued to be important components of El Saadawi's thought and activism. El Saadawi's second marriage was short lived; she asked for a divorce after her husband stipulated that she stop writing. Her third marriage to Sherif Hetata, a novelist and former political prisoner, lasted over 40 years but has also ended in divorce. She has a son from this marriage.

Upon graduation from medical school, El Saadawi returned to her village. As a physician working in the countryside, she was exposed to class and gender inequities that further helped shape her thinking. She witnessed firsthand the injurious consequences of entrenched patriarchal practices such as female genital cutting and defloration that were inflicted on the bodies of poor village women. She details some of her experiences in her book *Memoirs of a Woman Doctor* (1958). In 1963, she was appointed the director general for public health education. In that capacity, she was able to travel outside Egypt to participate in international forums and conferences. These travels, which she documents in her book *My Travels around the World* (1986), gave her an international and comparative perspective regarding the struggles of other women. She will always assert that patriarchy is a universal system of oppression and is not only restricted to Arab or Muslim societies. Thus while she does not hesitate to call female genital cutting "barbaric," she resists its sensationalization in the West as a mark of difference between first world and third world women and insists that all women are circumcised if not physically then "psychologically and educationally" (1980b, 177). Similarly, she rejects the idea that western women are needed to help liberate their Arab or African sisters—an idea she finds condescending and deleterious to true global feminist solidarity.

But it was the Arab defeat by Israel in the 1967 Six-Day War that pushed El Saadawi to a more radical public position regarding gender. This crushing military defeat created a crisis for Arab intellectuals generally, including El Saadawi, who felt the need to take a surgical look at their societies. El Saadawi believes that patriarchy and gender inequalities are root causes for Arab defeatism. It is not a coincidence that she rose to fame in the 1970s with a series of books that put her on the map as the foremost Arab feminist of her generation. *Woman and Sex* (1971) was the first of her feminist manifestos. In it, she condemned the violence committed against women's bodies including virginity tests, honor killings, wedding night defloration, and female genital cutting. She exposed her society's ignorance and double standards regarding women's bodies and sexuality. Her first chapter, for instance, was focused on the clitoris and its importance for women's sexual pleasure. She also challenged some sacrosanct social beliefs such as the traditional concepts of honor, virginity, romance, and marriage, arguing, for instance, that exploitative marriages are no different from prostitution. She used her medical knowledge to argue that the differences between the sexes are not natural but are socially constructed by patriarchal practices and therefore can be changed through legislation and education. However, she insisted that the liberation of women and the achievement of gender justice will not be possible under a capitalist society. Only socialism will grant women true equality and human dignity. Soon after this publication, she lost her job, and the magazine she had founded three years previously was closed down. But the positive reception of her work among the public encouraged her to publish other polemics and in multiple editions including *The Female is the Origin* (1974), *Woman and Psychological Struggle* (1976a), *Man and Sex* (1976b) and *The Hidden Face of Eve* (1977). In all of these books, she combined anecdotes of patients she treated, her biography, medical and social research, and polemic against gender injustice. She spoke with the authority of a physician, the knowledge of an intellectual, and the passion of an injured woman.

El Saadawi also used fiction to express many of her ideas regarding sex and society. Her first novel to attract attention is *Woman at Point Zero* (1975). Her main character, working class Firdaus, experiences sexual exploitation and assault and eventually is executed by the state for killing her pimp. Through Firdaus, El Saadawi indicts the violence of class, patriarchy, and the state. In *Two Women in One* (1968), El Saadawi exposes the double standards of society regarding female sexuality, a double standard that leads the main character to neurosis and schizophrenia. These novels are significant contributions to the Arab feminist novel and express fictionally the ideas El Saadawi presented in her other non-fictional works. But while El Saadawi views herself first and foremost as a novelist, her novels have been received less enthusiastically than her other work. They are criticized for being repetitive in theme, style, and structure, and her female characters are dismissed as one-dimensional mouthpieces of their author's ideology.

The creativity of fiction allowed El Saadawi a space to critique another taboo in Arab society—religion. While El Saadawi's earlier work was a product of the secular turn in Arab public life, and as such did not engage religion in any significant way, her later work, particularly her novels, were written in response to a religious backlash in public life in Egypt and beyond. In *The Fall of the Imam* (1987), for instance, she condemns the patriarchal regime of President Sadat for its use of the authority of religion to shore up political legitimacy and to marginalize leftist dissidents. The novel was banned by Al Azhar, the highest religious authority in Egypt, thus further convincing El Saadawi of the complicity of religious institutions with the autocratic state. She deals with the same theme of complicity of religion in oppression in *God Dies by the Nile* (1985). In both novels, the El Saadawian heroine kills the male authority figures who assume the language and legitimacy of religion to oppress them. In *The Innocence of the Devil* (1994), El Saadawi goes further: she makes God and the Devil into characters in a mental asylum and directly indicts both Islam and Christianity as oppressive of women. El Saadawi's critique of religion and its reactionary political uses made her an easy target for fundamentalists in Egypt who issued death threats against her. El Saadawi's hostility to political Islam is rooted in this personal experience of censorship and threats.

But aside from death threats, El Saadawi's critiques of religion alienated her from two kinds of readers: self-identified Muslims and liberal western academics. Because she was writing at a time religion was playing a more prominent role in public life in Egypt, a broad range of her compatriots found her views too radical and offensive. A case in point is her views on the veil. Writing in response to the widespread adoption of the veil by Egyptian women of all social classes, El Saadawi declared this new expression of religiosity a step backward for women and saw it as another manifestation of gender oppression. This view did not sit well with liberal academics who in the post-9/11 atmosphere of Islamophobia found that critiquing Islam head on is politically charged. In this period, Islamic feminism, as represented by Leila Ahmed, Amina Wadud, and Asmaa Barlas, expressed a more accommodating view of religion and feminism. In this political and intellectual climate, El Saadawi's secularism seemed out of place.

El Saadawi's uncompromising secularism is paralleled by her unwavering hostility to political oppression. She prides herself on never becoming a "state intellectual." For her dissent, she paid a price. In 1981 she was arrested by the Sadat regime and thrown into jail along with a thousand intellectuals who opposed the Camp David peace treaty between Egypt and Israel. In prison, she wrote her memoirs using an eye pencil smuggled to her by a sex worker on toilet paper given to her by a murderer. *Memoirs from the Women's Prison* (1983) details her three-month experience as a political prisoner. After her release, she formed The Arab Woman Solidarity Association (AWSA), but it was closed down by the Mubarak government in 1991 for its opposition to the Iraq War and for its criticism of her government's complicity in that war. Never wavering in her opposition to the government, she ran against Mubarak in the presidential elections of 2004. During the uprising that deposed Mubarak in 2011, El Saadawi, in her eighties, held seminars in tents in Tahrir Square to radicalize a new generation of Egyptian men and women.

El Saadawi's major writings

[1958] 1988a. *Memoirs of a Woman Doctor.* Trans. Catherine Cobham. London: Saqi. Reprint, San Francisco: City Lights, 1989.

[1968] 1985a. *Two Women in One.* Trans. Osman Nusairi and Jana Gough. London: Saqi.

1971. *Al-Mar'ah wal-jins.* Cairo: el-Shaab.

1974. *Al-Untha hiya al-asl.* Cairo: Maktabat Madbuli.

[1975] 1983. *Woman at Point Zero.* London: Zed.

1976a. *Al-Mar'ah wal-sira' al-nafsi.* Beirut: al-Mu'assasa al-'Arabiyah lil-Dirasat wal-Nashr.

1976b. *Al-Rajul wal-jins.* Beirut: al-Mu'assasa al-'Arabiyah lil-Dirasat wal-Nashr.

[1977] 1980a. *The Hidden Face of Eve: Women in the Arab World.* London: Zed.

[1979] 1987a. *She Has No Place in Paradise.* Trans. Shirley Eber. London: Methuen.

1980b. "Arab Women and Western Feminism: An Interview with Nawal El Saadawi." *Race and Class* 22(2):175–82.

[1983] 1987b. *Death of an Ex-Minister.* Trans. Shirley Eber. London: Methuen.

[1983] 1986. *Memoirs from the Women's Prison.* London: Women's Press. Reprint Berkeley: University of California Press, 1994.

1985b. *God Dies by the Nile.* Trans. Sherif Hetata. London: Zed.

[1986] 1991. *My Travels around the World.* Trans. Shirley Eber. London: Methuen.

[1987] 1988b. *The Fall of the Imam.* Trans. Sherif Hetata. London: Methuen.

[1993] 2013. *Love in the Kingdom of Oil.* London: Saqi.

1994. *The Innocence of the Devil.* Trans. Sherif Hetata. Berkeley: University of California Press.

1997. *The Nawal El Saadawi Reader.* London: Zed.

1999. *A Daughter of Isis: The Autobiography of Nawal El Saadawi*. London: Zed.

2002. *Walking through Fire: A Life of Nawal El Saadawi*. London: Zed.

[2004] 2008. *The Novel*. Trans. Omnia Amin and Rick London. Northampton, MA: Interlink.

[2009] 2011. *Zeina*. Trans. Amira Nowaira. London: Saqi.

2013. *The Essential Nawal El Saadawi: A Reader*. Ed. Adele Newson-Horst. London: Zed.

Further reading

Amireh, Amal. 2000. "Framing Nawal El Saadawi: Arab Feminism in a Transnational World." *Signs* 26(1): 215–49.

Emenyonu, Ernest and Maureen N. Eke, eds. 2010. *Emerging Critical Perspectives on Nawal El Saadawi*. Trenton, NJ: Africa World Press.

Hafez, Sabry. 1989. "Intentions and Realization in the Narratives of Nawal El-Saadawi." *Third World Quarterly* 11(3):188–99.

Hitchcock, Peter. 1993. "Firdaus; or, The Politics of Positioning." In *Dialogics of the Oppressed*, 25–52. Minneapolis: University of Minnesota Press.

Malti-Douglas, Fedwa. 1995. *Men, Women, and God(s): Nawal El Saadawi and Arab Feminist Poetics*. Berkeley: University of California Press.

Mitra, Madhuchhanda. 1995. "Angry Eyes and Closed Lips: Forces of Revolution in Nawal el Saadawi's God Dies by the Nile." In *Violence, Silence, and Anger: Women's Writing as Transgression*, ed. Deirdre Lashgari, 147–57. Charlottesville: University Press of Virginia.

Sussman, Anna Louie. 2011. "An Interview with Nawal El Saadawi." *The Nation*, March 21. www.thenation.com/article/interview-nawal-el-saadawi/

SAPPHO (c. 630–570 BCE)

Victoria Wohl

Someone will remember us / I say / even in another time

Sappho fr. 147[1]

In this fragment, Sappho accurately predicts her extraordinary status in Western history. Celebrated already in antiquity as the "tenth muse," Sappho is the only female author from ancient Greece whose work has survived in substantial, though highly fragmentary, form. Her singular status makes her a seminal figure for the history of both Western literature and feminist thought. Sappho herself seems to anticipate this unique position, for her poetry is concerned, centrally and self-consciously, with the construction of a female poetic and erotic subjectivity.

Sappho lived in Mytilene, on the island of Lesbos, at the end of the seventh century BCE. Mytilene at this time was a cosmopolitan place, a center of cultural exchange between Greece and the wealthy, sophisticated cities of Asia Minor. This cultural milieu is reflected in Sappho's aesthetic of *poikilia* (intricacy, subtlety) and the beautiful luxury objects that fill her poems. One fragment laments that there will be no "spangled (*poikilan*) headbinder" for her daughter (fr. 98b); the fragment's allusion to exile suggests that Sappho's family was involved in the intra-elite conflict that roiled Lesbos and features prominently in the poetry of Sappho's contemporary Alcaeus. It is typical of Sappho that this political turmoil is mentioned for its impact on her material world and personal relationships with other women.

These relationships are at the heart of Sappho's poetry, much of which describes scenes of intimacy and shared pleasure between women; but the social realities behind them remain obscure. Sappho is no longer imagined as a Victorian schoolmarm (Parker 1993; Stehle 1997, Ch. 6), but we don't know the nature of the elite circle of women of (and probably for) whom she wrote. Some fragments describe women leaving the group, perhaps to marry, so many scholars assume this homosocial sorority was preliminary to, if not preparatory for, married life. Maximus of Tyre in the second century CE compared Sappho with her circle of young beloveds to Socrates and his (Oration 18.9). But as we shall see, there were significant differences between Sapphic homosociality and Platonic, and we should be wary of assimilating Sappho to masculine models of desire or sociality.

Indeed, Sappho herself insists on the difference. Fragment 16 begins: "Some men say an army of horse and some men say an army on foot / and some men say an army of ships is the most beautiful thing / on the black earth. But I say it is / what you love." Sappho uses the traditional priamel form to highlight her own subject position, with the emphatic "But I say" (*egō de*). This position is set against masculine military preoccupations in general and the Homeric tradition in particular, both of which Sappho reads with what Jack Winkler (1981) terms "double consciousness," a gendered "bilingualism" that let Sappho speak the language of the dominant masculine culture while also acknowledging her alienation, as a woman, from it. The example Sappho offers of "what you love" is the *Iliad*'s Helen of Troy. In Greek tradition, Helen figures primarily as a fought-over object; to the extent that she is allowed subjectivity it is to blame her for adultery and the war fought in her name (e.g. Alcaeus fr. 42). But Sappho reimagines Helen's story: instead of offering her as an example of "the most beautiful thing on the black earth"—an object of desire—she presents Helen as a desiring subject, who left husband, children, and parents for her beloved Paris. Even as she evokes the misogynist tradition that vilified Helen, the poet identifies with her in her desire, as she herself thinks about "Anaktoria who is gone," and whose "lovely step / and the motion of light on her face" she would rather see "than chariots of Lydians or ranks of footsoldiers in arms."

Setting herself against traditional masculine values, the poet articulates not just her personal desire but an entire alternate ethics. Thus Page Du Bois (1995) reads fr. 16 as proto-philosophy. Sappho's definition of "the good" as what one loves anticipates the theoretization of eros in Plato's *Symposium*. But her insistence on the specificity of desire resists Plato's move toward the metaphysical, a move enabled (as Luce Irigaray argued) by the exclusion of feminine difference. Sappho insists upon both difference (the supreme value for each individual of what she or he loves) and the feminine (her own erotic subjectivity and Helen's). Prioritizing "the motion of light on [Anaktoria's] face" above the homogenizing light of Plato's paternal Sun, Sappho challenges Platonic ontology *avant la lettre*. Her fragments construct their own ontology, rooted in a sensual—physical and erotic—experience of the world.

This sensual ontology highlights the subject of sensation. The lyric poets of Archaic Greece are often credited with defining a new notion of the self. In Sappho that new self emerges as the subject of both desire and song. Fragment 1, for instance, is a dialogue between a poet named "Sappho" and the goddess Aphrodite. Again, as in fr. 16, Sappho uses the Homeric tradition to define her own voice. The poem begins with an apostrophe to the goddess of love that recalls the Homeric hero's battlefield invocation of his protecting deity. Sappho takes the roles of both hero—here a frustrated lover—and goddess, and constructs her poetic voice through the playful dialogue between the two. The poem is structured by a tension between past and present. The present scenario depicts the epiphanic power of the poet's desire: her passion bridges the distance to Olympus and makes Aphrodite appear. But Aphrodite's teasing questions of the poet—"what (now again) I have suffered and why / (now again) I am calling out"—suggest she has heard this prayer before, and thus cast an ironic light on the very desire that called the goddess into being. "Sappho" appears at this intersection between erotic urgency and poetic irony. "Who wrongs you, Sappho?"

asks the goddess. The poet is first named by an Aphrodite conjured by her own desire and made present through her poetry.

Poetic authority and erotic subjectivity emerge together for Sappho, both inextricable and in tension. Consider fr. 31. "He seems to me equal to the gods that man / whoever he is who opposite you / sits and listens close / to your sweet speaking / and lovely laughing." This poem, like fr. 16, defines the poet's desire in contrast to a generic masculine perspective. It goes on to catalogue its physical effects on her: ears rushing and eyes dimmed; cold sweat and "thin fire … racing under skin." The poem presents itself as unmediated mimesis of the sensation of desire, and the subject seems to fade behind her humming, burning body parts. There is no defiant *egō* here, as there is in fr. 16. Rather, the self emerges in the tension between this overwhelming experience and the exquisitely controlled verses that describe it, a tension Sappho highlights with irony: "no speaking / is left in me / no: tongue breaks …."

The insistent corporeality of fr. 31 raises the question of how specifically female is Sappho's erotic sensibility and poetic voice. Is Sappho an early example of *écriture féminine*? Although the grammatical forms identify the speaker as female, the physical symptoms in fr. 31 are not gendered, and similar images occur in contemporary male poets. Sapphic eros may reflect literary convention more than a specifically female experience. That experience, moreover, may have been entirely different from our own (itself, of course, far from unitary), and we must avoid retrojecting modern assumptions onto ancient bodies and, especially, essentializing female sexuality as timeless and unchanging.

But the contrast to the anonymous man in fr. 31 encourages us to consider the feminine specificity of Sappho's poetry. Thus we might note that desire in Sappho is generally reciprocal and non-hierarchical, in sharp distinction to Greek heterosexuality (with its hierarchy of man over woman) and homosexuality (which distinguished between the older active partner and the younger passive partner). In Sappho age differences between partners are not marked, and the rare metaphors of domination and subordination come with the recognition that these roles are labile, as when Aphrodite in fr. 1 promises the heartsick poet that the woman who now flees her will soon pursue, "even unwilling." This promise remains unfulfilled: Sappho's erotic scenarios don't culminate in erotic conquest (Stehle 1981). Indeed, they are conspicuously non-teleological or "anti-climactic": characteristic metaphors of sexual satisfaction are the mingling of nectar in golden cups (fr. 2), anointing with fragrant oils (fr. 94), dew flowing and flowers blossoming under spreading moonlight (fr. 96). Such synesthetic pleasures suggest an erotics of plenitude. This plenitude is fleeting, though, and such moments are often framed by loss or separation. Fragments 94 and 96, for instance, reconnect separated lovers through the memory of shared intimacy, of "beautiful times we had" (fr. 94). Memory transforms past pleasure into present desire, eternalized through song as remedy against a longing that "bites [the lover's] tender mind" (fr. 96) and makes her yearn to die (fr. 94).

The separation figured in these poems may be a result of marriage: a number of Sapphic fragments seem to come from *epithalamia* (wedding songs). It is tempting to contrast their rich homoerotic sensuality to marital heterosexuality, in which the bride is "like the hyacinth in the mountains that shepherd men / with their feet trample down" (fr. 105b). Marriage was an inevitable moment in a Greek woman's life (fr. 104, 114), and in later Greece, at least, represented the end of her (erotic) subjectivity. Yet if desire lives on through memory and poetry, as fr. 94 and 96 suggest, then the sexual subjectivity evoked by Sappho does not evanesce with the woman's entry into the patriarchal structures of kinship. Instead it persists within them as something men can glimpse but never grasp, like the "sweetapple" Sappho describes in another epithalamic fragment, that "reddens on a high branch / high on the highest branch and the applepickers forget − / no, not forgot: were unable to reach" (fr. 105a). Anticipating modern thinkers like Irigaray, Kristeva, and Cixous, this poignant fragment suggests that female subjectivity is never fully representable within the male symbolic order. The apple figures the experiential distance between men and women (then and perhaps still now) and the desire that seeks to bridge that divide. A fragmentary trace of a lost female experience, it also figures the modern reader's distance from and desire for Sappho, as it both invites and eludes our imaginative reach.

Note

1 Fragments are numbered following Voigt 1971. All translations are from Carson 2002. The fragments mostly come down to us on scraps of papyrus or quoted by later authors for their formal qualities or unusual diction. New fragments are still being unearthed, including a virtually complete poem on old age, discovered in 2004, and another, addressed to Sappho's brothers, published last year.

Further reading

Carson, A. 1986. *Eros the Bittersweet*. Princeton, NJ: Princeton University Press.

—. 2002. *If Not, Winter: Fragments of Sappho*. New York: Vintage.

Du Bois, P. 1995. *Sappho is Burning*. Chicago: University of Chicago Press.

Greene, E., ed. 1996a. *Reading Sappho: Contemporary Approaches*. Berkeley: University of California Press.

—. 1996b. *Re-Reading Sappho: Reception and Transmission*. Berkeley: University of California Press.

Parker, H. N. 1993. "Sappho Schoolmistress." *Transactions of the American Philological Association* 123: 309–51. [Reprinted in Greene 1996b.]

Prins, Y. 1999. *Victorian Sappho*. Princeton, NJ: Princeton University Press.

Raynor, D. J. 2014. *Sappho: A New Translation of the Complete Works*. Cambridge: Cambridge University Press.

Stehle [Stigers], E. 1981. "Sappho's Private World." In H. P. Foley, ed., *Reflections of Women in Antiquity*. New York and London: Gordon and Breach. 45–61.

—. 1990. "Sappho's Gaze: Fantasies of a Goddess and Young Man." *differences* 2: 88–125. [Reprinted in Greene 1996a.]

—. 1997. *Performance and Gender in Ancient Greece*. Princeton, NJ: Princeton University Press.

Voigt, E.-M. 1971. *Sappho et Alcaeus: Fragmenta*. Amsterdam: Athenaeum-Polak & Van Gennep.

Williamson, M. 1995. *Sappho's Immortal Daughters*. Cambridge, MA: Harvard University Press.

Winkler, J. J. 1981. "Gardens of Nymphs: Public and Private in Sappho's Lyrics." In H. P. Foley, ed., *Reflections of Women in Antiquity*. New York and London: Gordon and Breach. 63–90. [Reprinted in Greene 1996a.]

CINDY SHERMAN (1954–)

Charlotte Eyerman

Cindy Sherman is a titan of the contemporary art world, based on reputation, publications, exhibitions, and market evidence (Palmer 2015).[1] She is a woman and an artist, though does not tend to claim "feminist" as an identifier:

> As a woman artist, it's important to have a presence, to inspire other young women, and to discuss the disparity in the art world,

but personally I did not want to do it, perhaps as a relic of my upbringing. It's not shyness; I just didn't want to be bothered.

(Sherman 2015, 16)[2]

Her work, however, has addressed issues of gender, identity, and performance for forty years. Cindy Sherman's artistic practice raises key questions about how her photographs may be a form of feminist thinking: if not for the artist herself, then for those viewers for whom feminist thinking is a way of being in and understanding the world (Respini 2012, 13, 49), and of challenging normative notions of power, "femininity," and gendered positions.

While Sherman rather pointedly does not address matters of gender or feminism or gender identity in her words, her photographic output since the 1970s has been richly established on using different photographic media to interrogate identity in terms of gender, age, and social position as her core subject matter, most frequently employing herself as model. They are not, however, self-portraits, per se. Sherman expresses that while she employs herself in making photographs, she is not the subject. Rather, she creates characters and moments in a performative vein, and the camera is an accomplice in creating fictions, "one thing I've always known is that that camera lies" (Respini 2012, 23). As a contemporary artist, a woman artist, a "post-modern" artist—she has been labeled all of these things—Sherman empowers herself to draw upon the medium of photography and all of the tools and tricks and modes available to her to create her own worlds.

The creation of visual art as a form of feminist thinking is not limited to Cindy Sherman, or to photography as a medium, or even to women artists. In addition to her use of herself as primary subject, her investigation of femininity/ies and masculinity/ies and gender identity/ies as subject, her risk-taking approach to her work since her earliest days in the 1970s makes her a provocateur for and of gender politics. Sherman's various bodies of work index and reference art historical precedents that span centuries and cultures. Still, they related in direct and visceral ways to our own contemporary culture of late twentieth- and early twenty-first-century America: "From the very beginning, Sherman eschewed theory in favor of pop culture, film, television, and magazines—inspirations that remain at the heart of her work" (Respini 2012, 18).

Her first major body of work is the series "Untitled Film Stills," a project starting in 1977, following a series of untitled photographs in which she employed herself to take on various playful personae (1975–1976), and "A Play of Selves" (1976), which she made while still in college.[3] In a 1976 statement, Sherman addressed this pivotal choice:

I have been working with photography for about two years, at which point I decided to use the camera as means for exploring my experiences as a woman. My first attempts were with making up my face in order to become different characters which involved a total transformation of my personality. This grew into an involvement with transforming my whole body so that I could totally act out a given character ... Subsequently, this brought me to my present state of making characters with a multiplicity of purpose: stopped action and interaction.

(Stavitsky 2004, 29)

In Sherman's hands, the function of the photograph is to be a vessel for the creation of identity, which is always fluid, mutable, manipulable. As the curator of the 2012 Museum of Modern Art Cindy Sherman retrospective explains, enlisting Sherman's words to underscore the "madeness" and the fictional quality of her photographs:

For Sherman, performing for the camera was always undertaken in relation to the act of photographing: 'Once I'm set up, the camera starts clicking, then I just start to move and watch how I move in the mirror. It's not like I'm method acting or anything. I don't feel that I am that person ... I may be thinking about a certain story or situation, but I don't become her. There's this distance. The image in the mirror becomes her—the image the camera gets on film. And the one thing I've always known is that the camera lies.'

(Respini 2012, 23)

Indeed, visual art (particularly that vein of it that is representational, or seemingly so) is a vehicle for simulacra, imitation, verisimilitude. Sherman's photographs are intriguing, clever, mysterious, playful, ironic, deadpan, incisive. They are also capable of being disturbing, mocking, subversive, and mean. In her appropriation and transformations of genres, some of Sherman's photographs are intentionally disturbing, repellent even.

The range of subjects in her *oeuvre* from the 1970s to the present day includes female and male innocents and children or child-like characters; female and male bureaucrats, observers, seducers, subjects of fascination, objects of exploitation, victims, victors, trophies, pathetic specimens. In these provocative works, Sherman plays the whole keyboard: every role, age, gender. She hits all the notes: attractive, sympathetic, sad, pathetic, unattractive, powerful, vulnerable, oblivious, magnetizing.

The MoMA exhibition website provides a comprehensive compendium to explore Sherman's work.[4] In *Untitled Film Still #6*, 1977, a black-and-white photograph, Sherman plays the role of ingénue, as if from a movie. Scantily clad and gazing up dreamily as she reclines, coyly posed on a bed, mirror in hand, she invites our voyeuristic participation. Everything about her presentation of this "character" participates in conventional notions of femininity as passive, decorative, self-absorbed. She holds a mirror, an accouterment of vanity and self-regard, as well as a sly reference to self-portraiture in the history of art. For Sherman, the camera is the mirror and the canvas. Even though this work creates a narrative of normative, youthful femininity, presumably for the consumption of the male gaze, as the writer, director, cinematographer and actor in the scene, the vulnerability of the character is, ironically perhaps, an expression of Sherman's authority.

In the "Untitled Film Stills" and subsequent "Untitled" works, Sherman plays upon a panoply of archetypes and narratives. *Untitled #86*, 1981 seems to be a wan extension of the themes and narratives suggested by *#6* discussed above. Here, in a color photograph, the ingénue is dejected, depressed, possibly abused. This woman Sherman inhabits has dark hair, no make-up, and wears a t-shirt and shorts. Reclining but in an abject state, she is still the object of an interrogating gaze. However, the "come-hither" tones of the earlier work are displaced by an interiority that suggests withdrawal, fear, and resignation. She pushes this thematic further in *Untitled #140*, 1985, which echoes the composition of *#86*, but replaces the female character with a snout-nosed creature, shown in close-up with a bloodied and dirty face, and a cartoonish curly wig. Sherman's fearlessness comes through here, as she is willing to distort her features and push into confrontational terrain. The work from the late 1980s embraces this "anti-aesthetic" and sees Sherman employing prostheses and props to serve narratives of angst, ugliness, discomfort, even violence.

The experimentation with prosthetics led to a series that riffs on the conventions of historical portraiture in European painting, allowing Sherman to comment on the roots of the genre, with her particular flair for underscoring artifice. In many cases, she emulated (or aped) identifiable works by such canonical artists as Botticelli, Raphael, Caravaggio, Rubens, Boucher, Fragonard, David, Ingres, among others.[5] In *Untitled 201*, 1989, she plays the role of a male sitter, channeling modes of eighteenth- and nineteenth-century European, aristocratic self-satisfaction.

Sherman's feminism resides in her ability to access all these modalities of human emotional position and response as the maestro of the experience manifested in her photographs. In addition, Cindy Sherman owns Cindy Sherman's domain. She makes every creative decision, even when it is commercially counter-intuitive (Respini 2012, 44–47).[6] She is master and commander of—as well as the servant to—the project. The artist demonstrates insight and empathy as well as a critical distance—in the sense of both objectivity and a commitment to (sometimes uncomfortable) truth telling.

For forty years, Cindy Sherman has been in charge of her own show. As an artist and a businesswoman—and perhaps, herein lies the core of her feminism—she has experimented, evolved, provoked. Some of her work has been overtly, even crassly commercial (and yet, even then, she manages to be subversive), while in other modes both resolutely avant-garde and dialed into tradition. Her work is simultaneously consistent and inventive: deceptively mundane, seemingly banal, and sometimes shocking.

Sherman's singular approach is built into her inherently diverse body of work. We consider her a feminist thinker because she rejects labels, even that one. She is a woman, an artist, a maker of photographs, a participant in the art-world inflected rituals of high capitalism. As her viewers, we are in a dialogue with Sherman and the myriad narratives her photographs create.

For feminist thinkers, particularly those interested in visual art and photography, Cindy Sherman is an icon and a hero, for she is unapologetically and unrelentingly herself. She is a woman in charge and making photographs is the way that she expresses that power. The fact that powerful and wealthy collectors and museums chose to validate her authoritative position makes her status as a feminist thinker all the sweeter.

Notes

1 Sherman has been the subject of extensive publications (articles, books, exhibition catalogues), group, solo, and retrospective exhibitions, and was recently noted as #3 among living women artists in the art market. Sherman ranked #10 among living artists, one of two women, in August 2015.

2 Quoted in "Cindy Sherman Responds," *ARTNews*, June 2015. Her contribution was in response to an article in the previous issue, Maura Reilly, "Taking the Measure of Sexism: Facts, Figures, and Fixes," *ARTNews*, May, 2015.

3 Her earliest work is represented in the 2012 MoMA exhibition, and was the subject of a 2004 exhibition (see Stavitsky 2004). The best record of *A Play of Selves*, which was shown in Buffalo in 1976, her last year of college, is *Cindy Sherman: A Play of Selves* (Sherman 2007).

4 www.moma.org/interactives/exhibitions/2012/cindysherman/gallery/ chronology/
5 These works are presented in the MoMA exhibition and catalogue. For a focused reading of this series, see Döttinger 2012.
6 This series seems to parody patrons who purchase her works for enormous sums at galleries or auction houses. For a representative example, see *Untitled #476*, 2008.

Further reading

Döttinger, Christa. 2012. *Cindy Sherman: History Portraits/The Rebirth of the Painting after the End of Painting*. Translated by Daniel Mufson. Munich: Shirmer/Mosel. www.moma.org/interactives/exhibitions/2012/cindysherman/gallery/chronology/
Palmer, Laura. 2015. "Artnet News's Top 10 Most Expensive Living Women Artists 2015." *Artnet*, August 20.
Reilly, Maura, 2015. "Taking the Measure of Sexism: Facts, Figures, and Fixes," *ARTNews*, May. www.artnews.com/2015/05/26/taking-the-measure-of-www.artnews.com/2015/05/26/taking-the-measure-of-sexism-facts-figures-and-fixes/
Respini, Eva. 2012. "Will the Real Cindy Sherman Please Stand Up." In *Cindy Sherman*, 12–53. New York: Museum of Modern Art.
Sherman, Cindy. 2007. *Cindy Sherman: A Play of Selves*. Ostifildern: Hatje Cantz Verlag in collaboration with Metro Pictures, New York and Sprüth Magers, Cologne/Munich/London.
—. 2015. "Cindy Sherman Responds," *ARTNews*, June. www.artnews.com/2015/05/26/cindy-sherman-responds/
Stavitsky, Gail. 2004. *The Unseen Cindy Sherman: Early Transformations, 1975–1976*. Montclair: Montclair Art Museum.

GAYATRI CHAKRAVORTY SPIVAK (1942–)

Ritu Birla

As the Kyoto Prize in Arts and Philosophy celebrated, literary critic Gayatri Chakravorty Spivak, University Professor at Columbia, is a "critical theorist and educator speaking for the humanities against … colonialism in … the globalized world," a thinker who "exemplifies what intellectuals today should be."[1] Renowned for her English translation and indispensable introduction to Derrida's *Of Grammatology*, as a founding feminist force of postcolonial studies, and as a philosopher of globality forging theory and practice, Spivak resists autobiography. Her Kyoto Prize acceptance speech rejected any sole authorship or proprietorship of her life's work. "Who speaks when we speak?" she asked. "All our history speaks through us," though we can never fully chart it; as such, the prize "belongs to many others ... *more than I can tell.*"[2] Acknowledging the limits of narrativizing history as identity, these remarks underline Spivak's attention to what cannot be caught, conquered, codified: a grappling with the other—the peripheral, untranslatable, and even unknowable—as the ethico-political ground for justice. Deconstructive feminist and Marxist analysis exemplifies such inquiry and marks Spivak's exemplary critical moves.

In Spivak's thought, a commitment to the other cannot rest upon top-down benevolence, or any claims to the easy recovery and representation of subaltern subjects.[3] One must confront the double-bind of recognizing the other: practices of othering cannot be easily resolved by the giving of voice, a gesture too often conflated with the gift of agency. Processes of voice-giving always institutionalize a *politics of representation*, whether in the selective classification and documentation of the historical/empirical archive, or in the claims of sovereignty in the name of the people, or more specifically, the representative mechanics of democracy and the giving of the vote (furthering Derrida's reading of *la voix*, the French word for voice and vote—see Derrida 2009). Moreover representation, a process of abstraction, must be supplemented with attention to embodiment and inhabiting; Spivak does this through a critical feminist/Marxist approach to the body as text/ labor as episteme.

Responding thus to the question "who speaks when we speak?" Spivak uniquely charts *the disjuncture of subjectivity and agency*, deploying a deconstructive lever. How can we think democracy, equality and justice when we recognize that subjectivity and agency are not necessarily homologous; that speaking is not the same as being heard; that the philosophical Subject or "I" who wills and exercises Agency is different than the political subject, who is subjected to power and rendered its agent or instrument? A focus on the gendered exercise of power, in both the top-down as well as ostensibly bottom-up worlds of radical politics, structures these explorations.

From the influential "Can the Subaltern Speak" (Spivak 1988a) to the recent conceptualization of the "gendered epistemic body"[4] as counterpoint to the female target of developmentalist globalization, an attention to the *embodiment of social texts* has structured Spivak's readings of subjecthood and subjection, agency and instrumentality. Her revision of the historical study of *sati*—the statistically infrequent but highly visible subcontinental practice of immolating the widow on her husband's funeral pyre banned by the East India Company state in 1829—remains a powerful example of such analysis. Historical research demonstrated that while the imperial prohibition of sati challenged indigenous patriarchy, it foreclosed broader measures to support the livelihood of women and established the female body as ground for debates on "authentic" Indian tradition. Spivak pushed farther, theorizing that the banning of sati *staged a female subject who was exactly not her own agent*. Colonialism exposed a situation where "white men were saving brown women from brown men" (Spivak 1988a: 296). Here she exposed the *ventriloquizing of the subaltern*: the discursive production of the female subject fortified the agency of the colonial state and its exercise of benevolence from above. Her investigations of "the social text of sati-suicide" (1988a: 307) inform critical readings of (post)colonial globalization and the gendered staging of subjectivity and agency more broadly (Spivak 1999: 2012).

Since *A Critique of Postcolonial Reason* (Spivak 1999), which includes revisions of "Can the Subaltern Speak" and "The Rani of Sirmur: An Essay in Reading the Archives" (Spivak 1985), Spivak's recent work has clarified that the problem of speaking may be better understood as one of being heard (Spivak 2012; see Morris 2013: Introduction). This marks a shift from a cautious acceptance of the claiming of collective voice/identity for political justice—or what she called "strategic essentialism" (Spivak 1988c: 13)—to a critique of identity-politics and its politics of representation: its role as alibi for democratic practice and as symptom of a brand-making, capitalist globalization.

Still, a genealogy of the gendered, embodied question of being heard may begin with the key figure of "Can the Subaltern Speak"—Bhubaneshwari Bhaduri—a female ancestor of Spivak's entrusted with a political assassination in the Indian independence struggle. Her story, preserved by Spivak's mother and grandmother, tells of a woman who, unable to execute these orders, commits suicide by hanging herself while menstruating. Two generations later this political act is mistranslated as that of a woman who hung herself due to illicit pregnancy. Bhubaneshwari's agency (for independence but against her armed male compatriots) is lost, and the bodily writing of her subjectivity—her speech act—unheard.

These moves distinguishing subjectivity and agency open important investigations of identity, power and representation as a process of homogenizing abstraction. For example, Spivak warns that the transformative mapping of power and subject-effects that Foucault instigates can, in careless analysis, reduce Power into a universal historical Subject with Agency (Spivak 1999: 252–57). The subjectivity-agency disjuncture also informs an investigation of representation and its relationship to the concept of identity as the recognition of sameness. Here, a classic Spivakian reading exposes the double meaning of representation as political proxy (or speaking-for, as in the German *vertretung*) and as portrait (or re-presentation, as in the German *darstellung*) via Marx's analysis of the populist-authoritarian Louis Napoleon Bonaparte. This analysis illuminates Marx's mapping of a deferral between a political *speaking for* and an ethical *being the same as* the peasantry (Spivak 1999: 256–59), highlighting the space between as site of radical practice.

After *A Critique of Postcolonial Reason*, Spivak has further unpacked the concept of identity as sameness, and this as the ground for justice, through a careful investigation of globalizing discourses of democracy and development. Here she elaborates on iteration, or sameness-in-difference: every act of iteration is distinct, even as it repeats and performs sameness with what came before. Engaging the Derridian concept of *différance* that ties difference to the idea of deferral, and thus never resolvable into the self-same, Spivak vitalizes difference as an uncatchable outside that always already slips recognition, but that must nevertheless be understood. Embracing this dilemma, and launching political change accordingly, demands a consistent response to and from the other, a "response-ability" fueled by a rigorous practice of translation (Spivak 1999: 384).[5] This ethical responsibility works against a one-way doing good *to* others or making others in one's own image, the hallmark of civilizing missions (Spivak 2008).

Feminist analytics fuel the consistent supplementation of a politics of identity with an ethics of alterity that marks Spivak's thought. The female figure of her early work—the subject ventriloquized or whose agency is not acknowledged with subjectivity—opens questions for later analyses of global citizenship and political economy. Whose subjectivity is communicated, whose agency is activated in the benevolent dispensing of human rights or economic development? Attuned to gendered embodiment and its (mis)translation, Spivak reactivates Marx on capital as site for the social, and labor—intellectual and manual—as its medium.

Spivakian readings of international civil society and economic dogooding have thus offered a loving critique of the abstract, universal concept of the human built on the idea of self-sameness. Elaborating, Spivak has revitalized the pedagogy of *the humanities* and the role of literary: humanities training allows the imaginative inhabiting of other subject-positions, enabling a "learning from below" that asks us to listen in service of ethico-political responsibility. Such moves challenge the logic of development, which inserts "the subaltern into the circuit of capital, without the development of the subject of its ethical, or even appropriate social use" (Spivak 2014: 201). New capillaries of financialization harness subaltern agency for the global market with "insufficient attention to subject-formation" (Spivak 2015). Spivakian pedagogy thus cultivates "[h]umanities-style mind changing work" to "supplement statistical calculations as in the Human Development Index" (Spivak 2013).

Arguably the most potent site of the Spivakian text, to which Gayatri Chakravorty Spivak has personally committed over three decades of one-on-one teacher training amongst severely disenfranchised low caste and tribal groups, are the schools she has established in West Bengal, India. Elaborating a Gramscian commitment to education as critical awareness, they are experiments in response-ability and "learning from below." Their pedagogy challenges global habits of hegemony in which education for the subaltern means enforcing rote memory to reproduce social immobility and inequality. The schools sound the call of "other people's children," seizing the neoliberal biopolitics of childhood from below as a "weapon for democratic emancipation" (Spivak 2013). Remembering Marx's observation that "if everyone had rational judgment we would not need democracy," Spivak labors to produce "intuitions of democracy, above and below, rather than work in the acceptance of a world without it" (Spivak 2015).

Notes

1 www.kyotoprize.org/2012/en/28k-laureates-c.html
2 Ibid.
3 The Gramscian term "subaltern" marks those outside hegemony and is deployed by Subaltern Studies historians. For Spivak, "subaltern" refers to the outside/inside limits of hegemonic formations, marking a space with no access to institutional-political agency; subalternity is a position without identity. See Spivak 2012: 189, 431.
4 Spivak, personal communication, April 17, 2015.
5 These arguments on ethics and othering were initially informed by Irigaray's feminist critique of Levinas' *Totality and Infinity*, then fine-tuned via Levinas' *Otherwise than Being*: ethics "interrupts and postpones the epistemological—an undertaking to construct the other as object of knowledge, an undertaking never to be given up" (Spivak 2002: 17).

Spivak's major writings and works cited

1976. Translation and Introduction to Jacques Derrida, *Of Grammatology*. Revised translation and Afterword, 2016. Baltimore: Johns Hopkins University Press.

1985. "The Rani of Sirmur: An Essay in Reading the Archives." *History and Theory* 24(3): 247–72.

1988a. "Can the Subaltern Speak?" In *Marxism and the Interpretation of Culture*, edited by Carey Nelson and Lawrence Grossberg, 271–318. Urbana: University of Illinois Press.

1988b. *In Other Worlds: Essays in Cultural Politics.* New York: Routledge.

1988c. "Subaltern Studies: Deconstructing Historiography." In *Selected Subaltern Studies*, edited by Ranajit Guha and Gayatri Spivak, 3–34. Oxford: Oxford University Press.

1990. *The Post-Colonial Critic: Interviews, Strategies, Dialogues.* Edited by Sara Harasym. New York: Routledge.

1993. *Outside in the Teaching Machine.* New York: Routledge.

1999. *A Critique of Postcolonial Reason: Towards a History of the Vanishing Present.* Cambridge, MA: Harvard University Press.

2002. "Ethics and Politics in Tagore, Coetzee and Certain Scenes of Teaching." *Diacritics* 32(3–4): 17–31.

2003. *Death of a Discipline.* New York: Columbia University Press.

2008. *Other Asias.* London: Blackwell.

2012. *An Aesthetic Education in the Era of Globalization.* Cambridge, MA: Harvard University Press.

2013. "What Is It to Vote?" Manuscript of Lecture for Conference on Ida Blom. University of Bergen.

2014. "Crimes of Identity." In *Juliet Mitchell and the Lateral Axis*, edited by Robbie Duschinsky and Susan Walker, 207–28. New York: Palgrave Macmillan.

2015. "Housing the Body." Manuscript of Lecture for Panel on "Representation." Graduate School of Architecture, Planning and Preservation, Columbia University, New York.

Further reading

Abdalka, Ola. 2015. *Gayatri Spivak: Deconstruction and the Ethics of Postcolonial Literary Interpretation.* Cambridge: Cambridge Scholars Press.

Birla, Ritu. 2002. "History and the Critique of Postcolonial Reason: Limits, Secret, Value." *Interventions* 4(2): 175–86.

Derrida, Jacques. 2009. *La voix et le phenomène.* Paris: Press Universitaires de France.

Landry, Donna and Gerald M. MacLean. 1996. *The Spivak Reader: Selected Works.* New York: Routledge.

Morris, Rosalind, ed. 2013. *Can the Subaltern Speak: Reflections on the History of an Idea.* New York: Columbia University Press.

Sanders, Mark. 2006. *Spivak: Live Theory.* London: Continuum.

ELIZABETH CADY STANTON (1815–1902)

Andrea Foroughi

By the time that the Susan B. Anthony Amendment for women's suffrage was ratified in 1920, few American suffragists and feminists acknowledged that Elizabeth Cady Stanton had been the one to insist in 1848 that women had an "inalienable right to the elective franchise." The disavowal of Stanton as one of the most prominent voices in the nineteenth-century suffrage movement derives in large part from her refusal to focus solely on the vote as the means for women to achieve equality. Not only a suffragist, Stanton was a feminist. In her half-century of published works—speeches, articles, a newspaper, a history of the suffrage movement, a feminist interpretation of the Bible, and a memoir—Stanton explored the multiple sources of women's inequality in American political, legal, economic, educational, religious, and social life.

Born in Johnstown, New York in 1815, Elizabeth Cady grew up in a privileged household: her father was a lawyer, judge, and member of Congress, her mother descended from a prominent family, and an enslaved "manservant" watched over and cared for the Cady children (Kern 2001, 15, 22–29). In her memoir, Stanton describes a carefree childhood, but one overshadowed by loss. Of the eleven children born to the Cadys, only one son survived to the age of 20, while five daughters led long lives. Stanton provides several vignettes from her early years to highlight her awareness of female inequality: her father's devastation at her brother's death; her efforts to prove herself equally capable of the physical and educational accomplishments expected of boys; Judge Cady's failure to acknowledge her achievements and repeated wish that she had been a boy; her discovery that laws existed to prevent married women from owning property; and her recognition that the Bible and "every book taught the 'divinely ordained' headship of man, but my mind never yielded to this popular heresy" (Stanton 1993, 34).

As a young woman, Elizabeth Cady visited her cousin Gerrit Smith, an ardent abolitionist, at whose house she was exposed not only to abolitionist thought but also to discussions of temperance, and other social reforms. Elizabeth Cady gained more knowledge of reform causes when she married abolition lecturer Henry B. Stanton in 1840. This acquainted her with some of the abolitionist movement's key figures, particularly Lucretia Mott, whom Stanton met on her honeymoon at the World's Anti-Slavery Convention in London. Witnessing male abolitionists deny female delegates from anti-slavery societies speaking and voting privileges at the convention prompted Stanton to question how men who were committed to improving the plight of slaves would not do the same for "the equal wrongs of their own mothers, wives, and sisters, when, according to the common law, both classes occupied a similar state" (Stanton 1993, 79). Eight years later, Stanton articulated the "wrongs" against women in the Declaration of Sentiments in Seneca Falls, NY at the first women's rights convention.

Elizabeth Cady Stanton was not the first American female thinker to bring public attention to women's inequality or to point out the similarity between the legal status of enslaved people and women. Frances Wright, Sarah and Angelina Grimké, Margaret Fuller, and Lucy Stone all wrote and spoke publicly about inequalities women faced, doing so within the framework of existing reform movements, especially abolition, temperance, and transcendentalism. The Seneca Falls convention and Stanton's Declaration of Sentiments differ from these reformers' efforts because they established women's rights as a reform movement of its own with female suffrage as a stated goal (Davis 2008, 56–58; McMillen 2008, 71).

The Declaration of Independence served as a model for the Declaration of Sentiments, a calculated decision on the part of Stanton and her main collaborator, Elizabeth McClintock. By using the structure and phrasing from the Declaration of Independence, Stanton tapped into familiar natural rights rhetoric and America's revolutionary past, which seemed to legitimize the call for women's rights—"self-evident truths," "inalienable rights," "life, liberty, and the pursuit of happiness," listing "abuses and usurpations." However, the power that has exercised "absolute tyranny" is not the King but man (Davis 2008, 50–51). The sixteen grievances listed in the Declaration follow a repeated rhetorical pattern—"He has never," "He has denied her," "He has compelled her"—not only to follow the structure of the Declaration of Independence but also to emphasize the power differential between man and woman.

Man's "usurpations" against woman range widely: restricting access to education, professions, and positions of authority in the church and state; maintaining coverture laws preventing married women from owning property, having custody of their children, and divorcing. Moreover, single women who owned property faced taxation without representation, a familiar revolutionary-era grievance. Two charges sound hauntingly familiar today—man holds woman to a higher standard of morals and behaviors (i.e. the double standard) and man has undermined woman's self-confidence and independence.

The first grievance listed by Stanton, "He has never permitted her to exercise her inalienable right to the elective franchise," proved the most controversial for convention attendees as they discussed resolutions regarding the "repeated injuries" women face. It was the only resolution not passed unanimously. Stanton's insistence on women's suffrage departed from earlier women's rights thinkers and vexed some contemporary reformers who disavowed participation in politics. For Stanton, suffrage was a right of the individual, a right of citizenship that must be guaranteed to women and men alike (Gordon 2007, 112). More specifically, female suffrage would be the key to change laws that restrict women to a dependent position in society. However, as Lori D. Ginzberg explains, "her commitment to individual rights was never encompassed by the struggle to attain the vote for women" (2009, 64). She authored articles on dress reform, married women's property rights, and coeducation, among other topics, as well as wrote speeches for others, such as Susan B. Anthony, to deliver at conventions and meetings that she could not attend. This role suited Stanton's personal circumstances as the mother of seven children, born between 1842 and 1859, and wife of a frequently absent spouse.

Nevertheless, Stanton did speak in public on occasion. In May 1860, she addressed the New York state legislature to articulate a radical argument regarding divorce. She challenged marriage as a sacred union and instead framed it as a human contract with divorce as a necessary outcome should the marriage prove harmful to either party, but particularly to wives. Unlike most of her contemporaries, Stanton welcomed the increasing number of divorces occurring under more liberal state laws later in the century. Stanton viewed this as an indication that "[w]oman is in a transition period from slavery to freedom and she will not accept the conditions in married life that she has heretofore meekly endured" (Stanton 2007, 262).

During the Civil War, Stanton, like most women's rights leaders, focused primarily on abolition. By war's end, however, she worried that the thirteenth amendment signaled the post-war priorities of abolitionists, emancipation for and ensuring the rights of African Americans, rather than universal suffrage. When former allies supported the fourteenth amendment, which introduced the word "male" into the Constitution, and the fifteenth amendment, which enfranchised male citizens, Stanton felt betrayed by an "aristocracy of sex," which she characterized as "most odious and unnatural" because it places husbands above wives and sons above mothers (Stanton 2007, 192). She also lashed out with racist and xenophobic statements against the "lower orders" of men, who could vote before educated, native-born, white women could (Stanton 2007, 189, 202). Stanton's racism and elitism cannot be denied, and scholars offer a variety of explanations for her increased use of ascriptive arguments rooted in positivist and evolutionary thought after the Civil War (Mitchell 2007; Davis 2008, 140–46). What did not change for Stanton was her conviction that not only law but also custom kept women in a subordinate position, one with which most women were comfortable.

In "Solitude of Self," one of her most eloquent speeches, Stanton reiterated her argument for women's rights to equality in government, religion, education, professions, and society. However, unlike the Declaration of Sentiments, which argued for women as a class to gain rights, in "Solitude of Self" Stanton extended the argument for natural rights to women as individuals, each of whom have "a birthright to self-sovereignty" requiring her to be responsible for herself (Stanton in McMillen 2008, 243). When a woman exercises those rights, she will gain knowledge, training, and competencies that will help her meet the challenges of life and prepare for the solitude of self at death.

The final decade of Stanton's life proved her most prolific and provocative as a feminist author but also the most disappointing as a suffrage leader. In 1895, she and her co-authors completed the three-volume *History of Woman Suffrage*, which some suffragists thought was premature because women had not yet been granted the vote. For forty years Stanton used liberal and republican theories to assert women's rights, even as she questioned how the clergy invoked scripture to proscribe women. Her critique culminated in *The Woman's Bible*, published in two volumes (1895, 1898). Kathi Kern explains, "More polemical than scholarly, *The Woman's Bible* was at once a Bible commentary, a spiritual guidebook, and a political treatise," which Stanton intended individual women to read and "experience a conversion to a rationalist worldview, and thereby accelerate their own emancipation" (2001, 168, 169). Most suffragists considered *The Woman's Bible* heretical, and although she had only resigned her presidency in 1892, the National American Women's Suffrage Association censured her in 1896, fearing the damage the book and her radicalism would do to the suffrage cause.

Undaunted but not unscathed, Stanton published her memoir, *Eighty Years and More* (1898). Anecdotal and chatty, Stanton's autobiography has been interpreted as an effort to rehabilitate her reputation. Yet Stanton's memoir is also an "ideological manifesto," which defies conventions of female autobiography of her time, according to Lisa Shawn Hogan (2008). Stanton recounts her experiences and observations of sex inequality and her leadership in combating those inequalities, even when others thought she was going too far. After fifty years of effort, reforms that seemed impossibly radical—insisting on suffrage in 1848 and demanding changes to marriage and divorce laws in the 1850s, for example—are viewed in 1898 as "'steps in progress'"(Stanton 1993, 466–68), and she predicts the same will prove true for her theological critiques. Elizabeth Cady Stanton, like many feminists in their own time, discovered that the "trouble was not in what I said, but that I said it too soon, and before the people were ready to hear it. It may be, however, that I helped them to get ready; who knows?" (1993, 216).

Stanton's major writings

[1898] 1993. *Eighty Years and More: Reminiscences, 1815–1897.* Introduction by Ellen Carol DuBois. Afterword by Ann D. Gordon. Boston: Northeastern University Press.

1997–2013. *The Selected Papers of Elizabeth Cady Stanton and Susan B. Anthony*, 6 vols. Edited by Ann D. Gordon. Brunswick, NY: Rutgers University Press. http://ecssba.rutgers.edu/

2007. "A Selection of Speeches, Article, and Essays by Elizabeth Cady Stanton, 1854–1901." In Ellen Carol DuBois and Richard Cándida Smith (eds.), *Elizabeth Cady Stanton: Feminist as Thinker: A Reader in Documents and Essays*, 155–320. New York: NYU Press.

1881, 1882, 1886. Stanton, Elizabeth Cady, Susan B. Anthony, and Matilda Joslyn Gage (eds.). *History of Woman Suffrage*, 3 vols. New York and Rochester, NY: Fowler and Wells.

[1895, 1898] 1974. Stanton, Elizabeth Cady and the Revising Committee. *The Woman's Bible*. Seattle: Coalition Task Force on Women and Religion. In Kathryn Kish Sklar and Thomas Dublin (eds.), *Women and Social Movements in the United States, 1600–2000*. Accessed through Schaffer Library, Union College.

1922. Stanton, Theodore and Harriot Stanton Blatch (eds.). *Elizabeth Cady Stanton as Revealed in Her Letters, Diary, and Reminiscences*, 2 vols. New York: Harper & Row.

Further reading

Davis, Sue. 2008. *The Political Thought of Elizabeth Cady Stanton: Women's Rights and the American Political Traditions*. New York and London: New York University Press.

Ginzberg, Lori D. 2009. *Elizabeth Cady Stanton: An American Life*. New York: Hill and Wang.

Gordon, Ann D. 2007. "Stanton and the Right to Vote: On Account of Race or Sex." In Ellen Carol DuBois and Richard Cándida Smith (eds.), *Elizabeth Cady Stanton, Feminist as Thinker: A Reader in Documents and Essays*, 111–127. New York: NYU Press.

Hogan, Lisa Shawn. 2008. "The Politics of Feminist Autobiography: Elizabeth Cady Stanton's *Eighty Years and More* as Ideological Manifesto." *Women's Studies* 38(1): 1–22.

Kern, Kathi. 2001. *Mrs. Stanton's Bible*. Ithaca and London: Cornell University Press.

McMillen, Sally G. 2008. *Seneca Falls and the Origins of the Women's Rights Movement*. Oxford: Oxford University Press.

Mitchell, Michele. 2007. "'Lower Orders,' Racial Hierarchies, and Rights Rhetoric: Evolutionary Echoes in Elizabeth Cady Stanton's Thought During the Late 1860s." In Ellen Carol DuBois and Richard Cándida Smith (eds.), *Elizabeth Cady Stanton, Feminist as Thinker: A Reader in Documents and Essays*, 128–151. New York: NYU Press.

Stansell, Christine. 2007. "Missed Connections: Abolitionist Feminism in the Nineteenth Century." In Ellen Carol DuBois and Richard Cándida Smith (eds.), *Elizabeth Cady Stanton, Feminist as Thinker: A Reader in Documents and Essays*, 32–49. New York: NYU Press.

GERTRUDE STEIN (1874–1946)

Barbara Will

Author, art collector, muse, and avant-garde icon, Gertrude Stein was one of the most important figures in the modernist movement centered in Paris during the first four decades of the twentieth century. Celebrated in her time for her acquaintance with "everybody who was anybody," Stein spent much of her adult life in the company of famous friends like Pablo Picasso, Henri Matisse, and Ernest Hemingway, whose work she mentored and financially supported. In recent decades, Stein has become recognized as a major talent in her own right, a "pre-postmodernist" whose highly experimental writing continues to have a profound influence on contemporary literature, poetics, drama, and digital media. She has also been named a feminist or queer icon, celebrated for writing an expressive poetics of lesbian-feminist identity.

At the same time, Stein's lifelong political conservatism and aversion to "the cause of women" has troubled any easy or comfortable assessment of her feminism. The disconnect between her life and her work raises difficult and uncomfortable questions for feminist scholars. Nevertheless, readers continue to identify with Stein's writing for its fearless and joyful experimentation, and for the challenge it poses both structurally and thematically to what she herself referred to as "patriarchal poetry."

Gertrude Stein was twenty-nine when she left America in 1903 to set up permanent residence in Paris with her brother Leo. Located on the Left Bank, close to the Luxembourg Gardens and the artistic neighborhood of Montparnasse, the Stein home at 27 rue de Fleurus soon became a gathering point for artists, writers, and assorted colorful personalities. The regular Saturday evening salon at the Steins' allowed friends and acquaintances to come together to discuss topics of interest and to view Leo and Gertrude's impressive, growing collection of the work of as-yet relatively unknown artists: Paul Cézanne, Henri Matisse, Pierre-Auguste Renoir, and Pablo Picasso. The salon continued even after Leo was displaced by Stein's lover and lifelong companion, Alice Babette Toklas, who moved into the household in 1907 and managed his departure in 1913. After the war, the Stein-Toklas salon would again become a Parisian destination for a new generation of artists and writers, among them Hemingway, F. Scott Fitzgerald, Paul Bowles, and Sherwood Anderson. In her later years, Stein was considered one of the most important arbiters—male or female—of public taste regarding modernism in the first half of the twentieth century.

Stein's reputation as salon hostess—and her own cultivation of this reputation in her best-selling 1933 memoir *The Autobiography of Alice B. Toklas*—tended in her lifetime to overshadow the writing she composed from her earliest years in Paris to her death in 1946. Much of this writing remains among the most radical, experimental work ever written in English. Her now-famous short story "Melanctha" (1909), which Stein described, with typical assertiveness, as "the first definite step away from the nineteenth century and into the twentieth century in literature" (1990, 66), offered up a new kind of female character and a new modernist voice to describe this character. Sexually experimental, unfettered by social norms, restless and passionate, the African-American protagonist Melanctha defies conventional modes of female agency. Stein described her character as a "wanderer," traversing obstacles and transgressing boundaries, a melancholy figure of disruption and dissatisfaction who troubles and unsettles those around her. While Stein employed stereotypes of the "tragic mulatta" to set her character in motion—leading her story to be criticized for indulging in racist clichés—the singular course of Melanctha's "wandering" eventually delivers her from these stereotypes. So too does the strange language Stein adopted to tell Melanctha's story. Never one to follow conventional rules of grammar and syntax, Stein in "Melanctha" begins to develop a writing style based on an absolutely unprecedented use of the English language. Reduced vocabulary, relentless repetition, and a continuously present, non-developmental temporal frame transform "Melanctha" from a tragic mulatta cautionary tale into a radical literary breakthrough. With this "first definite step … into the twentieth century in literature," Stein set forth an uncompromising modernist manifesto.

"Melanctha" announced the originality of Stein's voice, and there would be no going back. By the time Stein composed the cubist word portraits of *Tender Buttons* (1914), her early stylistic experimentation had blossomed into an intense and sustained phenomenological exploration of the English language as both representational medium and object of analysis. English would never sound or look the same, as in the opening lines of *Tender Buttons*: "A kind in glass and a cousin, a spectacle and nothing strange a single hurt color and an arrangement in a system to pointing. All this and not ordinary, not unordered in not resembling. The difference is spreading" (1998, 313). *Abstract* is one term often used to describe this writing; *nonsensical* is another. Neither term is precise enough to capture the unique way in which Stein's words at once describe an object (here, a carafe); elicit its features (glass, a "hurt" or red color); proudly affirm its ordinariness ("nothing strange"); destabilize the ground of realism (juxtaposing a seemingly random collection of nouns, verbs, and prepositions); and comment on this process of mimetic destabilization ("not unordered in not resembling"). "The difference is spreading" is a triumphant closing salvo: difference rather than sameness, endless variation and creative free-play rather than contained ordinariness or "realism," will be the literary rule from now on.

Stein's innovative body of work has been extremely interesting to recent feminist and poststructuralist critics and theorists. The "difference" Stein's writing both embodies and celebrates directly speaks to core tenets in feminist and deconstructionist theory, particularly the emphasis upon non-unitary, anti-hierarchical writing. Marianne DeKoven reads Stein's "different" language in terms of "poststructuralist feminist notions of a subversive writing subject that is different from, incompatible with, the identity of the coherent, separate, uniquely individuated bourgeois-patriarchal self" (DeKoven 1990, 484). Rachel Blau DuPlessis refers to Stein's "'feminine' practice of otherness … a practice stirring up difference and undermining closure" (DuPlessis 2014, 41). And queer critics have frequently noted how much Stein's "practice of otherness" resonates with a politics of gendered embodiment and "intersubjective interplay" (Cope 2005, 8). In the way her work performs a "baffling of sexual or gendered identity categories and of normative categorization more generally," Stein poses a major challenge to (male) authorial tradition (Bennett 2010, 313).

Certainly Stein's most experimental writings—the texts she wrote during the sustained period of experimentation between *The Making of Americans* (1912) and *Stanzas in Meditation* (1932)—present a new kind of experience for the reader that relies upon a willingness to accept ambiguity and uncertainty and to engage in interpretive free-play. This experimental writing can be seen as "feminist" to the extent that it does not vest authority in the writer of the text or in the symbolic order but scatters authority across the textual field. The reader seeking to be assured of clear and unambiguous authorial intent will invariably become frustrated by her encounter with the Steinian text; yet this does not imply that authority is nowhere to be found. The most remarkable aspect of Stein's experimental writing is the way it enables a reader—*any* reader—to take on a temporary and provisional authorial role in the process of trying to make the text meaningful. Out of frustration at the text's opacity, readers of Stein often begin to produce their own speculative and creative interpretations, effectively "co-authoring" the text. As anyone knows who has taught Stein's writing to a group of skeptical or uncertain students, this is often the moment in which they begin to fall in love with Stein's writing. To this extent, Stein's experimental writing has a crucial pedagogical function, teaching readers a new mode of reading that echoes with the early childhood experience of language acquisition.

"Let the word-man in you come forth, dance for a time," Gertrude Stein is reported to have said to friends in encouraging their active participation as readers of her texts (Anderson 1934, 85). At other moments, Stein referred to her work in terms of an ideal process of "talking and listening," of a fluid and inconclusive conversational dynamic that might take place *within* the text or *around* the text (or both). Regarding the former modality, Stein often infuses her experimental texts with fragments of dialogue, literally showing in action the experience of "talking and listening." This can be seen in the following passage from *Ladies' Voices/Curtain Raiser* (1916): "Did you say they were different. I said it made no difference. / Where does it. Yes. / Mr. Richard Sutherland. This is a name I know. / Yes. / The Hotel Victoria. / Many words spoken to me have seemed English" (1993, 307). This meandering dialogue of two or more unnamed voices proceeds through free association and oblique or metonymic reference, presenting itself as a sort of primer on "talking and listening." The reader of *Ladies' Voices/Curtain Raiser* watches as the voices discuss, query, refer, expostulate, and even theorize about the meaning of English. The experience is disconcerting: like eavesdropping on a group of unknown women gossiping about an unknown set of interrelated subjects. Elsewhere in the text the reader is directly brought in on the act: "What are ladies voices. / Do you mean to believe me. / Have you caught the sun. / Dear me have you caught the sun" (1993, 307). In this second modality, the reader is directly solicited and asked to "believe" in the writing process, to hear and to respond to the women's voices that weave through the text in fragments—all without turning away in frustration. To believe in the text, to listen to it and talk back to it, to remain patient and attentive to all its multiple possibilities, is potentially an act of genius. It is, Stein writes, to "catch the sun."

In this and many other experimental texts from the early twentieth century, Gertrude Stein reorients the ground of what it means to write and read in English. Many of these texts remain to this day unpublished and unread, a sign perhaps that we have still not fully learned to appreciate Stein's remarkably prescient vision and voice. Enormously radical for her own time and perhaps for ours, Stein's writing remains a tantalizing mystery that both invites us in and eludes any final understanding.

Stein's major writings

[1909] 1990. "Melanctha." In *Three Lives*. New York: Penguin.

[1912] 1995. *The Making of Americans*. Normal, IL: Dalkey Archive Press.

[1914] 1998. "Tender Buttons." In *Writings 1903–1932*, 313–55. Ed. Catharine Stimpson and Harriet Chessman. New York: The Library of America.

[1916] 1993. "Ladies' Voices/Curtain Raiser." In *A Stein Reader*, 306–07. Ed. Ulla E. Dydo. Evanston, IL: Northwestern University Press.

[1932] 2012. *Stanzas in Meditation*. New Haven: Yale University Press.

[1933] 1990. *The Autobiography of Alice B. Toklas*. New York: Vintage.

[1935] 1988. *Lectures in America*. London: Virago.

[1941] 2012. *Ida*. New Haven: Yale University Press.

2008. *Gertrude Stein: Selections*. Ed. Joan Retallack. Berkeley: University of California Press.

Further reading

Anderson, Sherwood. 1934. *No Swank*. Philadelphia: Centaur Press.

Bennett, Chad. 2010. "'Ladies' Voices Give Pleasure': Gossip, Drama, and Gertrude Stein." *Modern Drama* 53(3): 311–31.

Cope, Karin. 2005. *Passionate Collaborations: Learning to Live with Gertrude Stein*. Victoria, BC: ELS editions.

DeKoven, Marianne. 1990. "Introduction" to Gertrude Stein entry. In Bonnie Kime Scott, ed. *The Gender of Modernism: A Critical Anthology*. Bloomington: Indiana University Press: 479–87.

DuPlessis, Rachel Blau. 2014. "Woolfenstein, the Sequel." In Janet Boyd and Sharon Kirsch, eds. *Primary Stein: Returning to the Writing of Gertrude Stein*. Lanham, MD: Lexington Books: 37–56.

Dydo, Ulla and William Rice. 2008. *Gertrude Stein: The Language That Rises: 1923–1934*. Chicago: Northwestern University Press.

North, Michael. 1994. *The Dialect of Modernism: Race, Language, and Twentieth-Century Literature*. New York: Oxford University Press.

Watson, Dana Cairns. 2005. *Gertrude Stein and the Essence of What Happens*. Nashville, TN: Vanderbilt University Press.

Will, Barbara. 2000. *Gertrude Stein, Modernism, and the Problem of "Genius."* Edinburgh: Edinburgh University Press.

—. 2011. *Unlikely Collaboration: Gertrude Stein, Bernard Faÿ and the Vichy Dilemma*. New York: Columbia University Press.

EDITH THOMAS (1909–1970)

Michelle Chilcoat

On vacation from her job in Paris as National Archives conservator, French Resistant, novelist, poet, short story writer, journalist, and women's historian Edith Thomas was working on a seventh novel in the family's summer home in Sainte-Aulde when she stopped to wonder what the point of writing was for an ex-communist. Twenty years earlier, when Thomas was first introduced to communism, she found in it nothing less than "a new explanation of the world"; now, three years after leaving the Party, she had lost her life's compass. The trained historian hoped to catch a glimpse of her future by looking back through her communist past, a twenty-year "adventure" which was, "like it or not, the adventure of our times" (*Le témoin* 44–45). Titling the manuscript *Le témoin compromis* (*The Compromised Witness*, published posthumously in 1995), Thomas described her need "to explain and justify myself, in your eyes and mine, so you will know who I am and love me in spite of everything, because I need to be loved for who I am" (30). Her appeal to former Party comrades likely imagined in this unnamed "you" had all the effectiveness of a ghost appealing to the wind; but Thomas harbored no illusions regarding the social death she would know the moment she quit the Party in 1949. And contrary to most, Thomas did so openly, in a letter published in the leftist newspaper *Combat* (December 15, 1949).

While she frequently lamented her solitude, Thomas did not fear it, actively seeking to set herself apart among others in situations that she believed called for an open demonstration of her commitment to a principled life. Born to non-practicing Catholic parents who, while politically conservative, were open-minded and tolerant, she described becoming a Protestant at age sixteen not as an expression of rebellion or religious belief but more succinctly as her "first act of freedom." She would continue to enact this freedom, which she understood as exercising the capacity to think and act independently of others, even those she deeply loved and respected (i.e., her parents, her mentors), or at the risk of incurring emotional or physical injury. In fact, commitment in and of itself remained a guiding principle for Thomas throughout her life.

Fascism was on the rise across Europe when the twenty-year-old Thomas entered the Ecole Nationale de Chartes in 1929 to pursue a degree in medieval history and archival studies. In *Le témoin compromis* she wrote that her "pseudo-Protestantism" and hostility toward the extreme right singled her out in the conservative Catholic milieu (43). Diagnosed with tuberculosis of the bone after graduating in 1931 (having contended with intense and persistent pain in her left knee throughout her studies), Thomas spent the greater part of the following two years in isolation and confined to bed. During this time, she discovered communism along with her need to write, "like a person needs to eat" (42), producing manuscripts for two novels, *La mort de Marie* (*The Death of Marie*) and *L'homme criminel* (*The Criminal Man*). *La mort de Marie*, a haunting and at times hallucinating account à la Faulkner of the main character's lonely yet ecstatic suffering and death of tuberculosis, claimed a First Novel Prize; both manuscripts were then published in 1934 by Gallimard (still one of France's most prestigious presses today).

The long, tortuous bout with the potentially fatal illness left Thomas emotionally and physically exhausted and with a permanent limp. Considering herself unmarriageable as an independent-minded and now handicapped woman, Thomas questioned the point of an existence so financially precarious that it would be principally consumed by concerns of how to insure her next meal. Profound depression and suicidal thoughts, however, turned into fuel for Thomas's resolve to revolt against suffering, both hers and that of others, especially after witnessing the brutalities of French colonialism during what was supposed to have been a brief period of recuperation in Algeria in 1934. Upon her return, she sought work writing for left-wing newspapers in Paris; the newly founded anti-fascist *Vendredi* published her first articles, a series on the hardships particular to women workers. Brief membership in the Association of Revolutionary Writers and Artists connected her with surrealist author Louis Aragon who hired her as a journalist for the communist newspaper he directed, *Ce Soir*. Between 1935 and 1938, Thomas penned articles on grave social problems in Paris, highlighting among other issues the lamentable living conditions of aged workers and spearheading health and education efforts for impoverished children. Despite her limp and fragile health, she also took on dangerous assignments reporting for the Republican side of the Spanish civil war (1936–1939) and in Austria in the year preceding the *Anschluss*.

Aragon fired Thomas from *Ce Soir* in mid-1938, due to differences of opinion related to his hardline communism. Meanwhile, she contracted tuberculosis again, of the lungs this time, and had to leave Paris for another long period of painful treatment. In September 1941, Thomas returned to an occupied Paris, fully committed to fight Hitler and Nazism. Despite misgivings in part stemming from her experiences with Aragon, she joined the Communist Party in 1942 as it offered the most efficacious way to hook up with the Resistance, which she had become determined to do the moment she learned of its activity. After the Gestapo arrested and executed its original editor, she signed on (anonymously of course) as co-editor of the clandestine *Lettres Françaises*, contributing hard-hitting yet compassionate articles such as "Crier la vérité!" ("Cry Out the Truth!"), in which she excoriates French literati who "isolate in their ivory tower" refusing to "break the silence" even as the cattle car of a French train passes them by, filled with children whose cries for their "Maman" go unanswered (Issue no. 2, October 1942). She also reported on the activity and conditions of Resistance fighters in several *maquis* throughout France after managing to visit them during the spring of 1944. The sole woman on the Comité National des Ecrivains (National Committee of Writers) along with Sartre and Camus among others, Thomas risked her life from February 1943 until the Liberation to hold the meetings of the "intellectual Resistance" in her apartment. Thomas also took part in founding the Editions de Minuit (Midnight Editions), the remarkable underground press whose first publication in 1942, Vercor's *Silence de la mer* (*Silence of the Sea*), managed to circulate throughout the world almost instantaneously. In 1943, the press published Thomas's pseudonymous *Contes d'Auxois* (*Tales by Auxois*), a collection of short stories narrating extraordinary acts of resistance by ordinary people, much based on what she witnessed personally. Upon word of the liberation of France's capital in August 1944, Thomas dared to leave her Paris apartment as bullets continued to fly to take notes on the event directly from the barricades. 1945 saw the publication of *La libération de Paris* based on that eyewitness account. In 1947 she wrote a Joan of Arc biography to reclaim the woman warrior from the far right's exploitation of the figure. At the Communist Party's behest she had also agreed to edit *Femmes Françaises*, a journal for the non-Communist Union des Femmes Françaises (French Women's Union), from which she would resign immediately after the war, unable to cope with the editorial board's limiting of "women's issues" to concerns for household and family.

Between 1947 and 1949, Thomas experienced two great heartbreaks. The first came with the ending of a brief but intense love affair with Gallimard editor Dominique Aury, the woman who anonymously authored *The Story of O*, a highly controversial novel featuring female masochistic erotica and a character based on Thomas (and with whom Thomas remained in close contact for the rest of her life). The second came with her decision—provoked by the Tito affair—to resign from the Communist Party. Resisting rather than succumbing to suicidal thoughts once again, she turned out several impressively documented historical biographies of powerful nineteenth-century women, including George Sand, Pauline Roland and Louise Michel, distinguishing Thomas as a pioneer in the discipline of women's history. In almost all of her writing, she turned to both fictional and real characters with whom she identified but who were at the same time specific individuals uniquely shaped by their particular moment and circumstances in history. Thomas's own particular moment and circumstances aligned perhaps most closely with the main character of the last novel she would write, published shortly before she died suddenly from viral hepatitis in 1970. In *Le jeu d'échecs* (*The Chess Game*), despite the potentially pessimistic title (which translates literally as *The Game of Failures*), the main character Aude, resolutely single and having just given birth to a little girl, finally sees that the reason for existence is "the adventure of bringing into the world the possibility of being human" (*Le jeu* 265). This challenge was especially great for women who at the same time had to confront and overcome obstacles in their continued struggle to find their own place in a world created by and for men.

All throughout her publication history—which, beyond seven novels, two short story collections and six historical biographies, included hundreds of articles and reviews written for newspapers, journals and magazines, academic as well as popular—runs the bright thread of Edith Thomas's unique approach to feminism, although she (much like her contemporary Simone de Beauvoir) considered the term itself an outdated reference to the political and social demands of "our grandmothers" (*Le témoin* 118). Thomas referred instead to "l'humanisme féminin" ("feminine humanism"), a concept, already stirring in her first publication *La mort de Marie*, that had crystalized in *Le jeu d'échecs* in what the character Aude calls "solidarity among women, in a world they didn't make" (*Le jeu* 261), shortly after observing that "it is without a doubt easier to be a man than it is to be a woman, because we have to invent everything for ourselves" (255). But Aude, whose life trajectory mimics Thomas's very closely, is neither bitter nor despairing here. The competitive disadvantage that has been women's lot throughout history has only rendered the so-called "weaker sex" that much more remarkable. Thus, each generation of women is deeply indebted to the one that came before for the particular improvements their own generation currently enjoys. It is in this vein that Thomas has Aude remark: "Only fifty years ago, I would not have been able to be who I was today: so aware, so willful, so responsible" (*Le jeu* 255–56).

Thomas's major writings

1934. *La mort de Marie*. Paris: Gallimard.
1934. *L'homme criminal*. Paris: Gallimard.
1935. *Sept-sorts*. Paris: Gallimard.
1936. *Le refus*. Paris: Éditions Sociales Internationales.
[1939–1944] 1995. *Pages de journal, (1940–1941)* followed by *Journal intime de monsieur Célestin Costedet*. Introduced and annotated by Dorothy Kaufmann. Paris:Viviane Hamy.
1943. *Contes d'Auxois (transcrits du réel)*. Paris: Éditions de Minuit.
1945. *Le champ libre*. Paris: Gallimard.
1945. *Étude de femmes*. Paris: Éditions Colbert.
1945. *La libération de Paris*. Paris: Mellottée (with photographs by Robert Doisneau, Henri Cartier-Bresson and others).
1947. *Berthie Albrecht, Pierre Arrighi, Général Brosset, D. Corticchiato, Jean Prevost, cinq parmi d'autres*. Paris: Éditions de Minuit (with René Char,Vercors and others).

1947. *Jeanne d'Arc.* Paris: Éditions Hier et Aujourd'Hui (re-edited by Gallimard, 1952).

1948. *Les femmes de 1848.* Paris: PUF.

1952. *Ève et les autres.* Paris: Gizard (re-edited by Mercure de France, 1970; translated into English as *Eve and the Others* by Estelle Eirenberg, Sioux City, IA: Continental Editions, 1976).

[1952] 1995. *Le témoin compromis.* Introduced and annotated by Dorothy Kaufmann. Paris: Viviane Hamy.

1956. *Pauline Roland, socialisme et féminisme au xixe siècle.* Paris: M. Rivière.

1959. *George Sand.* Paris: Éditions Universitaire.

1963. *Les "pétroleuses".* Paris: Gallimard (translated into English as *The Women Incendiaries* by James and Starr Atkinson, New York: George Braziller, 1966; paperback edition, Chicago: Haymarket Books, 2007).

1967. *Rossel (1844–1871).* Paris: Gallimard.

1970. *Le jeu d'échecs.* Paris: Grasset.

1971. *Louise Michel ou la Velléda de l'anarchie.* Paris: Gallimard (translated into English as *Louise Michel* by Penelope Williams, Montreal: Black Rose Books, 1980).

See also the singularly important, wonderfully readable, and thoroughly researched life and works study of Edith Thomas by Dorothy Kaufmann titled *Edith Thomas: A Passion for Resistance*, Ithaca, NY: Cornell University Press, 2004.

SOJOURNER TRUTH (1797–1883)

Laurie E. Naranch

Sojourner Truth: abolitionist, women's rights advocate, preacher, and former slave. Truth was a forceful, visible presence in public life in the nineteenth century. Venerated as an icon of determination fighting for freedom and remembered as a strong black woman, Truth could neither read nor write. Rather, her reputation derives from her dynamic public speech, the narratives of her life published and sold for her income, her image in etchings and photographs, the documentation from the three legal cases she brought and won, along with reports of her activities. She dictated her *Narrative of Sojourner Truth* to her neighbor Olive Gilbert (1850) and published another edition compiled by her friend and manager Frances Titus (1875) that included her "Book of Life," a scrapbook of articles, letters, and signatures of her admirers and famous figures with whom she came into contact. After her death Titus published a new edition of the *Narrative* including a chapter of memorials (1883). The challenge of textual authority and historical accuracy in the case of Truth is one with which scholars have wrestled. But what makes Truth most famous as an antislavery feminist and a women's rights advocate stems from her speech at a women's rights convention in Akron, Ohio in 1851—the famous "Aren't I a Woman?" speech.

Truth demonstrates at the level of her person the ongoing challenge to refigure the body politic of a nation that began as both a slave state and as a location for individual and collective self-determination. Her work reveals that a theory of individual freedom must recognize the conditions that make freedom possible—economic, spiritual, embodied, and legal. A black feminist in the nineteenth century, Truth shows how freedom takes shape in relation to dominant identities of whiteness, maleness, and property. Truth's powerful argumentative logic—working within authoritative discourses to expose hypocrisy and to reimagine slaves, blacks, and women, as human, moral beings, and citizens—serves as an illustration of the intersectional (Collins 2000) and embodied nature of identity and citizenship revealing the ongoing struggle to refigure the body politic with the legacy of racial and sexual oppression.

Sojourner Truth was born a slave in Ulster County, New York in the Hudson Valley around 1797. Her given name was Isabella Baumfree. She was the next to youngest daughter of James and Betsey who had maybe twelve children, most of whom were sold. Sold to five different owners, Truth's last owner was John Dumont who purchased her when she was thirteen. As a young woman Truth fell in love with another slave in the area, Robert, who was brutally beaten for visiting her; she never saw him again. She married an older slave, Thomas, with whom she had five children, three girls and two boys, one boy died in childbirth. Dumont had promised her freedom a year before New York State decreed emancipation on July 4, 1827 for those born before 1799 (children born after 1799 had to remain servants of their mother's owner until they were 21), but he broke that promise. Truth, steeled by a spiritual revelation, took her youngest daughter and walked away from slavery in 1826. Taken in by an antislavery family, Truth built connections, first to religious communities and then abolitionist and women's rights activists. However, her son Peter had been sold to a slave owner in Alabama, a cynical way to profit before state-mandated emancipation. Remarkably, Truth took the matter to court and won. Truth also won two other cases: she sued for libel in the 1830s and then in 1865 she challenged a Washington, D.C. law denying passengers a seat on street horse cars on the basis of race. Truth became an itinerant preacher and in 1843 gave herself the name Sojourner Truth (1998, 68).

As Nell Irvin Painter suggests, "Truth" "raises a host of issues regarding knowledge, representation, and communication" (1996, 75). "Sojourner" shows the travelling nature of truth. Truth dreamed of owning her own home, which she eventually did. She also traveled widely to speak at abolitionist meetings and women's rights conventions. She supported the Union effort in the Civil War and worked in the Freedman's Bureau in Washington, D.C. afterwards. Truth came into contact with key figures in abolition and women's rights politics such as Susan B. Anthony, William Lloyd Garrison, and Frederick Douglass, as well as meeting with President Lincoln and President Grant.

The most well-known version of Truth's "Aren't I a Woman?" speech was published by Frances Dana Gage in 1863. While this version has historical errors, for example, Gage presents Truth speaking in a Southern dialect reflecting the antislavery and feminist politics of the time given the Civil War (Painter 1996), it is the version that, if not as accurate as the report in the *Anti-Slavery Bugle* in 1851, certainly captures the wit, logic, and brilliance of Truth's words. Despite the errors, Truth included this version of her speech in her *Narrative*. By all accounts Truth was a brilliant public speaker. Reports remark on her physical appearance and voice—she was nearly six feet tall, with dark skin, and a booming, low voice still slightly accented by Dutch.

Truth challenges the unexamined view of women as represented in women's rights arguments. That view assumes "women" as white middle-class femininity; Truth argues instead for black women to have rights along with all other women. As reported:

Dat man ober dar say that womin needs to be helped into carriages, and lifted ober ditches, and to hab the best place everywhere. Nobody eber helps me into carriages, or ober mud-puddles, or gibs me any best place!" ... "And a'n't I a woman? Look at me! Look at my arm!" (and she bared her right arm to the shoulder showing tremendous muscular power). "I have ploughed, and planted, and gathered into barns, and no man could head me! And a'n't I a woman? I could work as much and eat as much as a man—when I could get it—and bear the lash as well! And a'n't I a woman? I have born thirteen chilern, and seen 'em mos' all sold

off to slavery, and when I cried with a mother's grief, none but
Jesus heard me! And a'n't I a woman?

(Lasser and Robertson 2010, 193–194)

Truth asks of those who claim to speak for women—which women
do you represent?

Moreover, Truth argues that women, like men, have entitlement through
the labor of their bodies to rights—a clever argument that simultaneously
transforms the laboring enslaved body to the laboring body that under-
girds liberal personhood in the U.S. She also takes on Church authorities. As reported: "Den dat little man in black dar, he say women can't
have as much rights as men, 'cause Christ wan't a woman! Whar did your
Christ come from? … From God and a woman! Man had nothing to do
wid Him" (Lasser and Robertson 2010, 194). Truth's ability to know and
exploit authoritative texts for persuasive purposes, and her humor in doing
so, also comes through in the 1851 version that ends with this section:

I can't read but I can hear. I have heard the Bible and have learned
that Eve caused man to sin. Well if women upset the world, do give
her a chance to set it right side up again. … And how came Jesus
into the world? Through God who created him and woman who
bore him. Man, where was your part?

(Lasser and Robertson 2010, 193)

Truth's public presence transgressed many social norms of gender, race,
and class. When a rumor circulated that Truth was a man in women's
clothing trying to solicit sympathy as a formerly enslaved woman,
Truth exposed her breasts to prove otherwise thus stepping into a
common experience of plantation slave women saying that her breasts
had suckled many a white child as she asked her audience if they too
wished to suck (1998, 95). We see here her performative embodiment
of the enslaved woman with whom she is in solidarity and with whom
she shares an identity. And, of course, in bold fashion she turns around
the objectification and use of black female breasts in a challenge to her
hostile white male interlocutors.

Truth wrestled with how she was represented: from the publicity
she got from Harriet Beecher Stowe's article about her as the "Libyan
Sybil" to the images made of her. Her 1875 *Narrative* includes an etching
based on a photograph where Truth appears as a respectable woman in
Quaker dress and not as a southern slave (Rohrbach 2010). Truth sold
these small photographs known as *cartes-de-vistes*. Truth copyrighted
the saying that accompanied her *cartes-de-vistes*, "The Shadow supports

the substance"—shadow was a typical way of referring to photography at the time—revealing that she knew enough about property laws to understand how to own her own words and her image.

In her 1875 "Preface" Truth says in response to the mention of a self-made man: "You call him a self-made man; well, I am a self-made woman." Acknowledging that she was a slave for whom "the paths of literature and science were forever closed" and then doubly burdened by poverty and "caste," Truth quickly reframes this narrative, saying she presents "this remarkable woman" to tell her story and advance "the cause of human rights." As noted frequently in the text, she will use proceeds from the sale of the book to support herself. Truth reveals the tension between the rhetoric of self-making and the reality of structural and personal vulnerability as she stages how freedom depends on circumstances and personal actions.

Truth saw labor as a source of the self, given the centrality of property to personhood in the liberal legal system of the U.S. She also used this as a fulcrum to argue for justice in light of the unpaid labor of slavery. She "looked about upon the imposing public edifices that grace the District of Columbia" and said, "We *helped* to pay this cost. We have been a source of wealth to this republic." She concludes, "Our unpaid labor has been a stepping-stone to its financial success. Some of its dividends must surely be ours" (1998, 132).

In 2009 Sojourner Truth became the first African-American woman memorialized with a bust installed in Emancipation Hall at the U.S. Capitol Visitor Center in Washington, D.C. after a decade-long push by the National Congress of Black Women. In her remarks Michelle Obama said: "I hope that Sojourner Truth would be proud to see me, a descendant of slaves, serving as the First Lady of the United States of America" (2009). That Truth serves as a heroic exemplar in the struggle for freedom was evident in her own lifetime and continues today. In numerous children's books, memorials, and scholarly writings she is held up as a symbol of strength, perseverance, and courage as a black woman—as she should be—but there are also lessons of vulnerability, sharp criticisms of racism and sexism, a case for reparations and social benefits as a result of uncompensated labor from slavery, recognition that slavery was not only a Southern institution, and the challenge of controlling the image of yourself in public life.

Truth's major writings

[1850, 1875, 1883] 1998. *Narrative of Sojourner Truth; A Bondswoman of Olden Time, With a History of her Labors and Correspondence Drawn*

from her 'Book of Life.' Also, A Memorial Chapter. Edited and introduced by Nell Irvin Painter. New York: Penguin.

Further reading

Collins, Patricia Hill. [2000] 2009. *Black Feminist Thought: Knowledge,
Consciousness, and the Politics of Empowerment.* New York: Routledge.

Lasser, Carol and Stacey Robertson (eds.). 2010. *Antebellum Women:
Private, Public, Partisan.* Lanham, MD: Rowman & Littlefield.

Mabee, Carlton with Susan Mabee. 1993. *Sojourner Truth: Slave, Prophet,
Legend.* New York: New York University Press.

Obama, Michelle. 2009. "Remarks by the First Lady at the Sojourner Truth Bust Unveiling," April 28. www.whitehouse.gov/
the-press-office/remarks-first-lady-sojourner-truth-bust-unveiling

Painter, Nell Irvin. 1996. *Sojourner Truth: A Life, a Symbol.* New York:
W. W. Norton.

Rohrbach, Augusta. 2012. "Shadow and Substance: Sojourner Truth
in Black and White." In *Pictures and Progress: Early Photography and
the Making of African American Identity.* Eds. Maurice O. Wallace
and Shawn Michelle Smith. Durham, NC: Duke University Press:
83–100.

MARINA WARNER (1946–)

Torrey Shanks

Marina Warner is a critic, essayist, and novelist whose work on myth
traces the layered historical and cultural meanings of feminine symbols and allegories. Her prolific body of work defies easy classification,
reaching audiences within and outside of the academy and crossing
diverse disciplinary fields, including but not limited to literature, art
history, cultural and political history, religion, philosophy, and women's
studies. Warner presents a rich and expansive archive of feminine figures circulating, often paradoxically, throughout cultural, political, and
aesthetic traditions, institutions, and imaginaries. She lavishes attention
on the embodied and poetic representations of universal figures and
their long-standing imbrication with the female body. Her sustained
interest in the feminine figures of religious, political, and literary history is a powerful reminder that the study of culture offers a far more
variegated and fertile field for imagining and re-visioning the feminine

than institutionalized forms of power would often admit. Yet those very institutions turn so often, particularly in times of crisis, to the signifying power of the figure of woman to reinvent and shore up their authority. Warner invites readers to consider how myths and fables circulate still in the verbal and visual languages of power and culture and how they may yet be re-visioned for more liberating futures.

Warner was born in London in 1946, raised in Cairo and the United Kingdom, and studied French and Italian as an undergraduate at Oxford. For much of her career, Warner has worked as an independent scholar, though she has been awarded numerous honorary doctorates and has held academic posts at the University of Essex and Birkbeck College, University of London. She belongs to the Order of the British Empire (DBE), the Chevalier de l'Ordre des Arts et des Lettres (France), and the Commendatore dell' Ordine della Stella di Solidarieta (Italy).

In her early work on myth and monuments, Warner traces the iterations and innovations of the myths of the Virgin Mary and Joan of Arc as well as the feminine form of national symbols such as Lady Liberty. In more recent work on fairytales such as the *Arabian Nights*, Warner explores the power of imagination in bodily metamorphosis and cultural hybridity. She attends to both the original figures and stories as well as to the subsequent fantasies, fables, and afterlives that these figures have inspired across centuries and around the globe.

Among her best known books, *Alone of All Her Sex: The Myth and the Cult of the Virgin Mary* explores the densely conflicted relation of religion and feminine sexuality in its mythic dimensions. She traces the Virgin Mary as "a polyvalent figure who appears under many guises … the Church's female paragon and ideal of the feminine personified" (1976, xxiv). Noting scant textual and historical evidence for the life of Mary, Warner finds in the silence openings for the storytelling that began in the earliest days of the Christian faith and extends into the present day. Woven together from classical and Jewish traditions as well as historical exigencies of the waxing and waning powers of the Church, the polyvocal myth of the Virgin Mary reflects Catholicism's "perennial ambivalence" toward women (ibid.).

Warner attends to the work of myth in articulating and maintaining conflicting institutional and cultural imperatives. In the myth of Mary, a central contradiction of the Christian tradition is given expression: a commitment to radical notions of equality and universality inclusive of women as believers, while assigning to women the value of humility construed as submission. The Virgin Mary is a symbol of adoration, honor, and power tightly linked to the identity of the Church itself.

Yet, "[t]he cult of Mary is inextricably interwoven with Christian ideas about the dangers of the flesh and their special connection with women" (1976, 67). Myth, in Warner's treatment, is never simply concerned with the ephemeral or abstract, but rather draws meaning and new life from its multiple material and aesthetic iterations. The many feminine guises of such mythological figures do not reveal a timeless truth about women or feminine difference per se. Instead, Warner draws readers into the constitutive contradictions of feminine symbols that are integral even in, or especially to, societies where women are socially and politically subordinated.

In *Joan of Arc: The Image of Female Heroism*, religious iconography combines with political imagination around a more robustly historical personage. While Joan brings a more substantial record of her life, trial, and death, she is for Warner "a universal figure who is female, but neither a queen, nor a courtesan, nor a beauty, nor a mother, nor an artist of one kind or another, nor – until the extremely recent date of 1920 when she was canonised – a saint" (6). It is the story of Joan of Arc's life and no less the afterlife of her story, resurrected and retold in the Renaissance, seventeenth-century France, and in the nineteenth century, that presents a figure of heroism in unexpected yet intelligible form. Joan presses at the conventional limits of female typologies, having grasped immortality and instant recognition in novel ways. She gestures not only toward heaven or a national future, but also to an unrealized possibility of a richer verbal and visual vocabulary for representing women in the sphere of action.

The meaning-making power of feminine icons in politics is brought more clearly into focus in *Monuments and Maidens: The Allegory of the Female Form*, where Warner tackles the feminine mythology of the nation-state. She invites readers to consider another long-standing paradox of feminine form: Why are the nation and its cherished values so frequently figured through the female body? She takes the Statue of Liberty, or Lady Liberty, as her point of departure on a trajectory that runs from classical myth through contemporary politics. She highlights what is right before our eyes as citizens and subjects – the images of justice, of wisdom, of power and empire that populate our buildings, memorials, and stamps of the state – to ask what it is that these feminine figures represent. It is surely not the liberty or justice traditionally denied women in the very societies – Greek, Roman, French, American, and British – whence these images come.

While these female forms appear most evidently in physical form – of stone, plaster, or copper – Warner trains our vision on their continued role in the living world of politics, exemplified in the persona crafted by Prime Minister Margaret Thatcher. Adopting and adapting the traditions inherited from British queens and the myth of Britannia, Thatcher taps into an allegorical language with which to negotiate an impoverished collective imagination for female authority. Her reinvention of these myths entails a selective emphasis among their plural dimensions, as between the constitutionalist and militaristic facets ascribed to Britannia over her long history. Warner depicts the artful ways in which Thatcher clothes herself in familiar feminine images – from Britannia's military prowess to the more pedestrian roles of nanny, matron, and governess – to define her role in Conservative political leadership where traditional roles would otherwise fail the first female Prime Minister. Warner's account of the manifold allegorical possibilities afforded by classical symbols strengthens our critical understanding of the uses of myths and allegories of power to shore up new modes of militaristic and imperial force as well as feminine authority.

Warner's work increasingly engages the expansive realm of fable and fairytales, where feminine figures remain central as both characters and creators. As with her treatment of feminine myths, Warner favors a capacious understanding of symbolic objects that attends to the diverse originary sources as well as their sometimes significantly altered future forms. *Stranger Magic: Charmed States and the Arabian Nights* maintains a central preoccupation with feminine figures, particularly the storyteller, Shahrazad, but it also follows the multilayered histories of these stories through many different cultural encounters. For Warner, such encounters are a fertile site for reconsidering and moving beyond Enlightenment antinomies of rationality and imagination that produces as its counterpart irrational cultures as the locus of magical thinking. Indeed, "[c]ontact or translation zones may be flashpoints for conflict and indeed fields of protracted oppression, but they are also areas of mingling and interfusion, of a process of Creolisation" (26). *Stranger Magic* considers the meaning of *Arabian Nights* for modern readers for whom magic appears in many cultural forms, but is only recognized as such "when it wears a foreign dress" (22). The text of the *Arabian Nights* is itself a hybrid object, collected out of multiple traditions, variously reproduced and translated, and abridged and expanded, especially as the focus of European, and later American, fantasy. There is no pure original just as the historical Mary or Joan do not determine the symbolic power of their myths over time. However, the layered historical treatment of these myths and fables brings into focus distinctive traditions as well as their points of contact, creative, conflicted, and ambivalent. Pursuing the various incarnations of jinns, carpets, enchanted objects, and other characters and objects of the *Arabian Nights*, Warner highlights the magical and imaginative dimensions of these stories as tales of power, property, and language. From the prodigious power of Shahrazad's memory, imagination, and language, Warner draws a vital and still unfolding contribution to an intellectual tradition of "reasoned imagination" that echoes through Freud, Benjamin, Borges, and a host of others.[1]

Note

1 The phrase is borrowed from Borges, quoted in *Stranger Magic*, p. 22.

Warner's major writings

Nonfiction

1976. *Alone of All Her Sex: The Myth and the Cult of the Virgin Mary*, New York: Alfred A. Knopf.

[1981] 1999. *Joan of Arc: The Image of Female Heroism*. Berkeley: University of California Press.

1985. *Monuments and Maidens: The Allegory of the Female Form*. London: Picador.

1994. *From the Beast to the Blonde: On Fairy Tales and Their Tellers*. New York: Farrar, Straus and Giroux.

1998. *No Go the Bogeyman: Scaring, Lulling, and Making Mock*. New York: Farrar, Straus and Giroux.

2002. *Fantastic Metamorphoses, Other Worlds: Ways of Telling the Self*. Oxford: Oxford University Press.

2006. *Phantasmagoria: Spirit Visions, Metaphors, and Media into the Twenty-First Century*. Oxford: Oxford University Press.

2011. *Stranger Magic: Charmed States and the Arabian Nights*. Cambridge: Harvard University Press.

2014. *Once Upon a Time: A Short History of Fairy Tale*. Oxford: Oxford University Press.

Novels

[1977] 1992. *In a Dark Wood*. New York: Penguin.

[1982] 1992. *The Skating Party*. New York: Random House.

1987. *The Lost Father*. New York: Simon & Schuster.

1992. *Indigo*. New York: Simon & Schuster.

2001. *The Leto Bundle*. New York: Farrar, Straus and Giroux.

Further reading

Marinawarner.com

Coupe, Laurence. 2006. *Marina Warner*. Tavistock: Northcote House.

IDA B. WELLS-BARNETT (1862–1931)

Crystal N. Feimster

Ida B. Wells-Barnett, a teacher-turned-journalist who was the co-owner of the Memphis *Free Speech*, launched the anti-lynching movement in 1892 after a mob murdered three Memphis storeowners, one of whom was a close friend. She urged African Americans to fight back, with guns if necessary but mainly through economic pressure. Spurred by her scathing editorials, thousands migrated to Oklahoma while those who stayed boycotted the newly opened streetcar line. Wells-Barnett began investigating other lynchings, and she soon discovered that few lynch victims were even accused of rape and that behind many rape charges lay interracial affairs. When she published an editorial arguing, "nobody in this section of the country believes the old threadbare lie that Negro men rape white women,"[1] a white mob destroyed her press and warned Wells-Barnett, who was in New York at the time, not to return to Memphis at the cost of her life.

Far from being silenced by this attack, Wells-Barnett transformed herself from a local leader into the architect of an international crusade. In exile, she wrote for the *New York Age* and published *Southern Horrors: Lynch Law in All its Phases* (1892), which offered an incisive analysis of the economic roots of lynching and linked violence against black men with the sexual exploitation of black women. Wells-Barnett revealed that less than 30 percent of all lynchings involved the charge of rape and documented consensual sexual contact between black men and white women. Wells-Barnett argued that the focus and attention placed on the image of the black rapist concealed lynching's motives and masked violence against black women who were victims of sexual assault and lynching. She lectured throughout the North and West. In 1893 and 1894, she traveled to England, where she inspired the formation of the British Anti-Lynching Society and published *A Red Record* in 1895.

Although Wells-Barnett continued to advocate black militancy and self-help, she also hoped to turn white public opinion against the South. The lynching-for-rape myth, accepted by white people, North and South, depicted white men as the manly protectors of virtuous white women against uncivilized black men. Wells-Barnett's genius lay in her ability to reverse this trope, casting white southern men as the lustful rapists of black women and the hypocritical murderers of innocent black men. In short, she subverted the equation between whiteness, manliness, and civilization, an equation that lay at the heart of Victorian notions of manhood and that helped to justify imperialism throughout the world. By the end of her second British tour, Wells-Barnett had made lynching a cause célèbre among British reformers, and white American men found that their tolerance of racial violence had placed them in the uncomfortable position of unmanly savages in the eyes of the "civilized" world. Her skillful manipulation of dominant cultural themes did not stop lynching, but it did put mob violence on the American reform agenda and made visible sexual assault against black women.

Wells-Barnett relied from the outset on the support of a network of black women. A fund-raising event held in New York's Lyric Hall—Wells-Barnett described it as "the greatest demonstration ever attempted by race women for one of their own number" (1970, 78)—made possible the publication of *Southern Horrors*. When the president of the Missouri Press Association reacted to Wells-Barnett's British tour by maligning the morality of black women, Josephine St. Pierre Ruffin (1842–1924), head of Boston's New Era Club, used the incident as the occasion for founding the National Federation of Afro-American Women, which merged in 1896 with two other groups to form the National Association of Colored Women (NACW). The NACW followed Well-Barnett's lead and argued that the sexual exploitation of black women by white men and the lynching of African Americans were intricately linked.

In 1886, almost a decade before initiating her anti-lynching crusade, twenty-four year old Ida B. Wells published an article protesting the lynching of Eliza Woods in Jackson, Tennessee for the alleged poisoning of Mrs. J. P. Wooten. In her journal she worried that her editorial in which she "almost advised murder" was too militant and expressed her fear that southern whites would retaliate. From the inception of her crusade, Wells claimed that white hysteria about the rape of white women by black men effectively masked violence against women, black and white. "To justify their own barbarism," she argued, southern white men "assume a chivalry which they do not possess" (1997a, 80). Lynching, she explained, was not about protecting southern womanhood, but had everything to do with shoring up white men's social and political power. Desperate to control white women's sexual behavior and maintain sexual control over black women, southern white men, reasoned Wells, had created a scapegoat in the figure of the black rapist.

By 1896 the lynching of African Americans for allegedly raping white women had become a weekly event in southern states. At the same time, whites intensified their assaults on the moral character of black womanhood and continued to ignore sexual and racial violence against black women. Inspired by Wells-Barnett, the NACW believed that negative stereotypes of African Americans, especially of women, served to justify rape and lynching. Thus, redeeming the image of black womanhood and dispelling the myth of the black rapist was for many black clubwomen the first of many steps in eradicating sexual and racial violence. According to Mary Church Terrell, the first president of the NACW and an outspoken anti-lynching advocate, the duty of black clubwomen was "setting a high moral standard and living up to it." To counter the slander circulated by the white press, it was necessary for black women who represented "the intelligence and virtue" of the race, to "avoid even the appearance of evil" in both their public and private lives. In short, Terrell, like many middle-class black women, espoused a "politics of respectability" that emphasized self-help and intra-group reform (Terrell 1900). Racial uplift, argued many black clubwomen, would chip away at white supremacy and guarantee African Americans equal protection under the law.

While the NACW focused much of its energy on morality, education, and temperance, the organization created anti-lynching committees at the local and national levels and made a special point of publicizing lynching and violence against black women. Wells-Barnett continued her anti-lynching efforts and in 1898, she along with the Michigan Federation of Colored Women's Clubs petitioned President William McKinley to appropriate forty thousand dollars for the widow of a lynched South Carolina postmaster. In 1899, Wells-Barnett published *Lynch Law in Georgia*. In 1904, at the NACW's St. Louis biennial meeting, the organization passed its first resolution calling on the federal government to take a firmer stance against lynching. By 1908, Mary Church Terrell was delivering anti-lynching lectures calling for white support and demanding federal protection against rape and lynching.

The founding of the National Association for the Advancement of Colored People (NAACP) in 1909 created another avenue for black clubwomen to campaign against lynching. From its inception the NAACP worked to investigate and publish the facts about southern lynchings and provided a broader base for black women's anti-lynching campaign. Wells-Barnett was one of the three black speakers asked to speak at the founding meeting. In her speech, "Lynching: Our National Crime," Wells-Barnett proposed a campaign for federal anti-lynching legislation and "a bureau for the investigation and publication of the details of every lynching." Wells-Barnett and Terrell were the only women who signed the "Lincoln's Birthday Call" for the creation of the NAACP.

The war years along with the Nineteenth Amendment, ratified in 1920, ushered in a New Negro Woman, committed to militant agitation. Black clubwomen sparked a new phase of the anti-lynching campaign that called on direct action and demanded white women's active participation. As black women advocated greater political and economic power, more justice, improved commitment to a reformed society, less discrimination, and embraced female suffrage as a weapon in the battle against lynching and the sexual exploitation of black women, their politics became decidedly more radical. Black clubwomen participated in and often led the NAACP's campaign for federal anti-lynching legislation, raised thousands of dollars, lectured about the evils of lynching and the realities of rape, participated in protest marches, lobbied senators, testified before Congress and wielded the franchise in a politically powerful way. Following in Wells' footsteps the NACW and the NAACP together engaged in speaking and petitioning campaigns against lynching and investigated instances of mob violence that kept lynching constantly before the American public.

Wells-Barnett embodied the New Negro Woman in her most radical incarnation. Committed to both woman suffrage and the struggle for racial equality, she led a variety of organizations and political protests in Chicago, where she had moved in the 1890s. While on the margins of the national movements, she still set the pace for a new generation of activists. Linking disfranchisement to rape and lynching of African Americans, she insisted that woman suffrage was the only way to affect local and national politics and ensure protection. Since Reconstruction, black men and women understood the power of the ballot and embraced black male suffrage as a means of acquiring and maintaining their rights as citizens. Wells-Barnett, however, like many black women, was not willing to entertain the idea that the dirty world of male politics was no place for a woman. Dedicated to ensuring equal rights and justice through direct political action, she embraced woman suffrage as essential to the survival of black communities. She understood that white anti-suffragists in part feared not the power the ballot would impart to white women, but the power it would extend to black women. While Wells-Barnett joined the suffrage movement, she defined suffrage not as a woman's issue but as part of the larger campaign for racial and human justice. Black women had done so since the

1880s, but this new generation who came on the scene after 1910 did so more pointedly. Wells–Barnett, ever in the vanguard, sharpened the edge. The 1908 race riot in Springfield, Illinois and the 1909 lynching in Cairo, Illinois of William James, a black man accused of raping and murdering a white woman, not only reinforced her belief that blacks needed federal protection, but also her commitment to the ballot as blacks' most powerful weapon.

In 1922, Wells–Barnett traveled to Washington, D.C. with a delegation of black clubwomen, who had recently attended the Thirteenth Biennial Session of the National Association of Colored Women (NACW) in Richmond, Virginia. The fifteen NACW delegates had an appointment with President Warren Harding to urge him to hasten final action on the Dyer Bill, the first anti-lynching law to reach the U.S. Senate. Thirty years had passed since Wells–Barnett single-handedly initiated the anti-lynching movement and first called on the federal government for protection against southern lynch mobs. A landmark year for Wells–Barnett, 1922 marked her sixtieth birthday and the thirtieth anniversary of the publication of *Southern Horrors*. The movement that she had initiated had grown from a one-woman campaign to a national effort.

In June 2005, almost seventy-five years after her death, Wells–Barnett's anti-lynching crusade was recognized on the floor of the United States Senate. Led by Democratic Senator Mary Landrieu of Louisiana, the 109th Congress passed a resolution apologizing for the Senate's failure to pass anti-lynching legislation.

Note

1 Quoted in *American Citizen*, July 1, 1892.

Wells–Barnett's major writings

[1895] 1997a. "A Red Record." In *Southern Horrors and Other Writings: The Anti-Lynching Campaign of Ida B. Wells, 1892–1900*, ed. Jacqueline Jones Royster. Boston and New York: Bedford: 73–157.

1970. *Crusade for Justice: The Autobiography of Ida B. Wells*. Ed. Alfeda M. Duster. Chicago: University of Chicago Press.

1995. *The Memphis Diary of Ida B. Wells*. Ed. Miriam DeCosta-Willis. Boston: Beacon.

1997b. *Southern Horrors and Other Writings: The Anti-Lynching Campaign of Ida B. Wells, 1892–1900*. Ed. Jacqueline Jones Royster. Boston and New York: Bedford.

2002. *On Lynchings*. Ed. Patricia Hill Collins. Amherst, NY: Humanity Books.

Further reading

Bay, Mia. 2010. *To Tell the Truth Freely: The Life of Ida B. Wells*. New York: Hill and Wang.

Carby, Hazel V. 1985. "'On the Threshold of Woman's Era': Lynching, Empire, and Sexuality in Black Feminist Theory." In *"Race," Writing, and Difference*, ed. Henry Louis Gates, Jr. Chicago: Chicago University Press.

Davidson, James. 2008. *"They Say": Ida B. Wells and the Reconstruction of Race*. Oxford: Oxford University Press.

Feimster, Crystal. 2009. *Southern Horrors: Women and the Politics of Rape and Lynching*. Cambridge, MA: Harvard University Press.

Giddings, Paula. 2008. *Ida, A Sword Among Lions: Ida B. Wells and the Campaign Against Lynching*. New York: Amistad.

McMurray, Linda O. 1998. *To Keep the Water Troubled: The Life of Ida B. Wells*. New York: Oxford University Press

Schechter, Patricia A. 2001. *Ida B. Wells-Barnett and American Reform, 1880–1930*. Chapel Hill: University of North Carolina Press.

Terrell, Mary Church. 1900. "The Duty of the National Quest for Equality." *AME Church Review* (January): 340–54.

MONIQUE WITTIG (1935–2003)

Linda M. G. Zerilli

Monique Wittig was a radical lesbian feminist, theorist, and avant-garde writer. Born on July 13, 1935 in Dannemarie, in the Haut-Rhin department of Alsace, France, she moved in 1950 to Paris and studied at the Sorbonne, eventually obtaining her Ph.D. in 1986 at the École des Hautes Études en Sciences Sociales. While a student in Paris, Wittig became deeply involved in the radical worker and student movements associated with May 1968. Quickly disenchanted with their masculinist and heteronormative ideas and practices, she refocused her energies and became a founding member of radical lesbian and feminist groups such as the Mouvement de la libération des femmes (MLF), Féministes Révolutionnaires, Petites Marguerites, and the Gouines Rouges. On August 26, 1970 she marched together with many other women to lay flowers under the Arc de Triomphe in honor of the wife of the Unknown Soldier—an event that later took on significant symbolic value as a founding gesture of French feminism.

Although Wittig shared some views of the older generation of famous feminist philosophers and writers, including Simone de Beauvoir, Nathalie Sarraute and Marguerite Duras, her literary and political voice developed in ways that were radically unprecedented and uniquely her own. In addition to creatively challenging established novelistic and prose traditions, Wittig was a masterful political essayist who addressed the standing temptation to blindly naturalize or wilfully reanimate historically and politically inscribed relations of power. Apart from the gender politics of May 1968, she became deeply disillusioned with the development of *écriture féminine*, *parler-femme* (womanspeak), and *la sémiotique* (the maternal semiotic), associated, respectively, with Hélène Cixous, Luce Irigaray, and Julia Kristeva, and other forms of "difference feminism" that developed in 1970s France, partly as a response to the disappointments associated with the earlier politics of sexual equality. Fiercely critical of this turn in feminist theory and practice, Wittig joined the editorial collective of France's major theoretical and materialist feminist journal, *Questions Féministes*. In 1976 she moved to the United States and taught at various universities, until taking up her last academic position in 1990 in Women's Studies and French at the University of Arizona, Tucson. She played an important role in complicating the trans–Atlantic translation and reception of French feminism, especially in her position as an advisory editor to an American journal, *Feminist Issues*, which made available English translations of important French materialist feminist works that challenged the turn to difference. Her own writing became increasingly bi-lingual as she found her audience in American feminist circles. She died in Tucson on January 3, 2003 at the age of 67.

A central concern that Wittig shares with feminists of Beauvoir's generation is how to make visible and critique the widely accepted view that "men" and "women" are natural categories of gender identity as they are given in the biology of sex difference. This naturalization of gender as the cultural expression of biological sex is part of the pervasive androcentrism of language, culture, and society that hides behind putatively neutral concepts of the "universal." Like Beauvoir, Wittig recognizes that "man" and "human being" have an equivalent status that, far from gender neutral, relegates women qua females to the sexed body and thus to the "particular." The challenge is how to refuse the term that marks individuals as members of the sex class called "women" and thus as always already "particular," regardless of any actual material claim to universality on their part. As Beauvoir had already seen, to treat "women" as a mere linguistic marker in the manner of nominalism or to deny one's own membership in this sex class was highly fraught: it did not automatically follow that one would be taken for a "human being." Although Wittig often rails against the wholly ideological and illusory character of what she calls "the category of sex," she recognizes that feminist critique must do more, for the category of sex has an "always already there" character that makes such denial the equivalent of trying to jump over one's own shadow. Out of that shared recognition, however, Wittig develops an ingenious political and rhetorical strategy that significantly radicalizes the insight of Beauvoir and her generation of French feminists that "one is not born, but rather becomes, a woman."

Wittig's revolutionary poetics emerge in the creative joining together of her radical critique of heterosexuality and her equally radical conception of how to intervene in the quotidian material culture of language in which the category of sex is reproduced. Within the frame of what she calls "the straight mind," sex seems to exist as pure universal form in nature, "a priori, before all society," hence, as that which resists critical examination. The straight mind is everywhere and nowhere; it seamlessly if invisibly structures, among other things, the "primitive concepts" of established knowledge practices such as anthropology, sociology, and linguistics (Wittig 1992a, 21–32). Organized around the ancient conception of form as the ultimate cause of the being of entities, the straight mind sets out "sex" as the necessary predetermination or boundary of the form of any phenomenon: "you-will-be-straight-or-you-will-not-be." What can appear is what is sexed, and what is sexed is what is.

The writer who would make visible and attack such a taken for granted heteronormative worldview, argues Wittig, needs a literary "war machine" akin to the famous "Trojan Horse" with which the Aegeans famously tricked and destroyed their enemy by appearing in a recognizable form. And

> if one wants to build a perfect war machine, one must spare oneself the delusion that facts, actions, ideas can dictate directly to words their form. There is a detour, and the shock of words is produced by their association, their disposition, their arrangement, and also by each one of them as used separately.
>
> (1992c, 72)

Accordingly, the "war machine" that the radical lesbian feminist writer Wittig would build cannot be what she calls "committed literature," i.e., literature "with a social theme … [which] attracts attention to a social problem" (1992b, 62–63) and which becomes "a symbol, a manifesto" (1992b, 62). Committed literature operates at the level of meaning, of the concept, rather than at the level of letter or form (i.e., "the sign solely in relation to language" (1992b, 65)). Committed literature may make one think but it can never bring forth something new: "What I am saying is that the shock of words in literature does not come out of the ideas they are supposed to promote," she explains (1992c, 72).

> And to come back to our horse, if one wants to build a perfect war machine, one must spare oneself the delusion that facts, actions, ideas can dictate directly to words their form. There is a detour, and the shock of words is produced by their association, their disposition, their arrangement, and also by each one of them used separately.
>
> (1992c, 72)

If one avoids this detour, says Wittig, one will produce a work populated with recognizable figures like 'the homosexual,' which is "interesting only to homosexuals" (1992b, 63), and which fails to transform the system of reference in which that very identity "appears like a ghost only dimly and sometimes not at all" (1992e, 41).

"Any important literary work is like the Trojan Horse at the time it is produced. Any work with a new form operates as a war machine, because its design and its goal is to pulverize the old forms and formal conventions," writes Wittig (1992c, 68–69). The central target of her war machine is the form of sex as it is reproduced through the grammatical logic of the pronoun. As "the pathways and the means of entrance into language" (1992d, 78) pronouns at once enforce the heterosexual logic of the straight mind by compelling (especially the French) speaker/writer to mark her sex in their use and open the space in which to challenge that logic.

In *L'opoponax* (1964), Wittig's first widely acclaimed war machine, the two girl protagonists refer to themselves in the third person as "*on*" ("one"), allowing Wittig to avoid problems of gendering and numbering "because *on* is 'neuter' and can represent a certain number of people successively or all at once while still remaining singular" (1964, 6), thus delegating both the universal and the particular. In her next literary work, *Les guérillères* (1969), the warriors who create a new society in the ruins of patriarchal culture are referred to as "*elles*," technically the plural third person feminine pronoun ("they"). The "shock of words" is to present this *elles* to the reader through the virtual elimination of an *"ils"* (they-he) that relativizes *"elles"* as "they-she" and so inscribes the category of sex. In the absence of *ils*, in other words, *elles* is no longer read as a sexed (plural) subject, and *elles* becomes the universal, "absolute subject of the world," comments Wittig.[1] And in *Le corps lesbien* (1973), the Trojan Horse pronoun "j/e" elides the distinction between "you" and "I," to signify a subject that is neither divided nor sexed but that once again claims universality.

Wittig's remarkable revolution in pronouns, however, tells only half the story of her creative feminist practice. To take the Wittigean Trojan Horse inside the walls of the straight mind is not so much to go on a journey into a mythical past or a utopian future unmarked by sex but to encounter "figures/forms of the newly thinkable." Echoing the spirit of the transformative power of radical imagination, *Les guérillères* beckons the reader:

> There was a time when you were not a slave, remember that. You walked alone, full of laughter, you bathed bare-bellied. You say you have lost all recollection of it, remember ... You say there are no words to describe this time, you say it does not exist. But remember. Make an effort to remember. Or, failing that, invent.
>
> (1985, 89)

Note

1 Infelicitously translated by David Le Vay into English as "the women," *elles* loses its war machine character, complains Wittig. "When *elles* is turned into *the women*," she writes, "the process of universalization is destroyed. All of a sudden *elles* stopped being *mankind*" (Wittig 1992d, 86).

Wittig's major writings

1964. *L'opoponax*. Paris: Union Générale d'Editions. (Winner of the Prix Médicis.)

[1969] 1985. *Les guérillères*. Translated by David Le Vay. Boston: Beacon.

[1973] 1975. *The Lesbian Body*. Translated by David Le Vay. New York: William Morrow.

[1980] 1992a. "The Straight Mind." In *The Straight Mind and Other Essays*. Boston: Beacon, 21–32.

[1982] 1992b. "The Point of View: Universal or Particular?" In *The Straight Mind and Other Essays*. Boston: Beacon, 59–67.

[1984] 1992c. "The Trojan Horse." In *The Straight Mind and Other Essays*. Boston: Beacon, 68–75.

[1985] 1987. *Across the Acheron*. Translated by David Le Vay and Margaret Crosland. London: Peter Owen.

[1985] 1992d. "The Mark of Gender." In *The Straight Mind and Other Essays*. Boston: Beacon, 76–89.

[1989] 1992e. "On the Social Contract." In *The Straight Mind and Other Essays*. Boston: Beacon, 33–45.

1992. *The Straight Mind and Other Essays*. Boston: Beacon.

1999. *Paris-la-Politique et Autre Histoires*. Paris: POL.

[1976] 1979. Wittig, Monique and Sande Zeig. *Lesbian Peoples: Material for a Dictionary*. New York: Avon.

The film *The Girl*, directed by Sande Zeig, Wittig's partner and collaborator, is made out of Wittig's first English short story (unpublished).

MARY WOLLSTONECRAFT (1759–1797)

Angela F. Maione

Mary Wollstonecraft was an eighteenth-century English political theorist who is most well known for two political pamphlets, both of which were published in the single most significant public intellectual debate around the French Revolution in Britain (Cobban 1950). Commonly known as the Revolution Controversy, this debate began with Edmund Burke's *Reflections on the Revolution in France* (1790) to which Wollstonecraft's *A Vindication of the Rights of Men* (1790) was the first reply. *Rights of Men* set the tone for the republican defense of the rights of men against hereditary monarchical rule, leading the outpour of pamphlets that followed it. First published anonymously at an historical moment when women did not take up their pens to write political disquisitions, *Rights of Men* was assumed to have been written by a male author. The immediate widespread warm reception to this first *Vindication* allowed Wollstonecraft, in a second edition, to disclose her own name as author and, with that, the fact that she was a woman (Gunther-Canada 2001). Though it was eventually overshadowed by Thomas Paine's reply to Burke with his own *Rights of Man* (1791–1792), the initial enthusiastic response to Wollstonecraft's *Rights of Men* created the conditions in which Wollstonecraft might have a place at the center of political debate in order, for the first time in history, to publish a book-length figuration and defense of the rights of women to participate in republican political community. With the publication of *A Vindication of the Rights of Woman* (1792), Wollstonecraft broke out of the domesticating mold that constrained women and prevented them from publicly participating in mainstream political debate in order to claim her rights to citizenship. Although she could not have known it at the time, it was precisely in this sense that Wollstonecraft met the prediction that she had made in a letter to her youngest sister that she would be "the first of a new genus" (Wardle 1979, 164).

While *Rights of Woman* is Wollstonecraft's greatest achievement as well as the text within her corpus that is of the most direct relevance to feminist scholarship, feminists have traditionally either favored many of Wollstonecraft's other works or, importantly, the telling and retelling of stories from her biographies. To a certain extent these preferences are understandable. Though Wollstonecraft only lived until her thirty-eighth year, the writings she left behind contribute to a range of areas beyond political theory including the eighteenth-century novel (*Mary, A Fiction*, 1788), children's literature (*Original Stories from Real Life*, 1788, the second edition of which was illustrated by William Blake), and travel literature (*Letters Written during a Short Residence in Sweden, Norway and Denmark*, 1796) in addition to pedagogy, history, book reviews, and translations. Moreover, as a feminist icon, it could be argued that it was Wollstonecraft's life almost as much as her works that inspired feminist movement beginning in the nineteenth-century all the way to the present. In fact, Wollstonecraft lived so thoroughly and yet seemingly with the most economical of fervent passions that it is tempting to see within every detail of her life's story a sign, if not an explanation, of the journey that enabled her to do what no woman before her had done.

Wollstonecraft was born in Spitalfields, London, on April 27, 1759 to Elizabeth Dickson from a Protestant family in Ireland, and Edward John Wollstonecraft, the son of a weaver whose financial success and early death ensured that Wollstonecraft's father could try his hand at gentleman farming. After having left the urban manufacturing neighborhood for the country, Wollstonecraft's family moved from farm to farm as the land around them gradually diminished as a result of the Enclosure Acts. Profitable farming proved elusive for Edward Wollstonecraft, keeping the very young Mary Wollstonecraft on the move and acquainting her with a variety of landscapes and worldly conditions. From the time that Wollstonecraft was nine until the age of fifteen, her family remained in one place; during this period she had almost all of her formal education in day schools before moving on.

Then, in search of independence at age nineteen, Wollstonecraft left the inhospitable home of her impecunious family against its wishes. Before publishing a number of works and becoming a professional writer for Joseph Johnson's *Analytical Review*, Wollstonecraft held most of the acceptable positions for women from her socio-economic background: a lady's companion (1778), a schoolmistress (1784), and a governess (1786). She wrote and traveled extensively, combining movement with writing. Throughout a long trip to Paris, for example, she produced *An Historical and Moral View of the Origin and Progress of the French Revolution* (1794). Her extraordinary career ended abruptly and prematurely when, as a result of complications in childbirth, she died on September 10, 1797.

With Wollstonecraft's biographical sketch in mind, it is enticing to interpret the impact of her personality and life experiences into her work. One might see in the first *Vindication* an understanding of the socio-political factors that contributed to her father's economic troubles in addition to a concern for those who were less fortunate than she within the context of her attunement to the broader political movement for democratic reform going on around her. One might even be astonished at the political acumen in interpreting and contesting the effect of early signs of a coming Industrial Revolution that she demonstrated by being the first to question Burke about the concentration of political and economic power in the hands of the few when, with paltry resources, her own education taught her that a girl needed to know nothing beyond how to attain some "corporeal accomplishment." And when, near the end of that text, Wollstonecraft writes that "virtue can only flourish amongst equals" (1995, 61), one might read not only a rejection of the domination that, on her view, plagued men, but also a growing consciousness of the obstacles in her own life that held her back as she came to see socio-economic disadvantage as an issue that was both distinct from and yet related to gender.

Indeed, one might see the exercise of the very virtue for which Wollstonecraft advocates in both *Vindications* in the way in which she threw open her own doors and rarely spared opportunities to both connect with others and to publish her hard-earned reflections. For example, by establishing a school at Newington Green, she both furnished herself with material for her first book, *Thoughts on the Education of Daughters* (1787), and she also positioned herself to meet notable members within the dissenting community, including Richard Price, with whom she identified in despite of having been born into the Church of England. This drive to reach out, which attained the height of its fulfillment with the publication of *Rights of Woman*, was necessary to her success; it was also linked to her ability to see gender in radical republican terms. Unlike her seventeenth-century predecessors like the high-Anglican Mary Astell, for example, Wollstonecraft was not interested merely in intellectual equality between men and women from the perspective of Tory politics; rather, the question of women's education could not, for her, be separated from a struggle for political equality for all against arbitrary rule. While less privileged girls had no access to education, the young Wollstonecraft was not among those who were privileged to have a governess or whose father or other male relative oversaw her studies (as was, by contrast, the case for many of the so-called bluestockings, that is, the elite women with whom Wollstonecraft is often, if erroneously, grouped). Wollstonecraft was obliged to self-educate, a herculean task that she accomplished not only by reading books but by endearing herself, from a young age forward, to various people from whom she might learn. Yet from the very beginning of her life, in despite of her efforts, Wollstonecraft could count on few women; it was radical men who were most responsive to her. Even those women who were sympathetic kept some distance from Wollstonecraft out of fear that the potential negative reaction to her political radicalism, which was inextricably linked to the way in which she flouted gender norms, would be redirected toward them.

After Wollstonecraft's death, the defeat of radical reform in Britain and the publication of the memoirs of her widower, William Godwin, conspired to turn Wollstonecraft into a symbolic scapegoat for political radicals. An anti-Wollstonecraft tradition that suppressed *Rights of Woman* was born (Todd 1975). From that moment forward anti-feminists and feminists alike became absorbed with the "scandalous" details of Wollstonecraft's life (Todd 1976). In their efforts to redeem the embattled memory of Wollstonecraft, feminists from Margaret Fuller to Emma Goldman to Virginia Woolf deradicalized and domesticated Wollstonecraft by excusing or celebrating her relationships to men in their homages to her.

Yet scorn for Wollstonecraft is currently alive and well. At the present historical juncture the derision often comes from twenty-first century feminists who rarely engage her work without recourse to biographical details that focus on her love life and sexuality divorced from historical context and the central political debate of which her key writings were part. When cited approvingly, Wollstonecraft is often hailed as the first defender of contemporary women's human rights, which is an anachronistic assessment that is belied by the loss of the radical republican rights that she figured. Wollstonecraft had no radical feminist inheritance on which she could draw and yet she politicized gender by contesting societal norms while also affirming public freedom for women as political actors. To the extent that it may still be held that gender hierarchy is a political problem, the historical model of Wollstonecraft's creativity in thought coupled with her courage to act could prove useful as an inspiration for action in future feminist thought and practice.

Wollstonecraft's major writings

[1790] 1995. *A Vindication of the Rights of Woman*. In *A Vindication of the Rights of Men with A Vindication of the Rights of Woman and Hints*, ed. Sylvana Tomaselli (Cambridge: Cambridge University Press).

1989. *The Works of Mary Wollstonecraft*, vols. 1–7, eds. Janet Todd and Marilyn Butler (Washington Square: New York University Press).

Further reading

Bahar, Saba. 2002. *Mary Wollstonecraft's Social and Aesthetic Philosophy: 'An Eve to Please Me'* (New York: Palgrave).

Botting, Eileen Hunt, and Carey, Christine. 2004. "Wollstonecraft's Philosophical Impact on Nineteenth-Century American Women's Rights Advocates." *American Journal of Political Science* 48(4): 707–22.

Cobban, Alfred. 1950. *The Debate on the French Revolution* (London: Adam and Charles Black).

Godwin, William. [1798] 2001. *Memoirs of the Author of A Vindication of the Rights of Woman*, ed. Pamela Cemit and Gina Luria Walker (Orchard Park, NY: Broadview Press).

Gunther-Canada, Wendy. 2001. *Rebel Writer: Mary Wollstonecraft and Enlightenment Politics* (DeKalb: Northern Illinois University Press).

Maione, Angela. Forthcoming. *Revolutionary Rhetoric: Wollstonecraft's Vindications*.

Modugno, Roberta A. 2002. *Mary Wollstonecraft: diritti umani e Rivoluzione francese* (Soveria Mannelli: Rubettino).

Sapiro, Virginia. 1992. *A Vindication of Political Virtue: Political Theory of Mary Wollstonecraft* (Chicago: University of Chicago Press).

Taylor, Barbara. 2003. *Mary Wollstonecraft and the Feminist Imagination* (Cambridge: Cambridge University Press).

Todd, Janet. 1975. "The Polwhelan Tradition and Richard Cobb." *Studies in Burke and His Time* 16(3): 271–77.

—. 1976. "The Biographies of Mary Wollstonecraft." *Signs* 1(3): 721–34.

Wardle, Ralph Martin (ed.). 1979. *Collected Letters of Mary Wollstonecraft* (Ithaca, NY and London: Cornell University Press).

Wardle, Ralph Martin. [c. 1951] 1966. *Mary Wollstonecraft: A Critical Biography* (Lincoln: University of Nebraska Press).

VIRGINIA WOOLF (1882–1941)

Susan Sellers

'Women have served all these centuries as looking-glasses possessing the magic and delicious power of reflecting the figure of man at twice its natural size', novelist and essayist Virginia Woolf argues in a series of lectures to women students in 1928. Published the following year as *A Room of One's Own*, Woolf highlights the economic and cultural conditions that have denied women access to education and prevented their participation in public life and the professions. While *A Room of One's Own* is particularly interested in the toll this has taken on women's contribution to literature, it is also attentive to the impact women's education and financial independence will have more widely. *A Room of One's Own* ends in anticipation of the changes that will ensue once more women begin to write and enter areas previously disbarred to them such as science. In 'Professions for Women', drafted two years later, Woolf argues that only then will it be possible to discuss women with any authority: 'What is a woman? … I do not believe that anybody can know until she has expressed herself in all the arts and professions open to human skill'.[1]

Virginia Woolf was born Adeline Virginia Stephen in London in 1882. Her father Sir Leslie Stephen was the founding editor of the *Dictionary of National Biography*, and allowed his intelligent daughter to read freely from his well-stocked library.[2] Like many women in her day, Virginia was home-educated, though her studies in Greek were overseen by the classical scholar Janet Case and in Latin by Clara Pater, and she attended degree-level classes in Greek, Latin, History and German at King's College, London, between 1897 and 1901. She remained a serious and avid reader of literature throughout her life, frequently rereading favourites such as the Elizabethans and the Romantic poets, and extending her reading to other national literatures. She read Classical Greek and French literature in the original, advised on translations of nineteenth-century Russian novels including Dostoyevsky's *The Devils*, encouraged the Chinese woman writer Ling Shuhua, and (from 1905) became a regular literary reviewer, initially battling against its predominantly male parameters as Hermione Lee has argued (2010, 92). She published two collections of essays on literature under the title *The Common Reader*. Through the Hogarth Press, which she established with her husband in 1917, she was responsible for bringing into print important modernist authors including women such as Vita Sackville-West and Katherine Mansfield. While literature remained her preoccupation, she read and wrote on a diverse range of subjects, including history, biography, women's lives, painting, the cinema, travel, London's streets and shops, the countryside, the solar eclipse of June 1927, the radio and, increasingly through the 1930s, polemical essays on politics, women and war. Married to Leonard Woolf in 1912 in a partnership that continued until her death in 1941, Virginia Woolf had intense and enduring relationships with a number of women friends, including Violet Trefusis, the writer Vita Sackville-West and the composer Ethel Smyth, as well as a lifelong bond with her elder sister, the artist Vanessa Bell.

The ten works of fiction that have secured Virginia Woolf's reputation as a pioneer of the modern novel all interrogate the gender norms of her time, whether through a focus on women's experience as in *The Voyage Out*, *Mrs Dalloway* and *To the Lighthouse*, or, as in *Orlando* and the posthumously published *Between the Acts*, by exploring the construction of gender through history. The eponymous 'hero' of *Orlando*, for example, begins the narrative as a young man living in England at the time of Queen Elizabeth I, but ends it in the present day of publication as a middle-aged woman. Consequently, Orlando witnesses first-hand the various legal and subtle behests directed at both sexes across different historical periods, exposing not only the flimsy and fluctuating nature of gender, but also its dependence on presentation and performance – on clothes worn and comportment – rather than biology. The novel abounds with sharply satirical observations of the absurdity and damage this causes, as in the legal challenges facing Orlando in the early eighteenth century over the ownership of her property: 'The chief charges against her were (1) that she was dead, and therefore could not hold any property whatsoever; (2) that she was a woman, which amounts to much the same thing'.[3] The novel's comic tone may in part have evolved to veil the same-sex relationships Orlando engages in. In an unpublished draft of *A Room of One's Own*, which Woolf worked on alongside the composition of *Orlando*, the consequences of intimating that women like each other are sketched in as the author imagines the knock of an arresting officer at her door. Shortly before *Orlando* appeared, Woolf signed a letter in support of the writer Radclyffe Hall, whose novel *The Well of Loneliness*, with its theme of love between two women, had been seized and withdrawn by order of the Home Secretary.

The published version of *A Room of One's Own* retains Woolf's original lecture format of a woman speaking to women. Using a novelist's technique of storytelling, Woolf describes the obstacles that have hampered the preparation of her lecture. For instance, in researching her topic of 'women and fiction' in the library of the British Museum in London, she discovered that although a great deal has been written about women, it is almost entirely by men. While she judges some of this praiseworthy, it shares a common feature: in the 'shadow' cast by the male author's 'I', any woman who appears 'has not a bone in her body'.[4] Woolf contrasts the wealth and traditions of the long-established men's colleges at Oxbridge (her shorthand for the universities of Oxford and Cambridge) with the new and impoverished women's colleges by comparing her markedly different experience of dining at each.[5] Among the story tellers of *A Room of One's Own* are Mary Beton, Mary Seton and Mary Carmichael, who feature in a sixteenth-century ballad about a fourth Mary Hamilton: a lady in waiting to the Queen of Scotland who is sentenced to death for infanticide after being made pregnant by the King. This intertextual reference to a historical woman prevented from living her life freely is echoed in a story about the imaginary Judith Shakespeare, sister to the playwright William. Woolf pictures this fictive sibling sharing her brother's talents, but not his success. While he was taught the tools of his trade (grammar, logic and the Classics) at school, Judith's girlhood would have been devoted to domestic duties in preparation for marriage to a man of her parents' choosing. She might have defied her parents and followed her brother to London, but would have been unable to find work as he did since at that time women were not permitted to act. Forced into prostitution, Woolf ends Judith Shakespeare's story when, discovering herself pregnant, she 'kill[s] herself one winter's night and lies buried at some cross-roads'.[6]

That Virginia Woolf is able to name so few women writers from history in *A Room of One's Own* leads her 'to guess that Anon, who wrote so many poems without signing them, was often a woman'.[7] Her search across past centuries on the grounds that 'we think back through our mothers if we are women'[8] paved the way for Anglophone feminist scholars in the 1970s to locate, re-value and disseminate women's writing. *A Room of One's Own* also prefigures more recent feminist enquiry as Woolf explores the alienation women experience reading what has been written from a male-only viewpoint, investigates how 'woman' has been appropriated and used within language and culture, and speculates on the form of a specifically women's 'sentence'. Her style in this essay, which is personal, circuitous, combative and involves the telling of multiple women's stories, may indicate Woolf's own sense of what a 'feminine' writing might be like. *A Room of One's Own* ends with the intimation that what counts is courage and collective endeavour; a belief that may have prompted Woolf to write the introduction to and publish a collection of autobiographical writings by workers from the Women's Co-operative Guild (*Life as We Have Known It*, 1931).

In 'Professions for Women', Woolf is emphatic that women must throw off the subservient role history has allotted us. Drawing on her own experience as an example, she cites the insidious 'phantom' of ideal womanhood (encapsulated in the 1854 poem by Coventry Patmore 'The Angel in the House') that has besieged her career as a writer. Aided by financial independence from a small inheritance and then her own earnings, Woolf delineates her daily struggle against the edicts of this 'phantom' which, if listened to, make it impossible for women to have 'a mind of your own' and express 'what you think to be the truth'.

In 1910, Woolf worked for a brief period for the women's suffrage movement, most probably for a body called the People's Suffrage Federation. Despite supporting the right to vote, she was ambivalent about feminist activism and in her novel *Night and Day* mocks the egoism and pettiness of some women's suffrage campaigners. Laura Marcus, following Alex Zwerdling, suggests that this ambivalence derived from a concern that the focus on suffrage was too narrow (2010, 211). As Marcus observes, in the epistolary *Three Guineas*, published in 1938, Woolf's agenda is a broader investigation into the workings of patriarchy and the difficulties women face in identifying and then liberating ourselves from it. Attentive to the close connection between patriarchy and patriotism, Woolf links the politics of gender with the rise of fascism across Europe. It is in this essay that she puts forward the hope that by embracing our 'outsider' status, women can transcend the power hierarchy of the father-dictator that tethers nations and leads to war: '[A]s a woman, I have no country. As a woman I want no country. As a woman my country is the whole world.'[9] In 'Thoughts on Peace in an Air Raid', written as a battle rages above her home in East Sussex in 1940, Woolf sees women's absence as either directors or active combatants in World War II as an opportunity. Since men appear unable to resist the tyrannies and lures that incite both sides to fight, women must do their thinking for them and create alternative scenarios founded on peace: 'there is another way of fighting for freedom without arms; we can fight with the mind'.[10]

Notes

1 'Professions for Women' was first delivered as a lecture to the National Society for Women's Service on 21 January 1931. It was published posthumously in 1942.
2 Leslie Stephen's editorship lasted from 1882 until 1891.
3 http://gutenberg.net.au/ebooks02/0200331.txt, Chapter 4.
4 http://gutenberg.net.au/ebooks02/0200791.txt, Chapter 6.
5 The lectures were given to the students of the two Cambridge women's colleges, Girton and Newnham. Woolf's other dining experience was at the all-male King's College, where her friend George Rylands was a Fellow.
6 http://gutenberg.net.au/ebooks02/0200791.txt, Chapter 3.
7 http://gutenberg.net.au/ebooks02/0200791.txt, Chapter 3.
8 http://gutenberg.net.au/ebooks02/0200791.txt, Chapter 4.
9 http://gutenberg.net.au/ebooks02/0200931.txt, Chapter 3.
10 http://gutenberg.net.au/ebooks02/0200771.txt.

Woolf's major writings

1915. *The Voyage Out*. London: Duckworth.

1919. *Night and Day*. London: Duckworth.

1922. *Jacob's Room*. London: Hogarth Press.

1925. *Mrs Dalloway*. London: Hogarth Press.

1925. *The Common Reader*, 1. London: Hogarth Press.

1927. *To the Lighthouse*. London: Hogarth Press.

1928. *Orlando*. London: Hogarth Press.

1929. *A Room of One's Own*. London: Hogarth Press.

1931. *The Waves*. London: Hogarth Press.

1932. *The Common Reader*, 2. London: Hogarth Press.

1933. *Flush*. London: Hogarth Press.

1937. *The Years*. London: Hogarth Press.

1938. *Three Guineas*. London: Hogarth Press.

1940. *Roger Fry*. London: Hogarth Press.

1941. *Between the Acts*. London: Hogarth Press.

1975–80. *The Letters of Virginia Woolf, 1888–1941*, 6 volumes, edited Joanne Trautmann Banks and Nigel Nicolson. London: Hogarth Press.

1977–84. *The Diary of Virginia Woolf 1915–1941*, 5 volumes, edited Anne Olivier Bell. London: Hogarth Press.

1986–2011. *The Essays of Virginia Woolf, 1904–1941*, 6 volumes, edited Andrew McNeillie and Stuart N. Clarke. London: Hogarth Press.

1990. *A Moment's Liberty: Shorter Diary of Virginia Woolf*, edited Anne Olivier Bell. London: Hogarth Press.

2002. *Moments of Being: Autobiographical Writings*, edited Jeanne Schulkind. London: Pimlico.
2008. *Selected Letters*, edited Joanne Trautmann Banks. London: Vintage.
2009. *Selected Essays of Virginia Woolf*, edited David Bradshaw. Oxford: Oxford University Press.

Further reading

Beer, Gillian. 1996. *Virginia Woolf: The Common Ground*. Edinburgh: Edinburgh University Press.
Bowlby, Rachel. 1997. *Feminist Destinations and Further Essays on Virginia Woolf*. Edinburgh: Edinburgh University Press.
Goldman, Jane. 2010. *The Cambridge Introduction to Virginia Woolf*. Cambridge: Cambridge University Press.
Lee, Hermione. 1999. *Virginia Woolf*. London: Vintage. (Originally published 1997.)
—. 2010. 'Virginia Woolf's Essays'. In *The Cambridge Companion to Virginia Woolf*, edited Susan Sellers. Cambridge: Cambridge University Press. 91–108.
Marcus, Laura. 1997. *Virginia Woolf*. Devon: Northcote House.
—. 2010. 'Woolf's Feminism and Feminism's Woolf'. In *The Cambridge Companion to Virginia Woolf*, edited Susan Sellers. Cambridge: Cambridge University Press. 209–44.
Sellers, Susan (ed.). 2010. *The Cambridge Companion to Virginia Woolf*. Cambridge: Cambridge University Press.
Whitworth, Michael H. (ed.). 2009. *Virginia Woolf (Authors in Context)*. Oxford: Oxford University Press.
Zwerdling, Alex. 1986. *Virginia Woolf and the Real World*. California: University of California Press.

IRIS MARION YOUNG (1949–2006)

Michaele Ferguson

Iris Young once described herself (borrowing from Linda Singer) as a *bandita*—a feminist bandit who selectively steals resources from male philosophers to serve her own political purposes, while leaving behind whatever of their work is sexist or unhelpful. Young regularly drew from a variety of intellectual traditions and thinkers that do not sit

comfortably with one another: feminist theory and practice, phenom-
enology, existentialism, analytic philosophy, and authors like Michel
Foucault, Jacques Derrida, and Jürgen Habermas. Yet she never bothered with the task of making the ideas she stole from various sources
philosophically compatible. Rather, Young was driven by what her
political needs were at any particular moment: if a thinker or tradition
was helpful to her in analyzing a political problem, then that was justification enough to do with it what she needed.

Indeed, unlike many of her fellow philosophers, Young always began
her theoretical inquiry with a practical issue: the challenges of inhabiting a female body in a culture that devalues and objectifies such bodies,
or the seeming impossibility of organizing a social movement around
the category of "woman" without being able to agree about what
makes women women, or the diverse claims of oppression articulated
by social justice activists. "I want to cling to the practical," she declared
in a 1999 interview. The practical, she explained, is "what is important
to me and to most other people when they are not doing philosophy" (Dhanda, 13). Her concern to make the practical the focus of her
theorizing is what makes Young's contributions to feminist thinking so
fresh, insightful, and urgent. She took up the important political questions of her time because they mattered to her and to others when they
were not doing philosophy.

Young's orientation to the practical grew out of a combination of
her training in philosophy and her political activism. As an undergraduate at Queens College, she studied existentialism—a school of
philosophy that stresses the importance of first-person experience of
existence. As a Ph.D. student at Pennsylvania State University, she studied Ludwig Wittgenstein, who showed that many philosophical dilemmas are dilemmas only for philosophers; in ordinary practice, these
problems simply disappeared. Her academic training prepared Young to
take the practical seriously and to be suspicious of abstract philosophical debates removed from everyday concerns.

After graduate school, Young became increasingly engaged in political activism. In the 1970s, she identified as a socialist feminist, but later
distanced herself from socialist orthodoxy. She embraced Jesse Jackson's
Rainbow Coalition in the 1980s as a model for social justice activism
that embraced yet went beyond socialism and feminism. As she moved
for different jobs, she became involved in various forms of community
organizing: in Worcester, Massachusetts, she volunteered for a candidate
for the school committee; in Pittsburgh, she participated in struggles
for greater police accountability. She also integrated activism into her
academic life, and was a valued participant and mentor in professional

groups devoted to radical political philosophy, engaged scholarship, and feminism.

As a result of her political engagement, Young's work became increasingly interdisciplinary—driven by the needs of her practical concerns, rather than the needs of the discipline of philosophy. Her remarkable breadth was on full display in the 1990 book that cemented her reputation as one of the most important political thinkers of her generation, *Justice and the Politics of Difference*. *Justice* spanned multiple fields—feminist theory, public policy, urban planning, and political theory—and took inspiration from a variety of social justice movements, earning her the American Political Science Association's Victoria Schuck Award for the best book on women and politics. 1990 also marked a professional turning point for Young: she left the field of philosophy to take a faculty position in the Graduate School of Public and International Affairs at the University of Pittsburgh. She later moved to the University of Chicago's Department of Political Science. Her interest in the practical had taken her far afield from philosophy.

Young came of age during the heyday of the Second Wave; her earliest feminist essays are interventions in the intense debates in the 1970s among activists and academics about how to conceptualize patriarchy. She was influenced by radical feminism, and in particular by its preoccupation with personal experience. However, as a socialist Young believed that personal experience could never be abstracted away from materiality—especially the materiality of bodies. Like other socialist feminists, Young sought to combine the insights of both radical feminism and socialism. Radical feminists theorized patriarchy as a system of universal male dominance; they drew on women's personal experiences in order to identify evidence of this ideological system. Socialists by contrast located the root cause of women's oppression in the material relations of capitalism. Young was critical of how many socialist feminists united these two social theories by treating capitalism and patriarchy as mutually exclusive phenomena. In an early essay, "Socialist Feminism and the Limits of Dual Systems Theory" (1980), she argued that socialist feminists should instead theorize capitalism and patriarchy as interrelated, albeit conceptually distinct.

To Young, combining the insights of radical feminism and socialism meant analyzing the symbolic (consciousness, culture, psychology, ideology) as well as the material (the built environment, relations of production, relations of reproduction, social structures). While this approach informed all of her scholarship, it is expressed most explicitly in her essays on female body experience (see *Throwing Like a Girl*, 1990 and *On Female Body Experience*, 2005). In these essays, Young theorized the body as the site of lived experience: experience shaped by both the material reality of the body and the ideological messages of patriarchal culture.

While many other feminists have theorized female embodiment (e.g., Sandra Bartky, Susan Bordo, Elizabeth Grosz, Luce Irigaray, and Julia Kristeva), Young's phenomenological approach to studying bodily experience is innovative and unique. Her analysis of the lived experience of the female body draws inspiration from Maurice Merleau-Ponty's studies of embodied experience and Simone de Beauvoir's understanding of the body as a "situation." Young's first essay on female embodiment is among her most well known, "Throwing Like a Girl" (1980). In this essay she theorized women's experience of habitually regulating their physical bodies to comport with patriarchal norms of femininity. This essay figured the body as a site of gendered oppression and unfreedom, but in later essays Young sought also to recover positive experiences in female embodiment. She studied "Breasted Experience" (1990), "Pregnant Embodiment" (1984), dressing and shopping for clothes, doing housework and maintaining a home. Young waited until she had experienced menopause herself before writing her "Menstrual Meditations" (2005). In each of these essays, she critically analyzed the bodily and cultural constraints on women, while also identifying positive experiences of female embodiment (for example, she argues that the periodicity of menstruation marks time and memory in women's lives).

Of course to speak of female body experience is to risk essentialism: claiming that all women share the same experiences. Young was acutely aware that women's experiences vary. Yet she refused to accept that the project of theorizing female body experience must therefore be incoherent. Consequently, while she rejected essentialism, she also rejected its counterpart, anti-essentialism. In the 1980s and early 1990s, feminist theorists such as Judith Butler, Ann Ferguson, Chandra Mohanty, Denise Riley, and Elizabeth Spelman debated these two alternatives to theorizing "the category of women." Young found their proposed solutions unhelpful because in various ways they called into question the ability of feminists to speak meaningfully about women.

Against the intellectual fashion of the time, Young insisted that feminist social theory and especially feminist politics require the ability to speak meaningfully about women as a collectivity. That is, she sought to redeem the category of women because of its practical value. Yet she did not offer the pragmatic response of Gayatri Chakravorty Spivak's "strategic essentialism" (which posits the existence of a subject only for the purposes of political action, while denying its conceptual coherence). On the contrary, Young argued in "Gender as Seriality" (1994) that the category of women could be both politically and theoretically coherent when "women" are understood as a series.

Young, acting as a *bandita*, lifted the concept of the series from Jean-Paul Sartre's *Critique of Dialectical Reason*. Sartre defined a series as a passive collection of people who are positioned in similar ways by their material environment, social structures, and cultural patterns. Women, Young argued, are those people who are positioned in similar ways by the combination of material and cultural constraints that constitute women as a collectivity (such as female bodies, compulsory heterosexuality, gendered language, and the sexual division of labor). The category of women refers to a structural position in a particular historical and material context. These structures do not determine individual-level experiences or group-level political identifications. Thus it is possible for two people to be positioned as women, and yet experience this positionality quite differently: one may experience the objectification of her body as a constraint, where another may experience this same phenomenon as liberating; one may experience pregnancy and childbirth, where another may not. Similarly, one person positioned as a woman may become politically active as a feminist, where another such person may be uninclined to see her gender as a site for political activity.

Gender theorized as seriality enabled Young to claim that the theoretical and political use of the word "women" has coherence and meaning, without assuming that all those positioned as women share any single experience in common. It also allowed her to theorize women as a collectivity while maintaining a socialist feminist orientation toward the material and structural conditions that create and constrain those who are positioned in society as women. While other feminist theorists since have offered novel ways out of the "category of women" debates (most notably Linda Zerilli), Young's approach remains the most materially oriented.

While many of her contemporaries abstracted away from actual politics in order to theorize it, Young made the lived experience and political activism of social justice movements the starting point for her philosophical inquiry. In *Justice*, she arrived at a novel account of justice by taking as her inspiration the specific claims of oppression and exclusion made by the women's, gay liberation, civil rights, and other social justice movements of the 1970s and 1980s. Yet she was deeply aware that her orientation to the practical meant her conclusions would be bound to a particular place and time. Practical philosophy does not offer general solutions, but rather responds to issues that arise in particular historical contexts. Young saw her own work in *Justice* as unfinished because she knew that new movements and new claims would surface. In the 2000s she took to analyzing the emergent anti-globalization and anti-sweatshop movements; today we might analyze fossil fuel divestment campaigns, trans activism, and nascent forms of feminism. And so, Young's orientation to theorizing the practical issues a call for permanent critique on the part of feminist scholars: to continue in her path to reflect on how the always-evolving practical concerns of social movements and political actors challenge and help us to rethink the concepts we use to imagine a transformed future.

Young's major writings

1990a. *Justice and the Politics of Difference*. Princeton, NJ: Princeton University Press.

1990b. *Throwing Like a Girl: And Other Essays in Feminist Philosophy and Social Theory*. Bloomington: Indiana University Press.

1997. *Intersecting Voices: Dilemmas of Gender, Political Philosophy, and Policy*. Oxford: Oxford University Press.

2000. *Inclusion and Democracy*. Oxford: Oxford University Press.

2005. *On Female Body Experience: "Throwing Like a Girl" and Other Essays*. Oxford: Oxford University Press.

2006. *Global Challenges: War, Self-Determination, and Responsibility for Justice*. Cambridge: Polity.

2011. *Responsibility for Justice*. Oxford: Oxford University Press.

Further reading

2008. "Special Issue: In Honor of Iris Marion Young: Theorist and Practitioner of Justice." *Hypatia* 23(3).

Dhanda, Meena. 2000. "Theorising with a Practical Intent: Gender, Political Philosophy and Communication—An Interview with Iris Marion Young." *Women's Philosophy Review* 26: 1–22.

Ferguson, Ann and Mechtild Nagel (eds.). 2009. *Dancing with Iris: The Philosophy of Iris Marion Young*. Oxford: Oxford University Press.

INDEX